Current Debates
in American Government

Ryan Emenaker

College of the Redwoods

James Morone

Brown University

New York   Oxford

OXFORD UNIVERSITY PRESS

Oxford University Press is a department of the University of Oxford.
It furthers the University's objective of excellence in research,
scholarship, and education by publishing worldwide.

Oxford   New York
Auckland   Cape Town   Dar es Salaam   Hong Kong   Karachi
Kuala Lumpur   Madrid   Melbourne   Mexico City   Nairobi
New Delhi   Shanghai   Taipei   Toronto

With offices in
Argentina   Austria   Brazil   Chile   Czech Republic   France   Greece
Guatemala   Hungary   Italy   Japan   Poland   Portugal   Singapore
South Korea   Switzerland   Thailand   Turkey   Ukraine   Vietnam

For titles covered by Section 112 of the US Higher Education
Opportunity Act, please visit www.oup.com/us/he for the
latest information about pricing and alternate formats.

Published by Oxford University Press
198 Madison Avenue, New York, New York 10016
http://www.oup.com

CIP data is on file at the Library of Congress
ISBN: 978-0-19-027276-0

Printing number: 9 8 7 6 5 4 3 2 1

Printed in the United States of America
on acid-free paper

I dedicate this book to all of the teachers and coaches who have taught me throughout my life (especially coaches Weber, Ahern, Bell, and Wells); my colleagues and teachers at College of the Redwoods, Brown University, Johns Hopkins University, and Humboldt State University who have taught me the collaborative nature of education; my students at CR who continue to teach me that education has a plurality of meanings; my close friends who taught me the joy of contemplating the solutions to problems that are both large and small (especially Tim, David, Jason, Matt, Gabe, Don, and Tim); my family who were my first teachers in life; my dad who taught me hard work and kindness; my mom who taught me intellectual curiosity and the lifelong joy of learning; and my partner Sofia who taught me to love life and travel as much as I love books and who continues to teach me every day. I hope all your lives are as full of teaching and learning as you have made mine.

Ryan Emenaker

I dedicate this book to all my wonderful graduate students, past and present, with a very special shout out to: Aaron Weinstein, Robert Hackey, Jason Barnosky, Elizabeth Fauquert, Joseph Coleman, Anthony Dell'Aera, Daniel Ehlke, Jennifer Fitzgerald, Eduardo Gomez, Daniel Gitterman, Carrie Nordlund; John Oberlander, David Blanding, Ravi Perry, Emily Ferris, Robin Schroeder, Kaitlin Sidorsky, Ravi Perry; Jeremy Johnson, Heather Silber Mohammed, Nick Coburn-Palo, Kevin McGravey, Dan Carrigg—and my super coauthor, Ryan Emenaker.

James Morone

Acknowledgments

Oxford University Press (OUP) has been amazing throughout this process. Without OUP not only would this book not exist, but as authors, we might not have met and collaborated. It was Andrea Hill's continued advocacy of OUP's introductory texts that first brought us together. Jennifer Carpenter was a champion of the project from the very beginning. Brianna Provenzano continually kept us on task (which was no easy task). Amy Gehl was a splendid editor who meticulously identified our formatting changes and awkward phrases. A huge thank you to the whole OUP team who helped make this book possible.

Brief Table of Contents

Table of Contents

Ryan Emenaker is a professor at College of the Redwoods (CR) where he serves as the area coordinator and lead faculty for political science. Ryan received his BA and MA from Humboldt State University. He also holds an MA in Government from The Johns Hopkins University.

His writings have appeared in the *Journal of Legal Metrics, PS: Political Science, Publius: The Journal of Federalism, the Journal of Political Science Education* and the *Encyclopedia of American Governance*. Ryan is an avid Supreme Court examiner and has attended numerous sessions of the Supreme Court and served as a Supreme Court analyst for several NBC affiliates. His research on Court-Congress relations has been featured on SCOTUSblog, the premier news and research website on the Supreme Court, including an article on why the Supreme Court should uphold the Voting Rights Act. In 2013 he won CR's Dr. Eugene Portugal Award given to the outstanding faculty researcher of the year.

James Morone is the John Hazen White Professor of Political Science and Public Policy and Director of the Taubman Center for Public Policy at Brown University. He grew up in Rio de Janeiro and New York, received his BA from Middlebury College and his Ph.D. at the University of Chicago. The Brown University classes of 1993, 1999, 2001, 2007, and 2008 voted him the Hazeltine Citation as the teacher that most inspired them. Jim has served as chair of the political science department, director of the public policy program, and chair of the Brown University faculty.

Professor Morone has published ten books and over 150 articles, reviews, and essays on American political history, health care policy, and social issues. Morone's first book, *The Democratic Wish*, was named a "notable book of 1991" by *The New York Times* and won the Political Science Association's Kammerer Award for the best book on the United States. His *Hellfire Nation: the Politics of Sin in American History* was nominated for a Pulitzer Prize and named a top book of 2003 by numerous newspapers and magazines. His *The Heart of Power: Health and Politics in the Oval Office* (written with David Blumenthal, MD) was featured on the front page of *The New York Times Book Review*. According to unreliable sources, President Obama was seen reading the book at his weekend retreat at Camp David.

Jim comments frequently on political issues for shows like The News Hour with Jim Lehrer, CBS Sunday Morning with Charles Osgood, The BBC, Fox News, C Span, NPR's Market Place, Morning Edition, Science Friday, The Take Away and other shows. He was distinguished Fulbright lecturer to Japan, has served on the editorial board of eight scholarly journals (chairing two of them), and has testified before the US Congress numerous times.

When he is not at Brown, Jim lives in a 19th century farmhouse in Lempster, New Hampshire and served for many years as the master of ceremonies at the town's annual Old Home Day talent show. Jim is especially proud of his canned tomatoes.

American politics changes quickly—just like the United States. There are constant arguments about what our politics (and our nation) are and what they should be next. The aim of this text is to bring you into these debates! Actually we have two aims: we want to introduce the debates that are defining America, and we want to help you to understand and analyze them.

Political debates surround us. They are captured in newspapers, blogs, Twitter feeds, magazines, online discussion boards, talk radio, and broadcast news. They are fascinating, sensational, exciting, often loud, and sometimes subtle. And they affect our lives. They shape the great issues: war, peace, economic inequality, health, safety, liberty, racial harmony, what Americans think, and who is going to govern the country.

But when you first tune in to the debates, you may find that you're missing the vital context. What's that? We call it the four I's of politics: the crucial role of the *Institutions*, the *Ideas*, the *Interests*, and the *Individuals* that constrain and shape political controversies. Here's the key point: the debates keep changing and political coverage focuses on the ever-shifting headlines. But savvy observers look beyond the headlines at the deeper trends. The four I's will help you see the trends and patterns quietly driving the political news.

The readings selected here address many current issues, controversies, and debates in American politics. But most importantly, the readings make sure that the deeper trend-lines are part of the story. The readings are pulled from a variety of sources—academic journals, scholarly books, magazines, and respected newspapers like *The New York Times*. The readings draw from both historical and contemporary sources. They illustrate the intense debates that have animated American politics in the past and energize it today. We selected them to show you multiple perspectives; the readings relate politics to our everyday lives and facilitate real-world applications of the theories discussed in your classroom. Most importantly, *Current Debates in American Government* is designed to convey our enthusiasm about American politics.

We agree with some of these articles, we disagree with others, and a few make us furious. But every one of them teaches an important lesson about the U.S. political system and how it really works. Over the years we have watched some of our students enjoy these debates so much they become political science majors. Many others pursue other goals. We know that most of you will not suddenly leap into a career in political science—but watch out, the discipline may reach out and grab you! Whether you become a major or are just briefly sampling politics, we have designed this collection to get you reading and debating politics in a more sophisticated way.

Each selection in *Current Debates in American Government* is accompanied by an introduction to guide your reading. The selected readings along with their introductions will get you started; subsequent classroom discussions will expand your ability to read the world of politics. We have seen students after class explaining to their friends how the news that was trending on their favorite site failed to adequately discuss the institutions limiting the political choices, or how the TV news reporter failed to discuss the importance of the ideas underlying the political actor's words, or how the comments on the Internet post didn't fully understand the interests of political actors. Once you start making similar connections, you will be reading as an intellectually savvy member of your community, debating ideas with your class, and, we hope, having some fun as well.

Let the debates begin!

A PERSONAL NOTE TO INSTRUCTORS

Like many creative endeavors, this reader was forged out of frustration and hope. Like many political science professors, we were frustrated when students failed to do the assigned readings. We tried the standard responses: we gave stern lectures on the importance of the readings, we handed out pop quizzes, and one of us went so far as to lock students out of class if they came unprepared (professors can be kind of a tough lot). However, as worked up as we got, none of these strategies changed the classroom dynamic. But we retained hope.

Fully subscribing to the belief that people pay attention to information that is interesting and relevant, we looked for a collection of readings to accompany our textbooks that were precisely that: interesting and relevant. However, these interesting readings still needed to teach the broader themes of American politics.

Most collections of readings in American politics focus on excerpts from the classic articles we read in graduate school. Such readings usually contain the important content our classes need, and a certain reliance on these articles is fine, but an overreliance can be a problem. Classic, discipline-specific articles often include detailed references to events that occurred before our students were born, making it hard for students to fully grasp the examples. Further, to make the classic selections fit into an introductory course, the readings often have to be edited so mercilessly that an author's carefully crafted argument is barely coherent. We wanted students to read the beginning, the middle, and the end of someone's argument. To engage their critical thinking, students need to see an entire argument develop.

The desire for relevant contemporary articles that didn't need to be heavily edited led us to focus on newspaper and magazine articles. But, for all the advantages that news articles provide (brevity and relevance), these advantages were counterbalanced by the fact that often something is lacking in the presentation. News coverage frequently focuses on the intricacies of evanescent conflicts, losing the deeper explanations. We needed articles that included contemporary applications of textbook theories. As noted in the preface, we needed readings that reflected the four I's of politics.

We started collecting articles. We tried different ones. Some we used for a few years; others were discarded quickly. Slowly we got a knack for what articles would work. Over time we gathered a collection of effective articles and created a formula to identify a small selection of new ones every year. Our students became very congenial partners. We eventually created a reader that generated the type of engagement, critical thinking, and discussion that worked.

We soon knew we were onto something. We overheard students discussing the articles in the halls. Our colleagues told us students were debating these articles in their math and biology classes. We had students start sending us links to news articles they thought should be included in the next course reader. Our teaching evaluations even began to include narratives praising the readings.

One of the most important aspects of *Current Debates in American Government*, and of particular assistance to you as an instructor, are the introductions that connect each reading to chapter themes. These introductions explain why the entry was included and provide background on the author and the publication. Further, each entry is paired with specific questions to stimulate in-class discussion and to assist you in teaching the material. The questions include one or two reading comprehension questions—to ensure that the students understood the author's argument—before moving into critical thinking questions that require synthesizing information and formulating arguments. You can use as many or as few of the articles as you like. They stand on their own, but they also connect well to the major themes found in each chapter of a typical introductory textbook.

The hard work was shifting through the tens of thousands of articles that could be included in *Current Debates in American Government* to ensure the final collection of articles is interesting and illustrative. But now the fun part begins: developing and debating the ideas with your class.

May you and your class have as much fun as we do in ours!

Ryan Emenaker
James Morone

Chapter 1

The Spirit of American Politics

The study of American politics answers four questions: (1) who governs? (2) how does American politics work? (3) what does government do?, and (4) who are we as a nation? These are perplexing questions with complex answers. In a totalitarian dictatorship it might be easy to identify who governs; in American politics the answer is less clear. For example, the Constitution established a republic with power derived from "we the people," but some people were granted more power than others and some (slaves, native Americans, women) were not granted any at all. The differences in power at the start of our republic illustrates the key point: answering the question of who rules in the United States is more complicated than reflexively shouting "the people." When examining who rules, we often want to know the specifics of how they rule. In other words: how does American politics actually work? To answer this we study the operations of American government.

Another fundamental question in American politics focuses on what government does and—and what government *should* do. Many people view politics as unsavory and consider government the problem. But government can also solve problems. Weighing the relative benefits of government is just the beginning; there are also conflicts about what we want government to do. Some people want government to provide lots of social services. Others think a government should protect people and their property—and nothing else. Finally, in the study of American politics we have to ask: who are we? If the people aspire to rule, we have to understand who the people are. American politics helps define who we are as a community, a people, and a nation. When we study American politics, we are engaged in the search for answers to these four questions.

The four I's—Ideas, Institutions, Interests, and Individuals—represent a set of tools that provide insight into the above questions. Let's look at each of these briefly before employing them to better understand the chapter's readings. Powerful ideas shape American politics. Essential ideas like liberty, equality, democracy, individualism, limited government, the American dream, and faith in God are at the heart of long, often loud controversies about what values and policies Americans should pursue. You may notice that political actors continually refer to these concepts. Policies that are viewed as consistent with these ideas may be adopted; ones that are perceived as inconsistent are typically discarded. Institutions also influence which policies are pursued. But here is a complication: Americans rarely agree on what these concepts mean. There are two sides to each of these great principles. So, as you'll see, there are great arguments about the meaning of equality or liberty or democracy.

Institutions—the organizations, norms, and rules that structure political action—allow some courses of action while restricting others. Majorities in the United States might be motived to adopt policies to expand (or restrict) democracy, but the structure of institutions (such as Congress, the presidency, and the courts) will contour the configuration of those policies. When trying to understand American politics, it is important to ask which institutions are involved and how they influence outcomes. Further, political action often springs from individuals, groups, and nations pursuing their interests. If you can discover someone's or some group's interests, you can better understand their actions. Finally, individuals make politics. Civic engagement by individuals—especially when those individuals work together in groups—can change the world. Examples of individuals working toward change are provided throughout this text. You will notice that employing the four I's will help you understand the readings as you proceed through the chapters, and it will help you better understand American politics.

The readings in this chapter address three of the four I's; the fourth I (ideas) is the subject of the second chapter. Adam Davidson, in "Why Are Some Countries Rich and Others Poor?," provides a review of the book *Why Nations Fail: The Origins of Power, Prosperity, and Poverty.* This review highlights the importance of institutions in shaping political life. As Davidson reports, the book's authors (Daron Acemoglu and James Robinson) assert that the wealth of a country is determined by its institutions. Their argument runs counter to many popular arguments about the role of geography, culture, or history in determining the level of a country's wealth. Acemoglu and Robinson argue that countries with institutions that fail to prevent a small elite from "crushing the poor and powerless" are more likely to be economically depressed. Based on the results of their comparative study of bordering countries, the authors argue that countries need to transition to having more inclusive institutions that facilitate more equitable wealth distributions.

Chris Cillizza accounts for interests as a critical component in understanding political behavior. In "The Failure of the Bailout Bill," Cillizza reports on the September 2008 House vote against a bill intended to secure U.S. financial institutions. To comprehend this, Cillizza analyzes which House members voted against the bill. His discovery: by an overwhelming margin, members of the House facing a tight reelection contest were the most likely to vote against the bill. Since public opinion was strongly opposed to the bill, this seems to indicate that members of Congress who were concerned about their reelection prospects voted to improve their reelection chances. It can be perplexing to understand the behavior of political actors, and challenging to make sense of political decision making, but interests are one of the four I's that demystify the political process.

Charles Wilson, in "The Other Movement That Rosa Parks Inspired," provides a moving example of the role of individuals in asserting political change. In this *Washington Post* article, Wilson reports that a dozen men and women rolled their wheelchairs in front of a Chicago bus to protest the lack of busses with wheelchair lifts. The disability rights activists all wore name tags that read "My name is Rosa Parks." This inscription was a tribute to the individual who sparked the 1955 boycott of segregated busses in Montgomery, Alabama. This is a powerful example of how individual actions can inspire the actions of others. As you will read in this example, and in other readings throughout this text, U.S. politics is ripe with examples of individuals—working together in groups—transforming society.

The three readings in this chapter do not cover everything that animates the spirit of American politics, but they do provide examples of how we can approach the four questions that underscore the study of American politics. The readings also illuminate how the four I's help us understand political life. These four questions and the four I's are worth keeping in mind as you engage with the readings in this chapter, debate the readings throughout this text, and continue to study American politics.

CHAPTER QUESTIONS

1) In what ways do the four I's help illuminate the readings in this chapter?
2) What recent political events can be better understood by employing the four I's?
3) Why is it important to answer the four questions that animate the study of American politics?

CHAPTER READINGS

1.1) Adam Davidson, "Why Are Some Countries Rich and Others Poor?" *Plant Money Blog, National Public Radio*, March 16, 2012.

1.2) Chris Cillizza, "The Failure of the Bailout Bill," *The Washington Post*, September 29, 2008.

1.3) Charles Wilson, "The Other Movement That Rosa Parks Inspired," *The Washington Post*, October 30, 2005.

1.1) Why Are Some Countries Rich and Others Poor?

Plant Money Blog, National Public Radio, March 16, 2012

ADAM DAVIDSON

Adam Davidson, in "Why Are Some Countries Rich and Others Poor?," reviews the book *Why Nations Fail: The Origins of Power, Prosperity, and Poverty* for *National Public Radio*. The authors of *Why Nations Fail*, Daron Acemoglu and James Robinson, enter the longstanding debate about what determines a country's economic status. To answer this question, they searched for geographic areas that shared similar climates, cultures, and histories but were separated by a border. In some areas of the globe—such as North and South Korea—they found a country struggling with poverty on one side of the border but an economically flourishing country on the other side. Based on the results of their study, Acemoglu and Robinson reject some of the common explanations (such as lack of natural resources, possession of an inhospitable climate, development of a bad culture, or indebtedness to a bad history) for what determines a country's economic status. Davidson summarizes the central finding of *Why Nations Fail* as the discovery that the "key difference between rich and poor countries is the degree to which a country has institutions that keep a small elite from grabbing all the wealth."

As Davidson notes, the authors argue that countries need to transition to having more inclusive institutions in order to improve their economic status. This is a similar finding to one derived by Nobel Prize economist Amartya Sen. Sen argues in *Democracy as Freedom* that democracies do not experience famines because in order to stay in power democratic leaders must be (at least somewhat) responsive to their people. Thus, Sen offers an argument for how understanding political actors' interest (of remaining in power), combined with an understanding of the pressures of democratic institutions, helps explain political behavior and the reduction of famines. Acemoglu and Robinson provide an example of institutions shaping political outcomes.

Why are some nations rich and others poor? In a new book called *Why Nations Fail*, a pair of economists argue that a lot comes down to politics.

To research the book, the authors scoured the world for populations and geographic areas that are identical in all respects save one: they're on different sides of a border.

The two Koreas are an extreme example. But you can see the same thing on the border of the U.S. and Mexico, Haiti and the Dominican Republic, and dozens of other neighboring countries. In all of these cases, the people and land were fairly similar, but the border changed everything.

"It's all about institutions," Daron Acemoglu, one of the authors, explained. "It's really about human-made systems, rules, regulations, formal or informal that create different incentives."

When these guys talk about institutions they mean it as broadly as possible: it's the formal rules and laws, but also the norms and common practices of a society. Lots of countries have great constitutions but their leaders have a practice of ignoring the rules whenever they feel like it.

Acemoglu and his co-author, James Robinson, say the key difference between rich countries and poor ones is the degree to which a country has institutions that keep a small elite from grabbing all the wealth. In poor countries, the rich and powerful crush the poor and powerless.

Think of a poor farmer in Haiti or the Congo today or medieval Europe 500 years ago. Sure, he could, maybe, irrigate his land and till the soil and grow more stuff. But they know that the institutions in place guarantee that a well-connected member of the elite will show up and claim the spoils. So what's the point? The poor have no incentive to invest in land or businesses or to accumulate savings. The result: undeveloped land and a poor nation.

James said, "Ultimately, what needs to change is that those countries have to make a transition to having inclusive institutions. And that's not something that throwing money at them can achieve."

This can seem discouraging but their message does offer hope, too. Poverty is not the simple result of bad geography, bad culture, bad history. It's the result of us: of the ways that people choose to organize their societies. And, that means, we can change things.

ARTICLE QUESTIONS

1) What is the cause of poverty according to Acemoglu and Robinson?
2) What method did they use to reach this conclusion?
3) Do you find their argument and methods convincing? Why or why not?

1.2) The Failure of the Bailout Bill

The Washington Post, September 29, 2008

CHRIS CILLIZZA

In September of 2008, the Great Recession hit; large financial institutions teetered on the brink of failure. There was growing panic concerning a potential financial meltdown. The George Bush administration proposed a bill to "bail out" the banks to strengthen the U.S. economy. The bill was supported by congressional leadership on both sides of the aisle as well as presidential candidates Barack Obama and John McCain. Despite the widespread support from political elites—and the perceived need by many in Congress—the House voted down the bill. Why? Chris Cillizza, in the "The Failure of the Bailout Bill," writes "the failure of the financial bailout bill in the House is a classic example of an old adage: all politics is local." What he means by "local" is the interest of each member of the House in representing his or her constituents. Cillizza's breakdown of the House vote is a great example of how interests (one of the four I's) help explain the political process.

As Cillizza notes, the House vote came just five weeks before the November election. Public opinion polls showed that a large portion of the public opposed bailing out failing financial institutions. The members of the House who were in the most competitive election districts (meaning they were facing a close election in November) were the most likely to vote against the bill. Those who were in safe districts (meaning they were assured victory in the November election) were the most likely to vote for the bill. If we understand the interests of members of Congress as getting reelected, then this voting pattern makes sense. Those who feared losing the election voted in line with public opinion; those assured victory could vote their conscience. Thus, Cillizza's breakdown of the data indicates that reelection interest influenced congressional voting patterns. The framers designed the Constitution with the idea that self-interest drives personal behavior. This vote seems to support the framers' suspicions. The voting pattern on the financial bailout bill demonstrates the power of accounting for interests in explaining political outcomes.

The failure of the financial bailout bill in the House is a classic example of an old adage: all politics is local.

Despite the fact that Republican President George W. Bush and the leadership of both parties lined up behind the bill, the rank and file of both parties—particularly on the Republican side—rebelled in light of polling that showed the American public is deeply skeptical about a planned $700 billion bailout for the financial industry.

With just over one month left before the November election, politicians of both partisan stripes are concerned primarily about one thing: their own political futures.

And, even a cursory glance at polling on the issue, shows why so many politicians voted against the bill.

In a recent USA Today/Gallup Poll, just 22 percent of the sample said they wanted Congress to "pass a plan similar to what the Bush Administration has proposed" while 56 percent wanted Congress to pass something "different" (although what that different plan would be was not made clear) and 11 percent wanted Congress to take no action at all.

The results were slightly more mixed in a *New York Times*/CBS News poll where 42 percent said they approved of the government's financial rescue plan while 46 disapproved, and in the Post/ABC poll where 44 percent expressed approval for the plan and 42 percent disapproved.

The data suggest that this bill was far from a political winner for members of Congress set to face voters in 36 days.

And, for vulnerable Republicans who believe that the free-spending attitude of Congress and the Bush Administration was either partially or primarily responsible for their ouster from majorities in the House and the Senate in 2006, the idea of floating the federal government another $700 billion was simply unpalatable.

It's no coincidence then that of the 205 Members who voted in support of the bill today, there are only two—Reps. Chris Shays (R-Conn.) and Jon Porter (R-Nev.)—who find themselves in difficult reelection races this fall. The list of the 228 "nays" reads like a virtual target list for the two parties.

ARTICLE QUESTIONS

1) How many members of Congress facing a tough reelection campaign voted for the financial bailout bill?
2) Do you think the concept of interests helps explain the voting pattern on this bill? What else besides self-interest might explain the voting patterns?
3) Often people bemoan the fact that the desire to get reelected drives congressional behavior; however, if the desire to get reelected caused members of Congress to vote in line with public opinion, why is it negative that reelection interests drive congressional behavior?

1.3) The Other Movement That Rosa Parks Inspired

The Washington Post, October 30, 2005

CHARLES WILSON

Individuals are another of the four I's key to understanding political decision making. "The Other Movement That Rosa Parks Inspired" provides a moving example of individuals in instigating social change. In this *Washington Post* article, Charles Wilson reports that a dozen men and women rolled their wheelchairs in front of a Chicago bus to protest a lack of busses with wheelchair lifts. The daring disability rights activists all wore name tags inscribed "My name is Rosa Parks" in tribute to the individual who sparked the 1955 boycott of segregated busses in Montgomery, Alabama. It is important to note that the 1955 Montgomery boycott came a year after the Supreme Court's *Brown v. Board of Education* decision, which ruled that separate but equal schools violated the Constitution. Despite the Court's decision in *Brown*, it took the actions of individuals to uproot segregation practices.

Decades after formal racial segregation has been outlawed, the work of individuals like Parks lives on through the changes they made and the inspiration they continue to provide. Parks inspired the disability rights activists in Chicago, and their actions have inspired others. It is sometimes hard to see the results of our efforts, but each of us has the potential to engage in actions that inspire others.

On an unseasonably warm September day in 1984, about a dozen men and women rolled their wheelchairs in front of a city bus that was pulling onto State Street in Chicago. Then they sat there and didn't move. The group had no secret agenda; they simply wanted to make a point. Days before, the Chicago Transit Authority had announced that it was purchasing 363 new public buses—and that none of them would be equipped with wheelchair lifts to serve disabled passengers because the lifts had been deemed too expensive. This ragtag group of wheelchair riders, who were affiliated with a disability rights organization called ADAPT, or Americans Disabled for Accessible Public Transit, decided to protest that decision by obstructing a bus until the police carted them away. Every one of them wore a simple paper name tag, the sort that you would normally see at a meet-and-greet. They all said: "My name is Rosa Parks."

Rosa Parks's act of courage in Montgomery, Ala., in 1955 did more than dismantle the system of racial segregation on public transportation. Her refusal to give up her seat to a white man also created a legacy she never could have foreseen. It was through Parks's example that the disabled community transformed its own often disorganized cause into a unified disability rights movement. "Had it not been for Parks and the bus boycott, there is no question that the disability rights movement would have been light-years behind, if it would have ever occurred," says Michael Auberger, a disability rights activist who was one of the first to place his wheelchair in front of a bus in the early 1980s. "Her genius was that she saw the bus as the great integrator: It took you to work, it took you to play, it took you to places that you were never before seen. We began to see the bus the same way, too, and it empowered a group of people who had been just as disenfranchised as African Americans."

The disability rights movement could in no sense have been called a movement when Parks refused to yield her seat. At that time, the unemployment rate for people with disabilities reached over 70 percent, and organizations that rallied for rights for people with disabilities focused on solutions that were specific to a single disorder. "The disability community was fragmented," says Bob Kafka, a quadriplegic who broke his neck in 1973 and who was an early organizer for ADAPT. "The deaf community wanted interpreters. People with mobility issues wanted curb cuts. The blind wanted more sensory communication. Everyone saw themselves as a deaf person, or a blind person, or a mental health person. We were tossed salad, not fondue."

Parks's action offered these separate communities a strategy that unified their various wishes. "Rosa Parks energized us in that she was the perfect symbol for when the meek become militant," says Kafka. "She was someone who was willing to cross the line." And the fight for accessible public transportation was to be the single issue that catalyzed disparate disability groups into a common cause.

By the 1960s and '70s, many cities had introduced paratransit services that picked up disabled patients. The officials who controlled city budgets, though, typically stipulated that these buses could be used by an individual only a few times a month and that the buses could be used only by appointment. So, in the late '70s and early '80s, some activists began to extend the logic of Parks's silent act of defiance to their own cause: Buses that divided people into separate categories, they said, were inherently unequal. Disabled people shouldn't be limited to using paratransit buses. They deserved to ride the city buses, just like everyone else.

"How could you go to school, or go on a date, or volunteer somewhere if the only trips deemed worth funding for you were medical trips?" wrote ADAPT member Stephanie Thomas in her introduction to "To Ride the Public's Buses," a collection of articles about the early bus actions that appeared in *Disability Rag*. "How could you get a job if you could only get 3 rides a week? If you were never on time?"

Parks's method of dissent—sitting still—was well suited to a community in which many people found themselves having to do that very thing all day long. Within two decades of her refusal to give up her seat, disabled people in cities across the country began staging their own "sit-ins" by parking their wheelchairs in front of ill-equipped city buses—or, alternatively, by ditching their wheelchairs and crawling onto the stairs of the bus vestibules.

Some of the sit-ins were individual acts of defiance. In Hartford, Conn., 63-year-old Edith Harris parked her wheelchair in front of 10 separate local buses on a single day after waiting nearly two hours for an accessible bus. Increasingly, though, the sit-ins were organized by ADAPT and involved many wheelchair users at a single location.

These actions began to change both how disabled people were perceived and how they perceived themselves. "Without the history of Parks and Martin Luther King, the only argument that the disability community had was the Jerry Lewis Principle," explains Auberger. "The Poor Pathetic Cripple Principle. But if you take a single disabled person and you show them that they can stop a bus, you've empowered that person. And you've made them feel they had rights."

The sit-ins also began to bring about concrete changes in the policies of urban transportation boards. In 1983, the city of Denver gave up its initial resistance and retrofitted all 250 of its buses with lifts after 45 wheelchair users blocked buses at the downtown intersection of Colfax Avenue and Broadway. Similar moves were made by Washington's Metro board in 1986 and by Chicago's transit authority in 1989. And in 1990, when the landmark Americans With Disabilities Act cleared Congress, the only provisions that went into effect immediately were those that mandated accessible public transportation.

If Rosa Parks left a lasting legacy on the disability rights movement, it is important to recognize that it is a legacy that is largely unfinished. A restored version of the bus that Rosa Parks rode in Montgomery recently went on display at the Henry Ford Museum near Detroit, the city where Parks lived her last decades and died last Monday.

Detroit's mayor, Kwame Kilpatrick, who is up for reelection on November 8, memorialized Parks by saying that "she stood up by sitting down. I'm only standing here because of her."

Kilpatrick failed to mention a further irony, though: The Justice Department joined a suit against his city in March. It was initially filed in August 2004, by Richard Bernstein, a blind 31-year-old lawyer from the Detroit suburb of Farmington Hills, on behalf of four disabled inner-city clients. His plaintiffs said that they routinely waited three to four hours in severe cold for a bus with a working lift. Their complaint cited evidence that half of the lifts on the city's bus fleet were routinely broken. The complaint did not ask for compensation. It demanded only that the Motor City comply with the Americans With Disabilities Act. The city recently purchased more accessible buses, but the mayor didn't offer a plan for making sure the buses stayed in good working order. He has publicly disparaged Bernstein on radio as an example of "suburban guys coming into our community trying to raise up the concerns of people when this administration is going to the wall on this issue of disabled riders."

Mayor Kilpatrick is not going to the wall, and neither are many other mayors in this country. A 2002 federal Bureau of Transportation Statistics study found that 6 million Americans with disabilities still have trouble obtaining the transportation they need. Many civic leaders and officials at transit organizations have made arguments about the economic difficulty of installing lifts on buses and maintaining them. But they are seeing only one side of the argument: More people in the disability community would pursue jobs and pay more taxes if they could only trust that they could get to work and back safely.

Public officials who offered elaborate eulogies to Parks's memory last week should evaluate whether they are truly living up to the power of her ideas. During a visit to Detroit in August to speak to disabled transit riders for a project I was working on, I met Robert Harvey, who last winter hurled his wheelchair in front of a bus pulling onto Woodward Avenue after four drivers in a row had passed him by. (He was knocked to the curb.) I met Carolyn Reed, who has spina bifida and had lost a job because she could rarely find a bus that would get her to work on time. Her able-bodied friends had also recently stopped inviting her to the movies. She guessed why: A few times over the past months, they had found themselves waiting late at night with her for hours to catch a bus with a working lift. "I'd say, 'Go ahead, go ahead, I'll be all right,'" she told me. "And they'd say, 'We're not leaving you out here.'" I also met Willie Cochran, a double amputee who once waited six hours in freezing temperatures for a bus that would take him home from dialysis treatment.

None of this should be happening in America. "Rosa Parks could get on the bus to protest," says Roger McCarville, a veteran in Detroit who once chained himself to a bus. "We still can't get on the bus." A true tribute to Parks would be to ensure that every American can.

ARTICLE QUESTIONS

1) Why specifically did the individuals in ADAPT roll their wheelchairs in front of a Chicago city bus?
2) What changes does the article attribute to the actions of the disability rights movement and groups such as ADAPT?
3) What actions of individuals and groups have you found inspiring?

Chapter 2

The Ideas That Shape America

The United States is built on ideas. Ideas touch every feature of government and politics. They affect the way Americans define their national ideals, their political goals, and their nation itself. Ideas have a power all their own. Ideas of liberty, democracy, or the American dream can move people to act. Of course it isn't always clear what actions these ideas require, and political actors employ these ideas in different and sometimes contradictory ways. The readings in this chapter will illustrate how these ideas are woven into diverse arguments and conflicting recommendations for courses of action.

The words of the Declaration of Independence include some of the most powerful ideas in the American historical tradition. The document makes appeals to human equality, liberty, and the just role of government. Political actors since 1776 have adopted the ideas and the framework of the Declaration to declare which new policies should be pursued. The first reading in this chapter comes from an 1852 speech by Fredrick Douglass titled "What to the Slave Is the Fourth of July?" Douglass uses the words of the Declaration to highlight contradictions between its equitable ideals and the maintenance of slavery in the United States. In the next reading, historian Howard Zinn makes an obvious allusion to the Declaration in "Some Truths Are Not Self-Evident." In this short piece written in 1987, the 200th anniversary of the signing of the Constitution, Zinn argues that the words in the Constitution are not enough to create a just society; the actions of citizens are required to ensure that the ideals of the Declaration are upheld.

Two other important American ideas are central in the next two readings; the concept of the American dream and the belief in American exceptionalism. In Nicholas Kristof's 2014 article, "It's the Canadian Dream Now," he laments the recent loss of wealth for the middle class and the poor in the United States, as well as condemning the loss of economic equality and opportunity for all Americans. These critiques are not particularly novel, but Kristof makes his case more powerful through his assertion that these developments mark the loss of the American dream. His final sentence, "It's time to bring the American dream home from exile," is a powerful plea to contest the inequities he bemoans. Clifford May, in "American Exceptionalism and Its Discontents," expresses concern that those critiquing American exceptionalism are both inaccurately defining the term and underestimating what makes the United States truly exceptional. May argues that the United States is truly exceptional because of the ideas on which it was founded. Further, he argues that the importance of these ideas, and the fact that other world superpowers have not fully embraced them, requires the United States to be a world leader.

George Will, in the final reading, shows how ideas in American politics can be contested and disputed. In "Progressives are Wrong about the Essence of the Constitution," he argues for a particular understanding behind the ideas of the Constitution. He rejects the belief that the Constitution was primarily about achieving democracy and asserts that it was primarily about securing individual liberties. Democracy and liberty are two ideas that motivate American politics, but as Will argues, these two ideas can be in conflict with one another. If democracy is defined as the power of the people to act through government, liberties can often be defined as limiting what majorities can do through government. This can mean that sometimes either liberty or democracy may have to be limited, as it is not always possible to have both.

As you read through this chapter, reflect upon the ideas that are used. These ideas touch almost everything we do as a nation. But as the articles illustrate, Americans rarely agree on what they mean. Instead, just as the articles in this chapter show, the meanings of important American ideas are contested, and the actions they compel disputed.

CHAPTER QUESTIONS

1) Which American ideas seem the most powerful and important to you?
2) What powerful ideas animate the Declaration of Independence? Do these ideas still animate the United States today?
3) Liberty is often defined as the most important American idea. How would you define liberty?
4) Think of an example where democracy and liberty conflict.

CHAPTER READINGS

2.1) Fredrick Douglass, "What to the Slave Is the Fourth of July?" 1852 speech delivered to Rochester Women's Antislavery Society.
2.2) Howard Zinn, "Some Truths Are Not Self-Evident," *The Nation*, August 1, 1987.
2.3) Nicholas Kristof, "It's the Canadian Dream Now," *The New York Times*, May 14, 2014.
2.4) Clifford May, "American Exceptionalism and Its Discontents," *National Review*, November 1, 2012.
2.5) George Will, "Progressives Are Wrong about the Essence of the Constitution," *The Washington Post*, April 16, 2014.

2.1) What to the Slave Is the Fourth of July?

FREDRICK DOUGLASS

Fredrick Douglass is one of the most remarkable figures in U.S. history. He was born into slavery in Maryland around 1818. Because it was against the law to teach slaves to read, he deceived and manipulated young white children into teaching him. Douglass described in his first autobiography how he fought back when his slave master whipped him; after that fight, the man never hit him again. He escaped from slavery and then hid in exile in England after he published the name of his owner in the first of his three autobiographies (a book that went on to become a bestseller). He is perhaps best known for becoming a leader of the abolitionist movement and for his fiery speeches calling for equal rights.

Douglass delivered his best-known speech, "What to the Slave Is the Fourth of July," a full-throttled assault against American slavery, in 1852, a full thirteen years before the Thirteenth Amendment outlawed slavery. Although he delivered the speech to a sympathetic crowd (the Ladies Anti-Slavery Society of Rochester, New York), it is still inspiring to fathom the depths of bravery required of a black man to speak so bluntly against American slavery in 1852. And Douglass surely does supply some harsh critiques of the United States. For example, near the end of his speech, he concludes that "there is not a nation on earth guilty of practices more shocking and bloody than are the people of the United States at this very hour." Despite the horrors of slavery, he still felt that "the great principles of political freedom and natural justice embodied in that Declaration of Independence" were important ideas that required expansion to those excluded. This speech is a powerful, moving display of the force of core American ideas. In the end Douglass' interpretation of the ideas embodied in the Constitution won out, and today it is unthinkable that slavery could be consistent with the philosophies of the Declaration or the Constitution.

Fellow citizens, pardon me, allow me to ask, why am I called upon to speak here today? What have I, or those I represent, to do with your national independence? Are the great principles of political freedom and of natural justice, embodied in that Declaration of Independence, extended to us? and am I, therefore, called upon to bring our humble offering to the national altar, and to confess the benefits and express devout gratitude for the blessings resulting from your independence to us?

Would to God, both for your sakes and ours, that an affirmative answer could be truthfully returned to these questions! Then would my task be light, and my burden easy and delightful. For who is there so cold that a nation's sympathy could not warm him? Who so obdurate and dead to the claims of gratitude that would not thankfully acknowledge such priceless benefits? Who so stolid and selfish that would not give his voice to swell the hallelujahs of a nation's jubilee, when the chains of servitude had been torn from his limbs? I am not that man. In a case like that the dumb might eloquently speak and the "lame man leap as an hart."

But such is not the state of the case. I say it with a sad sense of the disparity between us. I am not included within the pale of this glorious anniversary! Your high independence only reveals the immeasurable distance between us. The blessings in which you, this day, rejoice are not enjoyed in common. The rich inheritance of justice, liberty, prosperity, and independence bequeathed by your fathers is shared by you, not by me. The sunlight that brought light and healing to you has brought stripes and death to me. This Fourth of July is yours, not mine. You may rejoice, I must mourn. To drag a man in fetters into the grand illuminated temple of liberty, and call upon him to join you in joyous anthems, were inhuman mockery and sacrilegious irony. Do you mean, citizens, to mock me by asking me to speak today? If so, there is a parallel to your conduct. And let me warn that it is dangerous to copy the example of nation whose crimes, towering up to heaven, were thrown down by the breath of the Almighty, burying that nation in irrevocable ruin! I can today take up the plaintive lament of a peeled and woe-smitten people.

> By the rivers of Babylon, there we sat down. Yea! We wept when we remembered Zion. We hanged our harps upon the willows in the midst thereof. For there, they that carried us away captive, required of us a song; and they who wasted us required of us mirth, saying, Sing us one of the songs of Zion. How can we sing the Lord's song in a strange land? If I forget thee, O Jerusalem, let my right hand forget her cunning. If do not remember thee, let my tongue cleave to the roof of my mouth.

Fellow citizens, above your national, tumultuous joy, I hear the mournful wail of millions! Whose chains, heavy and grievous yesterday, are, today, rendered more intolerable by the jubilee shouts that reach them. If I do forget, if I do not faithfully remember those bleeding children of sorry this day, "may my right hand cleave to the roof of my mouth"! To forget them, to pass lightly over their wrongs, and to chime in with the popular theme would be treason most scandalous and shocking, and would make me a reproach before God and the world. My subject, then, fellow citizens, is American slavery. I shall see this day and its popular characteristics from the slave's point of view. Standing there identified with the American bondman, making his wrongs mine. I do not hesitate to declare with all my soul that the character and conduct of this nation never looked blacker to me than on this Fourth of July! Whether we turn to the declarations of the past or to the professions of the present, the conduct of the nation seems equally hideous and revolting. America is false to the past, false to the present, and solemnly binds herself to be false to the future. Standing with God and the crushed and bleeding slave on this occasion, I will, in the name of humanity which is outraged, in the name of liberty which is fettered, in the name of the Constitution and the Bible which are disregarded and trampled upon, dare to call in question and to denounce, with all the emphasis I can command, everything that serves to perpetuate slavery—the great sin and shame of America!

"I will not equivocate, I will not excuse"; I will use the severest language I can command; and yet not one word shall escape me that any man, whose judgment is not blinded by prejudice, shall not confess to be right and just. . . .

For the present, it is enough to affirm the equal manhood of the Negro race. Is it not as astonishing that, while we are plowing, planting, and reaping, using all kinds of mechanical tools, erecting houses, constructing bridges, building ships, working in metals of brass, iron, copper, and secretaries, having among us lawyers, doctors, ministers, poets, authors, editors, orators, and teachers; and that, while we are engaged in all manner of enterprises common to other men, digging gold in California, capturing the whale in the Pacific, feeding sheep and cattle on the hillside, living, moving, acting, thinking, planning, living in families as husbands, wives, and children, and above all, confessing and worshiping the Christian's God, and looking hopefully for life and immortality beyond the grave, we are called upon to prove that we are men! . . .

What, am I to argue that it is wrong to make men brutes, to rob them of their liberty, to work them without wages, to keep them ignorant of their relations to their fellow men, to beat them with sticks, to flay their flesh with the lash, to load their limbs with irons, to hunt them with dogs, to sell them at auction, to sunder their families, to knock out their teeth, to burn their flesh, to starve them into obedience and submission to their masters? Must I argue that a system thus marked with blood, and stained with pollution, is wrong? No! I will not. I have better employment for my time and strength than such arguments would imply. . . .

What, to the American slave, is your Fourth of July? I answer: a day that reveals to him, more than all other days in the year, the gross injustice and cruelty to which he is the constant victim. To him, your celebration is a sham; your boasted liberty, an unholy license; your national greatness, swelling vanity; your sounds of rejoicing are empty and heartless; your denunciation of tyrants, brass-fronted impudence; your shouts of liberty and equality, hollow mockery; your prayers and hymns, your sermons and thanksgivings, with all your religious parade and solemnity, are, to Him, mere bombast, fraud, deception, impiety, and hypocrisy—a thin veil to cover up crimes which would disgrace a nation of savages. There is not a nation of savages. There is not a nation on the earth guilty of practices more shocking and bloody than are the people of the United States at this very hour.

Go where you may, search where you will, roam through all the monarchies and despotisms—of the Old World, travel through South America, search out every abuse, and when you have found the last, lay your facts by the side of the everyday practices of this nation, and you will say with me that, for revolting barbarity and shameless hypocrisy, America reigns without a rival.

ARTICLE QUESTIONS

1) How does Fredrick Douglass answer the question: "What to the Slave Is the Fourth of July?"
2) Douglass offers some harsh critiques of the United States. Do you consider the speech un-American or unpatriotic?
3) Are there policies that the United States pursues today that are inconsistent with the ideas embodied in the Declaration? Is there widespread agreement that these policies are inconsistent with the Declaration's principles?
4) Can the ideas embodied in the Declaration still be successfully appealed to for change?

2.2) Some Truths Are Not Self-Evident

The Nation, August 1, 1987, volume 245, pp. 87–88

HOWARD ZINN

The title of Howard Zinn's 1987 article, "Some Truths Are Not Self-Evident," makes an obvious allusion to the Declaration. However, the majority of his article is actually about the role of the Constitution in protecting justice, liberty, and democracy. The crux of Zinn's argument is that the Constitution has little effect on the quality of our lives. He asserts this for two reasons: (1) even when the Constitution clearly defines rights to be protected, those provisions of the Constitution can be ignored; and (2) many important liberties are not covered by the Constitution. In other words, Zinn argues that sometimes the Constitution is "ignored," and sometimes the Constitution is "silent". After laying out this argument, the bulk of the article provides supporting examples.

Zinn's critique that "the Constitution . . . does not determine the degree of justice, liberty or democracy in our society" is similar to James Madison's concern that the Constitution was only a "parchment barrier" against tyranny. Zinn—in a similar fashion to Madison—concludes "the Constitution is of minor importance compared with the actions that citizens take, especially when those actions are joined in social movements." It might seem strange to use this article to showcase the importance of ideas, when it might appear Zinn is discounting the importance of the words of the Constitution. But Zinn does not argue "that the Constitution has no importance." Instead he argues that "words have moral power and principles can be useful." Even more to the point, think about Zinn's critique; he is expressing concern that the words of the Constitution fail to protect the important ideas—such as liberty, equality, and democracy—that are embodied in the Declaration. Further, he shows the importance of another core idea embedded in both the Declaration and the Constitution: the concept of citizens petitioning for change and altering their system of government to meet their needs.

This year Americans are talking about the Constitution but asking the wrong questions, such as, Could the Founding Fathers have done better? That concern is pointless, 200 years after the fact. Or, Does the Constitution provide the framework for a just and democratic society today? That question is also misplaced, because the Constitution, whatever its language and however interpreted by the Supreme Court, does not determine the degree of justice, liberty or democracy in our society.

The proper question, I believe, is not how good a document it is or was the Constitution but, What effect does it have on the quality of our lives? And the answer to that, it seems to me, is, Very little. The Constitution makes promises it cannot by itself keep, and therefore deludes us into complacency about the rights we have. It is conspicuously silent on certain other rights that all human beings deserve. And it pretends to set limits on governmental powers, when in fact those limits are easily ignored.

I am not arguing that the Constitution has no importance; words have moral power and principles can be useful even when ambiguous. But, like other historic documents, the Constitution is of minor importance compared with the actions that citizens take, especially when those actions are joined in social movements. Such movements have worked, historically, to secure the rights our human sensibilities tell us are self-evidently ours, whether or not those rights are "granted" by the Constitution.

Let me illustrate my point with five issues of liberty and justice:

First is the matter of racial equality. When slavery was abolished, it was not by constitutional fiat but by the joining of military necessity with the moral force of a great antislavery movement, acting outside the Constitution and often against the law. The Thirteenth, Fourteenth and Fifteenth Amendments wrote into the Constitution rights that extralegal action had already won. But the Fourteenth and Fifteenth Amendments were ignored for almost a hundred years. The right to equal protection of the law and the right to vote, even the Supreme Court decision in *Brown v. Board of Education* in 1954 underlining the meaning of the equal protection clause, did not become operative until blacks, in the fifteen years following the Montgomery bus boycott, shook up the nation by tumultuous actions inside and outside the law.

The Constitution played a helpful but marginal role in all that. Black people, in the political context of the 1960s, would have demanded equality whether or not the Constitution called for it, just as the antislavery movement demanded abolition even in the absence of constitutional support.

What about the most vaunted of constitutional rights, free speech? Historically, the Supreme Court has given the right to free speech only shaky support, seesawing erratically by sometimes affirming and sometimes overriding restrictions. Whatever a distant Court decided, the real right of citizens to free expression has been determined by the immediate power of the local police on the street, by the employer in the workplace and by the financial limits on the ability to use the mass media.

The existence of a First Amendment has been inspirational but its protection elusive. Its reality has depended on the willingness of citizens, whether labor organizers, socialists or Jehovah's Witnesses, to insist on their right to speak and write. Liberties have not been given; they have been taken. And whether in the future we have a right to say what we want, or air what we say, will be determined not by the existence of the First Amendment or the latest Supreme Court decision but by whether we are courageous enough to speak up at the risk of being jailed or fired, organized enough to defend our speech against official interference and can command resources enough to get our ideas before a reasonably large public.

What of economic justice? The Constitution is silent on the right to earn a moderate income, silent on the rights to medical care and decent housing as legitimate claims of every human being from infancy to old age. Whatever degree of economic justice has been attained in this country (impressive compared with others, shameful compared with our resources) cannot be attributed to something in the Constitution. It is the result of the concerted action of laborers and farmers over the centuries, using strikes, boycotts and minor rebellions of all sorts, to get redress of grievances directly from employers and indirectly from legislators. In the future, as in the past, the Constitution will sleep as citizens battle over the distribution of the nation's wealth, and will be awakened only to mark the score.

On sexual equality the Constitution is also silent. What women have achieved thus far is the result of their own determination, in the feminist upsurge of the nineteenth and early twentieth centuries, and the more recent women's liberation movement. Women have accomplished this outside the Constitution, by raising female and male consciousness and inducing courts and legislators to recognize what the Constitution ignores.

Finally, in an age in which war approaches genocide, the irrelevance of the Constitution is especially striking. Long, ravaging conflicts in Korea and Vietnam were waged without following Constitutional procedures, and if there is a nuclear exchange, the decision to launch U.S. missiles will be made, as it was in those cases, by the President and a few advisers. The public will be shut out of the process and deliberately kept uninformed by an intricate web of secrecy and deceit. The current Iran/contra scandal hearings before Congressional select committees should be understood as exposing not an aberration but a steady state of foreign policy.

It was not constitutional checks and balances but an aroused populace that prodded Lyndon Johnson and then Richard Nixon into deciding to extricate the United States from Vietnam. In the immediate future, our lives will depend not on the existence of the Constitution but on the power of an aroused citizenry demanding that we not go to war, and on Americans refusing, as did so many G.I.s and civilians in the Vietnam era, to cooperate in the conduct of a war.

The Constitution, like the Bible, has some good words. It is also, like the Bible, easily manipulated, distorted, ignored and used to make us feel comfortable and protected. But we risk the loss of our lives and liberties if we depend on a mere document to defend them. A constitution is a fine adornment for a democratic society, but it is no substitute for the energy, boldness and concerted action of the citizens.

ARTICLE QUESTIONS

1) What foundational American ideas does Zinn discuss in this article? Do any of these ideas overlap with the other articles in this chapter?

2) What are five areas of "liberty and justice" he uses to support his argument? Can you think of another area that would further his point?

3) Do you think Zinn underemphasizes the importance of the Constitution's role in protecting liberty and equality?

2.3) It's the Canadian Dream Now

The New York Times, May 14, 2014

NICHOLAS KRISTOF

The American dream—the belief that if you are talented and work hard you can achieve financial success—is an important part of any policy debate. Often people are championing a new policy because it will allow more people to achieve the American dream or decrying a policy because they argue it will stifle it. This is where Nicholas Kristof enters the debate. In his article "It's the Canadian Dream Now," he argues "the American dream has derailed, partly because of growing inequality." He therefore argues the United States needs to "create opportunity and dampen inequality" in order to make the American dream accessible again.

It was in 1931 that the historian James Truslow Adams coined the phrase "the American dream."

The American dream is not just a yearning for affluence, Adams said, but also for the chance to overcome barriers and social class, to become the best that we can be. Adams acknowledged that the United States didn't fully live up to that ideal, but he argued that America came closer than anywhere else.

Adams was right at the time, and for decades. When my father, an eastern European refugee, reached France after World War II, he was determined to continue to the United States because it was less class bound, more meritocratic and offered more opportunity.

Yet today the American dream has derailed, partly because of growing inequality. Or maybe the American dream has just swapped citizenship, for now it is more likely to be found in Canada or Europe—and a central issue in this year's political campaigns should be how to repatriate it.

A report last month in The Times by David Leonhardt and Kevin Quealy noted that the American middle class is no longer the richest in the world, with Canada apparently pulling ahead in median after-tax income. Other countries in Europe are poised to overtake us as well.

In fact, the discrepancy is arguably even greater. Canadians receive essentially free health care, while Americans pay for part of their health care costs with after-tax dollars. Meanwhile, the American worker toils, on average, 4.6 percent more hours than a Canadian worker, 21 percent more hours than a French worker and an astonishing 28 percent more hours than a German worker, according to data from the Organization for Economic Cooperation and Development.

Canadians and Europeans also live longer, on average, than Americans do. Their children are less likely to die than ours. American women are twice as likely to die as a result of pregnancy or childbirth as Canadian women. And, while our universities are still the best in the world, children in other industrialized countries, on average, get a better education than ours. Most sobering of all: A recent O.E.C.D. report found that for people aged 16 to 24, Americans ranked last among rich countries in numeracy and technological proficiency.

Economic mobility is tricky to measure, but several studies show that a child born in the bottom 20 percent economically is less likely to rise to the top in America than in Europe. A Danish child is twice as likely to rise as an American child.

When our futures are determined to a significant extent at birth, we've reverted to the feudalism that our ancestors fled.

"Equality of opportunity—the 'American dream'—has always been a cherished American ideal," Joseph Stiglitz, the Nobel-winning economist at Columbia University, noted in a recent speech. "But data now show that this is a myth: America has become the advanced country not only with the highest level of inequality, but one of those with the least equality of opportunity."

Consider that the American economy has, over all, grown more quickly than France's. But so much of the growth has gone to the top 1 percent that the bottom 99 percent of French people have done better than the bottom 99 percent of Americans.

Three data points:

- The top 1 percent in America now own assets worth more than those held by the entire bottom 90 percent.
- The six Walmart heirs are worth as much as the bottom 41 percent of American households put together.
- The top six hedge fund managers and traders averaged more than $2 billion each in earnings last year, partly because of the egregious "carried interest" tax break. President Obama has been unable to get financing for universal prekindergarten; this year's

proposed federal budget for pre-K for all, so important to our nation's future, would be a bit more than a single month's earnings for those six tycoons.

Inequality has become a hot topic, propelling Bill de Blasio to become mayor of New York City, turning Senator Elizabeth Warren into a star, and elevating the economist Thomas Piketty into such a demigod that my teenage daughter asked me the other day for his 696-page tome. All this growing awareness is a hopeful sign, because there are policy steps that we could take that would create opportunity and dampen inequality.

We could stop subsidizing private jets and too-big-to-fail banks, and direct those funds to early education programs that help break the cycle of poverty. We can invest less in prisons and more in schools.

We can impose a financial transactions tax and use the proceeds to broaden jobs programs like the earned-income tax credit and career academies. And, as Alan S. Blinder of Princeton University has outlined, we can give companies tax credits for creating new jobs.

It's time to bring the American dream home from exile.

ARTICLE QUESTIONS

1) What specific data does Kristof use to justify his argument that the "American dream has derailed"?
2) What policy solutions does Kristof propose to "create opportunity and dampen inequality"?
3) Do you agree with Kristof's argument that "today the American dream has derailed, partly because of growing inequality"?
4) Is making the American dream accessible achievable and/or worthwhile?

2.4) American Exceptionalism and Its Discontents

National Review, November 1, 2012

CLIFFORD MAY

Implicit in the title of Clifford May's article "American Exceptionalism and Its Discontents" is the fact that American exceptionalism is a hotly contested concept. Of course all countries are exceptional in some way, but some scholars and journalists fear that those employing the term "American exceptionalism" are implying a type of American chauvinism. May disagrees. He expresses frustration that those critiquing American exceptionalism are inaccurately defining the term, and they are neglecting what makes the United States truly exceptional.

May argues that the United States is exceptional in the fact that it was "founded on ideas" rather "than blood." May sees America's ideological founding as making it easier for immigrants to become full Americans than it is for immigrants to be accepted as naturalized citizens in other countries. May also argues that it is the validity of ideas that formed the United States, and the fact that other countries have not fully embraced them, that requires the United States to take a global leadership role. He cites the ideas of equality, consent of the governed, individual liberties, and limited government as ideas that define America and make it exceptional.

No, no, and no. American exceptionalism does not imply that [American voters "demand constant reassurance that their country, their achievements and their values are extraordinary"]—nor is it an assertion of "American greatness," as [Scott] Shane [a reporter for *The New York Times*] also claims. It is something simpler and humbler: recognition that America is, as James Madison said, the "hope of liberty throughout the world," and that America is different from other nations in ways that are consequential for the world. Let me briefly mention three.

Most nations are founded on blood. America, by contrast, was founded on ideas. This is why anyone from anywhere can move to America and become American. This is among the reasons so many people want to become American—and do. One cannot just as easily move to Japan and become Japanese. Nor can one simply become Ukrainian, Armenian, Azerbaijani, Portuguese, or Egyptian.

For those who do become Americans—and especially for their children—anything is possible. Consider such all-Americans as Colin Powell, Jeremy Lin, Bobby Jindal, Tiger Woods, and of course the most obvious example: An African student marries an American girl, and their son goes on to become the president of the United States. When I was a student in Russia years ago, I had friends from Africa and some married Russian girls. Does anyone believe that the children of these couples can hope to succeed Vladimir Putin?

A second way America is exceptional: The ideas on which this nation is based were revolutionary in the 18th century—and still are today. All men are created equal? Governments derive their powers only from the consent of the governed? We are endowed by our Creator with rights and freedoms that no one can take away? China is nowhere close to embracing such principles. Nor is most of the Middle East, the "Arab Spring" notwithstanding. Latin America and Africa have a long way to go. And in Europe, I fear, the commitment to individual liberty has been weakening.

Finally, there is leadership. If America does not accept this responsibility—and that's how it should

be seen, not as a privilege or entitlement, not as a reason to shout "We're No. 1!"—which nation will? Iran's theocrats would be eager—but that means they would impose their version of sharia, Islamic law, well beyond their borders. Putin will grab whatever power is within his reach but he would rule, not lead. There are those who see the U.N. as a transnational government. They don't get why it would be disastrous to give additional authority to a Security Council on which Russia and China have vetoes, or a General Assembly dominated by a so-called Non-Aligned Movement constituted largely of despotic regimes that recently elevated Iran as their president.

Among the evidence Shane gathers in an attempt to prove that America is unexceptional: America's high rates of incarceration and obesity and the fact that Americans own a lot of guns, consume a lot of energy, and have too few four-year-olds in pre-school. He maintains that one consequence of American exceptionalism is that there is little discussion, even during election campaigns, of America's "serious problems" and "difficult challenges" all because, he says, "we, the people, would rather avert our eyes."

His case in point is Jimmy Carter who "failed to project the optimism that Americans demand of their president," and therefore "lost his re-election bid to sunny Ronald Reagan, who promised 'morning in America' and left an indelible lesson for candidates of both parties: that voters can be vindictive toward anyone who dares criticize the country and, implicitly, the people."

Shane does not consider an alternative analysis: that Carter's policies contributed to the enfeebling economic phenomenon known as stagflation, and that he presided over a string of foreign-policy failures, among them America's humiliation at the hands of Iran's jihadist revolutionaries. He ignores this too: Reagan went on to restore the nation's economic health and to pursue policies that led to the collapse of the Soviet empire. Shane has every right to believe that America would have fared better under Carter than Reagan, but there is no historical or evidentiary basis to suggest he's right and a majority of American voters were wrong.

Shane writes that exceptionalism "has recently been championed by conservatives, who accuse President Obama of paying the notion insufficient respect." The issue is not respect but comprehension. Curiously, Shane omits Obama's most famous statement on exceptionalism. At a NATO summit in France in 2009, the president said:

> I believe in American exceptionalism, just as I suspect that the Brits believe in British exceptionalism and the Greeks believe in Greek exceptionalism.

This is really a way of saying that no nation is exceptional, that all are, as Garrison Keillor might put it, "above average." But it was America that began the modern democratic experiment. And if America does not fight for the survival of that experiment, what other nation will?

A half century ago, Reagan—not Carter—said: "Freedom is never more than one generation away from extinction." Today, freedom is under sustained assault by totalitarians, terrorists, and tyrants. It is America's exceptional burden to defend those who live in liberty, and support those who aspire to be free. This should be obvious. But, as Shane wrote in another context, too many of us "would rather avert our eyes."

ARTICLE QUESTIONS

1) In what ways does May see America as exceptional?
2) Do you agree with May that it is easier for immigrants and their children to be accepted as fully American than it might be for people immigrating to other countries?
3) What problems do you see with Americans' embracing a belief in American exceptionalism?
4) What problems do you see with Americans' not embracing American exceptionalism?

2.5) Progressives Are Wrong about the Essence of the Constitution

The Washington Post, April 16, 2014

GEORGE WILL

Almost everyone in the United States agrees the country's policies should be consistent with the ideals of the Constitution and the Declaration, yet there is disagreement about what those ideals are and what they mean. The Declaration itself sets up an inherent contradiction: It argues that governments' just powers derive from the consent of the governed, but it also contends that people have unalienable rights. A question never answered by the Declaration is this: What should be done when the consent of the governed is to restrict unalienable rights? In such cases, should we limit unalienable rights or ignore the consent of the governed? Another way to ask this is: When a majority uses democratic processes to limit liberty, should we promote democracy or defend liberty?

In "Progressives Are Wrong about the Essence of the Constitution." George Will clearly argues for restricting democracy to protect liberty. He is concerned that those who identify as "progressives" have determined that the intent of the Constitution is to promote democracy. Democracy and liberty are two ideas that motivate American politics, but as Will argues, these two ideas can be in conflict with one another. Will even cites the struggle over individual liberties as the right of the majority to govern as "the perennial conflict in American politics." As you read the article, reflect upon whether you think Will is correct in his assessment that progressives are wrong about the essence of the Constitution.

In a 2006 interview, Supreme Court Justice Stephen Breyer said the Constitution is "basically about" one word—"democracy"—that appears in neither that document nor the Declaration of Independence. Democracy is America's way of allocating political power. The Constitution, however, was adopted to confine that power in order to "secure the blessings of" that which simultaneously justifies and limits democratic government—natural liberty.

The fundamental division in U.S. politics is between those who take their bearings from the individual's right to a capacious, indeed indefinite, realm of freedom, and those whose fundamental value is the right of the majority to have its way in making rules about which specified liberties shall be respected.

Now the nation no longer lacks what it has long needed, a slender book that lucidly explains the intensity of conservatism's disagreements with progressivism. For the many Americans who are puzzled and dismayed by the heatedness of political argument today, the message of Timothy Sandefur's "The Conscience of the Constitution: The Declaration of Independence and the Right to Liberty" is this: The temperature of today's politics is commensurate to the stakes of today's argument.

The argument is between conservatives who say U.S. politics is basically about a condition, liberty, and progressives who say it is about a process, democracy. Progressives, who consider democracy the *source* of liberty, reverse the Founders' premise, which was: Liberty preexists governments, which, the Declaration says, are legitimate when "instituted" to "secure" natural rights.

Progressives consider, for example, the rights to property and free speech as, in Sandefur's formulation, "spaces of privacy" that government chooses "to carve out and protect" to the extent that these rights serve democracy. Conservatives believe that liberty, understood as a general absence of interference, and individual rights, which cannot be exhaustively listed, are natural and that governmental restrictions on them must be as few as possible and rigorously justified. Merely invoking the right of a majority to have its way is an insufficient justification.

With the Declaration, Americans ceased claiming the rights of aggrieved Englishmen and began asserting rights that are universal because they are natural, meaning necessary for the flourishing of human nature. "In Europe," wrote James Madison, "charters of liberty have been granted by power," but America has "charters of power granted by liberty."

Sandefur, principal attorney at the Pacific Legal Foundation, notes that since the 1864 admission of Nevada to statehood, every state's admission has been conditioned on adoption of a constitution consistent with the U.S. Constitution *and the Declaration*. The Constitution is the nation's fundamental law but is not the first law. The Declaration is, appearing on Page 1 of Volume 1 of the U.S. Statutes at Large, and the Congress has placed it at the head of the United States Code, under the caption, "The Organic Laws of the United States of America." Hence the Declaration "sets the framework" for reading the Constitution not as "basically about" democratic government—majorities—granting rights but about natural rights defining the limits of even democratic government.

The perennial conflict in American politics, Sandefur says, concerns "which takes precedence: the individual's right to freedom, or the power of the majority to govern." The purpose of the post-Civil War's 14th Amendment protection of Americans' "privileges or immunities"—protections vitiated by an absurdly narrow Supreme Court reading of that clause in 1873—was to assert, on behalf of emancipated blacks, national rights of citizens. National citizenship grounded on natural rights would thwart Southern states then asserting their power to acknowledge only such rights as they chose to dispense.

Government, the framers said, is instituted to improve upon the state of nature, in which the individual is at the mercy of the strong. But when democracy, meaning the process of majority rule, is the supreme value—when it is elevated to the status of what the Constitution is "basically about"—the individual is again at the mercy of the strong, the strength of mere numbers.

Sandefur says progressivism "inverts America's constitutional foundations" by holding that the Constitution is "about" democracy, which rejects the framers' premise that majority rule is legitimate "only within the boundaries" of the individual's natural rights. These include—indeed, are mostly—unenumerated rights whose existence and importance are affirmed by the Ninth Amendment.

Many conservatives should be discomfited by Sandefur's analysis, which entails this conclusion: Their indiscriminate denunciations of "judicial activism" inadvertently serve progressivism. The protection of rights, those constitutionally enumerated and others, requires a judiciary actively engaged in enforcing what the Constitution is "basically about," which is making majority power respect individuals' rights.

ARTICLE QUESTIONS

1) Name a situation where protecting individual liberties and promoting democracy come into conflict.
2) Can you think of a situation where it is better to protect liberty than promote democracy?
3) Can you think of a situation where promoting democracy is more important?

The Constitution

The Declaration of Independence sets out the ideas behind America. The Constitution takes those ideas and turns them into laws; in other words, it creates an institution to put the ideas into effect. Another way to think of the Constitution is like the owner's manual and the rule book for American government. It specifies how the government operates; it tells us what the government may do and how it should do it. If you want to learn about any feature of American politics, start by checking the Constitution.

There is a wrinkle in this concept of the Constitution guiding government; it is sometimes unclear how, or how well, the Constitution applies to modern dilemmas. After all, it is just 4,400 words written on four pages of parchment over 225 years ago. Many provisions can be read two (or more) different ways, and the document is silent on many topics. Some assert that even the constitutional provisions that are clearly understandable are no longer suitable for a twenty-first-century representative government.

This chapter has six readings on the Constitution, each of which shows that debates surrounding the Constitution are as alive today as they were between the Federalists and Anti-Federalists in the 1780s. The first reading is an op-ed in *The Sacramento Bee* by political scientists James Read and Alan Gibson. Read and Gibson attempt to debunk what they see as four myths about the Constitution. All of the myths relate back to the struggle over how to interpret the Constitution, which is a struggle that has persisted since the document was adopted.

The next reading is a chapter from Robert Dahl's book *How Democratic Is the American Constitution?* It is one of the longest readings in this text, but it is also one of the briefest synopses of the entire U.S. constitutional system. A solid understanding of this reading provides a foundation in the peculiarities of U.S. government. Rather than focusing on the vagueness of the Constitution, Dahl contends that some of the clearly laid-out structures of the Constitution (such as the Electoral College and the Senate) actually limit the possibility of democratic government. Dahl further asserts that other advanced democracies have rejected the U.S. constitutional model in favor of structures that are better suited to promote democratic government. Adam Liptak, a journalist for *The New York Times*, who studied at Yale Law School while Robert Dahl was a political scientist there, picks up on the theme of the U.S. Constitution as a model. In "'We the People' Loses Appeal with People around the World," Liptak argues that the influence of the U.S. Constitution as a model for constitution drafters around the world has waned since the 1980s. Liptak quotes heavily from scholars and practitioners who bemoan the Constitution's lack of rights, its age, and its inability to solve modern problems.

Supreme Court Justice Antonin Scalia, in his 2011 testimony before the Senate Judiciary Committee, hits upon a familiar theme by arguing that the U.S. constitutional system is unusual among contemporary countries. In this respect he expresses similar views to Dahl and Liptak, but in a sharp departure from them Scalia asserts: the relatively few rights protected by the Constitution, its potential for gridlock, its resistance to change, and its uniqueness from other representative governments should not be lamented but rather celebrated for allowing greater protection of liberties. Scalia wants Americans to embrace the gridlock built into the constitutional system. Compare Scalia's argument with that of Louis Seidman, a constitutional law professor at Georgetown University. In a *New York Times* op-ed Seidman argues that the "culprit" for the broken American system of government is "our insistence on obedience to the Constitution." He argues that historically citizens and political leaders were willing to engage in "constitutional disobedience" by ignoring the Constitution when it frustrated functional government. Seidman asserts that a renewed willingness to ignore the Constitution would require governmental actors to justify their decisions based on contemporary policy needs rather than on vague textual demands.

Louis Fisher, one of the most celebrated congressional and constitutional scholars over the last 40 years, penned the final reading in this chapter. His article follows the progression of a statute banning the sale and distribution of "crush videos"—videos that depict women in high heels crushing small animals for the sexual arousal of the viewers. In tracing this history he illuminates two of the unique aspects of the Constitution: the process of constitutional interpretation and the process of separating powers. The scenario described by Fisher underscores that interpretation of the Constitution is not confined to the Supreme Court; the president and Congress interpret the Constitution independently. Fisher's case study also highlights how separation of powers, which can lead to gridlock and confusion, can also lead to the protection of liberties and desirable policy outcomes.

All six of these readings highlight that the arguments over the proper way to interpret the Constitution and the proper role for the Constitution are alive and well. Some of the readings argue that the Constitution helps promote effective government; others point out that its unique features no longer promote representative government. However, each of the authors in his own way underscores that the Constitution has become more than a rulebook institutionalizing the ideas of the Declaration; the U.S. Constitution itself has become an idea to be revered and debated. As you read each of these pieces, keep this major question in your mind: Does the world's oldest constitution still maintain the best structures for a representative government 225 years after it was written?

CHAPTER QUESTIONS

1) How well, and in what ways, does the Constitution institutionalize the ideas introduced by the Declaration of Independence?
2) In what ways did the Constitution limit, and in what ways did it expand—as compared to the Articles of Confederation—the power of the federal government?
3) In what ways is the Constitution unique? Are these unique aspects advantageous? Does it matter if other countries use the U.S. Constitution as a model?
4) In what ways, if any, should the Constitution change?
5) Does the Constitution allow for a twenty-first-century representative government?
6) Is the Constitution likely to last another 200 years? Why or why not?

CHAPTER READINGS

3.1) James Read and Alan Gibson, "The Conversation: Four Myths about the Constitution," *The Sacramento Bee*, January 23, 2011.

3.2) Robert Dahl, "The Constitution as a Model: An American Illusion," Chapter 3 in *How Democratic Is the American Constitution?* Yale University Press, 2001, pp. 41–72.

3.3) Adam Liptak, "'We the People' Loses Appeal with People around the World," *The New York Times*, February 6, 2012.

3.4) Supreme Court Justice Antonin Scalia's comments before Senate Hearing 112-137, "Considering the Role of Judges under the Constitution of the United States," October 5, 2011.

3.5) Louis Seidman, "Let's Give Up on the Constitution," *The New York Times*, December 30, 2012.

3.6) Louis Fisher, "Crush Videos: A Constructive Dialogue," *The National Law Journal*, February 21, 2011.

3.1) The Conversation: Four Myths about the Constitution

The Sacramento Bee, January 23, 2011

JAMES H. READ AND ALAN GIBSON

Should the language of the Constitution be interpreted narrowly or broadly to adapt it to changing times?

> In this op-ed piece, political science professors James Read and Alan Gibson argue that Americans cannot understand and solve modern problems without properly understanding the Constitution. Read and Gibson are concerned that many Americans who "venerate" the Constitution for its flexibility (a flexibility that has allowed it to survive the last 220 years) simultaneously argue that the Constitution requires rigid interpretation. Read and Gibson challenge the view that fidelity to the Constitution requires an interpretation that circumscribes federal power.
>
> To make their case, Read and Gibson lay out what they argue are four myths underlying the misinterpretation of the Constitution. Their debunking efforts challenge the accuracy of narrowly interpreting the Constitution as a document intended to confine federal power. As you deconstruct their argument, notice the importance that historical knowledge can play in political arguments: These authors argue that the preexistence of the Articles of Confederation—with its weak national government—to the Constitution helps explain the Constitution's intent to centralize, energize, and expand the national government's powers to levy taxes.

Americans venerate our Constitution. And why not? It has guided our great republic for nearly 223 years and counting. The spare wording and broad clauses have made it flexible enough to adapt to more than two centuries of change. But these same characteristics have also made its *meaning* politically contested—and not just in Supreme Court cases.

Honoring a pledge to the tea party movement, the newly elected Republican majority in the House of Representatives has ignited a new round of constitutional contests.

Round One came in the ceremonial reading of the Constitution that House Republicans sponsored earlier this month with the opening of the 112th Congress. Round Two followed with Republicans' new rule that no bill or resolution be introduced in the House without "a statement citing as specifically as practicable the power or powers granted to Congress in the Constitution to enact it." The not-so-subtle implication is that health care legislation, cap and trade initiatives, the economic stimulus, among other Democratic-sponsored legislation, have no basis in the Constitution.

Many Democrats have dismissed Republicans' recent calls to constitutional fidelity as a political ploy. The occasion should be greeted instead as an opportunity for all citizens, whatever their political affiliations, to take seriously the Constitution and its history, including the history of arguments about how to interpret the document. Neither party can claim its constitutional interpretation is the only correct one. Neither party consistently practices the constitutional principles it preaches.

The soundest claim that Republicans and tea party members make is that no branch or level of government is entitled to do whatever it wants. It is not unreasonable to ask Democrats to provide constitutional justification for the legislation they introduce.

But the Republicans'—and tea party activists'—very constricted view of federal power rests on several myths about the Constitution.

Myth One: The Constitution was created to rein in an out-of-control federal government that was taxing people too much

Reality: Under the Articles of Confederation, which the Constitution replaced, the federal government was too weak and lacked the power to compel the payment of taxes. The Constitution created a stronger federal government able to "lay and collect Taxes," defend the country, pay its debts, regulate interstate and international commerce, and in general "secure the blessings of liberty" in ways the states acting individually could not. But at the same time the Constitution sought to define and limit this increased federal power and make it accountable to the people of the United States—above all through regularly scheduled elections. In the framers' view, government could be energetic and limited at the same time.

Myth Two: Strict adherence to the Constitution requires desiccated interpretations of congressional power

Reality: The framers intended the powers of Congress to be fully adequate to the real challenges the country would face. Article 1, Section 8 entrusts Congress with a pretty generous list of enumerated powers, including "to regulate commerce with foreign nations, and among the several states." Section 8 concludes by giving Congress the power "to make all Laws which shall be necessary and proper for carrying into Execution the foregoing Powers." This clause, which is the source of the Constitution's "implied powers," signals that Congress can pass laws on matters not directly named, as long as those laws have a "necessary and proper" relation to the specified purposes.

Together the "commerce clause" and the doctrine of implied powers have been the constitutional source of many programs—accepted by Democrats and Republicans alike—that the federal government uses to regulate trade and the economy and enhance the welfare of all Americans. They are also the constitutional source of recent Democratic programs in health care, cap and trade, and economic regulation.

Myth Three: The Constitution used to be followed strictly, but recently has been interpreted broadly

Reality: Debates about how broadly or narrowly to read the Constitution in general and the "necessary and proper" clause in particular date to the earliest years of the republic.

In 1791 Congress passed a law chartering a national bank, in certain respects the forerunner of today's Federal Reserve. Opponents challenged its constitutionality, since Article 1, Section 8 does not mention banks. President George Washington's Cabinet members Thomas Jefferson and Alexander Hamilton debated the constitutional question. Hamilton argued that the bank was a "necessary and proper" means of providing for national defense, paying the nation's debts and regulating interstate commerce. Jefferson argued for a much narrower interpretation of "necessary and proper," claiming that if there was any way of accomplishing these purposes without a bank, the bank was unnecessary and thus unconstitutional. Washington was persuaded by Hamilton and signed the bill. Later, as president, Jefferson took actions that contradicted his narrow view of constitutional power.

Myth Four: Only one party supports programs readily tied to the Constitution

Reality: A commitment to consistent constitutional principles is shaky on all sides of the political spectrum—including those most aggressive in their claims to own the document.

Democrats have at times passed legislation without troubling themselves to make serious constitutional arguments—like the Gun Free School Zones Act of 1990 later struck down by the Supreme Court. This purely symbolic law had no connection to commerce, and did nothing that state and local law enforcement couldn't accomplish better on their own.

But Republicans have their own constitutional lapses. For example, in its platform the Republican Party reiterates its full support of the Defense of Marriage Act, an attempted federal limit on state laws permitting same-sex marriage. What specific provision of the Constitution authorizes this legislation? Well, none. Under our Constitution marriage law is reserved to the states, unless state laws violate the 14th Amendment guarantee of "equal protection of the law."

Despite their veneration for the document, most Americans know very little about the Constitution or its history. We all know our Miranda rights from television. But unless we know Article 1,

Section 8—the powers of Congress—we will be unprepared for national politics in coming years. Is the health care law a legitimate exercise of Congress's constitutional power to regulate commerce?

Does the power to regulate commercial activity include regulating the pollution it generates?

These questions are for "we the people" to decide.

ARTICLE QUESTIONS

1) What are the four "myths" that Read and Gibson attempt to debunk?
2) Are the beliefs that Read and Gibson label as "myths" commonly held views on the proper way to understand the Constitution? Have you heard friends, neighbors, politicians, and political commentators express these views?
3) What examples do Read and Gibson offer of Democrats being inconsistent with constitutional principles? What examples do they offer of Republicans having "constitutional lapses"?
4) Do you agree with Read and Gibson's reason for why Americans' lack of knowledge of the Constitution matters?

3.2) The Constitution as a Model: An American Illusion

Chapter 3 in *How Democratic Is the American Constitution?* Yale University Press, 2001, pp. 41–72

ROBERT DAHL

This reading is Chapter 3, "The Constitution as a Model: An American Illusion," from *How Democratic Is the American Constitution?* The book was originally developed as a series of lectures by revered political scientist Robert Dahl. In service to his book's broader exploration of the U.S. constitutional system, Dahl uses this chapter to compare the U.S. constitutional system to other "advanced democracies." Dahl make it obvious from the title of the chapter, and in the first paragraph, that despite many Americans' belief that the U.S. Constitution has served as a model for other countries, Dahl's research concludes that in reality no other "advanced democracy" has adopted the U.S. constitutional system. Dahl acknowledges that his bold claim challenges a deeply held belief for many in the US. He therefore offers a detailed explanation of his methodology to meticulously back up his claim. Pay close attention to his methodology.

Also important to Dahl's argument is his assertion that these "advanced democracies"—despite their rejection of the U.S. constitutional system—have been equally proficient at providing stability and protecting human rights, and often better at encouraging democratic government. This reading serves as a a good example of employing a comparative approach to studying politics, and it also provides one of the best summations of the U.S. constitutional system.

Many Americans appear to believe that our constitution has been a model for the rest of the democratic world.[1] Yet among the countries most comparable to the United States and where democratic institutions have long existed without breakdown, not one has adopted our American constitutional system. It would be fair to say that without a single exception they have all rejected it. Why? . . .

. . . We could call [the countries where democracy is oldest and most firmly established] . . . the older democracies, the mature democracies, the stable democratic countries, and so on, but I'll settle on "the advanced democratic countries." Whatever we choose to call them, in order to compare the characteristics and performance of the American constitutional system with the characteristics and performance of the systems in other democratic countries, we need a set of reasonably comparable democratic countries. In short, we don't want to compare apples and oranges—or good apples and rotten apples.

I've noticed that we Americans often assure ourselves of the superiority of our American political system by comparing it with political systems in countries ruled by nondemocratic regimes or in countries that suffer from violent conflict, chronic corruption, frequent chaos, regime collapse or overthrow, and the like. On voicing or hearing criticism of political life in the United States, an American not infrequently adds, "Yes, but just compare it with X!," a favorite X being the Soviet Union during the Cold War and, after its collapse, Russia. One could easily pick more than a hundred other countries with political systems that by almost any standard are unquestionably inferior to our own. But comparisons like this are absurdly irrelevant.

To my mind, the most comparable countries are those in which the basic democratic political institutions have functioned without interruption for a fairly long time, let's say at least half a century, that is, since 1950. Including the United States, there are twenty-two such countries in the world.[2] Fortunately for our purposes, they are also comparable in their relevant social and economic conditions: not a rotten apple in the bunch. Not surprisingly, they are mostly European or English speaking, with a few outliers: Costa Rica, the only Latin American country; Israel, the only Middle Eastern country; and Japan, the only Asian country.

When we examine some of the basic elements in the constitutional structures of the advanced democratic countries, we can see just how unusual the American system is. Indeed, among the twenty-two older democracies, our system is unique.[3]

Federal or Unitary

To begin with, among the other twenty-one countries we find only seven federal systems, in which territorial units—states, cantons, provinces, regions, Länder—are endowed by constitutional prescription and practice with a substantial degree of autonomy and with significant powers to enact legislation. As in the United States, in these federal countries the basic territorial units, whether states, provinces, or cantons, are not simply legal creatures of the central government with boundaries and powers that the central government could, in principle, modify as it chooses. They are basic elements in the constitutional design and in the political life of the country.

As with the United States, so too in these other five countries federalism was not so much a free choice as a self-evident necessity imposed by history. In most, the federal units—states, provinces, cantons—existed before the national government was fully democratized. In the extreme case, Switzerland, the constituent units were already in place before the Swiss Confederation itself was formed from three Alpine cantons in 1291, five centuries before America was born. Throughout the following seven centuries the Swiss cantons, now twenty in number,[4] have retained a robust distinctiveness and autonomy. In the outlier, Belgium, federalism followed long after a unitary government had been imposed on its diverse regional groups. As the brilliant period of Flemish painting, weaving, commerce, and prosperity in the sixteenth and seventeenth centuries reminds us, profound territorial, linguistic, religious, and cultural differences between the predominantly Flemish and Walloon areas existed long before Belgium itself became an independent country in 1830. Despite the persistent cleavages between the Flemish and Walloons, however, federalism did not arrive until 1993 when the three regions—Wallonia, Flanders, and Brussels—were finally given constitutional status. . . .

The second and third features follow directly from the existence of federalism.

Strong Bicameralism

A natural, if not strictly necessary, consequence of federalism is a second chamber that provides special representation for the federal units. To be sure, unitary systems may also have, and historically all have had, a second chamber. However, in a democratic country with a unitary system, the functions of a second chamber are far from obvious. The question that was posed during the American constitutional convention is bound to arise: Exactly whom or whose interests is a second chamber supposed to represent? And just as the Framers could provide no rationally convincing answer, so too as democratic beliefs grow stronger in democratic countries with unitary governments, the standard answers become less persuasive—in fact, so unpersuasive to the people of the three Scandinavian countries that they have all abolished their second chambers. Like the state of Nebraska, Norway, Sweden, and Denmark also seem to do quite nicely without them. Even in Britain, the gradual advance of democratic beliefs created an inexorable force opposed to the historical powers of the House of Lords. As early as 1911 the Liberals wiped out the power of the Lords to veto "money bills" passed by the Commons. The continuing advance of democratic beliefs during the past century led in 1999 to the abolition of all but ninety-two hereditary seats. . . .

By the end of the twentieth century, then, a strongly bicameral legislature continued to exist in only four of the advanced democratic countries, all of them federal: in addition to the United States, these were Australia, Germany, and Switzerland. Their existence poses a question: What functions can and should a second chamber perform in a democratic country? And in order to perform its proper functions, if any, how should a second chamber be composed? . . .

Unequal Representation

A third characteristic of federal systems is significant unequal representation in the second chamber. By unequal representation I mean that the number of members of the second chamber coming from a federal unit such as a state or province is not proportional to its population, to the number of adult citizens, or to the number of eligible voters. The main reason, perhaps the only real reason, why second chambers exist in all federal systems is to preserve and protect *unequal* representation. That is, they exist primarily to

ensure that the representatives of small units cannot be readily outvoted by the representatives of large units. In a word, they are designed to construct a barrier to majority rule at the national level.

To make this clear, let me extend the range of the term unequal representation to include any system where, in contrast to the principle of "one person one vote," the votes of different persons are given unequal weights. Whenever the suffrage is denied to some persons within a system, we might say that their votes are counted as zero, whereas the votes of the eligible citizens are counted as one. When women were denied the vote, a man's vote effectively counted for one, a woman's for nothing, zero. When property requirements were required for the suffrage, property owners were represented in the legislature, those below the property threshold were not: like women their "votes" counted for zero. Some privileged members of Parliament, like Edmund Burke, referred to "virtual representation," where the aristocratic minority represented the best interests of the entire country. But the bulk of the people who were excluded easily saw through that convenient fiction, and as soon as they were able to they rejected these pretensions and gained the right to vote for their own M.P.s. In nineteenth-century Prussia, voters were divided into three classes according to the amount of their property taxes. Because each *class* of property owners was given an equal number of votes irrespective of the vast difference in numbers of *persons* in each class, a wealthy Prussian citizen possessed a vote that was effectively worth almost twenty times that of a Prussian worker.[6]

To return now to the United States: as the American democratic credo continued episodically to exert its effects on political life, the most blatant forms of unequal representation were in due time rejected. Yet, one monumental though largely unnoticed form of unequal representation continues today and may well continue indefinitely. This results from the famous Connecticut Compromise that guarantees two senators from each state.

Imagine a situation in which your vote for your representative is counted as one while the vote of a friend in a neighboring town is counted as seventeen. Suppose that for some reason you and your friend each change your job and your residence. As a result of your new job, you move to your friend's town. For the same reason, your friend moves to your town. Presto! To your immense gratification you now discover that simply by moving, you have acquired sixteen more votes. Your friend, however, has lost sixteen votes. Pretty ridiculous, is it not?

Yet that is about what would happen if you lived on the western shore of Lake Tahoe in California and moved less than fifty miles east to Carson City, Nevada, while a friend in Carson City moved to your community on Lake Tahoe. As we all know, both states are equally represented in the U.S. Senate. With a population in 2000 of nearly 34 million, California had two senators. But so did Nevada, with only 2 million residents. Because the votes of U.S. senators are counted equally, in 2000 the vote of a Nevada resident for the U.S. Senate was, in effect, worth about seventeen times the vote of a California resident. A Californian who moved to Alaska might lose some points on climate, but she would stand to gain a vote worth about fifty-four times as much as her vote in California.[7] Whether the trade-off would be worth the move is not for me to say. But surely the inequality in representation it reveals is a profound violation of the democratic idea of political equality among all citizens.

Some degree of unequal representation also exists in the other federal systems. Yet the degree of unequal representation in the U.S. Senate is by far the most extreme. In fact, among all federal systems, including those in more newly democratized countries—a total of twelve countries—on one measure the degree of unequal representation in the U.S. Senate is exceeded only by that in Brazil and Argentina.[8]

Or suppose we take the ratio of representatives in the upper chamber to the populations of the federal units. In the United States, for example, the two senators from Connecticut represent a population of slightly above 3.4 million, while the two senators from its neighbor New York represent a population of 19 million: a ratio of about

5.6 to 1. In the extreme case, the ratio of over-representation of the least populated state, Wyoming, to the most populous state, California, is just under 70 to 1.[9] By comparison, among the advanced democracies the ratio runs from 1.5 to 1 in Austria to 40 to 1 in Switzerland. In fact, the U.S. disproportion is exceeded only in Brazil, Argentina, and Russia.[10]

On what possible grounds can we justify this extraordinary inequality in the worth of the suffrage?

A Brief Digression: Rights and Interests

A common response is to say that people in states with smaller populations need to be protected from federal laws passed by congressional majorities that would violate their basic rights and interests. Because the people in states like Nevada or Alaska are a geographical minority, you might argue, they need to be protected from the harmful actions of national majorities. But this response immediately raises a fundamental question. *Is there a principle of general applicability that justifies an entitlement to extra representation for some individuals or groups?*

In searching for an answer, we need to begin with an eternal and elementary problem in any governmental unit:[11] whether the unit is a country, state, municipality, or whatever, virtually all of its decisions will involve some conflict of interests among the people of the relevant political unit. Inevitably, almost any governmental decision will favor the interests of some citizens and harm the interests of others. The solution to this problem, which is inherent in all governmental units, is ordinarily provided in a democratic system by the need to secure a fairly broad consent for its decisions by means, among other things, of some form of majority rule. Yet if decisions are arrived at by majority rule, then the possibility exists, as Madison and many others have observed, that the interests of *any* minority will be damaged by a majority. Sometimes, fortunately, mutually beneficial compromises may be found. But if the interests of a majority clash irreconcilably with those of a minority, then the interests of that minority are likely to be harmed.

Some interests, however, may be protected from the ordinary operation of majority rule. To a greater or lesser degree, all democratic constitutions do so.

Consider the protections that all Americans enjoy, not just in principle but substantially in practice as well. First, the Bill of Rights and subsequent amendments provide a constitutional guarantee that certain fundamental rights are protected whether a citizen lives in Nevada or California, Rhode Island or Massachusetts, Delaware or Pennsylvania. Second, an immense body of federal law and judicial interpretation based on constitutional provisions enormously extends the domain of protected rights—probably far beyond anything the Framers could have foreseen. Third, the constitutional division of powers in our federal system provides every state with an exclusive or overlapping domain of authority on which a state may draw in order to extend even further the protections for the particular interests of the citizens of that state.

The Basic Question

Beyond these fundamental and protected rights and interests, do people in the smaller states possess *additional* rights or interests that are entitled to protection from policies supported by national majorities? If so, what are they? And on what general principle can their special protection be justified? Surely they do not include a fundamental right to graze sheep or cattle in national forests or to extract minerals from public lands on terms that were set more than a century ago. Why should geographical location endow a citizen or group with special rights and interests, above and beyond those I just indicated, that should be given additional constitutional protection?

If these questions leave me baffled, I find myself in good company. "Can we forget for whom we are forming a government?" James Wilson asked at the Constitutional Convention. "Is it for *men,* or for the imaginary beings called *States?*" Madison was equally dubious about the need to protect the interests of people in the small states. "Experience," he said, "suggests no such danger. . . . Experience rather taught a contrary

lesson. . . . The states were divided into different interests not by their differences in size, but by other circumstances."[12]

Two centuries of experience since Madison's time have confirmed his judgment. Unequal representation in the Senate has unquestionably failed to protect the fundamental interests of the *least* privileged minorities. On the contrary, unequal representation has sometimes served to protect the interests of the *most* privileged minorities. An obvious case is the protection of the rights of slaveholders rather than the rights of their slaves. Unequal representation in the Senate gave absolutely no protection to the interests of slaves. On the contrary, throughout the entire pre–Civil War period unequal representation helped to protect the interests of slave owners. Until the 1850s equal representation in the Senate, as Barry Weingast has pointed out, gave the "the South a veto over any policy affecting slavery." Between 1800 and 1860 eight anti-slavery measures passed the House, and all were killed in the Senate.[13] Nor did the Southern veto end with the Civil War. After the Civil War, Senators from elsewhere were compelled to accommodate to the Southern veto in order to secure the adoption of their own policies. In this way the Southern veto not only helped to bring about the end of Reconstruction; for another century it prevented the country from enacting federal laws to protect the most basic human rights of African Americans.

So much for the alleged virtues of unequal representation in the Senate.

Suppose for a moment we try to imagine that we actually wanted the constitution to provide special protection to otherwise disadvantaged minorities by giving them extra representation in the Senate. What minorities most need this extra protection? How would we achieve it? Would we now choose to treat certain states as minorities in special need of protection simply because of their smaller populations? Why would we want to protect these regional minorities and not other, far weaker minorities? To rephrase James Wilson's question in 1787: Should a democratic government be designed to serve the interests of "the imaginary beings called States," or should it be designed instead to serve the interests of all its citizens considered as political equals?

As I have said, the United States stands out among twenty-two comparable democratic countries for the degree of unequal representation in its upper chamber. . . .

Strong Judicial Review of National Legislation

Not surprisingly, other federal systems among the older democracies also authorize their highest national courts to strike down legislation or administrative actions by the federal units—states, provinces, and the like—that are contrary to the national constitution. The case for the power of federal courts to review state actions in order to maintain a federal system seems to me straightforward, and I accept it here. But the authority of a high court to declare unconstitutional legislation that has been properly enacted by the coordinate constitutional bodies—the parliament or in our system the Congress and the president—is far more controversial.

If a law has been properly passed by the lawmaking branches of a democratic government, why should judges have the power to declare it unconstitutional? If you could simply match the intentions and words of the law against the words of the constitution, perhaps a stronger case could be made for judicial review. But in all important and highly contested cases, that is simply impossible. Inevitably, in interpreting the constitution judges bring their own ideology, biases, and preferences to bear. American legal scholars have struggled for generations to provide a satisfactory rationale for the extensive power of judicial review that has been wielded by our Supreme Court. But the contradiction remains between imbuing an unelected body—or in the American case, five out of nine justices on the Supreme Court—with the power to make policy decisions that affect the lives and welfare of millions of Americans. How, if at all, can judicial review be justified in a democratic order? . . .

Electoral Systems

. . .[O]ur electoral system was not the doing of the Framers, at least directly, for it was shaped less by them than by British tradition. The Framers simply left the whole matter to the states and Congress,[14] both of which supported the only system they knew, one that had pretty much prevailed in Britain, in the colonies, and in the newly independent states.

The subject of electoral systems is fearfully complex and for many people fearfully dull as well. I shall therefore employ a drastic oversimplification, but one sufficient for our purposes. Let simply divide electoral systems into two broad types, each with a variant or two. In the one we know best, typically you can cast your vote for only one of the competing candidates, and the candidate with the most votes wins. In the usual case, then, a single candidate wins office by gaining at least one more vote than any of his or her opponents. We Americans tend to call this one-vote margin a plurality; elsewhere, to distinguish it from an absolute majority it may be called a relative majority. To describe our system, American political scientists sometimes employ the cumbersome expression "single member district system with plurality elections." I prefer the British usage: on the analogy of a horse race where the winner needs only a fraction of a nose-length to win, the British tend to call it the "first-past-the-post" system.

If voters were to cast their ballots in the same proportion in every district, the party with the most votes would win every seat. In practice, as a result of variations from district to district in support for candidates, a second party generally manages to gain some seats, although its percentage of seats will ordinarily be smaller than its percentage of votes. But the representation of third parties usually diminishes to the vanishing point. In short, first-past-the-post favors two-party systems.

The main alternative to first-past-the-post is proportional representation. As the name implies, proportional representation is designed to ensure that voters in a minority larger than some minimal size—say, 5 percent of all voters—will be represented more or less in proportion to their numbers. For example, a group consisting of 20 percent of all voters might win pretty close to

20 percent of the seats in the parliament. Consequently, countries with proportional representation systems are also very likely to have multiparty systems in which three, four, or more parties are represented in the legislature. In short, although the relationship is somewhat imperfect, in general a country with first-past-the-post is likely to have a two-party.

The extent to which we take first-past-the-post for granted was clearly revealed in 1993, when it was discovered that a well-qualified candidate to head the Civil Rights Division of the Department of Justice had written an article in a law journal suggesting that a rather sensible system of proportional representation might be worth considering as a possible solution to the problem of securing more adequate minority representation.[16] From the comments the author's innocent heresy generated, you might have thought that she had burned the American flag on the steps of the Supreme Court. Her candidacy, naturally, was stone dead.

First-past-the-post was the only game in town in 1787 and for some generations thereafter. Like the locomotive, proportional representation had not yet been invented. It was not fully conceived until the mid-nineteenth century when a Dane and two Englishmen—one of them John Stuart Mill—provided a systematic formulation. Since then it has become the system overwhelmingly preferred in the older democracies.

After more than a century of experience with other alternatives, isn't it time at last to open our minds to the possibility that first-past-the-post may be just fine for horse races but might not be best for elections in a large and diverse democratic country like ours? . . .

Party Systems

Nearly a half-century ago, a French political scientist, Maurice Duverger, proposed what came to be called Duverger's Law: first-past-the-post electoral systems tend to result in two-party systems. Conversely, proportional representation systems are likely to produce multiparty systems.[17] Although the causal relation may be more complex than my brief statement of Duverger's Law suggests,[18] a country with a proportional representation system is likely to require coalition governments consisting of two or more parties. In a country with a first-past-the-post electoral system, however, a single party is more likely to control both the executive and the legislature. Thus in countries with proportional representation–multiparty systems and coalition governments, minorities tend to be represented more effectively in governing. By contrast, in countries with first-past-the-post and two-party systems, the government is more likely to be in the hands of a single party that has gained a majority of seats in the parliament and the most popular votes, whether by an outright majority, or more commonly, a plurality. To distinguish the two major alternatives, I'll refer to the proportional representation–multiparty countries as "proportional" and countries with first-past-the-post electoral systems and only two major parties as "majoritarian."[19]

Where does the United States fit in? As usual: in neither category. It is a mixed system, a hybrid, neither predominantly proportional nor predominantly majoritarian. three brief observations may help to put it in perspective here. First, the Framers had no way of knowing about the major alternatives to first-past-the-post, much less fully understanding them. Second, since the Framers' time most of the older and highly stable democratic countries have rejected first-past-the-post and opted instead for proportional systems. Third, our mixed design contributes even further to the unusual structure of our constitutional system.

Our Unique Presidential System

As we make our way through the list of countries that share some constitutional features with the United States, the list, short to begin with, diminishes even further. By the time we reach the presidency the United States ceases to be simply unusual. It becomes unique.

Among the twenty-two advanced democracies, the United States stands almost alone in possessing a single popularly elected chief executive endowed with important constitutional powers—a presidential system. Except for Costa Rica, all the other countries govern themselves with some variation of a parliamentary system in which the executive, a prime minister, is chosen by the national legislature. In the mixed systems of France and Finland, most of the important constitutional powers are assigned to the prime minister, but an elected president is also provided with certain powers—chiefly over foreign relations. This arrangement may lead, as in France, to a president from one major party and a prime minister from the opposing party, a situation that with a nice Gallic touch the French call "cohabitation." Yet even allowing for the French and Finnish variations, none of the other advanced democratic countries has a presidential system like ours.

Why is this? The question breaks down into several parts. Why *did* the Framers choose a presidential system? Why *didn't* they choose a parliamentary system? Why have all the other advanced democratic countries rejected our presidential system? Why have they adopted some variant of a parliamentary system instead, or as in France and Finland a system that is predominantly parliamentary with an added touch of presidentialism?

To answer these questions in detail would go beyond our limits here. But let me sketch a brief answer.

Before I do so, however, I want to admonish you not to cite the explanation given in the Federalist Papers. These were very far from critical, objective analyses of the constitution. If we employ a dictionary definition of propaganda as "information or ideas methodically spread to promote or injure a cause, nation, etc.," then the Federalist Papers were surely propaganda. They were written post hoc by partisans—Alexander Hamilton, John Jay, and James Madison—who wanted to persuade doubters of the virtues of the proposed constitution in order to secure its adoption in the forthcoming state conventions. Although they were very fine essays indeed, and for the most part much worth reading today, they render the work of the convention more coherent, rational, and compelling than it really was. Ironically, by the way, the task of explaining and defending the Framers' design for the presidency was assigned to Hamilton, who had somewhat injudiciously remarked in the Convention that as to the executive, "The English model was the only good one on this subject," because "the

hereditary interest of the king was so interwoven with that of the nation . . . and at the same time was both sufficiently independent and sufficiently controuled [*sic*], to answer the purpose." He then proposed that the executive and one branch of the legislature "hold their places for life, or at least during good behavior."[20] Perhaps as a result of these remarks, Hamilton seems to have had only a modest influence in the Convention on that matter or any other. . . .

But how was the independent executive to be chosen? How independent of the legislature and of the people should he be? How long should his term of office be? ("He" is, of course, the language of Article II and, like most Americans until recently, the only way the Framers could conceive of the office.) The British constitution was a helpful model for the Framers in some respects. But as a solution to the problem of the executive, it utterly failed them. Despite the respect of the delegates for many aspects of the British constitution, a monarchy was simply out of the question.[22]

Even so, they might have chosen a democratic version of the parliamentary system, as the other evolving European democracies were to do. Although they were unaware of it, even in Britain a parliamentary system was already evolving. Why then didn't the Framers come up with a republican version of a parliamentary system?

Well, they almost did. It has been too little emphasized, I think, that the Framers actually came very close to adopting something like a parliamentary system. . . .

. . . [T]he strange record suggests to me a group of baffled and confused men who finally settle on a solution more out of desperation than confidence. As events were soon to show, they had little understanding of how their solution would work out in practice.

So the question remains with no clear answer: Why, finally, did they fail to adopt the solution they had seemed to favor, a president elected by the Congress, a sort of American version of a parliamentary system? The standard answer no doubt has some validity: they feared that the president might be too beholden to Congress. And all the other alternatives seemed to them worse.

Among these alternatives was election by the people, which had been twice rejected overwhelmingly. Yet it was this twice-rejected solution, election by the people, that was quickly adopted de facto during the democratic phase of the American revolution.

How their solution failed. Perhaps in no part of their work did the Framers fail more completely to design a constitution that would prove acceptable to a democratic people. As I have mentioned, their hope for a group of electors who might exercise their independent judgments about the best candidate to fill the office came a cropper following the election of 1800. But as I shall describe in the next chapter, more was still to come. If the election of 1800 first revealed how inappropriate the electoral college was in a democratic order, the presidential election of 2000, two centuries later, dramatized for all the world to witness the conflict between the Framers' constitution and the democratic ideal of political equality. . . .

Andrew Jackson . . . [i]n justifying his use of the veto against Congressional majorities, as the only national official who had been elected by *all* the people and not just by a small fraction, as were Senators and Representatives, Jackson insisted that he alone could claim to represent *all* the people. Thus Jackson began what I have called the myth of the presidential mandate: that by winning a majority of popular (and presumably electoral) votes, the president has gained a "mandate" to carry out whatever he had proposed during the campaign.[25] Although he was bitterly attacked for this audacious assertion, which not all later presidents supported, it gained credibility from its reassertion by Lincoln, Cleveland, Theodore Roosevelt, and Wilson and was finally nailed firmly in place by Franklin Roosevelt.

Whatever we may think of the validity of the claim—I am inclined to think it is little more than a myth created to serve the political purposes of ambitious presidents—it is simply one part of a transformation of the presidency in response to democratic ideas and beliefs that has produced an office completely different from the office that the Framers thought they were creating, vague and uncertain as their intentions may have been.

And a good thing, too, you may say. But if you approve of the democratization of the presidency—or, as I would prefer to say, its pseudo-democratization—aren't you suggesting in effect that the constitutional system *should* be altered to meet democratic requirements?

Why other countries became parliamentary democracies. There is still one more reason why the Framers didn't choose a parliamentary system. They had no model to inspire them. One hadn't yet been invented. . . .

In addition, there was the problem of a monarch. How could a country have a parliamentary system without a symbolic head of state who would perform ceremonial functions, symbolize the unity of the country, and help to confer legitimacy on the parliament's choice by anointing him as prime minister? After the evolution of a parliamentary system in Britain, in due time monarchies also helped the Swedes, the Danes, and the Norwegians—and much later Japan and Spain—to move to a parliamentary system that the monarchy helped to legitimize. But in 1787 the full development of parliamentary democracy in countries with a monarchy was still a long way off. For Americans, a monarch, even a ceremonial monarch, was completely out of the question. So why didn't they split the two functions, ceremonial and executive, by creating a titular head of state to serve in the place of a ceremonial monarch, and a chief executive, the equivalent of a prime minister, to whom executive functions would be assigned? Although that arrangement may seem obvious enough to us now, for the Framers in 1787 it was even more distant than the system that was gradually evolving in Britain, the country they knew best. It was not until after 1875 and the installation of the Third Republic in France that the French evolved a solution that would later be adopted in many other democratizing countries: a president elected by the parliament, or in some cases by the people, who serves as formal head of state, and a prime minister chosen by and responsible to the parliament, who serves as the actual chief executive. But for the Framers this invention, which now seems obvious enough to us, was almost as far off and about as difficult to imagine, perhaps, as a transcontinental railroad.

Without intending to do so, then, the Framers created a constitutional framework that under the driving impact of the continuing American Revolution would develop a presidency radically different from the one they had in mind. In time American presidents would gain office by means of popular elections—a solution the Framers rejected and feared—and by combining the functions of a head of state with those of a chief executive the president would be the equivalent of monarch and prime minister rolled into one.

I can't help wondering whether the presidency that has emerged is appropriate for a modern democratic country like ours.

* * *

So: Among the Older Democracies our Constitutional system is not just unusual. It is unique.

Well, you might say, being unique isn't necessarily bad. Perhaps our constitutional system is better for it.

Better by what standards? Is it more democratic? Does it perform better in many ways? Or worse?

These questions are by no means easy to answer—probably impossible to answer with finality.

NOTES

1. In a 1997 survey, 34% strongly agreed and 33% somewhat agreed with the statement "The U.S. Constitution is used as a model by many countries." Only 18% somewhat or strongly disagreed. (Nationwide telephone survey of 1,000 adult U.S. Citizens conducted for the National Constitution Center, September, 1997.) To the statement "I am proud of the U.S. Constitution," 71% strongly agreed and 18% somewhat agreed. In 1999, 85% said the Constitution was a major reason for America's success in the twentieth century. (Survey of 1,546 adults for the Pew Research Center by the Princeton Survey Research Associates.)

2. Although India gained independence in 1947, adopted a democratic constitution, and has, except for one interval, maintained its democratic institutions in the face of extraordinary challenges of poverty and diversity, I have omitted it from the list for two reasons. First,

continuity was interrupted from 1975 to 1977 when the prime minister, Indira Gandhi, staged a coup d'etat, declared a state of emergency, suspended civil rights, and imprisoned thousands of opponents. Second, because India is one of the poorest countries in the world, comparisons with the wealthy democratic countries would make little sense.

3. For a summary of the constitutional differences among twenty-two older democracies, see Appendix B, Table 2. [Editors' note: Appendix B, Table 2 has been removed from this edited volume].

4. Plus six half-cantons.

6. For example, in the Prussian elections of 1858, 4.8% of the inhabitants were entitled to one-third of the seats, 13.4% to another third, and 81.8% to the remaining third. Thus members of the wealthiest third in effect possessed 17 times as many votes as members of the bottom third. Bernhard Vogel and Rainer-Olaf Schultze, "Deutschland," in *Die Wahl Der Parlamente,* Dolf Sternberger and Bernard Vogel, eds. (Berlin: Walter De Gruyter, 1969), 189–411, Tabelle A 4, p. 348.

7. Lest you think me biased against Nevada, the Rocky Mountain states, or small states in general: I have the greatest affection for Alaska, where I grew up in the days when it was still a territory, and for the Rocky Mountain states, where I like to spend some time every summer. And at just over 3 million people, Connecticut gives me a wholly undeserved voting advantage of nine to one over my sons in California.

8. Alfred Stepan, "Toward a New Comparative Analysis of Democracy and Federalism: Demos Constraining and Demos Enabling Federations," paper for the meeting of the International Political Science Association, Seoul, Aug. 17–22, 1997.

9. For a comprehensive description, analysis, and critique of unequal representation in the Senate, see Francis E. Lee and Bruce I.

Oppenheimer, *Sizing Up the Senate: The Unequal Consequences of Unequal Representation* (Chicago: University Chicago Press, 1999).

10. Stepan, supra n. 8.

11. More precisely, a governmental unit of a "State" defined as a territorial system with a government that successfully upholds a claim to the exclusive regulation of the legitimate use of physical force in enforcing its rules within a given territorial area.

12. For Mason, see *Records,* 1: 483; for Madison, see 447–48.

13. Barry R. Weingast, "Political Stability and Civil War: Institutions, Commitment, and American Democracy," in Robert H. Bates, Avner Greif, Margaret Levi, Jean-Laurent Rosenthal, and Barry R. Weingast, *Analytic Narratives* (Princeton: Princeton University Press, 1988), 148–93, 166, and Table 4.3, 168.

14. Article II, Section 4 provides: "The times, places, and manner of holding elections for Senators and Representatives, shall be prescribed in each State by the Legislature thereof; but the Congress may at any time by Law make or alter such regulations, except as to the place of choosing Senators." Article II, Section 1 provides: "Each state shall appoint, in such manner as the legislature therefore may direct, a number of Electors."

16. Lani Guanier, "No Two Seats: The Elusive Quest for Political Equality," *Virginia Law Review* 77 (1991).

17. Maurice Duverger, *Political Parties: Their Organization and Activity in the Modern State* (New York: John Wiley, 1954), 217.

18. In an appraisal of Duverger's propositions in 1958, John Grumm observed that "it may be more accurate to conclude that proportional representation is a result rather than a cause of the party system in a given country." "Theories of Electoral Systems," *Midwest Journal of Political Science* 2 (1958): 357–76, 375.

19. Arend Lijphart, *Patterns of Democracy, Government Forms and Performance in Thirty-Six Countries* (New Haven: Yale University Press, 1999) uses ten variables to distinguish "majoritarian" from "consensus" democracies. Table 14.1, p. 245. G. Bingham Powell, *Elections as Instruments of Democracy, Majoritarian and Proportional Visions* (New Haven: Yale University Press, 2000) uses the terms of his title: "majoritarian" and "proportional." See pp. 20ff and the classification of twenty democratic countries on p. 41.

20. *Records,* 1: 288, 299.

22. The only delegate recorded by Madison as speaking favorably about the British monarchy was Hamilton. See note 3 above. Ironically, the Federalist Papers defending the provisions of the Constitution on the executive—Nos. 67–77—were by Hamilton.

25. For a critical view, see my "The Myth of the Presidential Mandate," *Political Science Quarterly* 105, no. 3 (Fall 1990): 355–72.

ARTICLE QUESTIONS

1) Does Dahl believe other countries have adopted the U.S. constitutional model?
2) Explain Dahl's methodology. What countries does he compare, and what specifics does he compare among them?
3) Does Dahl believe that protecting the interest of "imaginary beings called States" led to protections of the "least privileged minorities"? What example related to slavery does he give to further his point?
4) Dahl is skeptical of providing extra representation to any group, and he is especially skeptical of providing "geographical minorities" extra protection through the Senate. This skepticism causes him to ask: "What minorities most need this extra protection? How would we achieve it?" How would you answer Dahl's question?

3.3) 'We the People' Loses Appeal with People around the World
The New York Times, February 6, 2012

ADAM LIPTAK

Adam Liptak, a journalist with *The New York Times* who specializes in legal studies, also explores the concept of the U.S. Constitution serving as a model constitution. Liptak begins by citing a *Time* magazine article (which used a different methodology from Robert Dahl's) that noted in 1987, 160 of 170 countries had written charters modeled on the U.S. Constitution. Citing a recent study from the *New York University (NYU) Law Review*, Liptak notes that this trend has since reversed. The *NYU Law Review* article concludes that by the start of the twenty-first century the world's democracies are less similar to the U.S. Constitution than they were in the 1940s. Some of the reasons offered for this reversal is that the U.S. Constitution "is terse and old, and it guarantees relatively few rights." Also, some of the scholars quoted by Liptak bemoan the immense difficulty of amending the U.S. Constitution (Of the 11,000 amendments that have been proposed, only 17 have been ratified since 1791).

As we have seen from the other readings, Liptak underscores the longstanding nature of the U.S. Constitution; he even cites that on average countries significantly rework their constitutions every 19 years. Like Robert Dahl, Liptak analyzes the U.S. Constitution using a comparative perspective. Directly comparing the Dahl and Liptak readings shows the how different methodologies yield different answers to the question of whether other constitutions are similar to the U.S. Constitution. Dahl found that *all advanced democracies rejected the U.S. model*, while the studies Liptak cites found that some countries have modeled their charters on the U.S. Constitution. One of the most fundamental questions in political science is "who rules?" or "who governs?" If the U.S. Constitution is difficult to amend and if it guarantees fewer rights than the constitutions of other countries, what does this say about "who governs" in America?

WASHINGTON—The Constitution has seen better days.

Sure, it is the nation's founding document and sacred text. And it is the oldest written national constitution still in force anywhere in the world. But its influence is waning.

In 1987, on the Constitution's bicentennial, *Time* magazine calculated that "of the 170 countries that exist today, more than 160 have written charters modeled directly or indirectly on the U.S. version."

A quarter-century later, the picture looks very different. "The U.S. Constitution appears to be losing its appeal as a model for constitutional drafters elsewhere," according to a new study by David S. Law of Washington University in St. Louis and Mila Versteeg of the University of Virginia.

The study, to be published in June in *The New York University Law Review*, bristles with data. Its authors coded and analyzed the provisions of 729 constitutions adopted by 188 countries from 1946 to 2006, and they considered 237 variables regarding various rights and ways to enforce them.

"Among the world's democracies," Professors Law and Versteeg concluded, "constitutional similarity to the United States has clearly gone into free fall. Over the 1960s and 1970s, democratic constitutions as a whole became more similar to the U.S. Constitution, only to reverse course in the 1980s and 1990s."

"The turn of the twenty-first century, however, saw the beginning of a steep plunge that continues through the most recent years for which we have data, to the point that the constitutions of the world's democracies are, on average, less similar to the U.S. Constitution now than they were at the end of World War II."

There are lots of possible reasons. The United States Constitution is terse and old, and it guarantees relatively few rights. The commitment of some members of the Supreme Court to interpreting the Constitution according to its original meaning in the 18th century may send the signal that it is of little current use to, say, a new African nation. And the Constitution's waning influence may be part of a general decline in American power and prestige.

In an interview, Professor Law identified a central reason for the trend: the availability of newer, sexier and more powerful operating systems in the constitutional marketplace. "Nobody wants to copy Windows 3.1," he said.

In a television interview during a visit to Egypt last week, Justice Ruth Bader Ginsburg of the Supreme Court seemed to agree. "I would not look to the United States Constitution if I were drafting a constitution in the year 2012," she said. She recommended, instead, the South African Constitution, the Canadian Charter of Rights and Freedoms or the European Convention on Human Rights.

The rights guaranteed by the American Constitution are parsimonious by international standards, and they are frozen in amber. As Sanford Levinson wrote in 2006 in "Our Undemocratic Constitution," "the U.S. Constitution is the most difficult to amend of any constitution currently existing in the world today." (Yugoslavia used to hold that title, but Yugoslavia did not work out.)

Other nations routinely trade in their constitutions wholesale, replacing them on average every 19 years. By odd coincidence, Thomas Jefferson, in a 1789 letter to James Madison, once said that every constitution "naturally expires at the end of 19 years" because "the earth belongs always to the living generation." These days, the overlap between the rights guaranteed by the Constitution and those most popular around the world is spotty.

Americans recognize rights not widely protected, including ones to a speedy and public trial, and are outliers in prohibiting government establishment of religion. But the Constitution is out of step with the rest of the world in failing to protect, at least in so many words, a right to travel, the presumption of innocence and entitlement to food, education and health care.

It has its idiosyncrasies. Only 2 percent of the world's constitutions protect, as the Second Amendment does, a right to bear arms. (Its brothers in arms are Guatemala and Mexico.)

The Constitution's waning global stature is consistent with the diminished influence of the Supreme Court, which "is losing the central role it once had among courts in modern democracies," Aharon Barak, then the president of the Supreme Court of Israel, wrote in *The Harvard Law Review* in 2002.

Many foreign judges say they have become less likely to cite decisions of the United States Supreme Court, in part because of what they consider its parochialism.

"America is in danger, I think, of becoming something of a legal backwater," Justice Michael Kirby of the High Court of Australia said in a 2001 interview. He said that he looked instead to India, South Africa and New Zealand.

Mr. Barak, for his part, identified a new constitutional superpower: "Canadian law," he wrote, "serves as a source of inspiration for many countries around the world." The new study also suggests that the Canadian Charter of Rights and Freedoms, adopted in 1982, may now be more influential than its American counterpart.

The Canadian Charter is both more expansive and less absolute. It guarantees equal rights for women and disabled people, allows affirmative action and requires that those arrested be informed of their rights. On the other hand, it balances those rights against "such reasonable limits" as "can be demonstrably justified in a free and democratic society."

There are, of course, limits to empirical research based on coding and counting, and there is more to a constitution than its words, as Justice

Antonin Scalia told the Senate Judiciary Committee in October. "Every banana republic in the world has a bill of rights," he said.

"The bill of rights of the former evil empire, the Union of Soviet Socialist Republics, was much better than ours," he said, adding: "We guarantee freedom of speech and of the press. Big deal. They guaranteed freedom of speech, of the press, of street demonstrations and protests, and anyone who is caught trying to suppress criticism of the government will be called to account. Whoa, that is wonderful stuff!"

"Of course," Justice Scalia continued, "it's just words on paper, what our framers would have called a 'parchment guarantee.'"

ARTICLE QUESTIONS

1) Detail two pieces of evidence that Liptak uses to support his claim that the Constitution's "influence is waning."
2) Is it a cause for concern that the U.S. Constitution is no longer serving as a model constitution? Why?
3) Is it a benefit or a detriment that the United States has the oldest written constitution?
4) If the United States were to write a constitution from scratch, should it use another country's constitution as a model?

3.4) Considering the Role of Judges under the Constitution of the United States

Supreme Court Justice Antonin Scalia's comments before Senate Hearing 112–137, October 5, 2011

Supreme Court Justice Antonin Scalia, in his 2011 testimony before the Senate Judiciary Committee, celebrates what he sees as an unusual governmental structure established by the U.S. Constitution. The uniqueness of the U.S. Constitution is a familiar theme running through the readings in this chapter. Like others in this chapter, Scalia asserts that the relatively few rights protected by the Constitution, its potential for gridlock, and its resistance to change make the U.S. constitutional system different from the systems established in other countries. However, in sharp contrast to the chapter's other readings, Scalia argues that these differences allow for the greatest protection of liberties.

Justice Scalia sees the real protections of liberties coming from the structures established by the U.S. Constitution rather than the listing of rights. Many of these constitutional structures are the same ones that Robert Dahl argued limited the potential for a democratic government. Justice Scalia asserts that the Framers thought that the listing of rights would only be "a parchment guarantee" for liberties, but the real protection would come from separating powers. He agrees with some of the other readings in this chapter that separating powers leads to gridlock; however, Scalia wants Americans to embrace the gridlock as a means to protect rights rather than lament gridlock as a means to frustrate representative government.

Thank you, Mr. Chairman, members of the committee. I am happy to be back in front of the Judiciary Committee where I started this pilgrimage.

I speak to students, especially law students but also college students and even high school students, quite frequently about the Constitution because I feel that we are not teaching it very well. I speak to law students from the best law schools, people presumably especially interested in the law, and I ask them: how many of you have read the Federalist Papers? Well, a lot of hands will go up. No, not just No. 48 and the big ones. How many of you have read the Federalist Papers cover to cover? Never more than about 5 percent. And that is very sad, especially if you are interested in the Constitution.

Here is a document that says what the Framers of the Constitution thought they were doing. It is such a profound exposition of political science that it is studied in political science courses in Europe. And yet we have raised a generation of Americans who are not familiar with it.

So when I speak to these groups, the first point I make—and I think it is even a little more fundamental than the one that [Justice] Stephen [Breyer] has just put forward—I ask them, what do you think is the reason that America is such a free country? What is it in our Constitution that makes us what we are? And the response I get—and you will get this from almost any American, including the woman that Stephen was talking to at the supermarket—is freedom of speech, freedom of the press, no unreasonable searches and seizures, no quartering of troops in homes, etc.—the marvelous provisions of the Bill of Rights.

But then I tell them, if you think that the Bill of Rights is what sets us apart, you are crazy. Every banana republic has a bill of rights. Every president for life has a bill of rights. The bill of rights of the former evil empire, the Union of Soviet Socialist Republics, was much better than ours. I mean that literally. It was much better. We guarantee freedom of speech and of the press. Big deal.

They guaranteed freedom of speech, of the press, of street demonstrations and protests, and anyone who is caught trying to suppress criticism of the government will be called to account. Whoa, that is wonderful stuff.

Of course, they were just words on paper, what our Framers would have called "a parchment guarantee." And the reason is that the real constitution of the Soviet Union—think of the word "constitution"; it does not mean a bill of rights, it means structure. When you say a person has a sound constitution, you mean he has a sound structure. Structure is what our Framers debated that whole summer in Philadelphia, in 1787. They did not talk about a Bill of Rights; that was an afterthought, wasn't it? The real constitution of the Soviet Union did not prevent the centralization of power in one person or in one party. And when that happens, the game is over. The bill of rights becomes what our Framers would call "a parchment guarantee."

So the real key to the distinctiveness of America is the structure of our Government. One part of it, of course, is the independence of the judiciary, but there is a lot more. There are very few countries in the world, for example, that have a bicameral legislature. England has a House of Lords for the time being, but the House of Lords has no substantial power. It can just make the Commons pass a bill a second time. France has a senate; it is honorific. Italy has a senate; it is honorific. Very few countries have two separate bodies in the legislature equally powerful. It is a lot of trouble, as you gentlemen doubtless know, to get the same language through two different bodies elected in a different fashion.

Very few countries in the world have a separately elected chief executive. Sometimes I go to Europe to speak in a seminar on separation of powers, and when I get there, I find that all we are talking about is independence of the judiciary. Because the Europeans do not even try to divide the two political powers, the two political branches—the legislature and the chief executive. In all of the parliamentary countries, the chief executive is the creature of the legislature. There is never any disagreement between the majority in the legislature and the prime minister, as there is sometimes between you and the President. When there is a disagreement, they just kick him out. They have a no-confidence vote, a new election, and they get a prime minister who agrees with the legislature.

You know, the Europeans look at our system and they say, well, the bill passes one House, it does not pass the other House (sometimes the other House is in the control of a different party). It passes both Houses, and then this President, who has a veto power, vetoes it. They look at this and they say, "It is gridlock."

And I hear Americans saying this nowadays, and there is a lot of that going around. They talk about a dysfunctional Government because there is disagreement. And the Framers would have said, "Yes, that is exactly the way we set it up. We wanted this to be power contradicting power because the main ill that besets us," as Hamilton said in the Federalist paper when he justified the inconvenience of a separate Senate, is an excess of legislation." This is 1787. They did not know what an excess of legislation was.

So unless Americans should appreciate that and learn to love the separation of powers, which means learning to love the gridlock that it sometimes produces. The Framers believed that would be the main protection of minorities—the main protection. If a bill is about to pass that really comes down hard on some minority, so that they think it terribly unfair, it does not take much to throw a monkey wrench into this complex system.

So Americans should appreciate that, and they should learn to love the gridlock. It is there for a reason: so that the legislation that gets out will be good legislation.

This is another respect, by the way, in which we differ from most of the countries of the world. Many foreigners cannot understand our affection for the Constitution. It is no big deal to amend the constitution in most of the countries of the world. In most of them, all you need is to have the legislature, a unicameral legislature, pass the amendment. Then there has to be an intervening election. And then they have to pass the amendment again.

Ours is very much more difficult to amend. And you are right, I have said that that is a good thing. Indeed, I have said that the only provision I am sure I would think about amending is the amendment provision because that sets a very, very high bar. But that is not going to happen.

Well, I suppose there is a point at which you do reach unbearable, dysfunctional gridlock. However, I think the attitude of the American people—and this is the point I was making—is largely a product of the fact that they do not understand our Constitution, that its genius is precisely this power contradicting power, which makes it difficult to enact legislation.

It is so much easier to enact legislation in France or in England, but, you know, the consequence of that is you have swings from one extreme to another as the legislature changes. That does not happen that much here, largely because of the fact that, as a general matter, only laws on which there is general agreement will get through.

So, I think that this is one of the reasons why we have to educate the American people, as we have not been doing for decades, about what our Constitution produces and what it is designed to produce.

ARTICLE QUESTIONS

1) According to Justice Scalia, what did the Framers think would be the "main protection of minorities"?

2) In what ways does Justice Scalia argue the United States differs from other countries?

3) Do you agree with Justice Scalia when he asserts that listing liberties in a document such as the Bill of Rights is less important for protecting liberties than the way a government is structured?

4) Do you agree with Justice Scalia that Americans should learn "to love the gridlock" produced by separation of powers?

3.5) Let's Give Up on the Constitution

The New York Times, December 30, 2012

LOUIS SEIDMAN

Louis Seidman, a constitutional law professor at Georgetown University, argues in this *New York Times* op-ed that the US "obsession with the Constitution has saddled us with a dysfunctional political system." He contends that this obedience reduces U.S. politics to debates "about what James Madison might have wanted done 225 years ago." He further argues that citizens and political leaders historically engaged in "constitutional disobedience" by ignoring the Constitution when it frustrated functional government. Seidman asserts that a renewed willingness to ignore the Constitution would create a more functional government by requiring governmental actors to justify their decisions based on contemporary needs rather than based on vague textual demands.

In what might be best described as pragmatism (or, as Seidman and many others term it, "living constitutionalism"), Seidman argues political debates have not and should not start and end based on the text of the Constitution or the Framers' original meaning; rather, political decisions should rest on current political necessities. By advocating that current political realities should shape constitutional interpretation, pragmatism often stands in stark contrast with originalism as a method of interpretation. Supreme Court Justice Antonin Scalia, whose Senate testimony appeared as the previous reading in this chapter, is one of the most ardent supporters of interpreting the Constitution through an originalist perspective. (An advocate of originalism argues that constitutional interpretations should be based on the original meaning of those who wrote the Constitution.) As you read Seidman's argument, assess if advocates of originalism would be likely to accept Seidman's promotion of "constitutional disobedience."

As the nation teeters at the edge of fiscal chaos, observers are reaching the conclusion that the American system of government is broken. But almost no one blames the culprit: our insistence on obedience to the Constitution, with all its archaic, idiosyncratic and downright evil provisions.

Consider, for example, the assertion by the Senate minority leader last week that the House could not take up a plan by Senate Democrats to extend tax cuts on households making $250,000 or less because the Constitution requires that revenue measures originate in the lower chamber. Why should anyone care? Why should a lame-duck House, 27 members of which were defeated for re-election, have a stranglehold on our economy? Why does a grotesquely malapportioned Senate get to decide the nation's fate?

Our obsession with the Constitution has saddled us with a dysfunctional political system, kept us from debating the merits of divisive issues and inflamed our public discourse. Instead of arguing about what is to be done, we argue about what James Madison might have wanted done 225 years ago.

As someone who has taught constitutional law for almost 40 years, I am ashamed it took me so long to see how bizarre all this is. Imagine that after careful study a government official—say, the president or one of the party leaders in Congress—reaches a considered judgment that a particular course of action is best for the country. Suddenly, someone bursts into the room with new information: a group of white propertied men who have been dead for two centuries, knew nothing of our present situation, acted illegally under existing law and thought it was fine to own slaves might have disagreed with this course of action. Is it even remotely rational that the official should change his or her mind because of this divination?

Constitutional disobedience may seem radical, but it is as old as the Republic. In fact, the Constitution itself was born of constitutional disobedience. When George Washington and the other framers went to Philadelphia in 1787, they were instructed to suggest amendments to the Articles of Confederation, which would have had to be ratified by the legislatures of all 13 states. Instead, in violation of their mandate, they abandoned the Articles, wrote a new Constitution and provided that it would take effect after ratification by only nine states, and by conventions in those states rather than the state legislatures.

No sooner was the Constitution in place than our leaders began ignoring it. John Adams supported the Alien and Sedition Acts, which violated the First Amendment's guarantee of freedom of speech. Thomas Jefferson thought every constitution should expire after a single generation. He believed the most consequential act of his presidency—the purchase of the Louisiana Territory—exceeded his constitutional powers.

Before the Civil War, abolitionists like Wendell Phillips and William Lloyd Garrison conceded that the Constitution protected slavery, but denounced it as a pact with the devil that should be ignored. When Abraham Lincoln issued the Emancipation Proclamation—150 years ago tomorrow—he justified it as a military necessity under his power as commander in chief. Eventually, though, he embraced the freeing of slaves as a central war aim, though nearly everyone conceded that the federal government lacked the constitutional power to disrupt slavery where it already existed. Moreover, when the law finally caught up with the facts on the ground through passage of the 13th Amendment, ratification was achieved in a manner at odds with constitutional requirements. (The Southern states were denied representation in Congress on the theory that they had left the Union, yet their reconstructed legislatures later provided the crucial votes to ratify the amendment.)

In his Constitution Day speech in 1937, Franklin D. Roosevelt professed devotion to the document, but as a statement of aspirations rather than obligations. This reading no doubt contributed to his willingness to extend federal power beyond anything the framers imagined, and to threaten the Supreme Court when it stood in the way of his New Deal legislation. In 1954, when the court decided *Brown v. Board of Education*, Justice Robert

H. Jackson said he was voting for it as a moral and political necessity although he thought it had no basis in the Constitution. The list goes on and on.

The fact that dissenting justices regularly, publicly and vociferously assert that their colleagues have ignored the Constitution—in landmark cases from *Miranda v. Arizona* to *Roe v. Wade* to *Romer v. Evans* to *Bush v. Gore*—should give us pause. The two main rival interpretive methods, "originalism" (divining the framers' intent) and "living constitutionalism" (reinterpreting the text in light of modern demands), cannot be reconciled. Some decisions have been grounded in one school of thought, and some in the other. Whichever your philosophy, many of the results—by definition—must be wrong.

In the face of this long history of disobedience, it is hard to take seriously the claim by the Constitution's defenders that we would be reduced to a Hobbesian state of nature if we asserted our freedom from this ancient text. Our sometimes flagrant disregard of the Constitution has not produced chaos or totalitarianism; on the contrary, it has helped us to grow and prosper.

This is not to say that we should disobey all constitutional commands. Freedom of speech and religion, equal protection of the laws and protections against governmental deprivation of life, liberty or property are important, whether or not they are in the Constitution. We should continue to follow those requirements out of respect, not obligation.

Nor should we have a debate about, for instance, how long the president's term should last or whether Congress should consist of two houses. Some matters are better left settled, even if not in exactly the way we favor. Nor, finally, should we have an all-powerful president free to do whatever he wants. Even without constitutional fealty, the president would still be checked by Congress and by the states. There is even something to be said for an elite body like the Supreme Court with the power to impose its views of political morality on the country.

What *would* change is not the existence of these institutions, but the basis on which they claim legitimacy. The president would have to justify military action against Iran solely on the merits, without shutting down the debate with a claim of unchallengeable constitutional power as commander in chief. Congress might well retain the power of the purse, but this power would have to be defended on contemporary policy grounds, not abstruse constitutional doctrine. The Supreme Court could stop pretending that its decisions protecting same-sex intimacy or limiting affirmative action were rooted in constitutional text.

The deep-seated fear that such disobedience would unravel our social fabric is mere superstition. As we have seen, the country has successfully survived numerous examples of constitutional infidelity. And as we see now, the failure of the Congress and the White House to agree has already destabilized the country. Countries like Britain and New Zealand have systems of parliamentary supremacy and no written constitution, but are held together by longstanding traditions, accepted modes of procedure and engaged citizens. We, too, could draw on these resources.

What has preserved our political stability is not a poetic piece of parchment, but entrenched institutions and habits of thought and, most important, the sense that we are one nation and must work out our differences. No one can predict in detail what our system of government would look like if we freed ourselves from the shackles of constitutional obligation, and I harbor no illusions

that any of this will happen soon. But even if we can't kick our constitutional-law addiction, we can soften the habit.

If we acknowledged what should be obvious—that much constitutional language is broad enough to encompass an almost infinitely wide range of positions—we might have a very different attitude about the obligation to obey. It would become apparent that people who disagree with us about the Constitution are not violating a sacred text or our core commitments. Instead, we are all invoking a common vocabulary to express aspirations that, at the broadest level, everyone can embrace. Of course, that does not mean that people agree at the ground level. If we are not to abandon constitutionalism entirely, then we might at least understand it as a place for discussion, a demand that we make a good-faith effort to understand the views of others, rather than as a tool to force others to give up their moral and political judgments.

If even this change is impossible, perhaps the dream of a country ruled by "We the people" is impossibly utopian. If so, we have to give up on the claim that we are a self-governing people who can settle our disagreements through mature and tolerant debate. But before abandoning our heritage of self-government, we ought to try extricating ourselves from constitutional bondage so that we can give real freedom a chance.

ARTICLE QUESTIONS

1) What are three historic examples of "constitutional disobedience" offered by Seidman?

2) According to Seidman, what has preserved U.S. political stability rather than a "poetic piece of parchment"?

3) Do you agree with Seidman that it is irrational to make modern political decisions based on the views of those who wrote the Constitution?

4) Seidman does not believe that all constitutional commands should be disobeyed. What process should be used to determine what aspects of the Constitution should be followed versus disobeyed? What are the potential problems with each person (or each new governmental administration) determining what constitutional provisions to follow?

3.6) Crush Videos: A Constructive Dialogue

The National Law Journal, February 21, 2011

LOUIS FISHER

Louis Fisher worked at the Library of Congress for four decades and is the author of many books, including The Constitution and 9/11: Recurring Threats to America's Freedoms.

In this reading Louis Fisher highlights the "constitutional dialogues" model of constitutional interpretation by tracing the history of congressional attempts to ban "crush videos." As described in Fisher's *National Law Journal* article, crush videos depict "the intentional torture and killing of helpless animals" to arouse a particular sexual fetish. In 1999 Congress banned the sale and distribution of such videos, but the statute was later struck down by the Supreme Court. Fisher explains that many Americans inaccurately believe that Court has the final word in constitutional interpretation; however, as Fisher's article illuminates, "the Court is only one of many participants" interpreting the Constitution and "often it is not the primary or dominant one."

Reading about crush videos can be disturbing, but Fisher's review of this particular constitutional dialogue highlights how separation of powers—which can lead to gridlock and confusion—can sometimes lead to the protection of liberties and desirable policy outcomes. At the same time, the planned outcomes took over a decade, numerous crush videos were legally produced during this time, and individuals were prosecuted for activities that the statute never intended to criminalize. Fisher's article provides a great example of how the separation-of-powers game is the game that never ends: Each branch of government is left with another action to resist or collaborate with its counterparts. This lack of an endpoint can be seen as advantageous or detrimental depending on one's perspective. One could imagine Justice Scalia using this example to underscore his point that Americans should learn "to love the gridlock" produced by separation of powers. One could also conceive Louis Seidman using this example to punctuate his point that when "our obsession with the Constitution" allows crush videos to remain legal for more than a decade after Congress tried to stop them, it means our constitutional obsession "has saddled us with a dysfunctional political system."

It is widely believed that the U.S. Supreme Court delivers the final word on the meaning of the Constitution. Yet the Court is only one of many participants. Often it is not the primary or dominant one. A recent Supreme Court decision, *U.S. v. Stevens,* helps illustrate this point. On April 20, 2010, it held that a statute passed by Congress to criminalize the commercial creation, sale or possession of certain depictions of animal cruelty was substantially overbroad and therefore invalid under the First Amendment. The Court split, 8-1, with only Justice Samuel Alito Jr. dissenting. It might appear that, at least on this particular constitutional dispute, the Court would have the final word.

In fact, the Court's decision was just one stage of many, and by no means the final stage. The Court explained that the legislative background of this statute focused primarily on the interstate market of "crush videos." These videos feature the intentional torture and killing of helpless animals, including cats, dogs, monkeys, mice and hamsters. They depict women slowly crushing animals to death with their bare feet or while wearing high-heeled shoes. Persons with a sexual fetish find the depictions sexually arousing and exciting. The problem with the statute, however, is that it was not written specifically for crush videos, even if that was the legislative intent. As a result, the Justice Department prosecuted someone for trafficking in videos of dog fighting. The statute was so broad, as the Court noted, that it could criminalize extremely popular hunting videos and hunting magazines.

How did this come about? In 1999, the House Judiciary Committee reported a bill to punish the depiction of animal cruelty. The committee report expressed concern about "a growing market in videotapes and still photographs depicting insects and small animals being slowly crushed to death." Women in bare feet and high-heeled shoes inflicted the torture. In some videos the woman's voice could be heard "talking to the animals in a kind of dominatrix patter. The cries and squeals of the animals, obviously in great pain, can be heard in the videos." The bill defined "depiction of animal cruelty" as any visual or auditory depiction (including photographs and video recordings) of conduct "in which a living animal is intentionally maimed, mutilated, tortured, wounded, or killed." That language could apply to hunting and fishing videos. The committee report explained that "depictions of ordinary hunting and fishing activities do not fall within the scope of the statute," but the bill did not make exceptions for those commercial activities.

The bill passed the House, 372-42. Like the committee report, floor debate focused on crush videos and stated that "the sale of depictions of legal activities, such as hunting and fishing, would not be illegal under this bill." That was legislative history, not legislative language. By unanimous consent, the Senate passed the bill. In signing the bill into law, President Clinton noted the concern that the bill "may violate the First Amendment of the Constitution." In an effort to ensure that the statute did not chill protected speech, he decided to "broadly construe the Act's exception and will interpret it to require a determination of the value of the depiction as part of a work or communication, taken as a whole. So construed, the Act would prohibit the types of depictions, described in the statute's legislative history, of wanton cruelty to animals designed to appeal to a prurient interest in sex. I will direct the Department of Justice to enforce the Act accordingly."

In this manner, Clinton attempted to refocus an overly broad statute and to correct features that should have been fixed during the legislative process. The statute put a stop to the market in crush videos. However, whatever direction Clinton decided to give the Justice Department in the enforcement of the statute would come to an end with his administration. The new administration, under George W. Bush, would not feel bound by his signing statement. Instead of prosecuting someone for trafficking in crush videos, the department brought criminal charges against an individual who sold dog-fighting videos. When the U.S. Court of Appeals for the 3d Circuit struck down the statute in 2008 as facially unconstitutional, the market for crush videos quickly revived.

Animals were once again being tortured to satisfy customers who asked for videos tailor-made for their tastes. Congress needed to act promptly. One month after the Court decided *Stevens*, a House subcommittee heard testimony from constitutional scholars and practitioners. They agreed that a new law, focusing exclusively on crush videos, would be constitutional. Although the House Judiciary Committee is often highly polarized, the bill was reported unanimously, 23-0. The legislative language expressly states that the bill does not apply to hunting, trapping or fishing. The bill passed the House on July 20, 2010. Although the contemporary Congress has a well-deserved reputation for partisanship and gridlock, the vote in the House was 416-3. After the Senate Judiciary Committee held a hearing, the Senate passed an amended bill by unanimous consent. The two chambers agreed on common language and sent the bill to President Obama, who signed it into law on December 9, 2010.

The Supreme Court played an important role in finding the 1999 statute to be overbroad. The more significant responsibility, however, fell to the elected branches. They were the driving force in identifying the problem, to hear from those in the private sector who wanted to put an end to crush videos, and to pursue whatever legislative language was needed to achieve the legislative purpose.

ARTICLE QUESTIONS

1) Why did the Supreme Court rule in 2010 that a congressional statute banning crush videos violated the Constitution?

2) What changed between the Clinton administration and the Bush administration that led to the statute being struck down?

3) If Fisher is correct that the Supreme Court doesn't have the final word in constitutional disputes, is this a cause for concern? Why or why not?

4) Do you view this article as depicting an example of separation of powers leading to (a) dysfunctional government that took too long to solve a problem or (b) a constructive dialogue that produced a better outcome than could a quicker response?

Chapter 4

Federalism and Nationalism

Federalism denotes the separate levels of government in the United States, sharing and sometimes squabbling over power. This complex interplay among state, local, and national governments stretches back to the debates between Federalists (who wanted a strong national government) and Anti-Federalists (who sought more power for the states). The controversy led to an elaborate division of power between national and state governments. The result is an overlapping, sometimes chaotic, often clashing division of political authority in America.

Issue after issue in U.S. politics returns to the question of where to locate governmental authority: federal, state, or local. Often people switch between support for state sovereignty and support for national preemption of state laws based on their policy preferences. For instance, an environmentalist might advocate for state sovereignty to allow California to adopt more stringent air-pollution standards than the existing national standards; the same environmentalist might switch and advocate national preemption when Texas proposes a law rejecting federal air-pollution regulations. A gun-rights supporter might endorse state sovereignty when Kansas adopts a law rejecting federal gun-control regulations, then champion national preemption when Connecticut enacts comprehensive gun-control polices.

The fluidity with which political actors switch between advocating state sovereignty and national preemption might make the debate about the proper location of authority seem like a political weapon used to mask partisan policy preferences. But conflicts among local, state, and national levels also reflect deeper questions about protecting values like democracy, fairness, and effective government. The three readings in this chapter depict how federalism, established by the Constitution and shaped by 200 years of political history, has made the United States a nation of divided loyalties and governments; this division can facilitate innovation, protect liberties, and create confusion.

The first two articles in this chapter focus on two conflicts inherent in federalism: conflicts between national and state sovereignty and conflicts among the sovereign states. George Annas's article, "Jumping Frogs, Endangered Toads, and California's Medical-Marijuana Law," provides examples of the sometimes clashing relationship between the states and the national government. The article focuses on the role of the

Interstate Commerce Clause, one of Congress' enumerated powers. Because it is a clearly listed power of Congress, when Congress regulates commerce between states, a conflicting state law is preempted by federal law. While the lines of authority based on this formulation might seem clear, as Annas highlights, when American federalism is involved, it is far from this simple. An article from *Governing*, "Could Gay Marriage, Guns and Marijuana Lead to a Fragmented United States of America?" places more emphasis on the second inherent complexity of federalism: states creating conflicting policies to each other. *Governing* sees the state adoption of policies on a diversity of issues becoming so divergent that we might be "returning to our roots as a loose confederation of culturally and geographically distinct governments." Note that the article appeared before the Supreme Court ruled, (in *Obergefell v. Hodges*, June 2015) that the Constitution guarantees all Americans the right to marry—wiping out state differences.

Where the first two articles concerned conflicts in state-by-state policy versus uniform national policy, Michael Powell's article, "Leery of Washington, Alaska Feasts on Its Dollars," proves that the national government holds a powerful tool to bend states to its will. The article provides an example of "fiscal federalism"—a phrase used to describe the national government's use of monetary incentives to influence state and local polices. Fiscal federalism is often employed when the national government finds it easier to enforce its policy preferences with economic incentives; often this is because the national government lacks clear constitutional authority to directly regulate.

Americans rarely think about the processes (such as federalism) behind policy, but federalism is one of the ways that the Constitution institutionalized the decision-making process. To understand U.S. politics you must understand the role of the states—both how they are united and how they are fragmented under the Constitution. These readings help us understand how U.S. politics works by engaging us in the classic debates over who rules, and who should rule.

CHAPTER QUESTIONS

1) Does it matter what level of government makes the decision as long as the policies you prefer are adopted?
2) How should we determine the types of policies best left to the states versus the types best left to the national government?

CHAPTER READINGS

4.1) George Annas, "Jumping Frogs, Endangered Toads, and California's Medical-Marijuana Law," *New England Journal of Medicine*, November 2005.
4.2) "Could Gay Marriage, Guns and Marijuana Lead to a Fragmented United States of America?" *Governing*, June 2013.
4.3) Michael Powell, "Leery of Washington, Alaska Feasts on Its Dollars," *The New York Times*, August 18, 2010.

4.1) Jumping Frogs, Endangered Toads, and California's Medical-Marijuana Law

New England Journal of Medicine, November 2005

GEORGE ANNAS

When Congress acts to regulate commerce between the states, a conflicting state law is preempted by federal law. As you read "Jumping Frogs, Endangered Toads, and California's Medical-Marijuana Law," you will become confused about what falls under the national government's interstate commerce authority. Do not dismay. This is Annas's point: what falls under the national government's Interstate Commerce Clause authority has been interpreted inconsistently and changes over time. Thus, what falls under state versus national authority is not always clear and not always the same.

In the 1990s and early 2000s, the Supreme Court went through what many legal scholars termed a "Federalism Revolution" because the Court struck down a string of federal laws regulating state activities. While the Federalism Revolution is sometimes seen as delegating power back to the states, the reality is more complex. For example, as Annas discusses in this article, the Court struck down the 1990 Gun Free School Zones Act (which made it a federal crime to bring a gun in or around a school) because it exceeded Congress' commerce clause authority. This decision was heralded as a victory for state sovereignty. However, one aspect not discussed by Annas is that several states filed legal briefs asking the Court to uphold the Gun Free School Zones Act because the legislation assisted state law-enforcement efforts. If states asked for the congressional law to be upheld but the Court struck the law down, is this properly seen as a victory for state sovereignty? How do we determine what counts as a victory for state sovereignty? What counts as a victory for national sovereignty?

The stories that unfold in Annas's article (and continue to evolve beyond his writing) highlight two tensions inherent in federalism: (1) states will sometimes defy federal law, and (2) the Court cannot compel political actors to follow its judgment. The same year the Court struck down the Gun Free School Zones Act, Congress adopted a nearly identical law, adding a few words about prohibiting guns with any connection to interstate commerce. Thus, while the Court might have ruled in favor of state sovereignty, Congress did not let that limit its authority. Similarly, the Court's decision to uphold federal criminalization of marijuana has not prevented state action; several states have modified their marijuana laws in defiance of congressional law. Ultimately, this article shows questions about which level of government has the authority, and the process for how to resolve political controversies remain at the heart of American federalism.

Mark Twain wasn't thinking about federalism or the structure of American government when he wrote "The Celebrated Jumping Frog of Calaveras County."[1] Nonetheless, he would be amused to know that today, almost 150 years later, the Calaveras County Fair and Jumping Frog Jubilee not only has a jumping-frog contest but also has its own Frog Welfare Policy. The policy includes a provision for the "Care of Sick or Injured Frogs" and a limitation entitled "Frogs Not Permitted to Participate," which stipulates that "under no circumstances will a frog listed on the endangered species list be permitted to participate in the Frog Jump."[2] This fair, like medical practice, is subject to both state and federal laws. Care of the sick and injured (both frogs and people) is primarily viewed as a matter of state law, whereas protection of endangered species is primarily regulated by Congress under its authority to regulate interstate commerce.

Not to carry the analogy too far, but it is worth recalling that Twain's famous frog, Dan'l Webster, lost his one and only jumping contest because his stomach had been filled with quail shot by a competitor. The loaded-down frog just couldn't jump. Until the California medical-marijuana case, it seemed to many observers that the conservative Rehnquist Court had succeeded in filling the commerce clause with quail shot—and had effectively prevented the federal government from regulating state activities. In the medical-marijuana case, however, a new majority of justices took the lead out of the commerce clause so that the federal government could legitimately claim jurisdiction over just about any activity, including the practice of medicine. The role of the commerce clause in federalism and the implications of the Court's decision in the California medical-marijuana case for physicians are the subjects I explore in this article.

The Commerce Clause

The U.S. Constitution determines the areas over which the federal government has authority. All other areas remain, as they were before the adoption of the Constitution, under the authority of the individual states. Another way to say this is that the states retain all governmental authority they did not delegate to the federal government, including areas such as criminal law and family-law matters. These are part of the state's "police powers," usually defined as the state's sovereign authority to protect the health, safety, and welfare of its residents. Section 8 of Article I of the Constitution contains 18 clauses specifying delegated areas (including the military, currency, postal service, and patenting) over which "Congress shall have power," and these include the commerce clause—"to regulate commerce with foreign nations, and among the several states, and with the Indian tribes."

Until the Great Depression (and the disillusionment with unregulated markets), the Supreme Court took a narrow view of federal authority that could be derived from the commerce clause by ruling consistently that it gave Congress the authority only to regulate activities that directly involved the movement of commercial products (such as pharmaceuticals) from one state to another. Since then, and at least until 1995, the Court's interpretation seemed to be going in the opposite direction: Congress was consistently held to have authority in areas that had almost any relationship at all to commerce.

Guns in Schools and Violence against Women

Under modern commerce clause doctrine, Congress has authority to regulate in three broad categories of activities: the use of the channels of interstate commerce (e.g., roads, air corridors, and waterways); the instrumentalities of interstate commerce (e.g., trains, trucks, and planes) and persons and things in interstate commerce; and "activities having a substantial relation to interstate commerce."[3] The first two categories are easy ones in that they involve activities that cross state lines. The third category, which does not involve crossing a state line, is the controversial one. The interpretation question involves the meaning and application of the concept of "substantially affecting" interstate commerce.

In a 1937 case that the Court characterized as a "watershed case" it concluded that the real question was one of the degree of effect. Intrastate activities that "have such a close and substantial relation to interstate commerce that their control is essential or appropriate to protect that commerce from burdens and obstructions" are within the power of Congress to regulate.[4] Later, in what has become perhaps its best-known commerce-clause case, the Court held that Congress could enforce a statute that prohibited a farmer from growing wheat on his own farm even if the wheat was never sold but was used only for the farmer's personal consumption. The Court concluded that although one farmer's personal use of homegrown wheat may be trivial (and have no effect on commerce), "taken together with that of many others similarly situated," its effect on interstate commerce (and the market price of wheat) "is far from trivial."[5]

The 1995 case that seemed to presage a states' rights revolution (often referred to as "devolution") involved the federal Gun-Free School Zones Act of 1990, which made it a federal crime "for any individual knowingly to possess a firearm at a place that the individual knows, or has reasonable cause to believe, is a school zone."[3] In a 5-to-4 opinion, written by the late Chief Justice William Rehnquist, the Court held that the statute exceeded Congress's authority under the commerce clause and only the individual states had authority to criminalize the possession of guns in school.[3]

The federal government had argued (and the four justices in the minority agreed) that the costs of violent crime are spread out over the entire population and that the presence of guns in schools threatens "national productivity" by undermining the learning environment, which in turn decreases learning and leads to a less productive citizenry and thus a less productive national economy. The majority of the Court rejected these arguments primarily because they thought that accepting this line of reasoning would make it impossible to define "any limitations on federal power, even in areas such as criminal law enforcement or education where States historically have been sovereign."[3]

In 2000, in another 5-to-4 opinion written by Rehnquist, using the same rationale, the Court struck down a federal statute, part of the Violence against Women Act of 1994, that provided a federal civil remedy for victims of "gender-motivated violence." In the Court's words:

> Gender-motivated crimes of violence are not, in any sense of the phrase, economic activity. . . . Indeed, if Congress may regulate gender-motivated violence, it would be able to regulate murder or any other type of violence since gender-motivated violence, as a subset of all violent crime, is certain to have lesser economic impacts than the larger class of which it is a part.[6]

The Court, specifically addressing the question of federalism, concluded that "the Constitution requires a distinction between what is truly national and what is truly local. . . . Indeed, we can think of no better example of the police power, which the Founders denied to the National Government and reposed in the States, than the suppression of violent crime and vindication of its victims."[6]

Medical Marijuana in California

The next commerce-clause case involved physicians, albeit indirectly, and the role assigned to them in California in relation to the protection of patients who used physician-recommended marijuana from criminal prosecution. The question

before the Supreme Court in the recent medical-marijuana case (*Gonzalez v. Raich*) was this: Does the commerce clause give Congress the authority to outlaw the local cultivation and use of marijuana for medicine if such cultivation and use complies with the provisions of California law?[7]

The California law, which is similar to laws in at least nine other states, creates an exemption from criminal prosecution for physicians, patients, and primary caregivers who possess or cultivate marijuana for medicinal purposes on the recommendation of a physician. Two patients for whom marijuana had been recommended brought suit to challenge enforcement of the federal Controlled Substances Act after federal Drug Enforcement Administration agents seized and destroyed all six marijuana plants that one of them had been growing for her own medical use in compliance with the California law. The Ninth Circuit Court of Appeals ruled in the plaintiffs' favor, finding that the California law applied to a separate and distinct category of activity, "the intrastate, noncommercial cultivation and possession of cannabis for personal medical purposes as recommended by a patient's physician pursuant to valid California state law," as opposed to what it saw as the federal law's purpose, which was to prevent "drug trafficking."[8] In a 6-to-3 opinion, written by Justice John Paul Stevens, with Justice Rehnquist dissenting, the Court reversed the appeals court's opinion and decided that Congress, under the commerce clause, did have authority to enforce its prohibition against marijuana—even state-approved, homegrown, noncommercial marijuana, used only for medicinal purposes on a physician's recommendation.

The majority of the Court decided that the commerce clause gave Congress the same power to regulate homegrown marijuana for personal use that it had to regulate homegrown wheat.[6] The question was whether homegrown marijuana for personal medical consumption substantially affected interstate commerce (albeit illegal commerce) when all affected patients were taken together. The Court concluded that Congress "had a rational basis for concluding that leaving home-consumed marijuana outside federal control" would affect "price and market conditions."[7] The Court also distinguished the guns-in-school and gender-violence cases on the basis that regulation of drugs is "quintessentially economic" when economics is defined as the "production, distribution, and consumption of commodities."[7]

This left only one real question open: Is the fact that marijuana is to be used only for medicinal purposes on the advice of a physician, as the Ninth Circuit Court had decided, sufficient for an exception to be carved out of otherwise legitimate federal authority to control drugs? The Court decided it was not, for several reasons. The first was that Congress itself had determined that marijuana is a Schedule I drug, which it defined as having "no acceptable medical use." The Court acknowledged that Congress might be wrong in this determination, but the issue in this case was not whether marijuana had possible legitimate medical uses but whether Congress had the authority to make the judgment that it had none and to ban all uses of the drug. The dissenting justices argued that personal cultivation and use of marijuana should be beyond the authority of the commerce clause. The Court majority disagreed, stating that if it accepted the dissenting justices' argument, personal cultivation for recreational use would also be beyond congressional authority. This conclusion, the majority argued, could not be sustained:

> One need not have a degree in economics to understand why a nationwide exemption for the vast quantity of marijuana (or other drugs) locally cultivated for personal use (which presumably would include use by friends, neighbors, and family members) may have a substantial impact on the interstate market for this extraordinarily popular substance. The congressional judgment that an exemption for such a significant segment of the total market would undermine the orderly enforcement of the entire [drug] regulatory scheme is entitled to a strong presumption of validity.[7]

The other primary limit to the effect of the California law on interstate commerce is the requirement of a physician's recommendation on the basis of a medical determination that a patient has an "illness for which marijuana provides relief."

And the Court's discussion of this limit may be the most interesting, and disturbing, aspect of the case to physicians. Instead of concluding that physicians should be free to use their best medical judgment and that it was up to state medical boards to decide whether specific physicians were failing to live up to reasonable medical standards—as the Court did, for example, in its cases related to restrictive abortion laws[9]—the Court took a totally different approach. In the Court's words, the broad language of the California medical-marijuana law allows "even the most scrupulous doctor to conclude that some recreational uses would be therapeutic. And our cases have taught us that there are some unscrupulous physicians who overprescribe when it is sufficiently profitable to do so."[7]

The California law defines the category of patients who are exempt from criminal prosecution as those suffering from cancer, anorexia, AIDS, chronic pain, spasticity, glaucoma, arthritis, migraine, and "any other chronic or persistent medical symptom that substantially limits the ability of a person to conduct one or more major life activities . . . or if not alleviated may cause serious harm to the patient's safety or physical or mental health." These limits are hardly an invitation for recreational-use recommendations.[7] Regarding "unscrupulous physicians," the Court cited two cases that involve criminal prosecutions of physicians for acting like drug dealers, one from 1919 and the other from 1975, implying that because a few physicians might have been criminally inclined in the past, it was reasonable for Congress (and the Court), on the basis of no actual evidence, to assume that many physicians may be so inclined today. It was not only physicians that the Court found untrustworthy but sick patients and their caregivers as well:

> The exemption for cultivation by patients and caregivers [patients can possess up to 8 oz of dried marijuana and cultivate up to 6 mature or 12 immature plants] can only increase the supply of marijuana in the California market. The likelihood that all such production will promptly terminate when patients recover or will precisely match the patients' medical needs during their convalescence seems remote; whereas the danger

that excesses will satisfy some of the admittedly enormous demand for recreational use seems obvious.[7]

Justice Sandra Day O'Connor's dissent merits comment, because it is especially relevant to the practice of medicine. She argues that the Constitution requires the Court to protect "historic spheres of state sovereignty from excessive federal encroachment" and that one of the virtues of federalism is that it permits the individual states to serve as "laboratories," should they wish, to try "novel social and economic experiments without risk to the rest of the country." Specifically, she argues that the Court's new definition of economic activity is "breathtaking" in its scope, creating exactly what the gun case rejected—a federal police power. She also rejects reliance on the wheat case, noting that under the Agricultural Adjustment Act in question in that case, Congress had exempted the planting of less than 200 bushels (about six tons), and that when Roscoe Filburn, the farmer who challenged the federal statute, himself harvested his wheat, the statute exempted plantings of less than six acres.[5,7]

In O'Connor's words, the wheat case "did not extend Commerce Clause authority to something as modest as the home cook's herb garden."[8] O'Connor is not saying that Congress cannot regulate small quantities of a product produced for personal use, only that the wheat case "did not hold or imply that small-scale production of commodities is always economic, and automatically within Congress' reach." As to potential "exploitation [of the act] by unscrupulous physicians" and patients, O'Connor finds no factual support for this assertion and rejects the conclusion that simply by "piling assertion upon assertion" one can make a case for meeting the "substantiality test" of the guns-in-school and gender-violence cases.[7]

It is important to note that the Court was not taking a position on whether Congress was correct to place marijuana in Schedule I or a position against California's law, any more than it was taking a position in favor of guns in schools or violence against women in the earlier cases. Instead, the Court was ruling only on the question of federal authority under the commerce clause. The Court noted, for example, that California and its supporters may one day prevail by pursuing the democratic process "in the halls of Congress."[7] This seems extremely unlikely. More important is the question not addressed in this case—whether suffering patients have a substantive due-process claim to access to drugs needed to prevent suffering or a valid medical-necessity defense should they be prosecuted for using medical marijuana on a physician's recommendation.[10] Also not addressed was the question that will be decided during the coming year: whether Congress has delegated to the U.S. attorney general its authority to decide what a "legitimate medical use" of an approved drug is in the context of Oregon's law governing physician-assisted suicide.[11,12] What is obvious from this case, however, is that Congress has the authority, under the commerce clause, to regulate both legal and illegal drugs whether or not the drugs in question actually cross state lines. It would also seem reasonable to conclude that Congress has the authority to limit the uses of approved drugs.

Federalism and Endangered Species

Because *Gonzales v. Raich* is a drug case, and because it specifically involves marijuana, the Court's final word on federalism may not yet be in. Whether the "states' rights" movement has any life left after medical marijuana may be determined in the context of the Endangered Species Act. Two U.S. Circuit Courts of Appeals, for example, have recently upheld application of the federal law to protect endangered species that, unlike the descendants of Mark Twain's jumping frog, have no commercial value. Even though the Supreme Court refused to hear appeals from both of the lower courts, the cases help us understand the contemporary reach of congressional power under the commerce clause. One case involves the protection of six tiny creatures that live in caves (the "Cave Species")—three arthropods, a spider, and two beetles—from a commercial developer. The Fifth Circuit Court of Appeals noted that the Cave Species are not themselves an object of economics or commerce, saying: "There is no market for them;

any future market is conjecture. If the speculative future medicinal benefits from the Cave Species makes their regulation commercial, then almost anything would be. . . . There is no historic trade in the Cave Species, nor do tourists come to Texas to view them."[13] Nonetheless, the court concluded that Congress had the authority, under the commerce clause, to view life as an "interdependent web" of all species; that destruction of endangered species can be aggregated, like homegrown wheat; and that the destruction of multiple species has a substantial effect on interstate commerce.[13]

The other case, from the District of Columbia Court of Appeals, involves the arroyo southwestern toad, whose habitat was threatened by a real-estate developer. In upholding the application of the Endangered Species Act to the case, the appeals court held that the commercial activity being regulated was the housing development itself, as well as the "taking" of the toad by the planned commercial development. The court noted that the "company would like us to consider its challenge to the ESA [Endangered Species Act] only as applied to the arroyo toad, which it says has no 'known commercial value'— unlike, for example, Mark Twain's celebrated jumping frogs [sic] of Calaveras County."[14] Instead, the court concluded that application of the Endangered Species Act, far from eroding states' rights, is consistent with "the historic power of the federal government to preserve scarce resources in one locality for the future benefit of all Americans."[14]

On a request for a hearing by the entire appeals court, which was rejected, recently named Chief Justice John Roberts—who at the time was a member of the appeals court —wrote a dissent that was not unlike Justice O'Connor's dissent in the marijuana case. In it he argued that the court's conclusion seemed inconsistent with the guns-in-school and gender-violence cases and that there were real problems with using an analysis of the commerce clause to regulate "the taking of a hapless toad that, for reasons of its own, lives its entire life in California."[15] The case has since been settled. The development is going ahead in a way that protects the toad's habitat.[16]

The Future of the Commerce Clause

Twain's short story has been termed "a living American fairy tale, acted out annually in Calaveras County."[1] In what might be termed a living American government tale, nominees to the Supreme Court are routinely asked to explain their judicial philosophy of constitutional and statutory interpretation to the Senate Judiciary Committee. Asked about his "hapless toad" opinion during the Senate confirmation hearings on his nomination to replace Rehnquist as chief justice, Roberts said: "The whole point of my argument in the dissent was that there was another way to look at this [i.e., the approach taken by the Fifth Circuit Court in the Cave Species case]. . . . I did not say that even in this case that the decision was wrong. . . . I simply said, let's look at those other grounds for decision because that doesn't present this problem." These hearings provide an opportunity for all Americans to review their understanding of our constitutional government and the manner in which it allocates power between the federal government and the 50 states. To the extent that this division of power is determined by the Court's view of the commerce clause, a return to an expansive reading of this clause seems both likely and, given the interdependence of the national and global economies, proper.

Of course, the fact that Congress has authority over a particular subject—such as whether to adopt a system of national licensure for physicians—does not mean that its authority is unlimited or even that Congress will use it. Rather, as Justice Stevens noted, cases such as the California medical-marijuana case lead to other central constitutional questions, as yet unresolved. These questions include whether patients, terminally ill or not, have a constitutional right not to suffer—at least, when their physicians know how to control their pain.[12]

NOTES

1. Charles Neider, ed. *The complete short stories of Mark Twain*. New York: Hanover House, 1957:1–6.

2. 39th District Agricultural Association. Animal welfare policy (Calaveras County Fair and Jumping Frog Jubilee). April 2003. (Accessed November 3, 2005, at http://www.frogtown.org.)

3. *U.S. v. Lopez*, 514 U.S. 549 (1995).

4. *NLRB v. Jones & Laughlin Steel Corp.*, 301 U.S. 1 (1937).

5. *Wickard v. Filburn*, 317 U.S. 111 (1942).

6. *U.S. v. Morrison*, 529 U.S. 598 (2000).

7. *Gonzales v. Raich*, 125 S.Ct. 2195 (2005).

8. *Raich v. Ashcroft*, 3352 F.3d 1222 (9th Cir. 2003).

9. Annas GJ, Glantz LH, Mariner WK. The right of privacy protects the doctor-patient relationship. *JAMA* 1990;263:858–61.

10. Annas GJ. Reefer madness—the federal response to California's medical-marijuana law. *N Engl J Med* 1997;337:435–9.

11. *Oregon v. Ashcroft*, 368 F.3d 1118 (2004).

12. Annas GJ. The bell tolls for a constitutional right to physician-assisted suicide. *N Engl J Med* 1997;337:1098–103.

13. *GDF Realty v. Norton*, 326 F.3d 622 (5th Cir. 2003).

14. *Rancho Viejo v. Norton*, 323 F.3d 1062 (D.C. Cir. 2003).

15. *Rancho Viejo v. Norton*, 357 F.3d 1158 (D.C. Cir. 2003).

16. Cummings J. Environmentalists uncertain on Roberts. *The Wall Street Journal*. August 15, 2005:A3.

ARTICLE QUESTIONS

1) Based on the information in the article, why is it important to determine if an activity is related to interstate commerce?

2) Describe *Gonzales v. Raich*. How did the case turn out? Did the state or national government ultimately have the power?

3) What was the Court's logic in overturning congressional laws banning guns in schools and the Violence against Women Act? Do you agree with the Court's argument? Why?

4) Describe the "Cave Species" cases and why two appellate courts ruled that the Interstate Commerce Clause allowed the federal government to protect endangered species.

4.2) Could Gay Marriage, Guns and Marijuana Lead to a Fragmented United States of America?

Governing, June 2013

The policies one experiences depends greatly upon which one of the states one finds themselves. In some parts of Alaska you can use food stamps to buy hunting and fishing equipment (such as nets, hooks, fishing line, harpoons, and knives), but this is not permitted in New York. In Alabama food is taxed; in California it is not. In Mississippi you can drive while drinking alcohol (as long as you are not over the legal blood-alcohol content limit of 0.08%). In Nevada, tied elections are resolved by going to a casino and playing high-card draw, and the state, unlike most others, also allows prostitution and gambling. However, on other issues, there is uniform national policy. Nevada cannot opt out of war if the federal government decides to engage in an armed conflict; all states are either at war or not. And since June 2015, no state may deny same sex couples the right to marry.

An increasing diversity among states on hot-button social issues is the focus of the *Governing* article "Could Gay Marriage, Guns and Marijuana Lead to a Fragmented United States of America?" (written before the Supreme Court guaranteed the right of all Americans to marry in *Obergefell v. Hodges*, June 2015). As is consistent with *Governing*'s focus on state and local government, it concludes that "if you want to change policy, look to the states . . . because that is where the action is." Yet, *Governing* sees a potential dark side to the "industrial efficiency" at which states are able to pass legislation. The article argues that states are adopting policies in opposition to national policy and in conflict with one another. Indeed, policies are becoming so divergent that we might be "returning to our roots as a loose confederation of culturally and geographically distinct governments." The Supreme Court decision on same sex marriage (which came after this article was published) only accentuates the article's points: that policy innovation lies in the states and that life and politics are very different in the different states—at least until the Supreme Court finds that some state innovations have uncovered a Constitutional right (like the right to marry) and ensures that right for all Americans regardless of the state they live in.

Less than five months after the massacre at Sandy Hook Elementary School, Connecticut enacted comprehensive gun control legislation. At the same time, 1,300 miles south and an ideological world away, Mississippi lawmakers considered a bill that would explicitly prohibit state officials from enforcing any new federal gun regulations. That last measure proved unnecessary. After months of controversy and extensive debate, Congress did not muster the votes to pass any federal law at all.

The same kind of split prevails on gay marriage. Last year, North Carolina joined more than 30 other states that have explicitly outlawed same-sex marriage. In just the past three months, Rhode Island, Delaware and Minnesota have legalized it, joining nine other states and the District of Columbia. The Supreme Court is currently deciding how far to wade into the gay marriage dispute—or whether it should wade in at all.

A third case: Voters in Colorado and Washington state chose to fully legalize marijuana in last November's election. On the same day, voters in Arkansas handily defeated a proposal to allow the drug even for medicinal purposes. The use of marijuana remains illegal under federal law; the Obama administration hasn't taken a position on last fall's actions but has made it clear that federal regulations will not be enforced.

This is more than just party polarization. It is part of a tectonic shift away from federal authority and toward power in the states. While the divided Congresses that have followed the 2010 Tea Party insurgency have been among the least productive in U.S. history, rife with partisan bickering and a chronic inability to compromise, robust action is common at the state level. Connecticut's quick and seamless movement from tragedy to statute is one of countless examples. In turn, ideologues and interest groups increasingly view states as the most promising venues for policymaking. Why waste your time in Washington—where you might pass a watered-down, largely impotent bill if you're lucky—when you can head to Austin or Sacramento and advance your agenda intact and with relative ease?

And while states pass legislation with an almost industrial efficiency, America, as is often noted these days, is becoming a more and more splintered nation. Red states are redder; blue states are bluer.

Take a look at a U.S. map colored by state party control. In the upper right-hand corner down to the Mid-Atlantic, it's all blue. In the South and across the Great Plains, you see a blanket of red. That crimson sea begins to break at the Rocky Mountains until you reach a stretch of blue along the West Coast. In a way, we are returning to our roots as a loose confederation of culturally and geographically distinct governments.

States led by Democrats are moving toward broader Medicaid coverage, stricter gun laws and a liberalized drug policy. They've legalized gay marriage, abolished the death penalty and extended new rights to undocumented immigrants. Republican strongholds are working quickly to remove government from the business sphere—reducing taxes, pushing anti-union right-to-work laws and rebelling against the Affordable Care Act (ACA). They're also pressing forward on some of their most valued social issues, promoting pro-life abortion policies and protecting the rights of gun owners.

The divisions generate fundamental questions about the nature of federalism. The sweeping national interventions of the New Deal and the comprehensive federal social legislation of the 1960s have been replaced by a more decentralized approach to governance. States are openly defying federal law and resurrecting the concept of nullification.

These are not merely legal or rhetorical exercises. They are fostering real change and real consequences for average Americans. If one bill that's currently pending in the Mississippi legislature is upheld by higher courts, the state will have effectively outlawed abortion altogether. In New York, meanwhile, Gov. Andrew Cuomo has introduced legislation that would make abortions easier for women in his state to obtain. Income taxes may go up this year in California and Massachusetts; several Republican governors say they want to abolish income taxes completely. Illinois will insure nearly 1 million additional people next year by expanding its Medicaid program under the federal health law, while Texas is expected to leave up to 2 million people without coverage because Gov. Rick Perry has steadfastly refused to do the same.

"Polarization has resulted in this changing relationship between the states and the federal government. There's a clear connection," says Alan Abramowitz, a political scientist at Emory University. "It's leading to gridlock at the federal level, which in turn is leading to many issues being decided at the state level because the federal government seems to be incapable of deciding anything."

"That's the hydraulics of political power. Power always seeks an outlet," agrees Heather Gerken, a law professor at Yale University. "When Congress is no longer doing anything, people are going to go to the states and localities."

This rebalancing of the federalist system has permeated almost every corner of public policy, taking center stage in the most controversial debates of the last few years. Last summer, Chief Justice John Roberts made the unexpected decision to join with his liberal colleagues and uphold the bulk of Obamacare and its individual mandate to purchase health insurance. But on the less publicized question of the law's Medicaid expansion, which was supposed to require states to extend eligibility for the program to those earning up to 138 percent of the federal poverty level, Roberts took a startling turn. He ruled, for the first time in the court's history, that the federal government had gone beyond its constitutional powers when it threatened to withhold all of a state's federal Medicaid funding if it refused to comply with the expansion.

The immediate implication was a dramatic reassertion of individual states' sovereignty. In the year since the court's decision, a Southern wall of conservative states, which fought against the ACA in the first place and have been encouraged by national Republican leaders, have decided to take this new option that Roberts legitimized and have refused to expand Medicaid.

On other issues, states have rebuffed federal policy or preempted it. The Real ID Act of 2005, mandating state adoption of what is effectively a national identification card, has been foiled in the last decade by states refusing to comply with its federal requirements. More than 40 states have agreed to adopt the Common Core State Standards for K-12 education, which involve new curricula and assessments developed by state policymakers, in part because they didn't want another federal education regime after the failure of No Child Left Behind. The distribution of medical marijuana in 17 states, paired with outright legalization in Colorado and Washington, is a clear flouting of the federal Controlled Substances Act.

Such assertiveness or outright defiance by the states is a dramatic shift from the assumptions of federal preeminence that have prevailed during most of the years since the enactment of comprehensive social legislation during the 1960s, which included the passage of the Civil Rights Act, the Voting Rights Act and Medicare. Some would place the beginning of the erosion of the federal model in the Reagan administration, which introduced the waiver concept to state-federal programs such as Medicaid.

But it is also a reflection of changing public opinion: The Pew Research Center found this April that people's trust in state and local government had settled comfortably above 50 percent. Trust in the federal government, meanwhile, sat at a dismal 28 percent in 2012. That's a far cry from the early 1960s, when public confidence in Washington approached 80 percent.

"People had lost confidence that states were really up to the task of dealing with problems of modern society, so the federal government filled that vacuum," says Ernest Young, a constitutional law scholar at Duke University. "We're living in a new era now where the opposite is true. People have more trust in their state and local governments than the federal government."

Coinciding with this movement toward more state-centric governance has been the ideological polarization of the two political parties. Conservative Southern Democrats and moderate Northeast Republicans have slowly disappeared both from Congress and from state legislatures in the last generation. The Democratic Party is more uniformly liberal, and the Republican Party more uniformly conservative, than either has ever been. They therefore command certain regions of the country more consistently; the turnover of conservative Southerners to the Republican Party has turned the Deep South impenetrably red. Republicans have become a weak minority in much of the Northeast and West Coast.

This natural political sorting has led to two very different outcomes. With the GOP controlling the U.S. House and the Democrats controlling the Senate and the White House, productivity in Washington is at a historic low. Multiple analyses

ranked the 112th Congress, which met in 2011 and 2012, at or near the bottom in terms of legislation passed and signed by the president. There was some optimism that the 113th Congress would see an uptick in action, due to the supposed mandates of the 2012 presidential election, but there is little to support that thesis so far.

While Capitol Hill trudges through political molasses, the states are as prolific as they have ever been—and the primary reason is the prevalence of single-party rule in the nation's statehouses. One party or the other is in full charge of both chambers of the legislative branch in 43 states. This is the highest concentration of partisan power since the 1940s. Half the legislatures have veto-proof supermajorities.

So when anti-abortion advocates want to roll back *Roe v. Wade*, they turn to conservative-controlled states. Arkansas and North Dakota are two of the most recent single-party legislatures to pass abortion restrictions, outlawing abortions after 12 and six weeks of pregnancy, respectively. Arkansas' Republican senate and house passed this legislation over the veto of Democratic Gov. Mike Beebe, one of only two Democratic governors left in the South.

On the other end of the spectrum, California, tired of waiting for federal action on climate change, established its own cap-and-trade system last year; the nation's largest and arguably most liberal state had little trouble charting its own course on legislation that's essentially been a pipe dream in Washington since the 2010 midterms.

Individual states or coalitions of states can increasingly be viewed as proxies for what their ruling party's elites would like to accomplish at the national level, but currently cannot. Take Washington state as the liberal example. The Democratic legislature and governor have legalized gay marriage, taken an active role in implementing Obamacare and begun work this year to meet the goal of reducing the state's greenhouse gas emissions to 1990 levels by 2020.

Conservative counterparts are plentiful: Texas has become the flagship opponent of the federal health law, leading a coalition that includes nearly every state below the Mason-Dixon Line. Its legislature voted to defund Planned Parenthood because of its ties to abortion providers. Kansas, Nebraska and Louisiana have weighed the elimination of their state income taxes this year. Republicans in Indiana and Michigan last year joined the anti-union right-to-work movement that conservatives have been promoting since the 1940s. At least 10 GOP-controlled states have passed laws this year loosening their gun regulations.

"As the parties become more distinct from each other, they're generating a lot of ideas. They've become very programmatic parties, and they've been doing a lot of policy implementation in the states," says Seth Masket, a political scientist at the University of Denver. "If you want to change the ways things are, you're almost invariably going to be frustrated at the federal level. If you're going to get anything done, a unified state government is the place to do it."

So where are we headed? Is this movement toward decentralization and polarization a momentary lapse in what once seemed an unavoidable march toward federal control? Or are we seeing a permanent revival of the 10th Amendment to the U.S. Constitution, under which most governmental power is reserved to the states and regional fracture is assumed to be the norm?

There is a good deal of evidence to suggest that political polarization across states and regions will solidify. One argument is that people seem to be choosing, consciously or unconsciously, to live in communities that share their ideological beliefs. This is known in sociological circles as "sorting." It offers a powerful explanation for the growing homogeneity within states and regions, and some statistical analysis backs the theory.

In 1976, 26 percent of Americans lived in "landslide counties," defined as those that voted for one presidential candidate by at least a 20-percentage-point margin over the other, according to an analysis by social commentator Bill Bishop and University of Texas sociologist Robert Cushing. By 2012, that number doubled to 52 percent. In the 1976 election, 20 states were decided by five percentage points or less in the race between Jimmy Carter and Gerald Ford; only four were that close in 2012 with Barack Obama and Mitt Romney on the ballot.

Some doubt the sorting thesis, both as a reason for polarization and as a predictor of future trends. They instead attribute the widening political gap to simple ideological reshuffling—conservatives coalescing in the Republican Party, and liberals on the Democratic side. Gerrymandering is sometimes blamed for appearing to sort like-minded people into the same jurisdictions.

Several variables could determine whether this movement persists in the coming years. In particular, the dispersion of Hispanics and other minority populations into new communities where they haven't historically lived could upset the political balance in those places. The Democratic goal of turning Texas blue within the next two decades is the most noteworthy endorsement of this belief. Or perhaps the millennial generation won't remain as thoroughly liberal as it seems to be right now.

But many prominent thinkers give credence to the sorting thesis, and if it does hold some truth, then ideological and geographic divisions should harden in the coming decades. New England would continue on its path toward liberalized social democracy; the South would move further toward laissez-faire or libertarian capitalism.

If the sorting rule bears out, and states and regions continue to drift further and further apart on public policy, people might increasingly decide where to live based on these differences. That would create a self-perpetuating cycle that would continue to decentralize political power and destabilize our concept of a national identity.

"The trouble is within these places, there's less diversity where you live, but there's more diversity from place to place. As a result, there's less of a sense of a country as a whole," says social commentator Bishop, who drew national attention to the idea in his 2008 book, "The Big Sort: Why the Clustering of Like-Minded America Is Tearing Us Apart." "So you have this phenomenon where like-minded people get together and they become more extreme in the way they're like-minded."

In this future as a sectarian nation, which some say has already arrived, states emerge as the best forum for meaningful policymaking. The federal government will always have a dominant role on some subjects—foreign relations and international trade being the most obvious—but as long as Washington is politically divided, the number of issues on which it can effectively act is likely to shrink.

"When states become very homogeneous inside, and more heterogeneous across state lines," says Michael Greve, a law professor at George Mason University and director of the Federalism Project at the American Enterprise Institute, "it becomes much, much harder to write federal legislation that wraps all of them under one federal cartel."

The Affordable Care Act, which might stand as the last significant legislative achievement of a single-party Congress and White House for the foreseeable future, has become a testament to how difficult it is to institute national initiatives when some states actively resist federal prescriptions.

The refusal of conservative states to expand Medicaid has undercut the law's ability to insure low-income Americans. More than 30 states have refused to set up health-care marketplaces, which has left the Obama administration scrambling to pick up the slack. Questions are mounting about what will happen in these conservative states in 2014, when the law's major changes are supposed to take effect. On the other hand, the liberal states that have embraced the law's policies will fundamentally overhaul their insurance markets next year, as was originally intended. But the law's goal of universal health coverage will be stifled by the dissenting states.

Supporters of a revised immigration law remain hopeful for federal action during the 113th Congress. But the resulting legislation, if it passes, will likely be an undesirable compromise for both parties, a vanilla law that really pleases no one. If you want ideological purity, look a few miles away to Democratic Maryland, where Gov. Martin O'Malley and his legislature have in the past year legalized gay marriage, cracked down on guns, passed a DREAM Act that eases access to education for undocumented immigrants and eliminated the death penalty. Or go to Republican Mississippi, where the Second Amendment is sacrosanct, abortion is being made extremely difficult and residents have one of the lowest tax burdens in the nation. It's still possible to achieve philosophical cohesion within a single-party state, and there are more of them than ever. If you want to change policy, look to the states. That's where the action is these days.

ARTICLE QUESTIONS

1) What are some examples of divergent state laws given in the article?
2) Why does the article argue that people are seeing states as the most promising venues for policymaking?
3) Explain the term "sorting" as described in the article. What evidence does the article provide that sorting is occurring?
4) Do you agree with the article that there is a "tectonic shift away from federal authority"? If such a shift is occurring, is it a cause for concern?

4.3) Leery of Washington, Alaska Feasts on Its Dollars

The New York Times, August 18, 2010

MICHAEL POWELL

Michael Powell's *New York Times* article, "Leery of Washington, Alaska Feasts on Its Dollars," provides two important examples of U.S. federalism in action. Implicit in the article is the reality that the federal government does not treat all states the same; Alaska gets significantly more in federal government funds than other states. This diversity of federal funding results from the diversity of federal programs throughout the states. For example, not all states need a bridge or make a good location for a military base, but the ones that do receive federal dollars not provided to neighboring states. Powell also discusses the national government's use of "fiscal federalism"—using monetary incentives to influence state and local policies. Two classic examples of fiscal federalism are the national government's reducing highway funding for any state with (a) speed limits in excess of 55 miles per hour (in the 1980s) and (b) a drinking age below 21. In both of these cases states could select the policies of their choice, but if they violated the federal policy they sacrificed part of the federally provided highway funding.

Powell's focus on fiscal federalism emphasizes a seeming contradiction: Some Alaskan lawmakers gladly accept federal money while complaining about the federal government. In what Powell terms "cognitive dissonance" he notes that many Alaskans identify "pork-barrel" spending by the federal government as a problem, but few Alaskans identify the benefits they receive from the spending. As you read Powell's article, think about whether you see it as a contradiction for Alaska (and other states) to take federal funds while complaining about the federal government and the requirements placed on the federal funds.

PALMER, Alaska—Backed by a blue row of saw-toothed mountain peaks, the Republican state lawmaker Carl Gatto finds himself on a fine roll.

Roll it back, he says, roll back this entire socialistic experiment in federal hegemony. Give us control of our land, let us drill and mine, and please don't let a few belugas get in the way of a perfectly good bridge.

"I've introduced legislation to roll back the federal government," he says. "They don't have solutions; they just have taxes."

And what of the federal stimulus, from which Alaska receives the most money per capita in the nation? Would he reject it?

Mr. Gatto, 72 and wiry, smiles and shakes his head: "I'll give the federal government credit: they sure give us a ton of money. For every $1 we give them in taxes for highways, they give us back $5.76."

He points to a new federally financed highway, stretching toward distant spruce trees. "Man, beautiful, right?"

Alaskans tend to live with their contradictions in these recessionary times. No place benefits more from federal largess than this state, where the Republican governor decries "intrusive" federal policies, officials sue to overturn the health care legislation and Senator Lisa Murkowski, a Republican, voted against the stimulus bill.

Although its unemployment rate sits at just 7.9 percent, about two percentage points below the national rate, Alaska has received $3,145 per capita in federal stimulus dollars, the most in the nation, according to figures compiled by Pro Publica, an investigative Web site. Nevada, by contrast, has an unemployment rate north of 14 percent and has received $1,034 per capita in recovery aid. Florida's jobless rate is 11.4 percent, and the state has obtained $914 per capita.

Alaska has budget woes, and, more perilously, oil production is slumping. But its problems are not mortal; the ax falls on new police headquarters and replacement Zamboni blades rather than on teachers and libraries. The state avoided the unemployment devastation visited on the Lower 48 in part because federal dollars support a third of Alaskan jobs, according to a university study.

Not that this has assuaged antigovernment rancor. The Alaskan Representative Don Young, a Republican, denounced the stimulus as appalling, done under the cover of night and without full disclosure. He also promised Alaskans that "if there are earmarks, we will have our fingerprints on them."

(Curiously, that pattern plays out in Louisiana, Wyoming and the Dakotas, states relatively low in unemployment but high in per capita stimulus aid and growling antigovernment animus.)

Sitting in valleys rimmed by mountains, glaciers and a vast alluvial delta, Matanuska-Susitna Borough, with its 83,000 residents, is a sub-Arctic suburb of Anchorage. Its largest city, Wasilla, is home to Sarah Palin. A year ago, while still governor, she took a stab at rejecting $28.6 million in federal stimulus for weatherization. As Alaska incurs a notable winter, Republican and Democratic state legislators overruled her and accepted the money.

Matanuska-Susitna Borough officials received about $111 million in federal stimulus, according to Pro Publica. There was $28 million for schools and $900,000 for a park-and-ride lot for commuters heading to Anchorage

(Wasillans have a practiced eye for federal dollars; when Ms. Palin was mayor, she hired a lobbying firm that reeled in $25 million in federal earmarks for a city of fewer than 7,000 residents.)

Fairbanks, Alaska's second-biggest city behind Anchorage, pulled in more than $4,000 per capita in stimulus aid. But Jay Ramras, its Republican state representative, who is running for lieutenant governor, says he feels a tug of suspicion as he looks at that cash.

"If you want to feed us federal money like it's a narcotic and make the state into a junkie of the U.S. Treasury, O.K.," he allows. "But we would like to be an Emersonian Alaska and just get control of our resources."

Here is the cognitive dissonance. More and more Alaskans, particularly of the Republican stripe, identify the federal government and pork-barrel spending as the enemy, although Alaska was built by both.

Alaska's appetite for federal dollars has always been voracious and is not confined to the stimulus. A study by Prof. Scott Goldsmith of the University of Alaska, Anchorage, noted that an "extraordinary increase" in federal spending drove the state's pile-driver growth of the last 15 years.

In 1996, federal spending in Alaska was 38 percent above the national average. Thanks to the late Republican Senator Ted Stevens, who was Senate appropriations chief for several years, and to the military, which keeps expanding its bases here, Alaska's share now is 71 percent higher than the national average.

Some of this owes to the expense of serving Alaska's rural reaches. But much is bred in the bone. The federal government carved this young state out of the northern wilderness, and officials here learn to manipulate federal budget levers at a tender age.

Still, many see strings attached. Lynn Gattis, a Republican Party official, lives by a lake in Wasilla, surrounded by aspens. She is a sourdough Alaskan, meaning she was born here, and she is a pilot, which means she threads her way around those cloud-hugging peaks. She knows that the federal government paid for the port of Anchorage and the highway that leads to Wasilla allowed Target and Sports Authority to take root.

But she sees a government that delays oil exploration, as President Obama did recently; that regulates timber and salmon harvests and hydropower; and that, in her view, cares more about polar bears than about Alaskans. (The government lists as endangered the beluga whales of Cook Inlet, a vast gray expanse that stretches out from Anchorage. Some Alaskans argue that this could stall construction of a multimillion-dollar bridge, which as it happens would be paid for by the federal government.)

"It just feels like the federal government intrudes everywhere," Ms. Gattis said. "Enough Ivy League lawyers—let's get people who can dig a mine and run a business."

This sentiment baffles Tony Knowles, a long drink of a man who worked on the North Slope oil rigs before becoming the governor of Alaska in 1994 as a Democrat. He understands the frustration that comes with bumping into federal officials at each turn. But the trade-off is not so terrible, he notes, such as having the feds pay to put broadband in Alaskan villages.

"Nobody likes to have all their eggs in one basket, and so you do feel vulnerable," he said. "But Ted Stevens, who was a Republican and beloved, was never shy about bringing money in."

Some Alaskans have made a founding narrative of their grievance. "Before statehood, when a distant federal bureaucracy managed our resources, Alaskans experienced devastating economic effects," Gov. Sean Parnell, a Republican, says on his Web site.

The historical record is a bit more complicated. Federal dollars, fishing and timber sustained Alaska until the discovery of oil in the 1960s. Victor Fischer, who helped write the state constitution in the 1950s, shrugs.

"There's all this verbiage that says we're the frontier, rough and ready," says Mr. Fischer, lithe and sardonic in his mid-80s. "The Feds paid for everything, but the conflict runs through our history."

Unemployment rose as the great recession blew through, although state residents still pay no sales or income tax. As an editorial in *The Anchorage Daily News* noted, Alaskans pride themselves on a libertarian ethos but the state makes so much money from the oil companies that it sends every man, woman and child a dividend check each autumn. The check this year will be about $1,300.

Still, uneasiness is palpable here, and perhaps it accounts for the political anger in the air. Oil production, the state's lifeblood, is winding down. Nonstimulus federal dollars have slowed, too.

All of which tends to reinforce that Alaska remains much as it was 50 years ago, dependent on drilling, mining and federal aid. The sense of history repeating itself is disquieting.

When Professor Goldsmith looks out his window, he sees more buildings than in the past. But the landscape—the snow-capped volcanoes and waters of Cook Inlet—is overpowering.

"Californians wait for a new entrepreneurial wave to lift them," Mr. Goldsmith says. "For us, the traditional extraction economy still rules."

That is why, he adds, "historically, we take whatever largess comes our way. A federal dollar is a good dollar."

ARTICLE QUESTIONS

1) How much money, according to the article, does Alaska get in return for every dollar Alaskan residents pay in federal highway tax?

2) What are some of the specific programs that, according to Powell, the federal government has paid for in Alaska?

3) Do you agree it creates "cognitive dissonance" for Alaskan officials to complain about the federal government while receiving significant funding from the federal government?

Chapter 5

Civil Liberties

Does freedom of religion allow a city government to open its council meetings with Christian prayers? Does freedom of speech shield protestors from lawsuits even when they disrupt a private funeral? When someone is arrested, can his or her cell phone be searched without a warrant? Does the death penalty violate the Eighth Amendment's prohibition of cruel and unusual punishment? The best answer to all these questions: "it depends." The context and the extenuating circumstances make a big difference.

One of the struggles in any society is balancing the rights of individuals against the rights and safety of the community. Often, civil rights and civil liberties demand opposite commitments from government. Civil rights *require government action* to secure individual rights; however, civil liberties *restrict government action* to protect individual rights. When governments enforce civil rights for some people, it can mean limiting the liberty of others. In some instances, as with the examples in the opening of this chapter, protecting one type of liberty may come at the expense of the other people's rights.

The struggle to find the limits to individual liberties is most complex when we make competing claims to civil liberties or civil rights. In all of the readings in this chapter, one type of liberty conflicts with a different type of right. The first two readings relate to two of the five liberties protected in the First Amendment: freedom of religion and freedom of speech. In "Freedom for Religion, Not From It" Jonathan Tobin analyzes the 2014 Supreme Court decision in *Town of Greece v. Galloway*. This case reviewed the First Amendment's establishment clause, which prohibits government from making laws establishing religion. What does it mean to "establish" a religion? The specific question presented to the Court in this case: did the town of Greece, NY, violate the establishment clause by continually opening its monthly town council meetings with only Christian prayers? Two citizens of the town, one an atheist and the other a Jew, felt their rights were violated by having to listen to denominational prayers at every council meeting. The council and many Christian members of the community felt they had a right to open the meetings with prayer. The 5-to-4 split of the Supreme Court in this case underscores the lack of agreement over what the establishment clause prohibits.

The second reading looks at another confrontational Supreme Court case addressing the First Amendment, this time over demarcating the limits to freedom of speech. Nina Totenberg, reporting for *National Public Radio* in October 2010, provides a summary of the oral argument in the Supreme Court case of *Snyder v. Phelps*. This case concerns whether First Amendment free-speech protections extend to outrageous and offensive speech even if that speech could inflict emotional harm. In this case, a father's burial of his son is marred by fanatical religious protestors. During the oral argument in *Snyder*, the justices struggled to simultaneously protect the liberties of the protestors and the rights of the father.

The next reading consists of excerpts from the Supreme Court's ruling in the case of *Riley v. California* (2014), where the justices had to interpret the limits of Fourth Amendment's protection against unreasonable searches. As you might expect, defining "unreasonable" can make interpreting the Fourth Amendment highly contestable. Adding to the interpretive challenge was the Court's need to determine what guidance the Fourth Amendment (ratified in 1791, before household electricity) provides regarding the legality of cell phone searches of an arrestee. In the decision, the Supreme Court noted that providing broad Fourth Amendment privacy protections for someone's cell phone can have repercussions for the ability of the police to protect victims of crime. How should a community's need for crime prevention be balanced against an individual's right to privacy?

The last reading in the chapter comes from an article in *The Economist* examining the declining use of the death penalty in the United States. The use of the death penalty can pit the interests of crime victims against the interests of those convicted of crimes. Numerous provisions in the Constitution protect the rights of the accused, but for various reasons, people are still wrongly convicted. As the article "The Slow Death of the Death Penalty" notes, one of the arguments against the death penalty is the fact that "since 1973, 144 death-row inmates have been exonerated." This shows that without additional appeals people who were later exonerated would have been executed. The article highlights the main theme of the chapter by illustrating how protecting the rights of those accused of crimes can sometimes pull against protecting the rights of those victimized in crimes.

The Declaration of Independence asserts that governments are created to protect rights; however, the document never explains how competing rights claims should be balanced. This balance represents the eternal dilemma of civil liberties and is one of the most important issues facing American democracy. While the readings in this chapter can explain how some recent controversies have been settled for now, the readings cannot tell us what will or should happen in the future. The very fact that these issues have been the subject of recent decisions shows us how much in flux the demarcations of liberties remain.

CHAPTER QUESTIONS

1) What are civil liberties?
2) Are some liberties more important than others?
3) How should competing rights be balanced?
4) Which liberties should receive stronger protections than they do now? Which ones should receive lesser protections? Do you think your classmates would agree?

CHAPTER READINGS

5.1) Jonathan Tobin, "Freedom for Religion, Not From It," *Commentary*, May 5, 2014.

5.2) Nina Totenberg, "High Court Struggles with Military Funerals Case," *National Public Radio*, October 6, 2010.

5.3) *Riley v. California* (2014). Unanimous Opinion of the U.S. Supreme Court delivered by Chief Justice John Roberts.

5.4) "The Slow Death of the Death Penalty," *The Economist*, April 26, 2014.

5.1) Freedom for Religion, Not From It

Commentary, May 5, 2014

JONATHAN TOBIN

The First Amendment provides two succinct commands regulating religion. The federal government may not make a law respecting an establishment of religion—known as the establishment clause—and it may not interfere with people's free exercise of religion—known as the free exercise clause. There are two different perspectives on how to interpret the establishment clause: a strict separation interpretation, meaning that governmental actions cannot be entangled with religion, and an accommodation interpretation, meaning government must simply avoid advantaging one religion over another. Which interpretation is applied can matter. For example, recent Court cases have upheld providing aid to religious schools to purchase computers or allowing the distribution of vouchers for parents to send their children to private religious schools. While an accommodation interpretation would not have a problem with such actions, a strict separation interpretation most likely would.

In *Town of Greece v. Galloway* (2014), the Supreme Court ruled that the town council was not prohibited by the establishment clause from opening its monthly meetings with a prayer, even if those prayers were sectarian in nature and predominantly Christian. In fact, from 1999 to 2007 every single prayer had been given by a Christian religious leader. This situation led two residents of Greece, NY (one Jewish and one an atheist), to sue the town to remove the sectarian nature of the opening prayers. Jonathan Tobin, writing for *Commentary* magazine, argues that the Court "simply affirmed a long American tradition of beginning public meetings with prayer . . . [and] refus[ed] to be drawn into the question of regulating the content of such prayers." He sees the position taken by the majority of the Court as preserving religious liberty. His article centers around two arguments: (1) there is no right not to be "put in a position where one must listen to the prayers of another faith" and (2) the separation between church and state that is required is not as robust as many liberals assert. No matter which outcome the Court would have reached, one of the parties would have perceived that their religious liberties had been infringed.

Today the U.S. Supreme Court once again affirmed that the so-called "wall of separation" that exists between church and state is not quite the edifice that liberals would like it to be. In *Town of Greece v. Galloway*, the court ruled today that a village in upstate New York did not violate the First Amendment in allowing members of clergy to begin town board meetings with prayers, some of which were explicitly sectarian (and usually Christian) rather than ecumenical. The narrow vote along the usual 5–4 conservative/liberal lines is bound to incite many on the left to express fears about the court trying to turn the U.S. into a "Christian nation."

But in upholding the rights of Greece, N.Y. to have meetings begin with a religious invocation, the court has done no such thing. Rather, it has simply affirmed a long American tradition of beginning public meetings with prayer. Even more to the point, by refusing to be drawn into the question of regulating the content of such prayers, the court has preserved religious liberty rather than constricting it. The decision also provides a timely reminder that for all the talk about separation walls, the main point of the First Amendment is to preserve freedom of religion, not freedom from any mention or contact with faith.

In recent decades, the "separationist" position on church/state interaction has grown more, rather than less, aggressive. In its 1962 *Engel v. Vitale* decision that banned public school prayers, the court rightly ruled that school districts had no business imposing what were often sectarian prayers on children. Given that students were not free agents who could accept or reject these prayers with impunity, it was clear that the practice could easily be considered an "establishment" of a state religion that is prohibited by the First Amendment. But purely ceremonial affairs such as invocations before legislative proceedings cannot be reasonably interpreted in the same light. Since, as Justice Anthony Kennedy noted in the majority opinion, such prayers go back to the First Congress and have been repeatedly upheld since then, any attempt to overturn these precedents was unwarranted.

It is true that for any member of a minority faith or for atheists, the repeated use of Christian prayers at Greece's public meetings might be tedious or possibly offensive. But in the absence of a more diverse group of local clergy in this hamlet not far from the shores of Lake Ontario, the town's choices were between either censoring the prayers of local clergy who were willing to take part or eliminating the practice. Clearly there are many on the left who would have been comfortable with the former and well pleased with the latter.

But what must be acknowledged is that being put in a position where one must listen to the prayers of another faith is not a violation of one's constitutional rights. A ceremonial prayer, like the words "In God We Trust" on our coinage, does not transform our republic into one with a state religion. So long as those participating in such gestures are not attacking other faiths or those who do not believe in religion, their words are not an establishment of religion or impinge on the freedom of those listening. Adults at a town board meeting are not like schoolchildren in a closed class. They can join in the prayer or not at their own pleasure with no fear of punishment.

At the heart of this issue is the notion that any expression of faith in the public square is a violation of a vast mythical wall that some believe must completely separate religion from state. But while the Founders explicitly and with good reason forbade any one sect, denomination, or faith from being empowered by and identified with the state, they did not intend the First Amendment to be used as a shield to prevent Americans from any contact with religion. To the contrary, they saw faith as having an important role in preserving a democratic nation and a civil society.

There may have been a time when religious minorities and non-believers felt that the identification of the state with the faith of the Christian majority resulted in discriminatory practices that compromised their rights. But what is at stake here are not cases of bias or religious rule but rather the desire of some to be insulated from expressions of faith, and that is a privilege that the First Amendment does not provide them.

. . . Americans have always defined religious freedom in a more open and expansive manner that allowed them to practice their faith on the public square rather than only in private. It is that rich legal tradition that the court has upheld in *Town of Greece*. Though only a narrow majority is defending that principle on the Supreme Court at present, it is one that is well worth preserving.

ARTICLE QUESTIONS

1) According to Tobin, what was the intent of the establishment clause?
2) Would you feel uncomfortable if, for nearly 10 years, every prayer offered at the start of your local government meeting was grounded in a religious background to which you didn't subscribe? Should the fact that some would feel uncomfortable and some would not have an effect on the interpretation of the establishment clause?
3) How much separation between government and religion is desirable?
4) Do you find Tobin's argument convincing? Why or why not?

5.2) High Court Struggles with Military Funerals Case

National Public Radio, October 6, 2010

NINA TOTENBERG

The First Amendment says that Congress shall make no law abridging the freedom of speech; the Fourteenth Amendment has extended this prohibition to state governments. In recent decades the Supreme Court has given free speech preferred treatment among protected liberties (something that has not always been true). But all liberties have limits: one person's exercise of liberties must be balanced against another's rights. Even with the Supreme Court's preferred treatment of free speech, the Court has allowed some limits to the "time, place and manner" of free speech. The difficulty is determining which limits to allow and which limits abridge too far.

In 2010 Nina Totenberg, the Supreme Court reporter for *National Public Radio*, reported on the oral arguments presented in *Snyder v. Phelps*. As described by Totenberg, the case "pit[ted] the father of a Marine killed in Iraq against seven religious picketers protesting the army's tolerance of gay individuals; they demonstrated at the soldier's funeral with signs that read 'God hates fags' and 'You're going to hell.'" As you could image, these protest were traumatic for the slain soldier's father (Albert Snyder); Mr. Snyder felt his right to peacefully bury his son was infringed. Mr. Snyder sued for "intentional infliction of emotional distress" and was awarded damages under federal civil law. The seven religious picketers—all members of the Westboro Baptist Church—appealed the decision. On the day that Totenberg filed this report, the Court had just finished hearing oral arguments about the seven picketers' actions and the boundaries of the First Amendment. The Supreme Court issued its opinion months after Totenberg's report, but Totenberg's story relays many of the questions posed by the justices during oral argument. The justices' questions frame how the Court tried to approach this First Amendment conflict. You will hear in their questions the difficulty of balancing First Amendment liberties against a parent's opportunity to bury his or her child in peace. If you don't already know the outcome of the case, try to envision how you would rule before looking up the decision. If you know the outcome, reflect upon the facts laid out in Totenberg's article and ask yourself: would you have joined the majority or dissenting opinion.

At an emotional argument before the U.S. Supreme Court on Wednesday, the justices struggled with a case testing whether picketers at a military funeral may be sued for inflicting emotional distress on the family of a dead soldier.

The case, *Snyder v. Phelps*, pits the father of a Marine killed in Iraq against seven religious picketers who demonstrated at the soldier's funeral with signs that read "God hates fags" and "You're going to hell." Though the Marine wasn't gay, the picketers say they were carrying God's message to condemn "sodomite enablers."

The picketers, all members of the Westboro Baptist Church in Topeka, Kan., traveled with their pastor, Fred Phelps, to Maryland to demonstrate at the funeral of Lance Cpl. Matthew Snyder, who died in Iraq. They have picketed at hundreds of other military funerals in recent years, preaching their message that the casualties of war are God's punishment for society tolerating, and even embracing, homosexuality.

Context

Cpl. Snyder's father, Albert Snyder, sued the picketers for intentional infliction of emotional distress and won a $5 million judgment, but a federal appeals court threw out the award, declaring that even outrageous and offensive opinion is protected by the First Amendment right of free speech.

Inside the courtroom, Snyder's lawyer, Sean Summers, told the justices that "if context ever matters, it matters at a funeral." But some justices pointed out that the picketers had obeyed all police instructions and stood 1,000 feet away from the church. Moreover, they noted that part of Snyder's emotional distress claim involves a derogatory Internet posting that he came across a month after the funeral.

"Suppose there had been no funeral protest, just the Internet posting," asked Justice Antonin Scalia. "Would you still have had a claim for damages?"

Summers answered yes, because of the "personal, targeted epithets directed at the Snyder family."

Moreover, he contended that just because the picketers were in compliance with the criminal law does not mean they are immune to lawsuits for civil damages.

Drawing The Line

Justice Stephen Breyer noted that Snyder had not seen the picketers' signs at the funeral, that he only saw the signs when he viewed TV coverage afterward. So, the justice asked, where do we draw the line on when you can sue for damages, and when you can't? It was a refrain heard repeatedly throughout the argument.

Summers repeatedly contended that the private, targeted nature of the speech is what makes it unprotected by the First Amendment.

But Chief Justice John Roberts wondered obliquely whether it was the content of the speech that was objectionable. "So you have no objection to a sign that said get out of Iraq?" Summers replied that he indeed would have no objection to such signs carried by picketers at a funeral.

Justice Scalia pounced on that answer, observing, "So the intrusion upon the privacy of the funeral isn't really what you are complaining about."

Justice Sonia Sotomayor moved back to the line-drawing dilemma asking: If you were a Marine and I went up to you, objecting to the Iraq war, and I said that "you are perpetuating the horrors" of that war, would the Marine have grounds to sue?

Summers first said yes, then no.

Free Speech

Justice Elena Kagan noted that the court has long been protective of even outrageous opinions because to impose damages based on a jury's tastes,

likes or dislikes is to undermine the whole idea of free speech. Why, she asked, wouldn't a general statute that simply bars demonstrations within 500 feet of a funeral take care of the problem?

Justice Samuel Alito interjected that a law like that wouldn't bar someone from coming up to Snyder at the funeral and spitting in his face. Justice Ruth Bader Ginsburg caustically pointed out that "you would have to be a lot closer than the law allows to spit in someone's face."

If Summers, representing Snyder, had a difficult time of it, Margie Phelps, representing the picketers, faced even tougher questioning. Phelps is the daughter of Pastor Phelps, the lead picketer in the case. And the justices threw one hypothetical after another at her.

First Amendment

"Suppose your group or some other group picks a wounded soldier and follows him around, demonstrates at his home, his workplace, at his church," postulated Justice Kagan. Suppose in doing that, they are saying offensive and outrageous things similar to those spouted by the protesters in this case. Does that soldier have a claim for intentional infliction of emotional distress?

Phelps answered that "any nonspeech activity like stalking, importuning, being confrontational" could indeed justify a damage suit.

Kagan followed up, asking whether there could be a claim for demonstrations, without disruption, at a person's home, workplace or church. Phelps said that in that case, there would be no basis for a lawsuit.

Justice Ginsburg neatly summed up the issue in its most basic terms: "This is a case about exploiting a private family's grief, and the question is: Why should the First Amendment tolerate exploiting this Marine's family when you have so many other forums for getting across your message?"

Phelps argued that if demonstrators abide by the law's requirements for time, place and manner of their protest, they know when they are acting legally. The notion of exploitation, however, is so wide open, she said, that it provides "no principle of law to guide people as to when they could or could not" protest.

Publicity

Chief Justice Roberts noted that the protesters here had selected the funeral as a demonstration site to get publicity for their cause. Does that matter, he asked?

No, Phelps said flatly, because every speaker tries to get maximum exposure for his cause.

Taking another tack, Justice Alito observed that the picketers' argument "depends on the proposition that this is speech on a matter of public concern," and he posed yet another hypothetical: What if someone believes that African-Americans are inferior and then berates an African-American on the street with epithets of racial hatred?

While contending that "the issue of race is matter of public concern," Phelps conceded that "approaching an individual up close to berate them gets you out of the zone of [First Amendment] protection."

What Is Appropriate?

Justice Anthony Kennedy, however, seemed to reject Phelps' conception of what constitutes a matter of public concern. "In a pluralistic society," anything can "turn into a public issue," he noted, while at the same time suggesting that can't be enough to justify allowing protesters to follow people around with pickets.

Justice Breyer, citing the right to be let alone, noted the First Amendment does not bar state damage suits when they are appropriate. But what is appropriate?

The justice again said he was "looking for a line."

Phelps replied that "there must be some actual physical sound, sight, intrusion if you are talking about invasion of privacy."

Justice Sotomayor inquired, what is the line between strong opinion on a public issue and personalizing it to create "hardship for an individual"?

That is the question facing the court—and Wednesday's argument gave few hints on how the justices will resolve it. It did appear, though, that some justices who just months ago expanded the right of free speech to allow corporations to spend unlimited amounts in candidate elections are looking for a way to limit the rights of picketers at funerals.

ARTICLE QUESTIONS

1) The justices asked the attorneys in the case several very difficult questions. What two questions do you think were the most difficult to answer? Which answers by the attorneys did you find the least convincing?
2) When, if ever, should speech be limited?
3) Are there important reasons to protect free speech even when it is offensive?

5.3) *Riley v. California* (2014)

Unanimous Opinion of the U.S. Supreme Court Delivered by Chief Justice John Roberts

The Fourth Amendment requires police to obtain a warrant from a judge before searching an individual's property. *Riley v. California* was the consolidation of two cases in which arrestees' cell phones were searched without a warrant, and the discovered information was used as evidence to convict the defendants. In a unanimous opinion, delivered by Chief Justice John Roberts, the Supreme Court ruled police could not search the content of someone's cell phone without first obtaining a warrant—even if that person was under arrest. As you will read in these excerpts from *Riley*, since the 1960s and 1970s the Court has ruled police can search an arrestee's immediate vicinity without a warrant. Such exemptions from the Fourth Amendment warrant requirement have been justified by the need for police protection and for the discovery of evidence that might be destroyed. California and the United States argued that searching a cell phone was simply an extension of these exemptions. Riley's attorneys argued that it was something significantly different, a position that ultimately swayed all nine members of the Court.

With each development of new technology, the courts, Congress, the states, and local police forces have to interpret the application of the Fourth Amendment. The Court acknowledges that its decision in *Riley* will make police work more difficult. However, the Court argued that because of the massive amount of personal information contained on a cell phone, the privacy interest outweighed the need to search without a warrant. The Court also acknowledged that part of the point of extending protections to those accused of crimes was to make it more difficult to convict someone.

These two cases raise a common question: whether the police may, without a warrant, search digital information on a cell phone seized from an individual who has been arrested.

In the first case, petitioner David Riley was stopped by a police officer for driving with expired registration tags. In the course of the stop, the officer also learned that Riley's license had been suspended. The officer impounded Riley's car, pursuant to department policy, and another officer conducted an inventory search of the car. Riley was arrested for possession of concealed and loaded firearms when that search turned up two handguns under the car's hood.

An officer searched Riley incident to the arrest and found items associated with the "Bloods" street gang. He also seized a cell phone from Riley's pants pocket. According to Riley's uncontradicted assertion, the phone was a "smart phone," a cell phone with a broad range of other functions based on advanced computing capability, large storage capacity, and Internet connectivity. The officer accessed information on the phone and noticed that some words (presumably in text messages or a contacts list) were preceded by the letters "CK"—a label that, he believed, stood for "Crip Killers," a slang term for members of the Bloods gang.

At the police station about two hours after the arrest, a detective specializing in gangs further examined the contents of the phone. The detective testified that he "went through" Riley's phone "looking for evidence, because . . . gang members will often video themselves with guns or take

pictures of themselves with the guns." Although there was "a lot of stuff" on the phone, particular files that "caught [the detective's] eye" included videos of young men sparring while someone yelled encouragement using the moniker "Blood." The police also found photographs of Riley standing in front of a car they suspected had been involved in a shooting a few weeks earlier.

Riley was ultimately charged, in connection with that earlier shooting, with firing at an occupied vehicle, assault with a semiautomatic firearm, and attempted murder. The State alleged that Riley had committed those crimes for the benefit of a criminal street gang, an aggravating factor that carries an enhanced sentence. Prior to trial, Riley moved to suppress all evidence that the police had obtained from his cell phone. He contended that the searches of his phone violated the Fourth Amendment, because they had been performed without a warrant and were not otherwise justified by exigent circumstances. The trial court rejected that argument. At Riley's trial, police officers testified about the photographs and videos found on the phone, and some of the photographs were admitted into evidence. Riley was convicted on all three counts and received an enhanced sentence of 15 years to life in prison. . . .

The Fourth Amendment provides:

"The right of the people to be secure in their persons, houses, papers, and effects, against unreasonable searches and seizures, shall not be violated, and no Warrants shall issue, but upon probable cause, supported by Oath or affirmation, and particularly describing the place to be searched, and the persons or things to be seized."

. . . The two cases before us concern the reasonableness of a warrantless search incident to a lawful arrest. In 1914, this Court first acknowledged in dictum "the right on the part of the Government, always recognized under English and American law, to search the person of the accused when legally arrested to discover and seize the fruits or evidences of crime." *Weeks v. United States* (1914). Since that time, it has been well accepted that such a search constitutes an exception to the warrant requirement. Indeed, the label "exception" is something of a misnomer in this context, as warrantless searches incident to arrest occur with far greater frequency than searches conducted pursuant to a warrant.

Although the existence of the exception for such searches has been recognized for a century, its scope has been debated for nearly as long. That debate has focused on the extent to which officers may search property found on or near the arrestee. Three related precedents set forth the rules governing such searches:

The first, *Chimel v. California* (1969), laid the groundwork for most of the existing search incident to arrest doctrine. Police officers in that case arrested Chimel inside his home and proceeded to search his entire three-bedroom house, including the attic and garage. In particular rooms, they also looked through the contents of drawers. . . .

The extensive warrantless search of Chimel's home did not fit within this exception, because it was not needed to protect officer safety or to preserve evidence.

Four years later, in *United States v. Robinson* (1973), the Court applied the *Chimel* analysis in the context of a search of the arrestee's person. A police officer had arrested Robinson for driving with a revoked license. The officer conducted a patdown search and felt an object that he could not identify in Robinson's coat pocket. He removed the object, which turned out to be a crumpled cigarette package, and opened it. Inside were 14 capsules of heroin. . . .

The Court thus concluded that the search of Robinson was reasonable even though there was no concern about the loss of evidence, and the arresting officer had no specific concern that Robinson might be armed. In doing so, the Court did not draw a line between a search of Robinson's person and a further examination of the cigarette pack found during that search. It merely noted that, "[h]aving in the course of a lawful search come upon the crumpled package of cigarettes, [the officer] was entitled to inspect it." A few years later, the Court clarified that this exception was limited to "personal property . . . immediately associated with the person of the arrestee." *United States v. Chadwick* (1977). . . .

These cases require us to decide how the search incident to arrest doctrine applies to modern cell phones, which are now such a pervasive and insistent part of daily life that the proverbial visitor from Mars might conclude they were an important feature of human anatomy. A smart phone of the sort taken from Riley was unheard of ten years ago; a significant majority of American adults now own such phones. . . .

Absent more precise guidance from the founding era, we generally determine whether to exempt a given type of search from the warrant requirement "by assessing, on the one hand, the degree to which it intrudes upon an individual's privacy and, on the other, the degree to which it is needed for the promotion of legitimate governmental interests." *Wyoming v. Houghton* (1999). . . .

Digital data stored on a cell phone cannot itself be used as a weapon to harm an arresting officer or to effectuate the arrestee's escape. Law enforcement officers remain free to examine the physical aspects of a phone to ensure that it will not be used as a weapon—say, to determine whether there is a razor blade hidden between the phone and its case. Once an officer has secured a phone and eliminated any potential physical threats, however, data on the phone can endanger no one. . . .

The United States and California both suggest that a search of cell phone data might help ensure officer safety in more indirect ways, for example by alerting officers that confederates of the arrestee are headed to the scene. There is undoubtedly a strong government interest in warning officers about such possibilities, but neither the United States nor California offers evidence to suggest that their concerns are based on actual experience. The proposed consideration would also represent a broadening of *Chimel*'s concern that an *arrestee himself* might grab a weapon and use it against an officer "to resist arrest or effect his escape." And any such threats from outside the arrest scene do not "lurk[] in all custodial arrests." Accordingly, the interest in protecting officer safety does not justify dispensing with the warrant requirement across the board. To the extent dangers to arresting officers may be implicated in a particular way in a particular case, they are better addressed through consideration of case-specific exceptions to the warrant requirement, such as the one for exigent circumstances. . . .

The United States and California focus primarily on the second *Chimel* rationale: preventing the destruction of evidence.

Both Riley and Wurie concede that officers could have seized and secured their cell phones to prevent destruction of evidence while seeking a warrant. . . . That is a sensible concession. . . . And once law enforcement officers have secured a cell phone, there is no longer any risk that the arrestee himself will be able to delete incriminating data from the phone.

The United States and California argue that information on a cell phone may nevertheless be vulnerable to two types of evidence destruction unique to digital data—remote wiping and data encryption. Remote wiping occurs when a phone, connected to a wireless network, receives a signal that erases stored data. This can happen when a third party sends a remote signal or when a phone is preprogrammed to delete data upon entering or leaving certain geographic areas (so-called "geofencing"). . . . Encryption is a security feature that some modern cell phones use in addition to password protection. When such phones lock, data becomes protected by sophisticated encryption that renders a phone all but "unbreakable" unless police know the password. . . .

We have also been given little reason to believe that either problem is prevalent. The briefing reveals only a couple of anecdotal examples of remote wiping triggered by an arrest. . . . Similarly, the opportunities for officers to search a password-protected phone before data becomes encrypted are quite limited. Law enforcement officers are very unlikely to come upon such a phone in an unlocked state because most phones lock at the touch of a button or, as a default, after some very short period of inactivity. . . . This may explain why the encryption argument was not made until the merits stage in this Court, and has never been considered by the Courts of Appeals.

Moreover, in situations in which an arrest might trigger a remote-wipe attempt or an officer discovers an unlocked phone, it is not clear that the ability to conduct a warrant-less search would make much of a difference. The need to effect the arrest, secure the scene, and tend to other pressing matters means that law enforcement officers may well not be able to turn their attention to a cell phone right away. . . . Cell phone data would be vulnerable to remote wiping from the time an individual anticipates arrest to the time any eventual search of the phone is completed, which might be at the station house hours later. Likewise, an officer who seizes a phone in an unlocked state might not be able to begin his search in the short time remaining before the phone locks and data becomes encrypted. . . .

The fact that an arrestee has diminished privacy interests does not mean that the Fourth Amendment falls out of the picture entirely. Not every search "is acceptable solely because a person is in custody." *Maryland v. King* (2013). To the contrary, when "privacy-related concerns are weighty enough" a "search may require a warrant, notwithstanding the diminished expectations of privacy of the arrestee." One such example, of course, is *Chimel*. *Chimel* refused to "characteriz[e] the invasion of privacy that results from a top-to-bottom search of a man's house as 'minor.'" Because a search of the arrestee's entire house was a substantial invasion beyond the arrest itself, the Court concluded that a warrant was required.

Robinson is the only decision from this Court applying *Chimel* to a search of the contents of an item found on an arrestee's person. In an earlier case, this Court had approved a search of a zipper bag carried by an arrestee, but the Court analyzed only the validity of the arrest itself.

See *Draper v. United States* (1959). Lower courts applying *Robinson* and *Chimel*, however, have approved searches of a variety of personal items carried by an arrestee. . . .

The United States asserts that a search of all data stored on a cell phone is "materially indistinguishable" from searches of these sorts of physical items. That is like saying a ride on horseback is materially indistinguishable from a flight to the moon. Both are ways of getting from point A to point B, but little else justifies lumping them together. Modern cell phones, as a category, implicate privacy concerns far beyond those implicated by the search of a cigarette pack, a wallet, or a purse. A conclusion that inspecting the contents of an arrestee's pockets works no substantial additional intrusion on privacy beyond the arrest itself may make sense as applied to physical items, but any extension of that reasoning to digital data has to rest on its own bottom.

Cell phones differ in both a quantitative and a qualitative sense from other objects that might be kept on an arrestee's person. The term "cell phone" is itself misleading shorthand; many of these devices are in fact minicomputers that also happen to have the capacity to be used as a telephone. They could just as easily be called cameras, video players, rolodexes, calendars, tape recorders, libraries, diaries, albums, televisions, maps, or newspapers.

One of the most notable distinguishing features of modern cell phones is their immense storage capacity. Before cell phones, a search of a person was limited by physical realities and tended as a general matter to constitute only a narrow intrusion on privacy. Most people cannot lug around every piece of mail they have received for the past several months, every picture they have taken, or every book or article they have read—nor would they have any reason to attempt to do so. And if they did, they would have to drag behind them a trunk of the sort held to require a search warrant in *Chadwick,* rather than a container the size of the cigarette package in *Robinson.*

But the possible intrusion on privacy is not physically limited in the same way when it comes to cell phones. The current top-selling smart phone has a standard capacity of 16 gigabytes (and is available with up to 64 gigabytes). Sixteen gigabytes translates to millions of pages of text, thousands of pictures, or hundreds of videos. Cell phones couple that capacity with the ability to store many different types of information: Even the most basic phones that sell for less than $20 might hold photographs, picture messages, text messages, Internet browsing history, a calendar, a thousand-entry phone book, and so on. We expect that the gulf between physical practicability and digital capacity will only continue to widen in the future.

The storage capacity of cell phones has several interrelated consequences for privacy. First, a cell phone collects in one place many distinct types of information—an address, a note, a prescription, a bank statement, a video—that reveal much more in combination than any isolated record. Second, a cell phone's capacity allows even just one type of information to convey far more than previously possible. The sum of an individual's private life can be reconstructed through a thousand photographs labeled with dates, locations, and descriptions; the same cannot be said of a photograph or two of loved ones tucked into a wallet. Third, the data on a phone can date back to the purchase of the phone, or even earlier. A person might carry in his pocket a slip of paper reminding him to call Mr. Jones; he would not carry a record of all his communications with Mr. Jones for the past several months, as would routinely be kept on a phone.

Finally, there is an element of pervasiveness that characterizes cell phones but not physical records. Prior to the digital age, people did not typically carry a cache of sensitive personal information with them as they went about their day. Now it is the person who is not carrying a cell phone, with all that it contains, who is the exception. According to one poll, nearly three-quarters of smart phone users report being within five feet of their phones most of the time, with 12% admitting that they even use their phones in the shower. A decade ago police officers searching an arrestee might have occasionally stumbled across a highly personal item such as a diary. But those discoveries were likely to be few and far between. Today, by contrast, it is no exaggeration to say that many of the more than 90% of American adults who own a cell phone keep on their person a digital record of nearly every aspect of their lives—from the mundane to the intimate. Allowing the police to scrutinize such records on a routine basis is quite different from allowing them to search a personal item or two in the occasional case.

Although the data stored on a cell phone is distinguished from physical records by quantity alone, certain types of data are also qualitatively different. An Internet search and browsing history, for example, can be found on an Internet-enabled phone and could reveal an individual's private interests or concerns—perhaps a search for certain symptoms of disease, coupled with frequent visits to WebMD. Data on a cell phone can also reveal where a person has been. Historic location information is a standard feature on many smart phones and can reconstruct someone's specific movements down to the minute, not only around town but also within a particular building. . . .

Mobile application software on a cell phone, or "apps," offer a range of tools for managing detailed information about all aspects of a person's life. There are apps for Democratic Party news and Republican Party news; apps for alcohol, drug, and gambling addictions; apps for sharing prayer requests; apps for tracking pregnancy symptoms; apps for planning your budget; apps for every conceivable hobby or pastime; apps for improving your romantic life. There are popular apps for buying or selling just about anything, and the records of such transactions may be accessible on the phone indefinitely. There are over a million apps available in each of the two major app stores; the phrase "there's an app for that" is now part of the popular lexicon. The average smart phone user has installed 33 apps, which together can form a revealing montage of the user's life.

In 1926, Learned Hand observed (in an opinion later quoted in *Chimel*) that it is "a totally different thing to search a man's pockets and use against him what they contain, from ransacking his house for everything which may incriminate him." *United States v. Kirschenblatt,* 16 F. 2d (CA2). If his pockets contain a cell phone, however, that is no longer true. Indeed, a cell phone search would typically expose to the government far *more* than the most exhaustive search of a house: A phone not only contains in digital form many sensitive records previously found in the home; it also contains a broad array of private information never found in a home in any form—unless the phone is. . . .

We cannot deny that our decision today will have an impact on the ability of law enforcement to combat crime. Cell phones have become important tools in facilitating coordination and communication among members of criminal enterprises, and can provide valuable incriminating information about dangerous criminals. Privacy comes at a cost.

Our holding, of course, is not that the information on a cell phone is immune from search; it is instead that a warrant is generally required before such a search, even when a cell phone is seized incident to arrest. Our cases have historically recognized that the warrant requirement is "an important working part of our machinery of government," not merely "an inconvenience to be somehow 'weighed' against the claims of police efficiency." *Coolidge v. New Hampshire,* (1971). Recent technological advances similar to those discussed here have, in addition, made the process of obtaining a warrant itself more efficient. . . .

In light of the availability of the exigent circumstances exception, there is no reason to believe that law enforcement officers will not be able to address some of the more extreme hypotheticals that have been suggested: a suspect texting an accomplice who, it is feared, is preparing to detonate a bomb, or a child abductor who may have information about the child's location on his cell phone. The defendants here recognize—indeed, they stress—that such fact-specific threats may justify a warrantless search of cell phone data. The critical point is that, unlike the search incident to arrest exception, the exigent circumstances exception requires a court to examine whether an emergency justified a warrantless search in each particular case.

Our cases have recognized that the Fourth Amendment was the founding generation's response to the reviled "general warrants" and "writs of assistance" of the colonial era, which allowed British officers to rummage through homes in an unrestrained search for evidence of criminal activity. Opposition to such searches was in fact one of the driving forces behind the Revolution itself. In 1761, the patriot James Otis delivered a speech in Boston denouncing the use of writs of assistance. A young John Adams was there, and he would later write that "[e]very man of a crowded audience appeared to me to go away, as I did, ready to take arms against writs of assistance." 10 Works of John Adams 247–248 (C. Adams ed. 1856). According to Adams, Otis's speech was "the first scene of the first act of opposition to the arbitrary claims of Great Britain. Then and there the child Independence was born." (quoted in *Boyd v. United States*, (1886)).

Modern cell phones are not just another technological convenience. With all they contain and all they may reveal, they hold for many Americans "the privacies of life," *Boyd*. The fact that technology now allows an individual to carry such information in his hand does not make the information any less worthy of the protection for which the Founders fought. Our answer to the question of what police must do before searching a cell phone seized incident to an arrest is accordingly simple—get a warrant.

ARTICLE QUESTIONS

1) What evidence obtained from the cell phone was used to convict David Riley?
2) Given that the evidence obtained from David Riley's phone will now be suppressed, a new jury—without the benefit of this evidence—is unlikely to determine he is guilty beyond a shadow of a doubt. Does this potential outcome frustrate you? Why or why not?
3) Do you think the Court made the correct ruling in this case? What arguments did you find the most/least convincing?
4) How far should individual liberties be protected against searches and seizures?

5.4) The Slow Death of the Death Penalty

The Economist, April 26, 2014

The Eighth Amendment prohibits the infliction of cruel and unusual punishment, but it is far from obvious if this prohibition bans capital punishment. An argument that the Eighth Amendment doesn't do this centers on the fact the Eighth Amendment was drafted when the death penalty was widely practiced. But a counterargument is that the use of the word "unusual" in the Eighth Amendment allows the meaning to change over time; now that 97% of nations have abolished the death penalty, it is an *unusual* punishment. In addition to the constitutional argument over the meaning of the Eighth Amendment, the death penalty inspires a debate over the punishment's merits. Proponents of capital punishment argue that some crimes are so terrible that justice demands its application in some cases. Opponents argue that social systems are imperfect; innocent people might be killed and the punishment is disproportionally leveled against the poor and minorities.

In this article from *The Economist,* the author surveys the changing landscape of the death penalty in America. The article notes that the death penalty has become "less common and less popular than it was." The article provides a great example of federalism in action: Some states allow the death penalty, others do not. States also vary widely in their use of the punishment. Federalism can become a major dilemma when civil liberties are involved. A common question in

U.S. politics is how much leeway a state should have to determine what liberties are protected. The debate over the death penalty again displays the struggle over competing rights: This time it is the rights of those accused of crimes and those who are victims of crimes.

On the afternoon of March 19th a ragtag group of protesters gathered outside the Huntsville Unit, home to America's busiest execution chamber. At 6pm Texas was set to execute Ray Jasper, convicted of murdering the owner of a recording studio. Protesters held up signs ("The Death Penalty: Guilty on All Counts: Shut it Down!"), made statements and read a few poems the condemned man had written. A priest rang a bell 14 times, once for every year Jasper had spent on death row. At 6:34 the prison door opened, letting out a few civilians whom protesters said they recognized as witnesses to the execution.

No one from the prison announced Jasper's death. A little after 7 the protesters dispersed, stowing signs and megaphones away in their trunks, ready for use at the next execution.

So far this year 19 prisoners have been put to death in America, seven of them in Texas. Another 14 are scheduled to die. According to Amnesty International, America executes more people than any country except China, Iran, Iraq and Saudi Arabia—disreputable peers for the land of the free. But capital punishment is less common and less popular than it was, and concerns over cost, efficacy and execution methods may be hastening its demise.

Even if all the executions scheduled for this year are carried out—which is unlikely—a total of 33 would be the lowest since 1994, and would have fallen by two-thirds from the peak of 98 in 1999 (see chart). In 2013 American juries handed out just 80 death sentences: a slight increase from the previous year, but still close to the lowest level in 40 years. As of October 1st 2013, 3,088 Americans were on death row—down from a peak in 2000 of 3,593.

Several factors have driven death sentences and executions down. The simplest may be that America's homicide rate has declined sharply—from 10.2 per 100,000 people in 1980 to 4.7 in 2012. With that broader decline has come a fall in the

most heinous murders; i.e., the sort that earn the harshest sentences. As Bob McCulloch, prosecuting attorney for St Louis County, explains: "In Missouri, most [murders] are second-degree . . . bar-room brawls, or some guys shooting each other over a bad dope deal." First-degree murders, he says, "rape and murder, killing a police officer—those are all way down."

Another shift is that most juries can now impose sentences of life without the possibility of parole. In 1972, when the Supreme Court suspended the death penalty (it was reinstated four years later), only seven states allowed such sentences. Now every state bar Alaska gives juries the option of making sure that a murderer will never be released (perhaps to kill again) without actually killing him.

That makes them warier of the needle. Texas, for instance, introduced life-without-parole sentences in 2005. "When that happened," says Craig Watkins, district attorney for Dallas County, the state's second-most populous county, "you saw a decrease in prosecutors even bringing death-penalty cases. . . . Now you have a choice. Before, you didn't." And indeed, Texas sentences fewer people to death now (nine in 2013) than in 2004 (23).

Most Americans still support capital punishment. But their majority has dwindled from 80% in 1994 to 60% in 2013, according to Gallup. Separate polls by the Pew Research Centre find that although most old and white Americans support it, young people are less keen and ethnic minorities such as blacks and Hispanics are solidly opposed. Since the young and non-white are America's future, that suggests that demography favors the abolitionists.

Earlier this month a vote to repeal the death penalty narrowly failed in New Hampshire, but similar measures succeeded in six states between 2007 and 2013, reducing the number of capital-punishment states to 32. Among those states, 15 have carried out no executions since

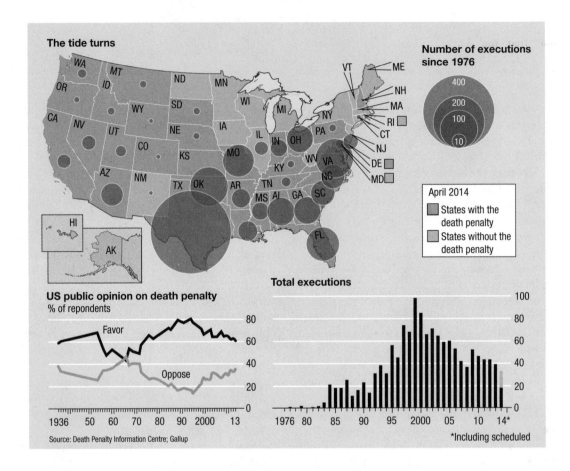

The tide turns

Number of executions since 1976

400
200
100
10

April 2014
■ States with the death penalty
▨ States without the death penalty

US public opinion on death penalty
% of repondents

Favor

Oppose

1936 50 60 70 80 90 2000 13

Total executions

1976 80 85 90 95 2000 05 10 14*

*Including scheduled

Source: Death Penalty Information Centre; Gallup

2010. Just four—Texas, Virginia, Oklahoma and Florida—are responsible for roughly 60% of the executions since 1976. Texas alone carried out 37% of the total. Within capital-punishment states, a mere 15 counties are responsible for 30% of executions. (Although capital punishment is state law, generally the decision to seek the death penalty is made by district attorneys at the county level.)

Fans of the death penalty say it deters murderers. The evidence for this is at best equivocal. The number of murders fluctuates each year and has fallen sharply over time, from 24,500 in 1993 to 14,800 in 2012. Many factors affect the murder rate: demography, policing, culture, the job market and so on. No one really knows how much weight to give to each. But it seems improbable that the death penalty has much effect. Murderers are

highly unlikely to be put to death (in 2012 there was one execution for every 345 murders). And they are staggeringly unlikely to be put to death before they reach middle age (the average wait on death row is more than a decade).

So when a social scientist claims to have shown that each execution prevents 2.5 murders (as one recent study found), it is reasonable to wonder if he was really able to separate the signal from the noise with such precision. A meta-study released by America's National Research Council in April 2012 found that "research to date . . . is not informative about whether capital punishment decreases, increases or has no effect on homicide rates."

The abolitionists' most emotive argument is that juries make mistakes. Since 1973, 144 death-row inmates have been exonerated. Death-penalty proponents say this shows that the system is working: that multiple safeguards have prevented anyone innocent from being put to death. But is that true? Although there are no proven cases in recent decades, the Death Penalty Information Centre, an abolitionist organisztion, points to ten executed men it suspects were innocent. The case of Cameron Todd Willingham is particularly compelling.

Another reason why some voters are falling out of love with the death penalty is that it now costs much more to execute a killer than to lock him up forever. In Maryland, for example, it cost three times more—until last year, when the state abolished capital punishment. Governor Martin O'Malley cited the cost as one reason for pressing for abolition.

An execution itself is not expensive, but the years of appeals that precede it are. Defendants facing death tend to have more, better and costlier lawyers. Death-row inmates are more expensive to incarcerate, too: they usually have their own cells, with meals brought to them and multiple guards present for every visit. "It's because of this myth that these people will be executed in a couple of months," explains Richard Dieter of the Death Penalty Information Centre.

All states that execute people do so principally by lethal injection. Until 2010 most used three drugs: sodium thiopental to induce unconsciousness, pancuronium bromide to stop breathing and potassium chloride to stop the heart. In January 2011, however, the sole American producer of sodium thiopental ceased production, fearing a regulatory backlash in Europe if its drug was used to kill people. European producers have been reluctant to sell to American states for the same reason.

So states have turned to less-tested drugs, sometimes with disastrous results. Michael Wilson complained "I feel my whole body burning" as he was executed in Oklahoma last January with a drug cocktail featuring pentobarbital rather than sodium thiopental. Some states have turned to compounding pharmacies (small firms that cobble together drugs from their active ingredients), and have enacted laws keeping the source of their drugs secret. This month Oklahoma's Supreme Court briefly stayed two imminent executions, concerned about secrecy. The Supreme Court ruled in 2008 that the three-drug protocol did not violate the constitution's bar on "cruel and unusual punishments," but newer injection methods remain legally untested, and have inspired lawsuits against several states.

The courts are unlikely to end the death penalty in America. But legislators and governors might. As Americans' support for capital punishment recedes, more of their representatives will back abolition. Granted, everything could change if the bad old days of high crime and widespread fear were to return, but that seems unlikely. It may be a long wait, but the death penalty's days are surely numbered.

ARTICLE QUESTIONS

1) What reasons does the article cite to explain why the support for and use of the death penalty have been decreasing?
2) What do you think is the strongest evidence for maintaining capital punishment as an option? What do you think is the strongest evidence against it?
3) Do you think the ultimate decision on the death penalty should be left to the Supreme Court, state legislatures, or juries?

Chapter 6

The Struggle for Civil Rights

Civil rights are the freedom to participate in the life of the community—to vote in elections, enjoy public facilities, and take advantage of economic opportunities like good jobs. People face discrimination when they are denied these opportunities because of their race, gender, ethnicity, religion, disabilities, age, or other personal characteristics. Throughout U.S. history, group after group has struggled for its right to participate. The successful struggles have required sustained efforts and mass mobilizations. These separate but still connected efforts are powerful stories that reveal the deepest truths about the United States and its values.

The long struggle for civil rights can be viewed through two different frameworks. Some observers see a steady march toward greater equality. Others perceive nothing inevitable—or continuous—in the expansion of civil rights; from this perspective, sometimes rights (and the number of groups afforded them) expand, but they are just as likely to contract. The readings in this chapter can be read through either lens— ever-expanding rights or continuous struggle with progressions and regressions. The readings include only a few of the groups that have pushed (and continue to push) for equal rights; however, it would be impossible to spotlight every civil rights struggle. Still, as observers of civil rights struggles, we can make connections among the distinct but associated quests for inclusion in "we the people."

One of the celebrated landmarks of the civil rights movement is the *Brown v. Board of Education* (1954) decision, in which, after years of constitutionally sanctioned segregation laws, the Supreme Court finally interpreted school segregation as being inconsistent with the Constitution. The ruling was one of the great landmark cases in American history. Despite that, Cass Sunstein cites data in "Did *Brown* Matter?" that challenges the notion that *Brown* led to integrated schools. In making this case, Sunstein highlights two important themes running through this chapter: the need for organized movements, and the existence of both progress and retreat in in the long quest for civil rights. Sunstein asserts that an organized, large-scale movement was required for the Court to reach its decision in *Brown*, and a movement was required for the decision to be implemented. In noting how little integration occurred immediately following *Brown*, Sunstein implies that the advance of civil rights is not a linear progression but rather one of occasional progress, much stagnation, and occasional retreat.

Stokely Carmichael's 1966 article "What We Want" is an important reminder that the civil rights movement was about more than integration; it was also about acquiring power. Carmichael's essay brings up an interesting question about how to evaluate the success of the civil rights movement. Often the movement is measured by the removal of segregation laws. But if the goal was for blacks and other groups to achieve power, how should we measure the successes of the movement, and further, how should we view the need for continued civil rights advances?

At the beginning of World War II President Roosevelt issued an executive order requiring Japanese-Americans to report to internment camps. In the process they were stripped of all their assets—bank accounts, homes, and all. Fred Korematsu refused to report and was arrested. He challenged his arrest and the constitutionality of Roosevelt's executive order, but lost in an infamous Supreme Court case *Korematsu v. United States* (1944). Fifty-four years later, in 1998, Korematsu was awarded the Medal of Freedom, the highest award given to a civilian. Like so many who have advanced civil rights, Korematsu's actions were initially seen as violating the law, but later his "illegal" actions were commended. In Korematsu's obituary, Richard Goldstein credits him with expressing concerns for civil rights protections after the September 11, 2001, terrorist attacks. In expressing this concern, Korematsu made a connection between his struggle—and the broader oppression of Japanese-Americans, who were unfairly accused of harboring sympathies for the Japanese after the bombing of Pearl Harbor—and the struggle of Arab-Americans facing discrimination after the bombing of the World Trade Center. People whose actions are perceived as illegal at the time but who are later vindicated, and the linking of one civil rights struggle to another are both important parts of the U.S. civil rights story.

Jose Antonio Vargas, in "Not Legal, Not Leaving," presents another link between two civil rights struggles in his story of "coming out" as an undocumented immigrant. In much the same way the gay rights movement used "coming out" as a strategy, he sees the strategy of undocumented immigrants coming out "as a game changer in the debate" on immigration. This article presents an emerging movement of those who are normally invisible to the public, and it also shows movements borrowing strategies from each other.

Jennifer Ludden, in "Despite New Law, Gender Salary Gap Persists," reports for *National Public Radio* that "women, on average, earn only 77 cents to a man's dollar." Today's gender pay discrepancy can be contrasted to the discrepancy in 1963 when "women earned 59 percent of men's wages." The changing of this discrepancy over time can be seen as reflective of the two ways of viewing the civil rights movement in the United States: we could emphasize "how far we've come" or we could focus on "how far we have to go."

No idea in the United States is more powerful than the idea of inalienable rights—but what rights are defined as inalienable? To whom should these rights be extended? What is the best way to ensure these rights are protected? These are hotly contested questions. Think about the movements for civil rights presented in this chapter as well as the ones that are left out. Each of the struggles has unique aspects, but they also share unifying themes. Movements borrow tactics and ideas from one another and each of these struggles can remind us how far "we the people" have come and how far we may still need to go.

CHAPTER QUESTIONS

1) Name some successful struggles for civil rights that have changed the way the United States functions today. Name some of the groups still excluded from equal civil rights protections.
2) What are some of the most pressing denials of civil rights in the United States today?
3) How do groups "win" civil rights?

CHAPTER READINGS

6.1) Cass Sunstein, "Did *Brown* Matter?" *The New Yorker*, May 3, 2004.

6.2) Stokely Carmichael, "What We Want," *The New York Review of Books*, September 22, 1966 (Vol. 7, pp. 5–6, 8).

6.3) Richard Goldstein, "Fred Korematsu . . . ," *The New York Times*, April 1, 2005.

6.4) Jose Antonio Vargas, "Not Legal, Not Leaving," *Time*, June 25, 2012.

6.5) Jennifer Ludden, "Despite New Law, Gender Salary Gap Persists," *National Public Radio*, April 19, 2010.

6.1) Did *Brown* Matter?

The New Yorker, May 3, 2004

CASS SUNSTEIN

On the fiftieth anniversary of the fabled desegregation case, not everyone is celebrating.

> On the 50th anniversary of *Brown v. Board of Education* (1954), Cass Sunstein asks an almost blasphemous question: "Did *Brown* matter?" *Brown* might be the most famous Supreme Court case of all time, and it is often cited as justification for why the federal courts need the power to strike down unfair legislation. But as you dig beyond the title and reflect upon Sunstein's more nuanced argument that "the Court on its own, brought about little desegregation," what at first seems a jaded critique of *Brown* begins to appear as a celebration of citizen action. If, as Sunstein claims, "social forces and political pressures were [more] responsible for the demise of segregation" than federal judges, then Sunstein is making an argument for why social movements are important.
>
> Sunstein's reflection on *Brown*'s impacts include some startling facts regarding the level of school segregation that remained following the decision. In providing these details, he gives a clear view of civil rights in America: it has not been a linear progression but a long struggle with advances, stagnations, and retreats. His observation seems all the more relevant in light of *The Washington Post*'s story on April 24, 2014 (the 60th anniversary of *Brown*), about the astonishing findings of educational policy specialist Richard Rothstein. Rothstein noted that "initial school integration gains following *Brown* stalled and black children are more racially and socioeconomically isolated today than at any time since . . . 1970." If the intention of *Brown* was to eliminate school segregation, not just to rule school segregation illegal, we may well ask "did *Brown* matter?"

On May 17, 1954, the Supreme Court announced its decision in the case of *Brown v. Board of Education*. "Separate educational facilities are inherently unequal," the Court ruled unanimously, declaring that they violated the equal-protection clause of the Fourteenth Amendment. It thus overturned the doctrine of "separate but equal," which had been the law of the land since 1896, when *Plessy v. Ferguson* was decided. The *Brown* ruling—the culmination of a decades-long effort by the N.A.A.C.P.—has today acquired an aura of inevitability. But it didn't seem inevitable at the time. And the fact that it was unanimous was little short of miraculous.

When the school-segregation cases first came before the Court, in 1952, the justices, all Roosevelt and Truman appointees, were split over the constitutional questions. Only four of them (William O. Douglas, Hugo L. Black, Harold H. Burton, and Sherman Minton) were solidly in favor of overturning *Plessy*. Though there is no official record of the Court's internal deliberations, scholars of the decision—notably Michael J. Klarman, a professor of law and history at the University of Virginia—have been able to reconstruct what went on through the justices' conference notes and draft opinions. Chief Justice Fred M. Vinson, a Truman appointee from Kentucky, argued that *Plessy* should be permitted to stand. "Congress has not declared there should be no segregation," Vinson observed, and surely, he went on, the Court must be responsive to "the long-continued interpretation of Congress ever since the Amendments." Justice Stanley F. Reed, also a Kentuckian, was even more skeptical of overturning segregation. "Negroes have not thoroughly assimilated," he said; segregation was "for the benefit of both" blacks and whites, and "states should be left to work out the problem for themselves." The notes for Justice Tom C. Clark, a Texan, indicate greater uncertainty, but he was clearly willing to entertain the position that "we had led the states on to think segregation is OK and we should let them work it out."

Justices Felix Frankfurter and Robert H. Jackson, though staunchly opposed to segregation, were troubled by the legal propriety of overturning a well-established precedent. "However passionately any of us may hold egalitarian views," Frankfurter, an apostle of judicial restraint, wrote in a memorandum, "he travels outside his judicious authority if for this private reason alone he declares unconstitutional the policy of segregation." During the justices' deliberations, Frankfurter pronounced that, considered solely on the basis of history and precedent, "*Plessy* is right." Jackson, for his part, composed a draft opinion reflecting his ambivalence. He acknowledged that the Court's decision "would be simple if our personal opinion that school segregation is morally, economically and politically indefensible made it legally so." But, he asked, "how is it that the Constitution this morning forbids what for three-quarters of a century it has tolerated or approved?" Both Frankfurter and Jackson had been deeply affected by the New Deal era, during which a right-wing Supreme Court had struck down progressive legislation approved by their beloved Franklin Delano Roosevelt, including regulations establishing minimum wages. Frankfurter and Jackson believed in democracy and abhorred judicial activism. They also worried that the judiciary would be unable to enforce a ban on segregation, and that an unenforceable decree would undermine the legitimacy of the federal courts. And so the justices were at odds. In an unusual step, the Court postponed its decision, and asked both sides to reargue the case.

In September of 1953, just before *Brown* was to be reargued, Vinson died of a heart attack, and everything changed. "This is the first indication that I have ever had that there is a God," Frankfurter told a former law clerk. President Eisenhower replaced Vinson with Earl Warren, then the governor of California, who had extraordinary political skills and personal warmth, along with a deep commitment to social justice. Through a combination of determination, compromise, charm, and intense work with the other justices (including visits to the hospital bed of an ailing Robert Jackson), Warren engineered something that might have seemed impossible the year before: a unanimous opinion overruling *Plessy*. Thurgood Marshall, a principal architect of the litigation strategy that led to *Brown*, recalled, "I was so happy I was numb." He predicted that school segregation would be entirely stamped out within five years.

That's how *Brown* looked fifty years ago. Not everyone thinks that it has aged well. Many progressives now argue that its importance has been greatly overstated—that social forces and political pressures, far more than federal judges, were responsible for the demise of segregation. Certainly, *Brown* has disappointed those who hoped that it would give black Americans equal educational opportunities. Some scholars on the left even question whether *Brown* was rightly decided. The experience of the past half century suggests that the Court cannot produce social reform on its own, and that judges are unlikely to challenge an established social consensus. But experience has also underlined *Brown's* enduring importance. To understand all this, we need to step back a bit.

A quiz: In 1960, on the sixth anniversary of the *Brown* decision, how many of the 1.4 million African-American children in the Deep South states of Alabama, Georgia, Louisiana, Mississippi, and South Carolina attended racially mixed schools? Answer: Zero. Even in 1964, a decade after *Brown*, more than ninety-eight per cent of African-American children in the South attended segregated schools. As Klarman shows in his magnificent "From Jim Crow to Civil Rights: The Supreme Court and the Struggle for Racial Equality" . . . the Court, on its own, brought about little desegregation, above all because it lacked the power to overcome local resistance.

Not that it made any unambiguous effort to do so. In the 1954 decision, the Court declined to specify the appropriate remedy for school segregation, asking instead for further arguments about it. The following year, in an opinion known as *Brown v. Board of Education II*, the Court declared that the transition to integration must occur "with all deliberate speed." Perhaps fearing that an order for immediate desegregation would result in school closings and violence, the justices held that lower-court judges could certainly consider administrative problems; delays would be acceptable. As Marshall later told the legal historian Dennis Hutchinson, "In 1954, I was delirious. What a victory! I thought I was the smartest lawyer in the entire world. In 1955, I was shattered. They gave us nothing and then told us to work for it. I thought I was the dumbest Negro in the United States." As a Supreme Court justice, Marshall—for whom I clerked in 1980—liked to say, "I've finally figured out what 'all deliberate speed' means. It means 'slow.'"

Real desegregation began only when the democratic process demanded it—through the 1964 Civil Rights Act and aggressive enforcement by the Department of Justice, which threatened to deny federal funds to segregated school systems. But Klarman doesn't claim that *Brown* was irrelevant to the desegregation struggle. In his view, the decision catalyzed the passage of civil-rights legislation by, in effect, heightening the contradictions: inspiring Southern blacks to challenge segregation—and Southern whites to defend it—more aggressively than they otherwise would have. Before *Brown*, he shows, Southern politics was dominated by moderate Democrats, who generally downplayed racial conflicts. The *Brown* ruling radicalized Southern politics practically overnight, and in a way that has had lasting consequences for American politics.

A case in point is Orval E. Faubus, who became a national figure in 1957, when, as the governor of Arkansas, he used the state's National Guard to defy the courts and stop African-American children from attending high school in Little Rock. But Klarman reminds us that, three years earlier, he had been elected on a liberal, race-neutral platform of spending more money on education and old-age pensions. (His father, a socialist organizer, gave him the middle name Eugene, in honor of Debs.) In the early days of his term, he appointed blacks to the Democratic Central Committee for the first time, and desegregated public transportation. Only after public indignation over *Brown*

swept through his state, and his chief political opponent accused him of being insufficiently zealous in resisting the decision, did he reposition himself as a racial hard-liner. . . .

Klarman's story doesn't stop there, however. Because "the post-*Brown* racial fanaticism of southern politics produced a situation that was ripe for violence," he writes, Northerners soon found themselves outraged by televised scenes of police brutality against peaceful black demonstrators. The civil-rights legislation of the sixties, including the very laws that led to the enforcement of *Brown*, arose from a sort of backlash to the backlash. Given these complicated causal chains, how important to our civil-rights history, in the end, was Chief Justice Vinson's fatal heart attack? Not very, in Klarman's accounting: "Deep background forces"—notably, the experience of the Second World War and the encounter with Nazi racial ideology—"ensured that the United States would experience a racial reform movement regardless of what the Supreme Court did or did not do."

. . . Was *Brown*, then, a failure? Suppose that this is the real meaning of the Court's decision: states may not, by law, separate citizens from one another by race, simply because forcible separation imposes a kind of stigma, or second-class citizenship, that offends the most minimal understanding of human equality. It is one thing to attend all-black schools. It is quite another to live under a legal system that announces, on a daily basis, that some children are not fit to be educated with others. *Brown* ruled that, under the Constitution, states may not humiliate a class of people in that way. It may have taken a while, but this ruling, at least, has stuck. And on the occasion of its fiftieth anniversary it justifies a celebration.

But it does not justify triumphalism. *Brown v. Board*, despite the unanimity of the decision, was the product of a divided Supreme Court and a divided nation. Its current meaning is up to us, not to previous generations or even to the Court that decided it. Cautious as that Court's justices were, Klarman notes a significant generational fact: nearly all of its clerks were in favor of overturning *Plessy*.

ARTICLE QUESTIONS

1) What case did *Brown v. Board of Education* overrule?
2) How many African-American children in the Deep South does Sunstein say attended racially mixed schools in 1960 (six years after the *Brown* decision)?
3) How do Court decisions, congressional and executive actions, and federalism all play a role in the expansion and protection of civil rights?
4) In what ways does Sunstein argue that *Brown* mattered?

6.2) What We Want

The New York Review of Books, September 22, 1966 (Vol. 7, pp. 5–6, 8)

STOKELY CARMICHAEL

All movements contain a multitude of voices making different demands. Even when a movement is successful, only some of its demands will be achieved; others will remain for future struggles. Stokely Carmichael's 1966 article "What We Want" is a militant reminder that the mid-twentieth-century African-American civil rights movement (often just called "the Movement" by people involved) cannot be reduced solely to a demand to end racial segregation. As Carmichael forcefully argues, the Movement was about acquiring power. Carmichael was a controversial voice in the Movement who helped popularize the slogan "black power." However, we should remember that in one of the first speeches where he used the term, he also asserted a need for yellow power for yellow people, red power for red people, brown power for brown people, and white power for white people. Invoking the word "power" often intimidates the listener—a strange realization when we remember that the definition of democracy is "power of the people." In one sense, then, "black power" was a call to include African-Americans in the decision-making power that is at the heart of democracy. But many saw it as a call for something more; you will have to judge what you think about Carmichael's intentions.

Carmichael's essay brings up an interesting question about how to evaluate the success of the civil rights movement. Often it is measured by the removal of segregation laws. But if the goal was for blacks (and other groups) to achieve power, how then should we measure the Movement's success, and how should we view the continued need for the Movement? Because Carmichael asserted that the Movement was about achieving power, he argues that earning the right to vote is not enough. About halfway through the essay he asks the powerful question "How do we make our vote meaningful?" The strategies that the Student Nonviolent Coordinating Committee (SNCC) devised to answer this question continue to provide models for civil rights struggles.

One of the tragedies of the struggle against racism is that up to now there has been no national organization which could speak to the growing militancy of young black people in the urban ghetto. There has been only a civil rights movement, whose tone of voice was adapted to an audience of liberal whites. It served as a sort of buffer zone between them and angry young blacks. None of its so-called leaders could go into a rioting community and be listened to. In a sense, I blame ourselves, together with the mass media, for what has happened in Watts, Harlem, Chicago, Cleveland, Omaha. Each time the people in those cities saw Martin Luther King get slapped, they became angry; when they saw four little black girls bombed to death, they were angrier; and when nothing happened, they were steaming. We had nothing to offer that they could see, except to go out and be beaten again. We helped to build their frustration.

For too many years, black Americans marched and had their heads broken and got shot. They were saying to the country, "Look, you guys are supposed to be nice guys and we are only going to do what we are supposed to do—why do you beat us up, why don't you give us what we ask, why don't you straighten yourselves out?" After years of this, we are at almost the same point—because we demonstrated from a position of weakness. We cannot be expected any longer to march and have our heads broken in order to say to whites: come on, you're nice guys. For you are not nice guys. We have found you out.

An organization which claims to speak for the needs of a community, as does the Student Nonviolent Coordinating Committee, must speak in the tone of that community, not as somebody else's buffer zone. This is the significance of black power as a slogan. For once, black people are going to use the words they want to use, not just the words whites want to hear. And they will do this no matter how often the press tries to stop the use of the slogan by equating it with racism or separatism.

An organization which claims to be working for the needs of a community, as SNCC does, must work to provide that community with a position of strength from which to make its voice heard. This is the significance of black power beyond the slogan.

Black power can be clearly defined for those who do not attach the fears of white America to their questions about it. We should begin with the basic fact that black Americans have two problems: they are poor and they are black. All other problems arise from this two-sided reality: lack of education, the so-called apathy of black men. Any program to end racism must address itself to that double reality.

Almost from its beginning SNCC sought to address itself to both conditions with a program aimed at winning political power for impoverished Southern blacks. We had to begin with politics because black Americans are a property-less people in a country where property is valued above all. We had to work for power, because this country does not function by morality, love, and nonviolence, but by power. Thus we determined to win

political power, with the idea of moving on from there into activity that would have economic effects. With power, the masses could *make or participate in making* the decisions which govern their destinies, and thus create basic change in their day-to-day lives.

But if political power seemed to be the key to self-determination, it was also obvious that the key had been thrown down a deep well many years earlier. Disenfranchisement, maintained by racist terror, makes it impossible to talk about organizing for political power in 1960. The right to vote had to be won, and SNCC workers devoted their energies to this from 1961 to 1965. They set up voter registration drives in the Deep South. They created pressure for the vote by holding mock elections in the Mississippi Freedom Democratic Party (MFDP) in 1964. That struggle was eased, though not won, with the passage of the 1965 Voting Rights Act. SNCC workers could then address themselves to the question: "Who can we vote for, to have our needs met—how do we make our vote meaningful?"

SNCC had already gone to Atlantic City for recognition of the Mississippi Freedom Democratic Party by the Democratic convention and been rejected; it had gone with the MFDP to Washington for recognition by Congress and been rejected. In Arkansas, SNCC helped thirty Negroes to run for School Board elections; all but one were defeated, and there was evidence of fraud and intimidation sufficient to cause their defeat. In Atlanta, Julian Bond ran for the state legislature and was elected—twice—and unseated—twice. In several states, black farmers ran in elections for agricultural committees which make crucial decisions concerning land use, loans, etc. Although they won places on a number of committees, they never gained the majorities needed to control them.

All of the efforts were attempts to win black power. Then, in Alabama, the opportunity came to see how blacks could be organized on an independent party basis. An unusual Alabama law provides that any group of citizens can nominate candidates for county office and, if they win 20 per cent of the vote may be recognized as a county political party. The same then applies on a state level. SNCC went on to organize in several counties such as Lowndes, where black people—who form 8 percent of the population and have an average annual income of $943—felt they could accomplish nothing within the frame work of the Alabama Democratic Party because of its racism and because the qualifying fee for this year's elections was raised from $50 to $500 in order to prevent most Negroes from becoming candidates. On May 3, five new county "freedom organizations" convened and nominated candidates for the offices of sheriff, tax assessor, members of the school boards. These men and women are up for election in November—if they live until then. Their ballot symbol is the black panther: a bold, beautiful animal, representing the strength of black demands today. A man needs a black panther on his side when he and his family must endure—as hundreds of Alabamians have endured—loss of job, eviction, starvation, and sometimes death, for political activity. He may also need a gun and SNCC reaffirms the right of black men everywhere to defend themselves when threatened or attacked. As for initiating the use of violence, we hope that such programs as ours will make that unnecessary; but it is not for us to tell black communities whether they can or cannot use any particular form of action to resolve their problems. Responsibility for the use of violence by black men, whether in self-defense or initiated by them, lies with the white community.

This is the specific historical experience from which SNCC's call for "black power" emerged on the Mississippi march last July. But the concept of "black power" is not a recent or isolated phenomenon: It has grown out of the ferment of agitation and activity by different people and organizations in many black communities over the years. Our last year of work in Alabama added a new concrete possibility. In Lowndes County, for example, black power will mean that if a Negro is elected sheriff, he can end police brutality. If a black man is elected tax assessor, he can collect and channel funds for the building of better roads and schools serving black people—thus advancing the move from political power into the economic arena. In such areas as Lowndes, where black men have a majority, they will attempt to use it to exercise control. This is what they seek: control. Where Negroes lack a majority, black power means proper representation and sharing of control. It means the creation of power bases from which black people can work to change statewide or nationwide patterns of oppression through pressure from strength—instead of weakness. Politically, black power means what it has always meant to SNCC: The coming together of black people to elect representatives and *to force those representatives to speak to their needs*. It does not mean merely putting black faces into office. A man or woman who is black and from the slums cannot be automatically expected to speak to the needs of black people. Most of the black politicians we see around the country today are not what SNCC means by black power. The power must be that of a community, and emanate from there.

SNCC today is working in both the North and South on programs of voter registration and independent political organizing. In some places, such as Alabama, Los Angeles, New York, Philadelphia, and New Jersey, independent organizing under the black panther symbol is in progress. The creation of a national "black panther party" must come about: it will take time to build, and it is much too early to predict its success. We have no infallible master plan and we make no claim to exclusive knowledge of how to end racism; different groups will work in their own different ways. SNCC cannot spell out the full logistics of self-determination but it can address itself to the problem by helping black communities define their needs, realize their strength, and go into action along a variety of lines which they must choose for themselves. Without knowing all the answers, it can address itself to the basic problem of poverty: to the fact that in Lowndes County 86 white families own 90 per cent of the land. What are black people going to do for jobs, where are they going to get money? There must be reallocation of land and money.

Ultimately, the economic foundations of this country must be shaken if black people are to control their lives. The colonies of the United States, and this includes the black ghettoes within its borders, north and south, must be liberated. For a century, this nation has been like an octopus of exploitation, its tentacles stretching from Mississippi and Harlem to South America, the Middle East, southern Africa, and Vietnam; the form of exploitation varies from area to area but the essential result has been the same, a powerful few have been maintained and enriched at the expense of the poor and voiceless colored masses. This pattern must be broken. As its grip loosens here and there around the world, the hopes of black Americans become more realistic. For racism to die, a totally different America must be born.

This is what the white society does not wish to face; this is why that society prefers to talk about integration. But integration speaks not at all to the problem of poverty, only to the problem of blackness. Integration today means the man who "makes it," leaving his black brothers behind in the ghetto as fast as his new sports car will take him. It has no relevance to the Harlem wino or to the cotton-picker making three dollars a day. As a lady I know in Alabama once said, "the food that Ralph Bunche eats doesn't fill my stomach."

Integration, moreover, speaks to the problem of blackness in a despicable way. As a goal, it has been based on complete acceptance of the fact that *in order to have* a decent house or education, blacks must move into a white neighborhood or send their children to a white school. This reinforces, among both black and white, the idea that "white" is automatically better and "black" is by definition inferior. This is why integration is a subterfuge for the maintenance of white supremacy. It allows the nation to focus on a handful of Southern children who get into white schools, at great price, and to ignore the 94 per cent who are left behind in unimproved all-black schools. Such situations will not change until black people have power, to control their own school boards, in this case. Then Negroes become equal in a way that means something, and integration ceases to be a one-way street. Then integration doesn't mean draining skills and energies from the ghetto into white neighborhoods; then it can mean white people moving from Beverly Hills into Watts, white people joining the Lowndes County Freedom Organization. Then integration becomes relevant. . . .

White America will not face the problem of color, the reality of it. The well-intended say:

"We're all human, everybody is really decent, we must forget color." But color cannot be "forgotten" until its weight is recognized and dealt with. White America will not acknowledge that the ways in which this country sees itself are contradicted by being black—and always have been. Whereas most of the people who settled this country came here for freedom or for economic opportunity, blacks were brought here to be slaves. . . .

Whites will not see that I, for example, as a person oppressed because of my blackness, have common cause with other blacks who are oppressed because of blackness. This is not to say that there are no white people who see things as I do, but that it is a black people I must speak to first. It must be the oppressed to whom SNCC addresses itself primarily, not to friends from the oppressing group.

From birth, black people are told a set of lies about themselves. We are told that we are lazy—yet I drive through the Delta area of Mississippi and watch black people picking cotton in the hot sun for fourteen hours. We are told, "If you work hard, you'll succeed"—but if that were true, black people would own this country. We are oppressed because we are black—not because we are lazy, not because we're stupid (and got good rhythm), but because we're black. . . .

This does not mean we don't welcome help, or friends. But we want the right to decide whether anyone is, in fact, our friend. In the past, Black Americans have been almost the only people whom everybody and his momma could jump up and call their friends. We have been tokens, symbols, objects, as I was in high school to many young whites, who liked having "a Negro friend." We want to decide who is our friend, and we will not accept someone who comes to us and says: "If you do X, Y, and Z, then I'll help you." We will not be told whom we should choose as allies. We will not be isolated from any group or nation except by our own choice. We cannot have the oppressors telling the oppressed how to rid themselves of the oppressor.

I have said that most liberal whites react to "black power" with the question: What about me? rather than saying: Tell me what you want me to do and I'll see if I can do it. There are answers to the right question. One of the most disturbing things about almost all white supporters of the movement has been that they are afraid to go into their own communities—which is where the racism exists—and work to get rid of it. They want to run from Berkeley to tell us what to do in Mississippi; let them look instead at Berkeley. They admonish blacks to be nonviolent; let them preach nonviolence in the white community. They come to teach me Negro history; let them go to the suburbs and open up freedom schools for whites. Let them work to stop America's racist foreign policy; let them press this government to cease supporting the economy of South Africa.

There is a vital job to be done among poor whites. We hope to see eventually a coalition between poor blacks and poor whites. That is the only coalition which seems acceptable to us, and we see such a coalition as the major internal instrument of change in American society. SNCC has tried several times to organize poor whites; we are trying again now, with an initial training program in Tennessee. It is purely academic today to talk about bringing poor blacks and whites together, but the job of creating a poor white power bloc must be attempted. The main responsibility for it falls upon whites. Black and white can work together in the white community where possible; it is not possible, however, to go into a poor Southern town and talk about integration. Poor whites everywhere are becoming more hostile—not

less—partly because they see the nation's attention focused on black poverty and nobody coming to them. Too many young middle-class Americans, like some sort of Pepsi generation, have wanted to come alive through the black community; they've wanted to be where the action is—and the action has been in the black community.

Black people do not want to "take over" this country. They don't want to "get whitey"; they just want to get him off their backs, as the saying goes. It was for example the exploitation by Jewish landlords and merchants which first created black sentiment toward Jews—not Judaism. This white man is irrelevant to blacks, except as an oppressive force. Blacks want to be in his place, yes, but not in order to terrorize and lynch and starve him. They want to be in his place because that is where a decent life can be had. . . .

As for white America, perhaps it can stop crying out against "black supremacy," "black nationalism," "racism in reverse," and begin facing reality. The reality is that this nation, from top to bottom, is racist; that racism is not primarily a problem of "human relations" but of an exploitation maintained, either actively or through silence, by the society as a whole. Camus and Sartre have asked, can a man condemn himself? Can whites, particularly liberal whites, condemn themselves? Can they stop blaming us, and blame their own system? Are they capable of the shame which might become a revolutionary emotion? . . .

ARTICLE QUESTIONS

1) What actions did SNCC workers engage in after working to win the passage of the 1965 Voting Rights Act in order to make their "vote meaningful"? Should any group that wants to make its vote meaningful engage in similar actions?

2) According to Carmichael, what are the two problems facing black Americans that any program to end racism must address? How does Carmichael see "all other problems aris[ing] from this two-sided reality"?

3) How does Carmichael employ the term "black power"? What does he mean? Does using this term help or hinder the push for African-American civil rights?

4) If we judge the success of the African-American struggle to acquire civil rights from the perspective of black power as articulated by Carmichael, how should we judge the success of the Movement?

6.3) Fred Korematsu, 86, Dies; Lost Key Suit on Internment

The New York Times, April 1, 2005

RICHARD GOLDSTEIN

In January 2011 California celebrated "Fred Korematsu Day of Civil Liberties and the Constitution." It was the first such day commemorating an Asian-American. Richard Goldstein notes that Korematsu was most famous for his refusal to report to one of the internment camps established for Japanese-Americans at the start of World War II. Some 120,000 individuals (more than 2,500 of whom were students at California public colleges and universities) were given short notice and forced to report to internment camps. In the process they lost all their possessions. Korematsu refused and was arrested. He challenged his arrest but ultimately lost in the infamous Supreme Court case *Korematsu v. United States* (1944). The conviction stayed on Korematsu's record until 1983, when a federal court reviewed new evidence and overturned his conviction.

Korematsu was later awarded the Medal of Freedom, the highest award given to a civilian. In 1988, the federal government provided payments and apologies to those interned, and by 2010 many California universities and colleges had awarded honorary degrees to the Japanese-American students who had been suddenly removed from their campuses nearly 70 years earlier. These are all important gestures—but, as Richard Goldstein notes in this obituary, Korematsu called for something more. Near the end of his life, he was concerned about civil rights protections after the September 11, 2001, terrorist attacks. In expressing such a concern Korematsu made a connection between his struggle and the struggle of other groups. He was also making an observation that in times of war, civil rights are often curtailed. But perhaps most importantly, he was challenging us to prevent civil rights denials rather than hoping for apologies many years after denials occur.

Fred T. Korematsu...lost a Supreme Court challenge in 1944 to the wartime internment of Japanese-Americans but gained vindication decades later when he was given the Medal of Freedom....

When he was arrested in 1942 for failing to report to an internment center, Mr. Korematsu was working as a welder and simply hoping to be left alone so he could pursue his marriage plans. He became a central figure in the controversy over the wartime removal of more than 100,000 Japanese-Americans and Japanese immigrants from the West Coast to inland detention centers. He emerged as a symbol of resistance to government authority.

When President Bill Clinton presented Mr. Korematsu with the Medal of Freedom, the nation's highest civilian award, in January 1998, the president likened him to Linda Brown and Rosa Parks in the civil rights struggles of the 1950's.

In February 1942, two months after the Japanese attacked Pearl Harbor, President Franklin D. Roosevelt signed an executive order authorizing the designation of military areas from which anyone could be excluded "as protection against espionage and sabotage."

In May 1942, the military command on the West Coast ordered that all people with Japanese ancestry be removed inland, considering them a security threat, and internment camps were built in harsh and isolated regions.

Mr. Korematsu, a native of Oakland, Calif., and one of four sons of Japanese-born parents, was jailed on May 30, 1942, in San Leandro, having refused to join family members who had reported to a nearby racetrack that was being used as a temporary detention center.

Mr. Korematsu had undergone plastic surgery in an effort to disguise his Asian features and had altered his draft registration card, listing his name as Clyde Sarah and his background as Spanish-Hawaiian. He hoped that with his altered appearance and identity he could avoid ostracism when he married his girlfriend, who had an Italian background.

A few days after his arrest, Mr. Korematsu was visited in jail by a California official of the American Civil Liberties Union who was seeking a test case against internment. Mr. Korematsu agreed to sue.

"I didn't feel guilty because I didn't do anything wrong," he told *The New York Times* four decades later. "Every day in school, we said the pledge to the flag, 'with liberty and justice for all,' and I believed all that. I was an American citizen, and I had as many rights as anyone else."

Mr. Korematsu maintained that his constitutional rights were violated by internment and that he had suffered racial discrimination. In the summer of 1942, he was found guilty in federal court of ignoring the exclusion directive and was sentenced to five years' probation. He spent two years at an internment camp in Utah with his family. In 1944, the A.C.L.U. took his case before the Supreme Court.

In December 1944 in *Korematsu v. the United States*, the Supreme Court upheld internment by a vote of 6 to 3. Justice Hugo L. Black, remembered today as a stout civil liberties advocate, wrote in the opinion that Mr. Korematsu was not excluded "because of hostility to him or his race" but because the United States was at war with Japan, and the military "feared an invasion of our West Coast."

In dissenting, Justice Frank Murphy wrote that the exclusion order "goes over the very brink of constitutional power and falls into the ugly abyss of racism."

The case was revisited long afterward when Peter Irons, a professor of political science at the University of California, San Diego, discovered documents that indicated that when it went to the Supreme Court, the government had suppressed its own findings that Japanese-Americans on the West Coast were not, in fact, security threats.

In light of that information, Judge Marilyn H. Patel of Federal District Court in San Francisco overturned Mr. Korematsu's conviction in November 1983. In 1988, federal law provided for payments and apologies to Japanese-Americans relocated in World War II.

Mr. Korematsu returned to California after the war, worked as a draftsman and raised a family. For many years, he withheld information about his case from his children, seeking to forget about his humiliation.

In recent years, Mr. Korematsu expressed concern about civil liberties in the United States after the Sept. 11, 2001, terrorist attacks. . . .

In her decision overturning Mr. Korematsu's conviction, Judge Patel said, "Korematsu stands as a constant caution that in times of war or declared military necessity our institutions must be vigilant in protecting constitutional guarantees."

ARTICLE QUESTIONS

1) What actions did Korematsu take to avoid being interned?
2) Why was the *Korematsu* case revisited long after the 1944 decision?
3) What lessons can we learn, and what connections to other civil rights struggles can we make, by reflecting upon the World War II internment of Japanese-Americans and the *Korematsu* case?

6.4) Not Legal, Not Leaving

Time, June 25, 2012

JOSE ANTONIO VARGAS

The wave after wave of immigrants coming to the United States is one of the nation's defining features. Almost every immigrant group has faced discrimination and struggled to gain civil rights. This discrimination has included restrictions on voting, serving on juries, holding public office, access to the legal system, and owning property. Today, an invisible struggle for immigration reform and access to citizenship rights is taking place. On one hand, the lack of visibility for many of those desiring immigration reform makes sense: People without legal status often hide in the shadows, hoping not to be noticed. On the other hand, this lack of visibility limits the prosepcts for change. Leaders in both the Republican and Democratic parties have promoted reform; both presidents Bush and Obama made it one of their top priorities. In May 2006, over 1.5 million marched in immigration reform rallies across the country; this was one of the largest days of protest in the country's history.

Jose Antonio Vargas, in "Not Legal, Not Leaving," presents a different strategy in the push for immigration reform: the idea of "coming out" as an undocumented immigrant. The "coming out" strategy was inspired by another movement that was pushed into the shadows, the gay rights movement. Coming out allows people to see that their friends and neighbors are some of the individuals affected by current immigration policies. The adoption of this tactic displays how civil rights struggles freely borrow strategies from other movements. Vargas himself came out very publically in an essay for *The New York Times.* Since coming out Vargas states, "I am now a walking conversation that most people are uncomfortable having." This uncomfortable conversation often includes a direct question about why he doesn't become a citizen or at least gain legal residency status. Vargas, referencing his own experience, explains that under current immigration policy gaining legal status is not that easy. In fact, after being brought to the United States by his parents from the Philippines, he has almost no options for gaining citizenship in the only country he has strong memories of living in.

"Why Haven't You Gotten Deported?"

That's usually the first thing people ask me when they learn I'm an undocumented immigrant or, put more rudely, an "illegal." Some ask it with anger or frustration, others with genuine bafflement. At a restaurant in Birmingham, not far from the University of Alabama, an inebriated young white man challenged me: "You got your papers?" I told him I didn't. "Well, you should get your ass home, then." In California, a middle-aged white woman threw up her arms and wanted to know: "Why hasn't Obama dealt with you?" At least once a day, I get that question, or a variation of it, via e-mail, tweet or Facebook message. Why, indeed, am I still here?

It's a fair question, and it's been hanging over me every day for the past year, ever since I publicly revealed my undocumented status. There are an estimated 11.5 million people like me in this country, human beings with stories as varied as America itself yet lacking a legal claim to exist here. Like many others, I kept my status a secret, passing myself off as a U.S. citizen—right down to cultivating a homegrown accent. I went to college and became a journalist, earning a staff job at *The Washington Post.* But the deception weighed on me. When I eventually decided to admit the truth, I chose to come out publicly—very publicly—in the form of an essay for *The New York Times* last June. Several immigration lawyers counseled against doing this. ("It's legal suicide," warned one.) Broadcasting my status to millions seemed tantamount to an invitation to the immigration cops: Here I am. Come pick me up.

So I waited. And waited some more. As the months passed, there were no knocks on my door, no papers served, no calls or letters from U.S.

Immigration and Customs Enforcement (ICE), which deported a record 396,906 people in fiscal 2011. Before I came out, the question always at the top of my mind was, What will happen if people find out? Afterward, the question changed to What happens now? It seemed I had traded a largely hidden undocumented life in limbo for an openly undocumented life that's still in limbo.

But as I've crisscrossed the U.S.—participating in more than 60 events in nearly 20 states and learning all I can about this debate that divides our country (yes, it's my country too)—I've realized that the most important questions are the ones other people ask me. I am now a walking conversation that most people are uncomfortable having. And once that conversation starts, it's clear why a consensus on solving our immigration dilemma is so elusive. The questions I hear indicate the things people don't know, the things they think they know but have been misinformed about and the views they hold but do not ordinarily voice.

I've also been witness to a shift I believe will be a game changer for the debate: more people coming out. While closely associated with the modern gay-rights movement, in recent years the term coming out and the act itself have been embraced by the country's young undocumented population. At least 2,000 undocumented immigrants—most of them under 30—have contacted me and outed themselves in the past year. Others are coming out over social media or in person to their friends, their fellow students, their colleagues. It's true, these individuals—many brought to the U.S. by family when they were too young to understand what it means to be "illegal"—are a fraction of the millions living hidden lives. But each becomes another walking conversation. We love this country. We contribute to it. This is our home. What happens when even more of us step forward? How will the U.S. government and American citizens react then?

The contradictions of our immigration debate are inescapable. Polls show substantial support for creating a path to citizenship for some undocumenteds—yet 52% of Americans support allowing police to stop and question anyone they suspect of being "illegal." Democrats are viewed as being more welcoming to immigrants, but the Obama Administration has sharply ramped up deportations. The pro-business GOP waves a KEEP OUT flag at the Mexican border and a HELP WANTED sign 100 yards in, since so many industries depend on cheap labor.

Election-year politics is further confusing things, as both parties scramble to attract Latinos without scaring off other constituencies. President Obama has as much as a 3-to-1 lead over Mitt Romney among Latino voters, but his deportation push is dampening their enthusiasm. Romney has a crucial ally in Florida Senator Marco Rubio, a Cuban American, but is burdened by the sharp anti-immigrant rhetoric he unleashed in the primary-election battle. This month, the Supreme Court is expected to rule on Arizona's controversial anti-immigrant law. A decision either way could galvanize reform supporters and opponents alike.

But the real political flash point is the proposed Dream Act, a decade-old immigration bill that would provide a path to citizenship for young people educated in this country. The bill never passed, but it focused attention on these youths, who call themselves the Dreamers. Both the President and Rubio have placed Dreamers at the center of their reform efforts—but with sharply differing views on how to address them.

ICE, the division of the Department of Homeland Security (DHS) charged with enforcing immigration laws, is its own contradiction, a tangled bureaucracy saddled with conflicting goals. As the weeks passed after my public confession, the fears of my lawyers and friends began to seem faintly ridiculous. Coming out didn't endanger me; it had protected me. A Philippine-born, college-educated, outspoken mainstream journalist is not the face the government wants to put on its deportation program. Even so, who flies under the radar, and who becomes one of those unfortunate 396,906? Who stays, who goes, and who decides? Eventually I confronted ICE about its plans for me, and I came away with even more questions.

I am not without contradictions either. I am 31 and have been a working journalist for a decade.

I know I can no longer claim to be a detached, objective reporter, at least in the traditional sense. I am part of this evolving story and growing movement. It is personal. Though I have worked hard to approach this issue like any other, I've also found myself drawn to the activists, driven to help tell their story.

This is the time to tell it.

"Why don't you become legal?" asked 79-year-old William Oglesby of Iowa City, Iowa. It was early December, a few weeks before the Iowa caucuses, and I was attending a Mitt Romney town hall at an animal-feed maker. Romney had just fielded questions from a group of voters, including Oglesby and his wife Sharon, both Republicans. Addressing immigration, Romney said, "For those who have come here illegally, they might have a transition time to allow them to set their affairs in order and then go back home and get in line with everybody else."

"I haven't become legal," I told William, "because there's no way for me to become legal, sir."

Sharon jumped in. "You can't get a green card?"

"No, ma'am," I said. "There's no process for me." Of all the questions I've been asked in the past year, "Why don't you become legal?" is probably the most exasperating. But it speaks to how unfamiliar most Americans are with how the immigration process works.

As Angela M. Kelley, an immigration advocate in Washington, told me, "If you think the American tax code is outdated and complicated, try understanding America's immigration code." The easiest way to become a U.S. citizen is to be born here—doesn't matter who your parents are; you're in. (The main exception is for children of foreign diplomatic officials.) If you were born outside the U.S. and want to come here, the golden ticket is the so-called green card, a document signifying that the U.S. government has granted you permanent-resident status, meaning you're able to live and, more important, work here. Once you have a green card, you're on your way to eventual citizenship—in as little as three years if you marry a U.S. citizen—as long as you don't break the law and you meet other requirements such as paying a fee and passing a civics test.

Obtaining a green card means navigating one of the two principal ways of getting permanent legal status in the U.S.: family or specialized work. To apply for a green card on the basis of family, you need to be a spouse, parent, child or sibling of a citizen. (Green-card holders can petition only for their spouses or unmarried children.) Then it's time to get in line. For green-card seekers, the U.S. has a quota of about 25,000 green cards per country each year. That means Moldova (population: 3.5 million) gets the same number of green cards as Mexico (population: 112 million). The wait time depends on demand. If you're in Mexico, India, the Philippines or another nation with many applicants, expect a wait of years or even decades. (Right now, for example, the U.S. is considering Filipino siblings who applied in January 1989.)

Taking the employment route to a green card means clearing a pretty high bar if you have an employer who's willing to hire you. There are different levels of priority, with preference given to people with job skills considered crucial, such as specialized medical professionals, advanced-degree holders and executives of multinational companies. There's no waiting list for those. If you don't qualify for a green card, you may be able to secure one of the few kinds of temporary work visas—including the now famous H1-B visas that are common in Silicon Valley. For those already in the U.S. without documentation—those who have sneaked across a border or overstayed a temporary visa—it's even more complicated. Options are extremely limited. One route is to marry a U.S. citizen, but it's not as easy as the movies would have you think. The process can take years, especially if a sham marriage is suspected. I couldn't marry my way into citizenship even if I wanted to. I'm gay. Same-sex marriage is not recognized by the federal government—explicitly so, ever since Congress passed the Defense of Marriage Act. From the government's perspective, for me to pursue a path to legalization now, I would have to leave the U.S., return to the Philippines and hope to qualify via employment, since I don't have any qualifying family members here. But because I have admitted to being in the U.S. illegally, I would be subject to a 10-year bar before any application would be considered.

The long-stalled Dream Act is the best hope for many young people. The original 2001 version would have created a path to legal status—effectively a green card—for undocumented people age 21 and under who had graduated from high school and resided in the U.S. for five years. As the bill stalled in Congress and Dreamers got older, the age requirement went up, getting as high as 35. Rubio is expected to introduce his own variation, granting nonimmigrant visas so Dreamers could legally stay in the U.S., go to school and work. Its prospects are dim in a gridlocked Congress. Obama, meanwhile, is said to be weighing an Executive Order that would halt deportation of Dream Act–eligible youth and provide them with work permits. Under both Rubio's bill (details of which are not yet confirmed) and Obama's Executive Order (which is being studied), Dreamers could become legal residents. However, both proposals are only the first steps of a longer journey to citizenship.

"Why did you get your driver's license when you knew it wasn't legal? Do you think you belong to a special class of people who can break any laws they please?"

These were the questions of a polite, mild-mannered man named Konrad Sosnow, who I later learned was a lawyer. In late March, Sosnow and I participated in what was billed as a "civility roundtable" on immigration in my adopted hometown of Mountain View, Calif. About 120 people attended. Sosnow had read my coming-out story and wanted to know why I had such disregard for laws.

"I don't think I belong to a special class of people—not at all," I remember telling Sosnow. "I didn't get the license to spite you or disrespect you or because I think I'm better than you. I got the license because, like you, I needed to go to work. People like me get licenses because we need to drop kids off at school and because we need to pick up groceries. I am sorry for what I did, but I did it because I had to live and survive." Sosnow nodded, not exactly in agreement but at least with some understanding. We shook hands as the evening drew to a close. Months later, Sosnow told me he's written e-mails to the President and other elected officials, asking for immigration reform.

Everyday life for an undocumented American means a constant search for loopholes and back doors. Take air travel, for instance. Everyone knows that in the post-9/11 era, you can't fly without a government-issued ID. The easiest option for most people is their driver's license. Most states will not issue a license without proof of legal residency or citizenship. But a few grant licenses to undocumented immigrants, New Mexico and Washington State among them. Like many others, I had falsely posed as a Washington State resident in order to get a license. Weeks after my coming-out essay was published last year, Washington revoked the license—not because I'm undocumented but because I don't actually live in Washington.

For those who don't have a driver's license—that includes me now—a passport from our native country can serve as ID. But it makes every flight a gamble. My passport, which I got through the Philippine embassy, lacks a visa. If airport security agents turn the pages and discover this, they can contact Customs and Border Protection, which in turn can detain me. But for domestic flights, security usually checks just the name, photo and expiration date, not for the visa.

We may be nonpeople to the TSA but not to the IRS. Undocumented workers pay taxes. I've paid income taxes, state and federal, since I started working at 18. The IRS doesn't care if I'm here legally; it cares about its money. Some undocumented people, of course, circumvent the system, just like some citizens. But according to the nonpartisan Institute on Taxation and Economic Policy, households headed by undocumented workers collectively paid $11.2 billion in state and local taxes in 2010—$1.2 billion in income taxes, $1.6 billion in property taxes (because undocumented immigrants do own property) and $8.4 billion in consumption taxes. We also pay into Social Security. Even as many of us contribute, we cannot avail ourselves of a great deal of the services those tax dollars pay for.

When you lack legal status, the threat of deportation is a constant concern. In three years, Obama has deported 1.2 million; it took President George W. Bush eight years to deport 1.6 million. "Under both the Bush and Obama administrations, we have reversed ourselves as a nation of immigrants," Bill Ong Hing, a veteran immigration lawyer, told me. (Indeed, nations like Canada now have higher percentages of immigrants than the "melting pot" of the U.S.)

A big driver of the deportation numbers is ICE's Secure Communities program, which was meant to target terrorists and serious criminals but also winds up snaring those whose only crimes are civil violations connected to being undocumented (like driving without a license). Students and mothers have been detained and deported alongside murderers and rapists.

Depending on how the politics plays to the local electorate, many states wind up writing their own immigration laws. Two years ago, Arizona passed SB 1070—its "Show me your papers" bill—then the strictest immigration law in the country. It embodies an attrition-through-enforcement doctrine: the state will so threaten the livelihood of its undocumented population that they will just give up and self-deport. Among the bill's most controversial provisions, currently being reviewed by the Supreme Court, is one giving law-enforcement officials the power to stop anyone whom they suspect to be "illegal." Arizona's law inspired copycat bills across the country.

For all the roadblocks, though, many of us get by thanks to our fellow Americans. We rely on a growing network of citizens—Good Samaritans, our pastors, our co-workers, our teachers who protect and look after us. As I've traveled the country, I've seen how members of this underground railroad are coming out about their support for us too.

"So you're not Mexican?" an elderly white woman named Ann (she declined to give her last name) asked me when I told her about my undocumented status last October. We stood in front of a Kohl's department store in Alabama, which last year outdid Arizona by passing HB 56, the country's most draconian immigration law. HB 56 requires public schools to collect the immigration status of new students and their parents and makes it a felony for anyone to transport or house an undocumented immigrant. Both provisions are currently blocked by federal courts pending a ruling.

Ann, a registered Republican, was born and raised in the South, where immigration is introducing a new variable into the old racial divide. Alabama's immigrant population, though still relatively small, has nearly doubled in the past decade. The state's Latino population alone grew from 1.7% of the overall population in 2000 to nearly 4% in 2010—about 180,000 people, according to Census figures. But when I told Ann I am Filipino, she scrunched her forehead. "My border," I explained, "was the Pacific Ocean."

Though roughly 59% of the estimated 11.5 million undocumented immigrants in the U.S. are from Mexico, the rest are not. About 1 million come from Asia and the Pacific Islands, about 800,000 from South America and about 300,000 from Europe. Others come from Nigeria, Israel, pretty much everywhere. In the case of countries that don't share a border with the U.S., these are almost always people who entered the country legally—as vacationers or on temporary visas—and overstayed the time permitted.

But perception has become reality. What's cemented in people's consciousness is the television reel of Mexicans jumping a fence. Reality check: illegal border crossings are at their lowest level since the Nixon era, in part because of the continued economic slump and stepped-up enforcement. According to the Office of Immigration Statistics at DHS, 86% of undocumented immigrants have been living in the U.S. for seven years or longer.

Still, for many, immigration is synonymous with Mexicans and the border. In several instances, white conservatives I spoke to moved from discussing "illegals" in particular to talking about Mexicans in general—about Spanish being overheard at Walmart, about the onslaught of new kids at schools and new neighbors at churches, about the "other" people. The immigration debate, at its core, is impossible to separate from America's unprecedented and culture-shifting demographic makeover. Whites represent a shrinking share of the total U.S. population. Recently the U.S. Census reported that for the first time, children born to racial- and ethnic-minority parents represent a majority of all new births.

According to the Pew Hispanic Center, there are also at least 17 million people who are legally living in the U.S. but whose families have at least one undocumented immigrant. About 4.5 million U.S.-citizen kids have at least one undocumented parent. Immigration experts call these mixed-status families, and I grew up in one. I come from a large Filipino clan in which, among dozens of cousins and uncles and aunties and many American-born nieces and nephews, I'm the only one who doesn't have papers. My mother sent me to live with my grandparents in the U.S. when I was 12. When I was 16 and applied for a driver's permit, I found out that my green card—my main form of legal identification—was fake. My grandparents, both naturalized citizens, hadn't told me. It was disorienting, first discovering my precarious status, then realizing that when I had been pledging allegiance to the flag, the republic for which it stands didn't have room for me.

"Why did you come out?" asked 20-year-old Gustavo Madrigal, who attended a talk I gave at the University of Georgia in late April. Like many Dreamers I've met, Madrigal is active in his community. Since he grew up in Georgia, he's needed to be. A series of measures have made it increasingly tough for undocumented students there to attend state universities.

"Why did you come out?" I asked him in turn.

"I didn't have a choice," Madrigal replied.

"I also reached a point," I told him, "when there was no other choice but to come out." And it is true for so many others. We are living in the golden age of coming out. There are no overall numbers on this, but each day I encounter at least five more openly undocumented people. As a group and as individuals, we are putting faces and names and stories on an issue that is often treated as an abstraction.

Technology, especially social media, has played a big role. Online, people are telling their stories and coming out, asking others to consider life from their perspective and testing everyone's empathy quotient. Some realize the risks of being so public; others, like me, think publicity offers protection. Most see the value of connecting with others and sharing experiences—by liking the page of United We Dream on Facebook, for example, or watching the Undocumented and Awkward video series on YouTube.

This movement has its roots in the massive immigrant-rights rallies of 2006, which were held in protest of HR 4437, a Republican-backed House bill that would have classified undocumented immigrants and anyone who helped them enter and remain in the U.S. as felons. Though the bill died, it awakened activism in this young generation. Through Facebook, Twitter and YouTube, I encountered youths who were bravely facing their truths.

"For many people, coming out is a way of saying you're not alone," says Gaby Pacheco of United We Dream. Her parents came from Ecuador and brought her to the U.S. in 1993, when she was 7. Immigration officials raided her home in 2006, and her family has been fighting deportation since. Now 27, she has three education degrees and wants to be a special-education teacher. But her life remains on hold while she watches documented friends land jobs and plan their futures. Says Pacheco: "In our movement, you come out for yourself, and you come out for other people."

The movement, as its young members call it, does not have a single leader. News travels by tweet and Facebook update, as it did when we heard that Joaquin Luna, an undocumented 18-year-old from Texas, killed himself the night after Thanksgiving and, though this is unproved, we instantly connected his death to the stresses of living as a Dreamer. Some Dreamers, contemplating coming out, ask me whether they should pretend to be legal to get by. "Should I just do what you did? You know, check the citizenship box [on a government form] and try to get the job?" a few have asked me. Often I don't know how to respond. I'd like to tell them to be open and honest, but I know I owe my career to my silence for all those years. Sometimes all I can manage to say is "You have to say yes to yourself when the world says no."

"What next?" is the question I ask myself now. It's a question that haunts every undocumented person in the U.S. The problem is, immigration has become a third-rail issue in Washington, D.C.—more controversial even than health care because it deals with issues of race and class, of entitlement and privilege, that America has struggled with since its founding. As much as we talk about the problem, we rarely focus on coming up with an actual solution—an equitable process to fix the system.

Maybe Obama will evolve on immigrant rights, just as he's evolved on gay rights, and use his executive powers to stop the deportations of undocumented youths and allow us to stay, go to school and work, if only with a temporary reprieve. The Republican Party can go one of two ways. It will either make room for its moderate voices to craft a compromise; after all, John McCain, to name just one, was a supporter of the Dream Act. Or the party will pursue a hard-line approach, further isolating not just Latinos, the largest minority group in the U.S., but also a growing multiethnic America that's adapting to the inevitable demographic and cultural shifts. In 21st-century politics, diversity is destiny.

As for me, what happens next isn't just a philosophical question. I spend every day wondering what, if anything, the government plans to do with me. After months of waiting for something to happen, I decided that I would confront immigration officials myself. Since I live in New York City, I called the local ICE office. The phone operators I first reached were taken aback when I explained the reason for my call. Finally I was connected to an ICE officer.

"Are you planning on deporting me?" I asked.

I quickly found out that even though I publicly came out about my undocumented status, I still do not exist in the eyes of ICE. Like most undocumented immigrants, I've never been arrested. Therefore, I've never been in contact with ICE.

"After checking the appropriate ICE databases, the agency has no records of ever encountering Mr. Vargas," Luis Martinez, a spokesman for the ICE office in New York, wrote me in an e-mail.

I then contacted the ICE headquarters in Washington. I hoped to get some insight into my status and that of all the others who are coming out. How does ICE view these cases? Can publicly revealing undocumented status trigger deportation proceedings, and if so, how is that decided? Is ICE planning to seek my deportation?

"We do not comment on specific cases," is all I was told.

I am still here. Still in limbo. So are nearly 12 million others like me—enough to populate Ohio. We are working with you, going to school with you, paying taxes with you, worrying about our bills with you.

What exactly do you want to do with us? More important, when will you realize that we are one of you?

UPDATE: *Shortly after Jose Antonio Vargas' story on the issue of the undocumented was published in* TIME, *the U.S. Department of Homeland Security announced that it would no longer deport young undocumented residents who qualify for the DREAM act. Those eligible will receive work permits.*

ARTICLE QUESTIONS

1) What does Vargas mean when he states, "I haven't become legal . . . because there's no way for me to become legal"?

2) Is "coming out" an effective strategy for promoting immigration reform? Why or why not? Is it worth the risks for those who come out?

3) The Declaration of Independence never mentions citizenship as a prerequisite for who is endowed with inalienable rights. Is this significant? What rights should be possessed just by citizens? What rights should be extended to all residents of the United States?

4) While many agree the immigration system is broken, few agree on a solution. What are some of the reasons it is difficult to reach agreement on immigration policy reforms?

6.5) Despite New Law, Gender Salary Gap Persists

National Public Radio, April 19, 2010

JENNIFER LUDDEN

Jennifer Ludden, in "Despite New Law, Gender Salary Gap Persists," cites Bureau of Labor Statistics data from 2008 showing "women, on, average earn only 77 cents to a man's dollar." The article provides a diversity of opinions on the causes of this wage discrepancy. These opinions range from governmental policies to independent employee choices. Because the roots of the salary gap are debated, research methods attempting to isolate its causes are an important component of Ludden's story. Thus, this article highlights the role of social science in developing policy and shaping social change.

Two themes central in civil rights struggles come out in this article. The first is the ability to see civil rights struggles through two divergent frameworks. Women earning 77% of men's wage wages could be seen as a steady march toward greater equality. Given in 1963—prior to the adoption of the Equal Pay Act—"women earned 59 percent of men's wages," we can see things as improving; indeed, some argue that given more time, this salary gap could rectify itself. From another perspective, women's wages could be seen as remaining unacceptably low compared to men's, and women's wages could be viewed as just as likely to stagnate (if not contract) without continued efforts. Such a perspective emphasizes the long struggle that remains to achieve pay equity. The debate between these two frameworks leads into another important civil rights theme: What is the proper role of governmental intervention in promoting civil rights? For example, in the 1950s, many who lamented the presence of segregation remained uncertain if the federal government should mandate changes. Today it is widely accepted that the federal government had a role in eliminating even private segregation. But what about the federal government's role in reducing wage disparity? At the end of Ludden's article, a critic of governmental efforts to achieve pay equity asks, "Do we want government deciding what is a business necessity?" The debate surrounding the proper limits of governmental action in securing civil rights is ever present, and as the example of segregation shows, how we conceptualize the role of governmental action for promoting civil rights changes with time.

The very first bill that President Obama signed into law dealt with equal pay for women, but activists say it's done little to close the ongoing difference between what men and women earn.

The law—the Lilly Ledbetter Fair Pay Restoration Act—may have extended the amount of time victims have to file discrimination cases, but it hasn't changed this fact: Women, on average, earn only 77 cents to a man's dollar, and the disparity is greater for women of color.

New legislation in Congress aims to close the pay equity gap, even as administration officials prepare to step up enforcement of the existing law.

Economists say part of the gap is because women are more likely to take time off work for child care, and an even bigger part is because of "occupational segregation": Women tend to work disproportionately in lower-paying fields. To be sure, many women's groups see this as a vestige of discrimination. (Another bill, the Fair Pay Act, seeks to address this, though that legislation is considered less likely to gain congressional passage.)

But even when you control for occupation and a host of other variables, economists still find an unexplained gender gap of anywhere from around a nickel to a dime or more on the dollar. Ilene Lang with the women's research group Catalyst recently studied MBA graduates.

"From their very first job after getting their MBA degree, women made less money than men," Lang says. "On average, they were paid $4,600 less."

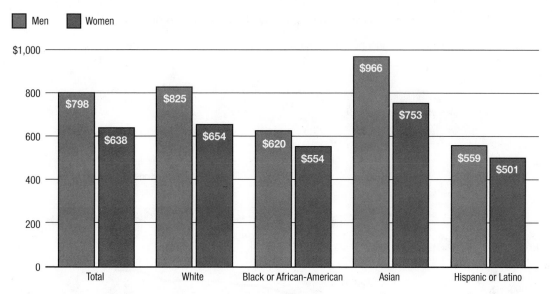

Men **Women**

The Pay Gap, By Sex, Race And Ethnicity (Weekly Earnings)
Source: Bureau of Labor Statistics (2008 annual averages)
Credit: Alyson Hurt/NPR

Paycheck Fairness Act Builds on 1963 Law

Catalyst's findings held even when those studied had no children. For Lang, this says that decades-old stereotypes persist.

"There are assumptions that women don't care about money, which is crazy!" Lang says. "There are assumptions that women will always have men who will take care of them, that women will get married, have children and drop out of the labor force. All those assumptions are just not true."

The pay gap has certainly narrowed since Congress first passed the Equal Pay Act in 1963, when women earned 59 percent of men's wages. But economists say this is largely because men's wages in the decades since have either fallen or were flat. Today, the recession—in which so many more men have lost jobs that some dub it the "mancession"— has left more women than ever as primary breadwinners.

As Obama has noted, the pay disparity means they're losing hundreds of thousands of dollars over the course of a career. "It's about parents who find themselves with less money for tuition and child care," Obama said last year. It's about "couples who wind up with less to retire on. [In] households where one breadwinner is paid less than she deserves, it's the difference between affording the mortgage or not."

The Paycheck Fairness Act would make it easier to prove gender discrimination and would toughen penalties. It would also try to erode what advocates say is a paralyzing secrecy around salaries: The bill would ban companies from retaliating if workers talk to each other about pay. Rep. Rosa DeLauro reminded a Senate hearing last month that Lilly Ledbetter's case only came about because someone left an anonymous note on her windshield.

"Just ask Lilly Ledbetter how much sooner she could have found out that she was being discriminated against had this protection been in place," DeLauro said.

Equal Pay for Different Work?

Women's groups say that fields traditionally dominated by women tend to be undervalued, and that this accounts for much of the ongoing gender pay

The Pay Gap, 1963–2008
Source: U.S. Census Bureau

gap. This is a contentious claim, with critics offering a number of other reasons, such as the danger associated with many mostly male fields. In any case, the Fair Pay Act—which is considered unlikely to pass Congress—would have companies evaluate their salary structure to ferret out such bias. Many large corporations, countries like Sweden and Canada, and a number of U.S. state governments already do this. The state of Minnesota has a gender pay equity law and uses an outside consultant to help set wage levels.

In 1982, a state evaluation found a sex-based wage disparity between delivery van drivers and clerk typists. The two jobs were deemed to be "equal work," yet the drivers (mostly men) at the time earned $1,900 a month, while the typists (mostly women) earned $1,400.

Pay Inequity Crackdown

Economist Heather Boushey of the Center for American Progress testified that the pay gap grows over time. Research shows that women are less likely than men to negotiate for a higher salary. Then "as a woman goes through her career," she said, "you're asked at every job, 'Well, how much did you make at your last job?' And then that exacerbates the pay gap."

Critics worry the Paycheck Fairness Act would encourage a surge of unfounded class-action lawsuits. Labor and employment lawyer Jane McFetridge said small businesses would also find the new requirements cumbersome. For example, an employer who pays a man more than a woman for the same job might have to show that it's a "business necessity."

"Do we want the government deciding what is business necessity?" McFetridge asked lawmakers at the hearing. "Isn't that for the business owner to decide?"

Whether or not the Paycheck Fairness Act becomes law, the Obama administration plans to crack down on pay inequity. Labor agencies, which saw their budgets shrink under the Bush administration, are getting a new infusion of staff and money. Pay equity consultant Tom McMullen says companies should prepare.

"They better get their foundation right soon, because I think there's a new wind blowing in Washington that this is on their radar screen," McMullen says.

In February, the Obama administration announced a task force to coordinate enforcement of equal pay laws. It plans an education campaign to make sure that companies know: Equal work means equal pay.

ARTICLE QUESTIONS

1) What are some reasons cited in the article for the pay disparity between men and women? Which reasons seem the most likely to you?

2) According to the Catalyst study of recent MBA graduates, how much less do women with an MBA make in their first job versus men with an MBA? What is the importance of comparing men's and women's salaries in this very controlled way?

3) Does government have a role in trying to reduce this pay disparity? What actions could be taken?

Chapter 7

Political Participation

Intense popular participation has been a hallmark of the United States since its founding, and Americans remain among the globe's most participatory-minded people. But even though Americans volunteer for public service projects at unusually high rates, they score poorly on other indices of national participation. Compared to other advanced democracies, the voting rate in the United States ranks near the bottom of the pack, as does the level of participation with political parties. This raises a question about how to describe Americans' political participation: Should Americans be described as highly engaged participants or a people with little interest in public affairs? The answer is of more than just academic concern. Rates of public participation are important because they improve personal and community health. Americans who join a civic group, vote regularly, or engage in other types of political participation are on average healthier, wealthier, and generally more satisfied with their lives. Public involvement tends to increase our willingness to trust other people and escalate our optimism about achieving our goals and aspirations. Further, the strong social connections created through civic participation are shown to improve the quality of life for the community in many ways, from crime reduction to increased community health.

Given that public participation provides a host of positive outcomes, an obvious question is how participation can be increased. While there are no definitive answers, decades of research into what motivates political involvement indicate that certain conditions can inspire participation. This research can be employed to increase and direct participation. In the intriguing book *Nudge: Improving Decisions About Health, Wealth, and Happiness*, Richard Thaler and Cass Sunstein argue public officials can and should design forms, buildings, roads, and other structures in a manner that leaves people free to choose, but still nudges their decisions in a particular direction. One of many examples highlighted in the book includes nudges for increasing voter turnout. The authors explain that by asking people "the day before the election whether they intend to vote, you can increase the probability of their voting by as much as 25 percent!" In the book, the authors evaluate nudging as a mechanism for increasing organ donations, increasing investments in retirement funds, expanding healthy food consumption, and a host of activities that would potentially improve peoples' lives.

The authors see nudging as preferable to government mandates such as compulsory voting. An obvious concern about government nudging concerns public officials choosing to promote some types of political participation over others.

Social change movements have often debated the legitimacy of using civil disobedience as a means of political participation. In a 1971 speech, Historian Howard Zinn attempts to flip this debate by arguing that the real problem is "civil obedience." Zinn never explicitly states the means of participation in which people should engage, but he argues that people need "to get back to the principles and aims and spirit of the Declaration of Independence." He sees this spirit as "resistance to illegitimate authority." This implies that participation should extend beyond electoral activities and civic volunteerism. Zinn's speech brings up some intriguing questions. What would a society look like that used civil disobedience as a primary means of political participation? Would those currently serving in public office be equally likely to nudge the public toward all types of participation, from planting trees to protesting against those in power? Should they?

We noted in the first paragraph that U.S. residents actively engage in some types of participatory activities but not in others. But political analysts, including Zinn, do not rate all forms of political participation equally, and how they rate these types of participation will influence the level of civic engagement they observe. In an excerpt from *The Good Citizen: How a Younger Generation is Reshaping American Politics*, Russell Dalton distinguishes between two categories of participation: "duty-based citizenship," which includes voting, paying taxes and joining a political party, and "engaged citizenship," which involves a broader definition of citizenship that focuses on "social concerns and the welfare of others." Whereas many political analysts lament the current downturn in civic participation based on a decline of duty-based citizenship, Dalton celebrates the rise of engaged citizenship. He recognizes that this is "an unconventional view," but it helps U.S. residents rank higher on the scale of participation; it also gives a particular boost to the participation rates of Generations X and Y.

Internet activism as a form of political participation has been rapidly increasing. For example, in 2001 there were 500 politically themed blogs; by 2012 this number had exploded to 93,500. But does using the Internet and social media as a means of political involvement provide the same benefits of more traditional forms of participation? In her article "Does Slacktivism Work?" political scientist Laura Seay reviews research on advocacy groups that rely on social media to build support for their causes. Seay notes that "such forms of advocacy . . . are often derisively referred to as 'slacktivism'" because they require minimal effort. This article raises many questions: Can Internet activism be used to nudge people into other forms of political participation? Does relying on the Internet nudge people away from more public acts of participation? Do you think Internet activism counts as a type of engaged citizenship that Dalton would celebrate? Would Zinn be as inspired by slacktivism as he is by civil disobedience that is achieved through other forms of mass action?

Participating in civic and political life is a longstanding American tradition. Today, while Americans still exhibit higher levels of volunteerism than citizens of other countries, our rates of participation in politics and government have fallen. The readings in this chapter raise important questions about the level of American political participation and the value of divergent means of participation. We need to ask ourselves how participation can be increased, and what ethical methods could be used to encourage greater participation.

CHAPTER QUESTIONS

1) What types of participatory activities have you, your family, and your friends engaged in?
2) What participatory activities would you like to engage in? Are some methods of political participation more valuable than others?
3) What are ethical ways of increasing participation?

CHAPTER READINGS

7.1) Richard Thaler and Cass Sunstein, "Introduction" in *Nudge: Improving Decisions About Health, Wealth, and Happiness*, Penguin Books, 2009, pp. 1–14.

7.2) Howard Zinn, "The Problem Is Civil Obedience," 1971 speech given at Johns Hopkins University.

7.3) Russell Dalton, "Citizenship and the Transformation of American Society," in *The Good Citizen: How a Younger Generation Is Reshaping American Politics*, CQ Press, 2008, pp. 1–16.

7.4) Laura Seay, "Does Slacktivism Work?" *The Monkey Cage Blog*, March 12, 2014.

7.1) Introduction in *Nudge: Improving Decisions About Health, Wealth, and Happiness*

Penguin Books, 2009, pp. 1–14

RICHARD THALER AND CASS SUNSTEIN

In *Nudge: Improving Decisions About Health, Wealth, and Happiness*, Richard Thaler and Cass Sunstein review studies of human behavior to show how the simple design choices made when creating forms, erecting buildings, constructing roads, and crafting other structures can significantly modify people's decisions. Fittingly, the authors label the designers of these structured choices "choice architects." Many of us are familiar with the nudges we receive when we make the "choice" to select the default settings for our cell phone or when we enter a credit card number to be automatically billed each month. If choice architects had created different defaults, many of our phones, computers, and billing cycles would be different. Sunstein and Thaler suggest that this knowledge of human behavior should be harnessed to nudge people to make choices that will make people's lives better. The process of designing structures to influence people's choices can seem like a strange blend of manipulation and free choice; the authors adopt the term "libertarian paternalism" to describe the process of nudging. They argue that a nudge can be seen as consistent with libertarian principles of free choice because it allows for individual choices (as opposed to prohibiting certain actions), but it is paternalistic because "it tries to influence choices" to make people better off.

Many of the examples provided in the text describe nudges that have public policy repercussions. For example, electoral participation, organ donation, retirement contributions, and consumption of healthy foods can all be increased by nudges. Many of us don't think twice about a private cell phone company nudging us toward default settings—but do we feel differently when public policy is affected by how we are nudged? Since we know political participation benefits ourselves and our society, should governmental choice architects nudge us toward participation? Perhaps an even better question: Since *all* design structures nudge people in a particular direction, should public officials disregard nudging people toward participation?

The Cafeteria

A friend of yours, Carolyn, is the director of food services for a large city school system. She is in charge of hundreds of schools, and hundreds of thousands of kids eat in her cafeterias every day. Carolyn has formal training in nutrition (a master's degree from the state university), and she is a creative type who likes to think about things in nontraditional ways.

One evening, over a good bottle of wine, she and her friend Adam, a statistically oriented management consultant who has worked with supermarket chains, hatched an interesting idea. Without changing any menus, they would run some experiments in her schools to determine whether the way the food is displayed and arranged might influence the choices kids make. Carolyn gave the directors of dozens of school cafeterias specific instructions on how to display the food choices. In some schools the desserts were placed first, in others last, in still others in a separate line. The location of various food items was varied from one school to another. In some schools the French fries, but in others the carrot sticks, were at eye level.

From his experience in designing supermarket floor plans, Adam suspected that the results would be dramatic. He was right. Simply by rearranging the cafeteria, Carolyn was able to increase or decrease the consumption of many food items by as much as 25 percent. Carolyn learned a big lesson: school children, like adults, can be greatly influenced by small changes in the context. The influence can be exercised for better or for worse. For example, Carolyn knows that she can increase consumption of healthy foods and decrease consumption of unhealthy ones.

With hundreds of schools to work with, and a team of graduate student volunteers recruited to collect and analyze the data, Carolyn believes that she now has considerable power to influence what kids eat. Carolyn is pondering what to do with her newfound power. Here are some suggestions she has received from her usually sincere but occasionally mischievous friends and coworkers:

1. Arrange the food to make the students best off, all things considered.
2. Choose the food order at random.
3. Try to arrange the food to get the kids to pick the same foods they would choose on their own.
4. Maximize the sales of the items from the suppliers that are willing to offer the largest bribes.
5. Maximize profits, period.

Option 1 has obvious appeal, yet it does seem a bit intrusive, even paternalistic. But the alternatives are worse! Option 2, arranging the food at random, could be considered fair-minded and principled, and it is in one sense neutral. But if the orders are randomized across schools, then the children at some schools will have less healthy diets than those at other schools. Is this desirable? Should Carolyn choose that kind of neutrality, if she can easily make most students better off, in part by improving their health?

Option 3 might seem to be an honorable attempt to avoid intrusion: try to mimic what the children would choose for themselves. Maybe that is really the neutral choice, and maybe Carolyn should neutrally follow people's wishes (at least where she is dealing with older students). But a little thought reveals that this is a difficult option to implement. Adam's experiment proves that what kids choose depends on the order in which the items are displayed. What, then, are the true preferences of the children? What does it mean to say that Carolyn should try to figure out what the students would choose "on their own"? In a cafeteria, it is impossible to avoid some way of organizing food.

Option 4 might appeal to a corrupt person in Carolyn's job, and manipulating the order of the food items would put yet another weapon in the arsenal of available methods to exploit power. But Carolyn is honorable and honest, so she does not give this option any thought. Like Options 2 and 3, Option 5 has some appeal, especially if Carolyn thinks that the best cafeteria is the one that makes the most money. But should Carolyn really try to maximize profits if the result is to make children less healthy, especially since she works for the school district?

Carolyn is what we will be calling a *choice architect*. A choice architect has the responsibility for organizing the context in which people make decisions. Although Carolyn is a figment of our imagination, many real people turn out to be choice architects, most without realizing it. If you design the ballot voters use to choose candidates, you are a choice architect. If you are a doctor and must describe the alternative treatments available to a patient, you are a choice architect. If you design the form that new employees fill out to enroll in the company health care plan, you are a choice architect. If you are a parent, describing possible educational options to your son or daughter, you are a choice architect. If you are a salesperson, you are a choice architect (but you already knew that).

There are many parallels between choice architecture and more traditional forms of architecture. A crucial parallel is that there is no such thing as a "neutral" design. Consider the job of designing a new academic building. The architect is given some requirements. There must be room for 120 offices, 8 classrooms, 12 student meeting rooms, and so forth. The building must sit on a specified site. Hundreds of other constraints will be imposed—some legal, some aesthetic, some practical. In the end, the architect must come up with an actual building with doors, stairs, windows, and hallways. As good architects know, seemingly arbitrary decisions, such as where to locate the bathrooms, will have subtle influences on how the people who use the building interact. Every trip to the bathroom creates an opportunity to run into colleagues (for better or for worse). A good building is not merely attractive; it also "works."

As we shall see, small and apparently insignificant details can have major impacts on people's behavior. A good rule of thumb is to assume that "everything matters." In many cases, the power of these small details comes from focusing the attention of users in a particular direction. A wonderful example of this principle comes from, of all places, the men's rooms at Schiphol Airport in Amsterdam. There the authorities have etched the image of a black housefly into each urinal. It seems that men usually do not pay much attention to where they aim, which can create a bit of a mess, but if they see a target, attention and therefore accuracy are much increased. According to the man who came up with the idea, it works wonders. "It improves the aim," says Aad Kieboom. "If a man sees a fly, he aims at it." Kieboom, an economist, directs Schiphol's building expansion. His staff conducted fly-in-urinal trials and found that etchings reduce spillage by 80 percent.

The insight that "everything matters" can be both paralyzing and empowering. Good architects realize that although they can't build the perfect building, they can make some design choices that will have beneficial effects. Open stairwells, for example, may produce more workplace interaction and more walking, and both of these are probably desirable. And just as a building architect must eventually build some particular building, a choice architect like Carolyn must choose a particular arrangement of the food options at lunch, and by so doing she can influence what people eat. She can nudge.

Libertarian Paternalism

If, all things considered, you think that Carolyn should take the opportunity to nudge the kids toward food that is better for them, Option 1, then we welcome you to our new movement: *libertarian paternalism*. We are keenly aware that this term is not one that readers will find immediately endearing. Both words are somewhat off-putting, weighted down by stereotypes from popular culture and politics that make them unappealing to many. Even worse, the concepts seem to be contradictory. Why combine two reviled and contradictory concepts? We argue that if the terms are properly understood, both concepts reflect common sense—and they are far more attractive

together than alone. The problem with the terms is that they have been captured by dogmatists.

The libertarian aspect of our strategies lies in the straightforward insistence that, in general, people should be free to do what they like—and to opt out of undesirable arrangements if they want to do so. To borrow a phrase from the late Milton Friedman, libertarian paternalists urge that people should be "free to choose."[2] We strive to design policies that maintain or increase freedom of choice. When we use the term *libertarian* to modify the word *paternalism,* we simply mean liberty-preserving. And when we say liberty-preserving, we really mean it. Libertarian paternalists want to make it easy for people to go their own way; they do not want to burden those who want to exercise their freedom.

The paternalistic aspect lies in the claim that it is legitimate for choice architects to try to influence people's behavior in order to make their lives longer, healthier, and better. In other words, we argue for self-conscious efforts, by institutions in the private sector and also by government, to steer people's choices in directions that will improve their lives. In our understanding, a policy is "paternalistic" if it tries to influence choices in a way that will make choosers better off, *as judged by themselves.*[3] Drawing on some well-established findings in social science, we show that in many cases, individuals make pretty bad decisions— decisions they would not have made if they had paid full attention and possessed complete information, unlimited cognitive abilities, and complete self-control.

Libertarian paternalism is a relatively weak, soft, and nonintrusive type of paternalism because choices are not blocked, fenced off, or significantly burdened. If people want to smoke cigarettes, to eat a lot of candy, to choose an unsuitable health care plan, or to fail to save for retirement, libertarian paternalists will not force them to do otherwise—or even make things hard for them. Still, the approach we recommend does count as paternalistic, because private and public choice architects are not merely trying to track or to implement people's anticipated choices. Rather, they are self-consciously attempting to move people in directions that will make their lives better. They nudge.

A nudge, as we will use the term, is any aspect of the choice architecture that alters people's behavior in a predictable way without forbidding any options or significantly changing their economic incentives. To count as a mere nudge, the intervention must be easy and cheap to avoid. Nudges are not mandates. Putting the fruit at eye level counts as a nudge. Banning junk food does not.

Many of the policies we recommend can and have been implemented by the private sector (with or without a nudge from the government). Employers, for example, are important choice architects in many of the examples we discuss in this book. In areas involving health care and retirement plans, we think that employers can give employees some helpful nudges. Private companies that want to make money, and to do good, can even benefit from environmental nudges, helping to reduce air pollution (and the emission of greenhouse gases). But as we shall show, the same points that justify libertarian paternalism on the part of private institutions apply to government as well.

Humans and Econs: Why Nudges Can Help

Those who reject paternalism often claim that human beings do a terrific job of making choices, and if not terrific, certainly better than anyone else would do (especially if that someone else works for the government). Whether or not they have ever studied economics, many people seem at least implicitly committed to the idea of *homo economicus,* or economic man—the notion that each of us thinks and chooses unfailingly well, and thus fits within the textbook picture of human beings offered by economists.

If you look at economics textbooks, you will learn that homo economicus can think like Albert Einstein, store as much memory as IBM's Big Blue, and exercise the willpower of Mahatma Gandhi. Really. But the folks that we know are not like that. Real people have trouble with long division if they don't have a calculator, sometimes forget their spouse's birthday, and have a hangover on New Year's Day. They are not homo economicus; they are homo sapiens. To keep our Latin usage to a

minimum we will hereafter refer to these imaginary and real species as Econs and Humans.

Consider the issue of obesity. Rates of obesity in the United States are now approaching 20 percent, and more than 60 percent of Americans are considered either obese or overweight. There is overwhelming evidence that obesity increases risks of heart disease and diabetes, frequently leading to premature death. It would be quite fantastic to suggest that everyone is choosing the right diet, or a diet that is preferable to what might be produced with a few nudges.

Of course, sensible people care about the taste of food, not simply about health, and eating is a source of pleasure in and of itself. We do not claim that everyone who is overweight is necessarily failing to act rationally, but we do reject the claim that all or almost all Americans are choosing their diet optimally. What is true for diets is true for other risk-related behavior, including smoking and drinking, which produce more than five hundred thousand premature deaths each year. With respect to diet, smoking, and drinking, people's current choices cannot reasonably be claimed to be the best means of promoting their well-being. Indeed, many smokers, drinkers, and overeaters are willing to pay third parties to help them make better decisions.

But our basic source of information here is the emerging science of choice, consisting of careful research by social scientists over the past four decades. That research has raised serious questions about the rationality of many judgments and decisions that people make. To qualify as Econs, people are not required to make perfect forecasts (that would require omniscience), but they are required to make unbiased forecasts. That is, the forecasts can be wrong, but they can't be systematically wrong in a predictable direction. Unlike Econs, Humans predictably err. Take, for example, the "planning fallacy"—the systematic tendency toward unrealistic optimism about the time it takes to complete projects. It will come as no surprise to anyone who has ever hired a contractor to learn that everything takes longer than you think, even if you know about the planning fallacy.

Hundreds of studies confirm that human forecasts are flawed and biased. Human decision making is not so great either. Again to take just one example, consider what is called the "status quo bias," a fancy name for inertia. For a host of reasons, which we shall explore, people have a strong tendency to go along with the status quo or default option.

When you get a new cell phone, for example, you have a series of choices to make. The fancier the phone, the more of these choices you face, from the background to the ring sound to the number of times the phone rings before the caller is sent to voice mail. The manufacturer has picked one option as the default for each of these choices. Research shows that whatever the default choices are, many people stick with them, even when the stakes are much higher than choosing the noise your phone makes when it rings.

Two important lessons can be drawn from this research. First, never underestimate the power of inertia. Second, that power can be harnessed. If private companies or public officials think that one policy produces better outcomes, they can greatly influence the outcome by choosing it as the default. As we will show, setting default options, and other similar seemingly trivial menu-changing strategies, can have huge effects on outcomes, from increasing savings to improving health care to providing organs for lifesaving transplant operations.

The effects of well-chosen default options provide just one illustration of the gentle power of nudges. In accordance with our definition, a nudge is any factor that significantly alters the behavior of Humans, even though it would be ignored by Econs. Econs respond primarily to incentives. If the government taxes candy, they will buy less candy, but they are not influenced by such "irrelevant" factors as the order in which options are displayed. Humans respond to incentives too, but they are also influenced by nudges. By properly deploying both incentives and nudges, we can improve our ability to improve people's lives, and help solve many of society's major problems. And we can do so while still insisting on everyone's freedom to choose.

A False Assumption and Two Misconceptions

Many people who favor freedom of choice reject any kind of paternalism. They want the government to let citizens choose for themselves. The standard policy advice that stems from this way of thinking is to give people as many choices as possible, and then let them choose the one they like best (with as little government intervention or nudging as possible). The beauty of this way of thinking is that it offers a simple solution to many complex problems: Just Maximize (the number and variety of) Choices—full stop! The policy has been pushed in many domains, from education to prescription drug insurance plans. In some circles, Just Maximize Choices has become a policy mantra. Sometimes the only alternative to this mantra is thought to be a government mandate which is derided as "One Size Fits All." Those who favor Just Maximize Choices don't realize there is plenty of room between their policy and a single mandate. They oppose paternalism, or think they do, and they are skeptical about nudges. We believe that their skepticism is based on a false assumption and two misconceptions.

The false assumption is that almost all people, almost all of the time, make choices that are in their best interest or at the very least are better than the choices that would be made by someone else. We claim that this assumption is false—indeed, obviously false. In fact, we do not think that anyone believes it on reflection.

Suppose that a chess novice were to play against an experienced player. Predictably, the novice would lose precisely because he made inferior choices—choices that could easily be improved by some helpful hints. In many areas, ordinary consumers are novices, interacting in a world inhabited by experienced professionals trying to sell them things. More generally, how well people choose is an empirical question, one whose answer is likely to vary across domains. It seems reasonable to say that people make good choices in contexts in which they have experience, good information, and prompt feedback—say, choosing among ice cream flavors. People know whether they like chocolate, vanilla, coffee, licorice, or something else. They do less well in contexts in which they are inexperienced and poorly informed, and in which feedback is slow or infrequent—say, in choosing between fruit and ice cream (where the long-term effects are slow and feedback is poor) or in choosing among medical treatments or investment options. If you are given fifty prescription drug plans, with multiple and varying features, you might benefit from a little help. So long as people are not choosing perfectly, some changes in the choice architecture could make their lives go better (as judged by their own preferences, not those of some bureaucrat). As we will try to show, it is not only possible to design choice architecture to make people better off; in many cases it is easy to do so.

The first misconception is that it is possible to avoid influencing people's choices. In many situations, some organization or agent *must* make a choice that will affect the behavior of some other people. There is, in those situations, no way of avoiding nudging in some direction, and whether intended or not, these nudges will affect what people choose. As illustrated by the example of Carolyn's cafeterias, people's choices are pervasively influenced by the design elements selected by choice architects. It is true, of course, that some nudges are unintentional; employers may decide (say) whether to pay employees monthly or biweekly without intending to create any kind of nudge, but they might be surprised to discover that people save more if they get paid biweekly because twice a year they get three pay checks in one month. It is also true that private and public institutions can strive for one or another kind of neutrality—as, for example, by choosing randomly, or by trying to figure out what most people want. But unintentional nudges can have major effects, and in some contexts, these forms of neutrality are unattractive. . . .

Some people will happily accept this point for private institutions but strenuously object to government efforts to influence choice with the goal of improving people's lives. They worry that governments cannot be trusted to be competent or benign. They fear that elected officials and bureaucrats will place their own interests first, or pay attention to the narrow goals of self-interested private groups. We share these concerns. In particular, we emphatically agree that for government, the risks of mistake, bias, and overreaching are real and sometimes serious. We favor nudges over commands, requirements, and prohibitions in part for that reason. But governments, no less than cafeterias (which governments frequently run), have to provide starting points of

one or another kind. This is not avoidable. As we shall emphasize, they do so every day through the rules they set, in ways that inevitably affect some choices and outcomes. In this respect, the antinudge position is unhelpful—a literal nonstarter.

The second misconception is that paternalism always involves coercion. In the cafeteria example, the choice of the order in which to present food items does not force a particular diet on anyone, yet Carolyn, and others in her position, might select some arrangement of food on grounds that are paternalistic in the sense that we use the term. Would anyone object to putting the fruit and salad before the desserts at an elementary school cafeteria if the result were to induce kids to eat more apples and fewer Twinkies? Is this question fundamentally different if the customers are teenagers, or even adults? Since no coercion is involved, we think that some types of paternalism should be acceptable even to those who most embrace freedom of choice. . . .

. . . [B]y insisting that choices remain unrestricted, we think that the risks of inept or even corrupt designs are reduced. Freedom to choose is the best safeguard against bad choice architecture. . . .

A New Path

. . . [M]any of the most important applications of libertarian paternalism are for government, and we will offer a number of recommendations for public policy and law. Our hope is that that those recommendations might appeal to both sides of the political divide. Indeed, we believe that the policies suggested by libertarian paternalism can be embraced by Republicans and Democrats alike. A central reason is that many of those policies cost little or nothing; they impose no burden on taxpayers at all.

Many Republicans are now seeking to go beyond simple opposition to government action. As the experience with Hurricane Katrina showed, government is often required to act, for it is the only means by which the necessary resources can be mustered, organized, and deployed. Republicans want to make people's lives better; they are simply skeptical, and legitimately so, about eliminating people's options.

For their part, many Democrats are willing to abandon their enthusiasm for aggressive government planning. Sensible Democrats certainly hope that public institutions can improve people's lives. But in many domains, Democrats have come to agree that freedom of choice is a good and even indispensable foundation for public policy. There is a real basis here for crossing partisan divides.

Libertarian paternalism, we think, is a promising foundation for bipartisanship. In many domains, including environmental protection, family law, and school choice, we will be arguing that better governance requires less in the way of government coercion and constraint, and more in the way of freedom to choose. If incentives and nudges replace requirements and bans, government will be both smaller and more modest. So, to be clear: *we are not for bigger government, just for better governance.*

NOTES

2. Friedman, Milton and Rose Friedman. Free to Choose: A Personal Statement. New York: Harcourt Brace Jovanovich, 1980.

3. For a similar definition, see Van De Veer, Donald. Paternalistic Intervention: The Moral Bounds on Benevolence. Princeton: Princeton University Press, 1986.

ARTICLE QUESTIONS

1) What are the five ways that, according to the authors, Carolyn, the director of food services of a large school system, could organize the cafeteria food to influence what the kids eat? What do you think is the most ethical choice?

2) Think of an example of a nudge that is not provided in the text. Who is the choice architect, and why is he or she creating the nudging?

3) What are some of the different concerns that might arise when government officials versus private companies nudge public choices?

7.2) The Problem Is Civil Obedience

1971 speech given at Johns Hopkins University

HOWARD ZINN

Howard Zinn provocatively argues for a particular type of civic participation, civil disobedience, in his speech "The Problem Is Civil Obedience." Civil disobedience can be incredibly effective, but some people believe it is not a legitimate means of political participation. Zinn suggests that obeying "the dictates of leaders" has led to worse atrocities around the world than civil disobedience. While Zinn focuses on the particular problem of obedience to authority, there are obvious problems with civil disobedience as well. For example, white racists in the South engaged in civil disobedience against laws that required integration; Zinn would hardly endorse this type of civil disobedience. If we accept that civil disobedience is sometimes legitimate, how do we know *when* it is a legitimate form of political participation and when it is simply breaking the law? Obviously, allowing each person to choose for himself or herself which laws to follow is too simplistic; if each person is choosing which laws to follow, then we are no longer following laws—each person is doing what he or she chooses. And obviously the white racists in our example were choosing for themselves which laws to disobey.

Zinn never explicitly states the means of participation that people should engage in, but he argues that people need "to get back to the principles and aims and spirit of the Declaration of Independence," a spirit he sees as "resistance to illegitimate authority." But almost all those who commit acts of civil disobedience in the United States see themselves as the rightful inheritors of the spirit of the Declaration. The United States that we have inherited was created from multiple forms of political participation, including civil disobedience. While participation through civic volunteerism and electoral activities is almost always celebrated, the very fact that Zinn had to engage in a debate about civil disobedience indicates that the merits of this form of participation are fiercely debated.

[By the latter part of May, 1970, feelings about the war in Vietnam had become almost unbearably intense. In Boston, about a hundred of us decided to sit down at the Boston Army Base and block the road used by buses carrying draftees off to military duty. We were not so daft that we thought we were stopping the flow of soldiers to Vietnam; it was a symbolic act, a statement, a piece of guerrilla theater. We were all arrested and charged, in the quaint language of an old statute, with "sauntering and loitering" in such a way as to obstruct traffic. Eight of us refused to plead guilty, insisting on trial by jury, hoping we could persuade the members of the jury that ours was a justified act of civil disobedience. We did not persuade them. We were found guilty, chose jail instead of paying a fine, but the judge, apparently reluctant to have us in jail, gave us forty-eight hours to change our minds, after which we should show up in court to either pay the fine or be jailed. In the meantime, I had been invited to go to Johns Hopkins University to debate with the philosopher Charles Frankel on the issue of civil disobedience. I decided it would be hypocritical for me, an advocate of civil disobedience, to submit dutifully to the court and thereby skip out on an opportunity to speak to hundreds of students about civil disobedience. So, on the day I was supposed to show up in court in Boston I flew to Baltimore and that evening debated with Charles Frankel. Returning to Boston I decided to meet my morning class, but two detectives were waiting for me, and I was hustled before the court and then spent a couple of days in jail. What follows is the transcript of my opening statement in the debate at Johns Hopkins. It was included in a book published by Johns Hopkins Press in 1972, entitled Violence: The Crisis of American Confidence.*]*

I start from the supposition that the world is topsy-turvy, that things are all wrong, that the wrong people are in jail and the wrong people are out of jail, that the wrong people are in power and the wrong people are out of power, that the wealth is distributed in this country and the world in such a way as not simply to require small reform but to require a drastic reallocation of wealth. I start from the supposition that we don't have to say too much about this because all we have to do is think about the state of the world today and realize that things are all upside down. Daniel Berrigan is in jail—A Catholic priest, a poet who opposes the war—and J. Edgar Hoover is free, you see. David Dellinger, who has opposed war ever since he was this high and who has used all of his energy and passion against it, is in danger of going to jail. The men who are responsible for the My Lai massacre are not on trial; they are in Washington serving various functions, primary and subordinate, that have to do with the unleashing of massacres, which surprise them when they occur. At Kent State University four students were killed by the National Guard and students were indicted. In every city in this country, when demonstrations take place, the protesters, whether they have demonstrated or not, whatever they have done, are assaulted and clubbed by police, and then they are arrested for assaulting a police officer.

Now, I have been studying very closely what happens every day in the courts in Boston, Massachusetts. You would be astounded—maybe you wouldn't, maybe you have been around, maybe you have lived, maybe you have thought, maybe you have been hit—at how the daily rounds of injustice make their way through this marvelous thing that we call due process. Well, that is my premise.

All you have to do is read the Soledad letters of George Jackson, who was sentenced to one year to life, of which he spent ten years, for a seventy-dollar robbery of a filling station. And then there is the U.S. Senator who is alleged to keep 185,000 dollars a year, or something like that, on the oil depletion allowance. One is theft; the other is legislation. Something is wrong, something is terribly wrong when we ship 10,000 bombs full of nerve gas across the country, and drop them in somebody else's swimming pool so as not to trouble our own. So you lose your perspective after a while. If you don't think, if you just listen to TV and read scholarly things, you actually begin to think that things are not so bad, or that just little things are wrong. But you have to get a little detached, and then come back and look at the world, and you are horrified. So we have to start from that supposition—that things are really topsy-turvy.

And our topic is topsy-turvy: civil disobedience. As soon as you say the topic is civil disobedience, you are saying our problem is civil disobedience. That is not our problem.... Our problem is civil obedience. Our problem is the numbers of people all over the world who have obeyed the dictates of the leaders of their government and have gone to war, and millions have been killed because of this obedience. And our problem is that scene in *All Quiet on the Western Front* where the schoolboys march off dutifully in a line to war. Our problem is that people are obedient all over the world, in the face of poverty and starvation and stupidity, and war and cruelty. Our problem is that people are obedient while the jails are full of petty thieves, and all the while the grand thieves are running the country. That's our problem. We recognize this for Nazi Germany. We know that the problem there was obedience, that the people obeyed Hitler. People obeyed; that was wrong. They should have challenged, and they should have resisted; and if we were only there, we would have showed them. Even in Stalin's Russia we can understand that; people are obedient, all these herdlike people.

But America is different. That is what we've all been brought up on. From the time we are this high and I still hear it resounding in Mr. Frankel's statement—you tick off, one, two, three, four, five lovely things—about America that we don't want disturbed very much. But if we have learned anything in the past ten years, it is that these lovely things about America were never lovely. We have been expansionist and aggressive and mean to other people from the beginning. And we've been aggressive and mean to people in this country, and we've allocated the wealth of this country in a very unjust way. We've never had justice in the courts for the poor people, for black people, for radicals. Now how can we boast that America is a very special place? It is not that special. It really isn't.

Well, that is our topic, that is our problem: civil obedience. Law is very important. We are talking about obedience to law—law, this marvelous invention of modern times, which we attribute to Western civilization, and which we talk about proudly. The rule of law, oh, how wonderful, all these courses in Western civilization all over the land. Remember those bad old days when people were exploited by feudalism? Everything was terrible in the Middle Ages—but now we have Western civilization, the rule of law. The rule of law has regularized and maximized the injustice that existed before the rule of law, that is what the rule of law has done. Let us start looking at the rule of law realistically, not with that metaphysical complacency with which we always examined it before.

When in all the nations of the world the rule of law is the darling of the leaders and the plague of the people, we ought to begin to recognize this. We have to transcend these national boundaries in our thinking. Nixon and Brezhnev have much more in common with one another than we have with Nixon. J. Edgar Hoover has far more in common with the head of the Soviet secret police than he has with us. It's the international dedication to law and order that binds the leaders of all countries in a comradely bond. That's why we are always surprised when they get together—they smile, they shake hands, they smoke cigars, they really like one another no matter what they say. It's like the Republican and Democratic parties, who claim that it's going to make a terrible difference if one or the other wins, yet they are all the same. Basically, it is us against them.

Yossarian was right, remember, in *Catch-22*? He had been accused of giving aid and comfort to the enemy, which nobody should ever be accused of, and Yossarian said to his friend Clevinger: "The enemy is whoever is going to get you killed, whichever side they are on." But that didn't sink in, so he said to Clevinger: "Now you remember that, or one of these days you'll be dead." And remember? Clevinger, after a while, was dead. And we must remember that our enemies are not divided along national lines, that enemies are not just people who speak different languages and occupy different territories. Enemies are people who want to get us killed.

We are asked, "What if everyone disobeyed the law?" But a better question is, "What if everyone obeyed the law?" And the answer to that question is much easier to come by, because we have a lot of empirical evidence about what happens if everyone obeys the law, or if even most people obey the law. What happens is what has happened, what is happening. Why do people revere the law? And we all do; even I have to fight it, for it was put into my bones at an early age when I was a Cub Scout. One reason we revere the law is its ambivalence. In the modern world we deal with phrases and words that have multiple meanings, like "national security." Oh, yes, we must do this for national security! Well, what does that mean? Whose national security? Where? When? Why? We don't bother to answer those questions, or even to ask them.

The law conceals many things. The law is the Bill of Rights; in fact, that is what we think of when we develop our reverence for the law. The law is something that protects us; the law is our right— the law is the Constitution. Bill of Rights Day, essay contests sponsored by the American Legion on our Bill of Rights, that is the law. And that is good.

But there is another part of the law that doesn't get ballyhooed—the legislation that has gone through month after month, year after year, from the beginning of the Republic, which allocates the resources of the country in such a way as to leave some people very rich and other people very poor, and still others scrambling like mad for what little is left. That is the law. If you go to law school you will see this. You can quantify it by counting the big, heavy law books that people carry around with them and see how many law books you count

that say "Constitutional Rights" on them and how many that say "Property," "Contracts," "Torts," "Corporation Law." That is what the law is mostly about. The law is the oil depletion allowance— although we don't have Oil Depletion Allowance Day, we don't have essays written on behalf of the oil depletion allowance. So there are parts of the law that are publicized and played up to us—oh, this is the law, the Bill of Rights. And there are other parts of the law that just do their quiet work, and nobody says anything about them.

It started way back when the Bill of Rights was first passed, remember, in the first administration of Washington? Great thing. Bill of Rights passed! Big ballyhoo. At the same time Hamilton's economic program was passed. Nice, quiet, money to the rich—I'm simplifying it a little, but not too much. Hamilton's economic program started it off. You can draw a straight line from Hamilton's economic program to the oil depletion allowance to the tax write-offs for corporations. All the way through—that is the history. The Bill of Rights publicized; economic legislation unpublicized.

You know the enforcement of different parts of the law is as important as the publicity attached to the different parts of the law. The Bill of Rights, is it enforced? Not very well. You'll find that freedom of speech in constitutional law is a very difficult, ambiguous, troubled concept. Nobody really knows when you can get up and speak and when you can't. Just check all of the Supreme Court decisions. Talk about predictability in a system—you can't predict what will happen to you when you get up on the street corner and speak. See if you can tell the difference between the Terminiello case and the Feiner case, and see if you can figure out what is going to happen. By the way, there is one part of the law that is not very vague, and that involves the right to distribute leaflets on the street. The Supreme Court has been very clear on that. In decision after decision we are affirmed an absolute right to distribute leaflets on the street. Try it. Just go out on the street and start distributing leaflets. And a policeman comes up to you and he says, "Get out of here." And you say, "Aha! Do you know *Marsh v. Alabama*, 1946?" That is the reality of the Bill of Rights. That's the reality of the Constitution, that part of the law which is portrayed to us as a beautiful and marvelous thing. And seven years after the Bill of Rights was passed, which said that "Congress shall make no law abridging the freedom of speech," Congress made a law abridging the freedom of speech. Remember? The Sedition Act of 1798.

So the Bill of Rights was not enforced. Hamilton's program was enforced, because when the whisky farmers went out and rebelled, you remember, in 1794 in Pennsylvania, Hamilton himself got on his horse and went out there to suppress the rebellion to make sure that the revenue tax was enforced. And you can trace the story right down to the present day, what laws are enforced, what laws are not enforced. So you have to be careful when you say, "I'm for the law, I revere the law." What part of the law are you talking about? I'm not against all law. But I think we ought to begin to make very important distinctions about what laws do what things to what people.

And there are other problems with the law. It's a strange thing, we think that law brings order. Law doesn't. How do we know that law does not bring order? Look around us. We live under the rules of law. Notice how much order we have? People say we have to worry about civil disobedience because it will lead to anarchy. Take a look at the present world in which the rule of law obtains. This is the closest to what is called anarchy in the popular mind—confusion, chaos, international banditry. The only order that is really worth anything does not come through the enforcement of law, it comes through the establishment of a society which is just and in which harmonious relationships are established and in which you need a minimum of regulation to create decent sets of arrangements among people. But the order based on law and on the force of law is the order of the totalitarian state, and it inevitably leads either to total injustice or to rebellion—eventually, in other words, to very great disorder.

We all grow up with the notion that the law is holy. They asked Daniel Berrigan's mother what she thought of her son's breaking the law. He burned draft records—one of the most violent acts of this century—to protest the war, for which he was sentenced to prison, as criminals should be. They asked his mother who is in her eighties, what she thought of her son's breaking the law. And she looked straight into the interviewer's face, and she said, "It's not God's law." Now we forget that. There is nothing sacred about the law. Think of who makes laws. The law is not made by God, it is made by Strom Thurmond. If you have any notion about the sanctity and loveliness and reverence for the law, look at the legislators around the country who make the laws. Sit in on the sessions of the state legislatures. Sit in on Congress, for these are the people who make the laws which we are then supposed to revere.

All of this is done with such propriety as to fool us. This is the problem. In the old days, things were confused; you didn't know. Now you know. It is all down there in the books. Now we go through due process. Now the same things happen as happened before, except that we've gone through the right procedures. In Boston a policeman walked into a hospital ward and fired five times at a black man who had snapped a towel at his arm—and killed him. A hearing was held. The judge decided that the policeman was justified because if he didn't do it, he would lose the respect of his fellow officers. Well, that is what is known as due process—that is, the guy didn't get away with it. We went through the proper procedures, and everything was set up. The decorum, the propriety of the law fools us.

The nation, then, was founded on disrespect for the law, and then came the Constitution and the notion of stability which Madison and Hamilton liked. But then we found in certain crucial times in our history that the legal framework did not suffice, and in order to end slavery we had to go outside the legal framework, as we had to do at the time of the American Revolution or the Civil War. The union had to go outside the legal framework in order to establish certain rights in the 1930s. And in this time, which may be more critical than the Revolution or the Civil War, the problems are so horrendous as to require us to go outside the legal framework in order to make a statement, to resist, to begin to establish the kind of institutions and relationships which a decent society should have.

No, not just tearing things down; building things up. But even if you build things up that you are not supposed to build up—you try to build up a people's park, that's not tearing down a system; you are building something up, but you are doing it illegally—the militia comes in and drives you out. That is the form that civil disobedience is going to take more and more, people trying to build a new society in the midst of the old.

But what about voting and elections? Civil disobedience—we don't need that much of it, we are told, because we can go through the electoral system. And by now we should have learned, but maybe we haven't, for we grew up with the notion that the voting booth is a sacred place, almost like a confessional. You walk into the voting booth and you come out and they snap your picture and then put it in the papers with a beatific smile on your face. You've just voted; that is democracy. But if you even read what the political scientists say—although who can?—about the voting process, you find that the voting process is a sham. Totalitarian states love voting. You get people to the polls and they register their approval. I know there is a difference—they have one party and we have two

parties. We have one more party than they have, you see.

What we are trying to do, I assume, is really to get back to the principles and aims and spirit of the Declaration of Independence. This spirit is resistance to illegitimate authority and to forces that deprive people of their life and liberty and right to pursue happiness, and therefore under these conditions, it urges the right to alter or abolish their current form of government—and the stress had been on abolish. But to establish the principles of the Declaration of Independence, we are going to need to go outside the law, to stop obeying the laws that demand killing or that allocate wealth the way it has been done, or that put people in jail for petty technical offenses and keep other people out of jail for enormous crimes. My hope is that this kind of spirit will take place not just in this country but in other countries because they all need it. People in all countries need the spirit of disobedience to the state, which is not a metaphysical thing but a thing of force and wealth. And we need a kind of declaration of interdependence among people in all countries of the world who are striving for the same thing.

ARTICLE QUESTIONS

1) What are some of the critiques of the rule of law that Zinn offers when he asks us to "start looking at the rule of law realistically"?
2) When, if ever, is civil disobedience a legitimate means of participation? When is it not?

7.3) Citizenship and the Transformation of American Society in *The Good Citizen: How a Younger Generation Is Reshaping American Politics*

CQ Press, 2008, pp. 1–16

RUSSELL DALTON

Russell Dalton's book, *The Good Citizen: How a Younger Generation is Reshaping American Politics*, opens with the provocative question: "What does it mean to be a 'good citizen' in today's society?" Dalton enthusiastically notes that "many young people in America . . . are concerned about their society and others in the world. And they are willing to contribute their time and effort to make a difference." But despite this civic concern, Dalton observes that "a host of political analysts now bemoans . . . too few of us are voting, we are disconnected from our fellow citizens and lacking in social capital, we are losing our national identity, we are losing faith in our government, and the nation is in social disarray." These two observations seem fundamentally at odds with one another. Dalton seeks to explain this paradox by analyzing the ebbs and flows of different methods of public participation.

Dalton's research confirms what those political analysts bemoan: People today, especially younger Americans, are less likely to participate in what Dalton calls "duty-based citizenship," which includes voting, paying taxes, and joining a political party. Again in confirmation of civic engagement scholars, Dalton observes that people are simultaneously expressing increased concern over "the welfare of others." Dalton describes these concerns as part of an "engaged citizenship," which includes a broader definition of citizenship. Thus Dalton sees an increase in engaged citizenship replacing the decreasing levels of duty-based citizenship, and ultimately he celebrates this transformation. Dalton recognizes this as "an unconventional view." Is it a view we agree with?

> Every age since the ancient Greeks fashioned an image of being political [is] based upon citizenship
>
> Engin Isin, *Being Political*

What does it mean to be a "good citizen" in today's society?

In an article on the 2005 annual UCLA survey of college freshmen, the *Los Angeles Times* presented an interview with a California university student who had spent his semester break as a volunteer helping to salvage homes flooded by Hurricane Katrina.[1] The young man had organized a group of student volunteers, who then gave up their break to do hard labor in the devastated region far from their campus. He said finding volunteers willing to work "was easier than I expected." Indeed, the gist of the article was that volunteering in 2005 was at its highest percentage in the 25 years of the college survey.

Later I spoke with another student who also had traveled to the Gulf Coast. Beyond the work on Katrina relief, he was active on a variety of social and political causes, from problems of development in Africa, to campus politics, to the war in Iraq. When I asked about his interest in political parties and elections, however, there was stark lack of interest. Like many of his fellow students, he had not voted in the last election. He had not participated at all in the 2004 campaign, which was his first opportunity to vote. This behavior seems paradoxical considering the effort involved; it's just a short walk from the campus to the nearest polling station, but almost a two-thousand-mile drive along Interstate 10 to New Orleans.

These stories illustrate some of the ways that the patterns of citizenship are changing. Many young people in America—and in other Western democracies as well—are concerned about their society and others in the world. And they are willing to contribute their time and effort to make a difference. They see a role for themselves and their government in improving the world in which we all live. At the same time, they relate to government and society in different ways than their elders. Research in the United States and other advanced industrial democracies shows that modern-day citizens are the most educated, most cosmopolitan, and most supportive of self-expressive values than any other public in the history of democracy.[2] So from both anecdotal and empirical perspectives, most of the social and political changes in the American public over the past half-century would seem to have strengthened the foundations of democracy.

Despite this positive and hopeful view of America, however, a very different story is being told today in political and academic circles. An emerging consensus among political analysts would have us believe that the foundations of citizenship and democracy are crumbling. Just recently, a new study cosponsored by the American Political Science Association and the Brookings Institution begins:

> American democracy is at risk. The risk comes not from some external threat but from disturbing internal trends: an erosion of the activities and capacities of citizenship. Americans have turned away from politics and the public sphere in large numbers, leaving our civic life impoverished. Citizens participate in public affairs less frequently, with less knowledge and enthusiasm, in fewer venues, and less equally than is healthy for a vibrant democratic polity.[3]

A host of political analysts now bemoans what is wrong with America and its citizens.[4] Too few of us are voting, we are disconnected from our fellow citizens and lacking in social capital, we are losing our national identity, we are losing faith in our government, and the nation is in social disarray. The *lack* of good citizenship is the phrase you hear most often to explain these disturbing trends.

What you also hear is that the young are the primary source of this decline. Authors from Robert Putman to former television news anchor Tom Brokaw extol the civic values and engagement of the older, "greatest generation" with great hyperbole.[5] Putnam holds that the slow, steady, and ineluctable replacement of older, civic-minded generations by the disaffected Generation X is the most important reason for the erosion of social capital in America.[6] Political analysts and politicians seemingly agree that young Americans are dropping out of politics, losing faith in government, and even becoming disenchanted with their personal lives.[7] Perhaps not since Aristotle held that "political science is not a proper study for the young" have youth been so roundly denounced by their elders.

Here we have two very different images of American society and politics. One perspective says American democracy is "at risk" in large part because of the changing values and participation patterns of the young. The other view points to new patterns of citizenship that have emerged among the young, the better educated, and other sectors of American society. These opposing views have generated sharp debates about the vitality of our democracy, and they are the subject of this book.

Perhaps the subtitle for this volume should be: "The good news is . . . the bad news is wrong." Indeed, something is changing in American society and politics. But is it logical to conclude, as many do, that if politics is not working as it did in the past, then our entire system of democracy is at risk? To understand what is changing, and its implications for American democracy, it is more helpful first to ask that simple but fundamental question:

What does it mean to be a good citizen in America today?

Take a moment to think of how you would answer. What are the criteria you would use? Voting? Paying taxes? Obeying the law? Volunteer work? Public protests? Being concerned for those in need? Membership in a political party? Trusting government officials?

[P]eople answer [this question] . . . in different ways. [I] argue that the changing definition of what it means to be a good citizen—what I call the *norms of citizenship*—provides the key to understanding what is really going on . . .

Changing living standards, occupational experiences, generational change, the entry of women into the labor force, expanding civil rights, and other societal changes are producing two reinforcing effects. First, people possess new skills and resources that enable them to better manage the complexities of politics—people today are better educated, have more information available to them, and enjoy a higher standard of living. This removes some of the restrictions on democratic citizenship that might have existed in earlier historical periods when these skills and resources were less commonly available. Second, social forces are reshaping social and political values. Americans are more assertive and less deferential to authority, and they place more emphasis on participating in the decisions affecting their lives. The expansion of these self-expressive values has a host of political implications.[8]

These social changes have a direct effect on the norms of citizenship, if for no other reason than that citizenship norms are the encapsulation of the nation's political culture. They essentially define what people think is expected of them as participants in the political system, along with their expectations of government and the political process.

Most definitions of citizenship typically focus on the traditional norms of American citizenship—voting, paying taxes, belonging to a political party—and how these are changing. I call this **duty-based citizenship** because these norms reflect the formal obligations, responsibilities, and rights of citizenship as they have been defined in the past.

However, it is just as important to examine new norms that make up what I call **engaged citizenship.** These norms are emerging among the American public with increasing prominence. Engaged citizenship emphasizes a more assertive role for the citizen and a broader definition of the elements of citizenship to include social concerns and the welfare of others. As illustrated by the Katrina volunteers, many Americans believe they are fully engaged in society even if they do not vote or conform to traditional definitions of citizenship. Moreover, the social and political transformation of the United States over the past several decades has systematically shifted the balance between these different norms of citizenship. Duty-based norms are decreasing, especially among the young, but the norms of engaged citizenship are increasing. . . .

. . . [S]ocial and demographic changes affect citizenship norms, which in turn affect the political values and behavior of the public. For instance, duty-based norms of citizenship stimulate turnout in elections and a sense of patriotic allegiance to the elected government, while engaged citizenship may promote other forms of political action, ranging from volunteerism to public protest. These contrasting norms also shape other political values, such as tolerance of others and public policy priorities. Even respect for government itself is influenced by how individuals define their own norms of citizenship.

American politics and the citizenry are changing. Before anyone can deliver a generalized indictment of the American public, it is important to have a full understanding of how citizenship norms are changing and the effects of these changes. It is undeniable that the American public at the beginning of the twenty-first century is different from the American electorate in the mid-twentieth century. However, some of these differences actually can benefit American democracy, such as increased political tolerance and acceptance of diversity in society and politics. Other generational differences are just different—not a threat to American democracy unless these changes are ignored or resisted. A full examination of citizenship norms and their consequences will provide a more complex, and potentially more optimistic, picture of the challenges and opportunities facing American democracy today.

In addition, it is essential to place the American experience in a broader cross-national context. Many scholars who study American politics still study *only* American politics. This leads to an introspective, parochial view of what is presumably unique about the American experience and how patterns of citizenship may, or may not be, idiosyncratic to the United States. American politics is the last field of area-study research in which one nation is examined by itself. Many trends apparent in American norms of citizenship and political activity are common to other advanced industrial democracies. Other patterns may be distinctly American. Only by broadening the field of comparison can we ascertain the similarities and the differences.

The shift in the norms of citizenship does not mean that American democracy does not face challenges in response to new citizen demands and new patterns of action. Indeed, the vitality of democracy is that it must, and usually does, respond to such challenges, and this in turn strengthens the democratic process. But it is my contention that political reforms must reflect a true understanding of the American public and its values. By accurately recognizing the current challenges, and responding to them rather than making dire claims about political decay, American democracy can continue to evolve and develop. The fact remains, we cannot return to the politics of the 1950s, and we probably should not want to. But we can improve the democratic process if we first understand how Americans and their world are really changing.

The Social Transformation of America

I recently took a cab ride from Ann Arbor, Michigan, to the Detroit airport, and the cab driver retold the story of the American dream as his life story. Now, driving a cab is not a fun job; it requires long hours, uncertainty, and typically brings in a modest income. The cab driver had grown up in the Detroit area. His relatives worked in the auto plants, and he drove a cab as a second job to make ends meet. We started talking about politics, and when he learned I was a university professor, he told me of his children. His son had graduated from the University of Michigan and had begun a successful business career. He was even prouder of his daughter, who was finishing law school. "All this on a cab driver's salary," he said with great pride in his children.

If you live in America, you have heard this story many times. It is the story of American society. The past five decades have seen this story repeated over and over again because this has been a period of exceptional social and political change.[9] There was a tremendous increase in the average standard of living as the American economy expanded. The postwar baby boom generation reaped these benefits, and, like the cab driver's children, were often the first in their family to attend college. The civil rights movement of the 1960s and 1970s ended centuries of official governmental recognition and acceptance of racial discrimination. The women's movement of the 1970s and 1980s transformed gender roles that had roots in social relations since the beginning of human history. (A generation ago, it was unlikely that the cab driver's daughter would have attended law school regardless of her abilities.) America also became a socially and ethnically diverse nation—even more so than its historic roots as an immigrant society had experienced

in the past. Changes in the media environment and political process have transformed the nature of democratic politics in America, as citizens have more information about how their government is, or is not, working for them, and more means of expressing their opinions and acting out their views.

In *The Rise of the Creative Class,* Richard Florida has an evocative discussion of how a time traveler from 1950 would view life in the United States if he or she was transported to 1900, and then again to 2000.[10] Florida suggests that *technological* change would be greater between 1900 and 1950, as people moved from horse-and-buggy times all the way to the space age. But *cultural* change would be greater between 1950 and 2000, as America went from a closed social structure to one that gives nearly equal status to women, blacks, and other ethnic minorities. Similarly, I suspect that if Dwight D. Eisenhower and Adlai E. Stevenson returned to observe the next U.S. presidential election, they would not recognize it as the same electorate as the people they encountered in their 1952 and 1956 campaigns for the Oval Office.

In the same respect, many of our scholarly images of American public opinion and political behavior are shaped by an outdated view of our political system. The landmark studies of Angus Campbell, Philip Converse, Warren Miller, and Donald Stokes remain unrivaled in their theoretical and empirical richness in describing the American public.[11] However, they examined the electorate of the 1950s. At an intellectual level, we may be aware of how the American public and American politics have changed since 1952, but since these changes accumulate slowly over time, it is easy to overlook their total impact. The electorate of 1956, for instance, was only marginally different from the electorate of 1952; and the electorate of 2004 is only marginally different from that of 2000. As these gradual changes accumulated over fifty years, however, a fundamental transformation in the socio-economic conditions of the American public occurred, conditions that are directly related to citizenship norms.

None of these trends in and of themselves is likely to surprise the reader. But you may be struck by the size of the total change when compared across a long span of time.

Perhaps the clearest evidence of change, and the carrier of new experiences and new norms, is the generational turnover of the American public. The public of the 1950s largely came of age during the Great Depression or before, and had lived through one or both world wars—experiences that had a strong formative influence on images of citizenship and politics. We can see how rapidly the process of demographic change transforms the citizenry by following the results of the American National Election Studies, which have tracked American public opinions over the past half-century. . . . In the electorate of 1952, 85 percent of Americans had grown up before the outbreak of World War II (born before 1926). This includes the "greatest generation" (born between 1895 and 1926) heralded by Tom Brokaw and other recent authors. Each year, with mounting frequency, a few of this generation leave the electorate, to be replaced by new citizens. In 1968, in the midst of the flower-power decade of the 1960s, the "greatest generation" still composed 60 percent of the populace. But by 2004, this generation accounts for barely 5 percent of the populace. In their place, a third of the contemporary public are post-World War II baby boomers, another third is the flower generation of the 1960s and early 1970s, and a full 20 percent are the Generation-Xers who have come of age since 1993 (born after 1975).

The steady march of generations across time has important implications for norms of citizenship. Anyone born before 1926 grew up and became socialized in a much different political context, where citizens were expected to be dutiful, parents taught their children to be obedient, political skills were limited, and social realities were dramatically different from contemporary life. These citizens carry the living memories of the Great Depression, four-term president Franklin Delano Roosevelt and World War II and its aftermath—and so they also embody the norms of citizenship shaped by these experiences.

The baby boom generation experienced a very different kind of life as American social and economic stability was reestablished after the war.

In further contrast, the 1960s generation experienced a nation in the midst of traumatic social change—the end of segregation, women's liberation, and the expansion of civil and human rights around the world. The curriculum of schools changed to reinforce these developments, and surveys show that parents also began emphasizing initiative and independence in rearing their children.[12] And most recently, Generation X and Generation Y are coming of age in an environment where individualism appears dominant, and both affluence and consumerism seem overdeveloped (even if unequally shared). If nothing else changed, we would expect that political norms would change in reaction to this new social context.

Citizenship norms also reflect the personal characteristics of the people. Over the past several decades, the politically relevant skills and resources of the average American have increased dramatically. One of the best indicators of this development is the public's educational achievement. Advanced industrial societies require more educated and technically sophisticated citizens, and modern affluence has expanded educational opportunities. University enrollments grew dramatically during the latter half of the twentieth century. By the 1990s, graduate degrees were almost as common as bachelor's degrees were in mid-century.

These trends have steadily raised the educational level of the American public. For instance, two-fifths of the American public in 1952 had a primary education or less, and another fifth had only some high school. In the presidential election that year, the Eisenhower and Stevenson campaigns faced a citizenry with limited formal education, modest income levels, and relatively modest sophistication to manage the complexities of politics. It might not be surprising that these individuals would have a limited definition of the appropriate role of a citizen. By 2004, the educational composition of the American public had changed dramatically. Less than a tenth have less than a high school degree, and more than half have at least some college education—and most of these have earned one or more degrees. The contemporary American public has a level of formal schooling that would have been unimaginable in 1952.

There is no direct, one-to-one relationship between years of schooling and political sophistication. Nonetheless, research regularly links education to a citizen's level of political knowledge, interest, and sophistication.[13] Educational levels affect the modes of political decision-making that people use, and rising educational levels increase the breadth of political interests.[14] A doubling of the public's educational level may not double the level of political sophistication and political engagement, but a significant increase should and does occur. The public today is the most educated in the history of American democracy, and this contributes toward a more expansive and engaged image of citizenship.

In addition, social modernization has transformed the structure of the economy from one based on industrial production and manufacturing (and farming), to one dominated by the services and the information sectors. Instead of the traditional blue-collar union worker, who manufactured goods and things, the paragon of today's workforce has shifted to the "knowledge worker" whose career is based on the creation, manipulation, and application of information.[15] Business managers, lawyers, accountants, teachers, computer programmers, designers, database managers, and media professionals represent different examples of knowledge workers.

If one takes a sociological view of the world, where life experiences shape political values, this shift in occupation patterns should affect citizenship norms. The traditional blue-collar employee works in a hierarchical organization where following orders, routine, and structure are guiding principles. Knowledge workers, in contrast, are supposed to be creative, adaptive, and technologically adept, which presumably produces a different image of what one's role should be in society. Richard Florida calls them the "creative class" and links their careers to values of individuality, diversity, openness, and meritocracy.[16]

These trends are a well-known aspect of American society, but we often overlook the amount of change they have fomented in politics over the past five decades. plots the broad employment patterns of American men from 1952 until 2004. (We'll track only males at this point to separate out the shift in the social position of women, which is examined below). In the 1950s, most of the labor force was employed in working class occupations, and another sixth had jobs in farming. The category of professionals and managers, which will stand here as a surrogate for knowledge workers (the actual number of knowledge workers is significantly larger), was small by comparison. Barely a quarter of the labor force held such jobs in the 1950s.

Slowly but steadily, labor patterns have shifted. By 2000–2004, blue-collar workers and knowledge workers are almost at parity, and the proportions of service and clerical workers have increased (some of whom should also be classified as knowledge workers). Florida uses a slightly more restrictive definition of the creative class, but similarly argues that their proportion of the labor force has doubled since 1950.[17] Again, if nothing else had changed, we would expect that the political outlook of the modern knowledge worker would be much different than in previous generations.

The social transformation of the American public has no better illustration than the new social status of women. At the time Angus Campbell and colleagues published *The American Voter* in 1960, women exercised a very restricted role in society and politics. Women were homemakers and mothers—and it had always been so. One of the co-authors of *The American Voter* noted that their interviewers regularly encountered women who thought the interviewer should return when her husband was home to answer the survey questions, since politics was the man's domain.

The women's movement changed these social roles in a relatively brief span of time. Women steadily moved into the workplace, entered universities, and became more engaged in the political process. Employment patterns illustrate the changes . . . In 1952, two-thirds of women described themselves as housewives. The image of June Cleaver, the stay-at-home-mom on the popular TV show *Leave it to Beaver,* was not an inaccurate portrayal of the middle class American woman of that era. By 2004, however, three-quarters of women were employed and only a sixth described themselves as housewives. The professional woman is now a staple of American society and culture. The freedom and anxieties of the upwardly mobile women in *Friends* and *Sex and the City* are more typical of the contemporary age.

The change in the social status of women also affects their citizenship traits. For instance, the educational levels of women have risen even more rapidly than men. By 2000, the educational attainment of young men and women were essentially equal. As women enter the workforce, this should stimulate political engagement; no longer is politics a male preserve. For instance, although women are still underrepresented in politics, the growth in the number of women officeholders during the last half of the twentieth century is quite dramatic.[19] Rather than being mere spectators or supporters of their husbands, women are now engaged on their own and create their own political identities. Though gender inequity and issues of upward professional mobility remain, this transformation in the social position of half the public has clear political implications.

Race is another major source of political transformation within the American electorate. In the 1950s, the American National Election Studies found that about two-thirds of African-Americans said they were not registered to vote, and few actually voted. By law or tradition, many of these Americans were excluded from the most basic rights of citizenship. The civil rights movement and the transformation of politics in the South finally incorporated African-Americans into the electorate.[20] In the presidential elections of 2000 and 2004, African-Americans voted at rates equal to or greater than white Americans. In other words, almost a tenth of the public was excluded from citizenship in the mid-twentieth century, and these individuals are now both included and more active. Moreover, Hispanic and Asian-Americans are also entering the electorate in increasing numbers, transforming the complexion of American politics. If Adlai Stevenson could witness the Democratic National Convention in 2008, he would barely recognize the party that nominated him for president in both 1952 and 1956.

Though historically seismic, these generational, educational, gender, and racial changes are not the only ingredients of the social transformation of the United States into an advanced industrial society.[21] The living standards of Americans have grown tremendously over this period as well, providing more resources and opportunities to become politically engaged. The great internal migration of Americans from farm to city during the mid-twentieth century stimulated changes in life expectations and lifestyles. The urbanization—and, more recently, the "suburbanization"—of American society has created a growing separation of the home from the workplace, a greater diversity of occupations and interests, an expanded range of career opportunities, and more geographic and social mobility. The growth of the mass media and now the Internet create an information environment that is radically different from the experience of the 1950s: information is now instantaneous, and it's available from a wide variety of sources. The expansion of transportation technologies has shrunk the size of the nation and the world, and increased the breadth of life experiences.[22]

These trends accompany changes in the forms of social organization and interaction. Structured forms of organization, such as political parties run by backroom "bosses" and tightly run political machines, have given way to voluntary associations and ad hoc advocacy groups, which in turn become less formal and more spontaneous in organization. Communities are becoming less bound by geographical proximity. Individuals are involved in increasingly complex and competing social networks that divide their loyalties. Institutional ties are becoming more fluid; hardly anyone expects to work a lifetime for one employer anymore.

None of these trends are surprising to analysts of America society, but too often we overlook the size of these changes and their cumulative impact over more than fifty years. In fact, these trends are altering the norms of citizenship and, in turn, the nature of American politics. They have taken place in a slow and relatively silent process over several decades, but they now reflect the new reality of political life. . . .

In many ways this book presents an unconventional view of the American public. Many of my colleagues in political science are skeptical of positive claims about the American public—and they are especially skeptical that any good can come from the young. Instead, they warn that democracy is at risk and that American youth are a primary reason.

I respect my colleagues' views and have benefited from their writings—*but, this book tells the rest of the story.* Politics in the United States and other advanced industrial societies is changing in ways that hold the potential for strengthening and broadening the democratic process. The old patterns are eroding—as in norms of duty-based voting and deference toward authority—but there are positive and negative implications of these trends if we look for both. The new norms of engaged citizenship come with their own potential advantages and problems. America has become more democratic since the mid-twentieth century, even if progress is still incomplete. Understanding the current state of American political consciousness is the purpose of this book. If we do not become preoccupied with the patterns of democracy in the past, but look toward the potential for our democracy in the future, we can better understand the American public and take advantage of the potential for further progress.

NOTES

1. Stuart Silverstein, "More freshmen help others, survey finds." *Los Angeles Times,* January 26, 2006.

2. Ronald Inglehart and Christian Welzel. *Modernization, Cultural Change and Democracy.* New York: Cambridge University Press, 2005; Wayne Baker, *America's Crisis of Values Reality and Perception.* Princeton: Princeton University Press, 2004; Russell Dalton, *Citizen Politics,* 4th ed. Washington, DC: CQ Press, 2006.

3. Stephen Macedo et al., *Democracy at Risk: How Political Choices Undermine Citizen Participation, and What We Can Do about It.* Washington, DC: Brookings Institution Press, 2005: 1.

4. Some of the most prominent examples of this genre are Alan Wolfe, *Does American Democracy Still Work?* New Haven: Yale University Press, 2006; Fareed Zakaria, *The Future of Freedom: Illiberal Democracy at Home and Abroad.* New York: Norton, 2003; Samuel Huntington, *Who Are We? The Challenges to America's Identity.* New York: Simon & Schuster, 2004; Stephen Craig, *The Malevolent Leaders: Popular Discontent in America.* Boulder, CO: Westview Press, 1993; E. J. Dionne, *Why Americans Hate Politics.* New York: Simon & Schuster, 1991; John Hibbing and Elizabeth Theiss-Morse, *Congress as Public Enemy: Public Attitudes toward American Political Institutions.* New York: Cambridge University Press, 1995; Joseph Nye, Philip Zelikow, and David King, eds., *Why Americans Mistrust Government.* Cambridge, MA: Harvard University Press, 1997; and perhaps the best-researched and most well-reasoned project, Robert Putnam, *Bowling Alone: The Collapse and Renewal of American Community.* New York: Simon and Schuster, 2000. Some might add to this list Russell Dalton, *Democratic Challenges, Democratic Choices.* Oxford: Oxford University Press, 2004; but I disagree.

5. Putnam, *Bowling Alone*; Tom Brokaw, *The Greatest Generation.* New York: Random House, 1998.

6. Putnam, *Bowling Alone,* 283.

7. William Damon, "To not fade away: Restoring civil identity among the young." In Diane Ravitch and Joseph Viteritti, eds., *Making Good Citizens: Education and Civil Society.* New Haven: Yale University Press, 2001. Also see Wattenberg, *Is Voting for the Young?* New York: Longman, 2006; Jean Twenge, *Generation Me: Why Today's Young Americans Are More Confident, Assertive,*

Entitled—and More Miserable Than Ever Before. New York: Free Press, 2006.

8. Ronald Inglehart, *Culture Shift in Advanced Industrial Society*; Baker, *America's Crisis of Values*; Inglehart and Welzel. *Modernization, Cultural Change and Democracy*; Terry Clark and Michael Rempel, eds., *Citizen Politics in Post-Industrial Societies.* Boulder, CO: Westview Press, 1998.

9. Clark and Rempel, *Citizen Politics in Post-Industrial Societies*; Inglehart, *Culture Shift in Advanced Industrial Society.*

10. Richard Florida, *The Rise of the Creative Class: And How It's Transforming Work, Leisure, Community and Everyday Life.* New York: Perseus Books, 2002: 1–3.

11. Angus Campbell et al., *The American Voter.* New York: Wiley, 1960; Angus Campbell et al., *Elections and the Political Order.* New York: Wiley, 1966.

12. Neil Nevitte, *The Decline of Deference.* Petersborough, Canada: Broadview Press, 1996.

13. Norman Nie, Jane Junn, and Kenneth Stehlik-Barry, *Education and Democratic Citizenship in America.* Chicago: Chicago University Press, 1996.

14. Samuel Popkin, *The Reasoning Voter.* Chicago: University of Chicago Press, 1991.

15. Peter Drucker, *Post-Capitalist Society.* New York: Harper Business, 1993; also see Erik Wright, *Class Counts: Comparative Studies in Class Analysis.* Cambridge: Cambridge University Press, 1996. The comparative politics literature notes a similar development in most other Western democracies, labeling this group as the "new middle class," or the "salatariat." Oddbjørn Knutsen, *Class Voting in Western Europe.* Lanham, MD: Lexington Books, 2006.

16. Florida, *The Rise of the Creative Class,* 77–80; also see Morley Winograd and Dudley Buffa, *Taking Control: Politics in the Information Age.* New York Henry Holt, 1996.

17. Florida, *The Rise of the Creative Class,* ch. 3.

18. The Center for American Women and Politics (www.cawp.rutgers.edu) reports that only twenty-six women were members of the 83rd U.S. Congress in 1953, and by the 108th Congress (elected in 2004) this had increased to 172 women—a six-fold increase. Twenty-three women held statewide elective offices in 1969; this increased to eighty-one in 2004. In 1971, there were 244 women in all the state legislatures combined, and by 2003 this increased to 1,654—also a six-fold increase.

19. Katherine Tate, *From Protest to Politics: The New Black Voters in American Elections.* Cambridge: Harvard University Press, 1993.

20. Daniel Bell, *Postindustrial Society.* New York: Free Press, 1973; Ronald Inglehart, *The Silent Revolution.* Princeton: Princeton University Press, 1977; Inglehart, *Culture Shift in Advanced Industrial Society.*

21. There is a tendency, however, to idealize the past, implying that Americans had access to more and better information in the past, when newspaper readership was higher and television was still uncommon; Putnam, *Bowling Alone*; Wattenberg, *Is Voting for Young People?* Certainly access to information is much greater today than in the 1950s: this seems indisputable.

ARTICLE QUESTIONS

1) What are the specific types of engaged citizenship that Dalton sees as increasing? What are the specific types of duty-based citizenship that Dalton sees as decreasing?

2) Are there some types of participation that should be more valued than others? Why? What are they?

3) What do you think it means to be a good citizen in today's society?

7.4) Does Slacktivism Work?

The Monkey Cage Blog, March 12, 2014

LAURA SEAY

Laura Seay is an Assistant Professor of Government at Colby College. She studies African politics, conflict, and development, with a focus on central Africa. She has also written for Foreign Policy, The Atlantic, Guernica, and Al Jazeera English.

> Political scientist Laura Seay notes in "Does Slacktivism Work?" that an increasing form of political participation involves the use of social media by advocacy groups seeking to build support for their causes. Seay notes that even without evidence, "many large U.S. advocacy organizations are convinced that asking new participants for token forms of support is a strong path to deeper engagement." Seay summarizes a new paper by a graduate student at the University of British Columbia who used "a series of field and laboratory experiments, [and] . . . found that those who engage in slacktivism can and do sometimes engage more deeply." Since this only sometimes occurs, it indicates that not all types of slacktivism are the same—so what's the difference between slacktivism that encourages further participation and that which doesn't? According to the study, it appears that "those whose initial act of support is done more privately (for example, writing to a member of Congress) are more likely to engage in deeper, more costly forms of engagement later on." In contrast, "those whose initial support is public (i.e., through posting to Facebook or Twitter) are less likely to engage more deeply." This seems to show that those who are willing to engage in more participatory actions that require a greater personal investment (like letter writing) are likely to continue down this path than those who simply click "like" on Facebook. Thus, this study implies that those likely to engage in purely slacktivism-style actions aren't inclined to engage in further actions simply through social media prodding.

In our information-rich world, activist and advocacy groups trying to get attention for particular causes increasingly rely on social media as a means of building support for their causes. Users are urged to "like" posts and pages on Facebook, share Twitter and blog posts with everyone they know, and to create videos or take a picture for Instagram relating to their cause. Advocates often ask supporters to wear a particular color of clothing on a certain day or purchase bracelets or show other signs of support for a cause.

Such forms of advocacy, particularly those related to social media, are often derisively referred to as "slacktivism" or "armchair activism." These activities pose a minimal cost to participants; one click on Facebook or retweet on Twitter and the slacktivist can feel that he or she has helped to support the cause. While a percentage of the purchase price of a T-shirt or piece of jewelry may go to support program activities, for the most part, these activities of support for a cause require minimal cost—and the activist gets something tangible in return rather than donating the full amount to the cause. Slacktivists don't have to spend a Saturday doing hard labor to build a home or sacrifice a portion of their monthly entertainment budget to a cause. They don't even have to move from behind the screens of their electronic devices.

Campaigns targeting slacktivists are usually based on the logic that increased awareness of a cause is in and of itself a worthy reason to pursue them. There is some limited evidence that asking supporters to "Please retweet" a Twitter post increases the number of retweets a post will get, but many large U.S. advocacy organizations are convinced that asking new participants for token forms of support is a strong path to deeper engagement. Their logic assumes that the more attention a cause receives, the more likely public officials are to pay attention to a cause, and thus the more tangible benefits (like legislation, a policy change, or money allocated to help victims of a crisis) there will be.

Campaigns for attention also often implicitly assume that more attention will lead to a greater likelihood of increased participant engagement, including providing forms of financial support.

A new paper (gated) by University of British Columbia graduate student Kirk Kristofferson and co-authors Katherine White and John Peloza tests the notion that slacktivist-style "token displays of support" lead participants to engage in more costly and meaningful contributions to the cause. Using a series of field and laboratory experiments, they found that those who engage in slacktivism can and do sometimes engage more deeply. What's the determining factor? The extent to which a slacktivist's activism is public or private. Note Kristofferson et al:

> Importantly, the socially observable nature (public vs. private) of initial token support is identified as a key moderator that influences when and why token support does or does not lead to meaningful support for the cause. Consumers exhibit greater helping on a subsequent, more meaningful task after providing an initial private (vs. public) display of token support for a cause.

In other words, those whose initial act of support is done more privately (for example, writing to a member of Congress) are more likely to engage in deeper, more costly forms of engagement later on. Those whose initial support is public (i.e., through posting to Facebook or Twitter) are less likely to engage more deeply. Moreover, the researchers find that most appeals for token engagement "promote slacktivism among all but those highly connected to the cause."

As Kristofferson and his co-authors point out, these findings have several practical applications for advocacy organizations seeking to promote their cause. One of the team's experiments found that value alignment—the idea that a person's public actions reflect his or her private beliefs—was more likely to produce deeper engagement as well, and they suggest that charities should promote the values underlying their causes if they want to turn more slacktivists into committed, policy-changing activists.

ARTICLE QUESTIONS

1) Is creating awareness of an issue, through slacktivism or any other type of activism, a good in itself? Why and why not?
2) Have you engaged in "slackitivism"? What were the advantages and limitations of this style of participation?
3) Based on the results of the study from the University of British Columbia, how could you make "slacktivist-style 'token displays of support'" more effective at promoting more engaged actions?

Chapter 8

Public Opinion

Public opinion serves as shorthand for how a nation's population collectively views policy issues and evaluates political leaders. For the public to have any meaningful say in ruling, political leaders must listen to the people's views—but how much should leaders heed public opinion? Do the people know enough about complex, highly technical matters to form opinions consistent with outcomes they want? When the Constitution was framed, there were fierce disagreements about how much leaders should follow public opinion. The debate continues today. Somehow, the government must reflect popular views; at other times, government officials balance public opinion with their own best judgment. How do public officials achieve the right mix of following the public and doing what they believe to be best? That difficult question lies at the heart of our debates about how to govern.

For public officials to listen to the people, they need to be able to measure public opinion. Elections provide insight into which leaders the people desire, but elections are sporadic and do not provide enough information about the long list of public concerns. Most often public opinion is measured through polling. Polling has become such a dominant method of measuring public sentiment that polling results are often thought to be synonymous with public opinion. And it is true that when polls are done well, they provide an accurate snapshot of what people believe at a given moment. However, the statistical accuracy that underlies polling does not mean that polling results are merely reflecting public opinion. Political scientist Benjamin Ginsberg, in "The Perils of Polling," presents a scathing critique of the practice of developing policy based on polling results. Since the public knows very little about most issues, writes Ginsberg, recorded opinions do not reflect true desires; instead, poll results are a culmination of off-the-cuff responses to questions on issues most people do not understand. If polls are only measuring fickle responses to polling questions, then public opinion as measured by polls is highly malleable. From this perspective, if a political leader tries to implement the public opinion of today, he or she is likely to be working against the public opinion of tomorrow. Further, Ginsberg sees changes in public opinion as often driven by the polling process itself. He argues that polling results are used to shape arguments to build support for the opinions that political leaders already have, as opposed to seeing polling results—and the public opinion they attempt to measure—as shaping governmental policy.

Robert Pear, in his *New York Times* article "White House Works to Shape Debate Over Health Law," reports that in the lead-up to the 2012 Supreme Court arguments on the Affordable Care Act (ACA), White House officials met with dozens of leaders from nonprofit organizations supporting the health law so that they could coordinate plans for showing public support for it. This seems to confirm Ginsberg's concern that political leaders try to shape public opinion rather than heed it. At the same time, the article mentions that much of the information the White House was supplying was data on how the law was operating. Seen in a particular light, this could show that public officials were actually educating the people about the ACA. If people are unaware of the provisions in the law, how can they form accurate opinions? After reading this article, think about whether it provides an example of manipulating public opinion or an example of public officials relying on their own judgment to educate the public about the ACA as a means of implementing the law.

In "Dysfunction: Maybe It's What the Voters Want," Peter Schrag argues that Californians "want a set of incompatible things." Schrag compares responses to polling questions and the results of recent elections to identify a series of contradictory signals sent by the California public. The people of California have responded in public opinion polls (by wide margins) that "they want good schools, roads, low university tuition—and they say they're willing to pay more taxes." But when pollsters asked about a series of different taxes that Californians would be willing to pay, they responded "no" to all specific tax increases. Likewise, Californians have voted for a series of policies that have increased spending on prisons, but polling shows that prison funding is the one area where Californians are most supportive of spending cuts. Think about the implications of these mixed signals. A government official who desired nothing more than to implement the desires of the California public would have no clear indication of what policies to pursue; almost any action could simultaneously support and contradict public opinion as measured by these polling results and election returns.

We surely don't want a government that ignores public opinion, but how much do we want government to follow it? The readings in this chapter present some of difficulties in trying to find the correct balance between being responsive to public opinion and allowing representatives to use their judgment.

CHAPTER QUESTIONS

1) How should the United States balance public opinion against representatives' judgment?
2) What are some of the advantages and disadvantages of using public opinion polling?
3) Should the public be upset when public officials fail to adopt policies that are consistent with public opinion?
4) Do you believe that the public is basically ignorant or collectively wise?

CHAPTER READINGS

8.1) Benjamin Ginsberg, "The Perils of Polling," Has Polling Killed Democracy Conference, University of Virginia, April 2008.

8.2) Robert Pear, "White House Works to Shape Debate Over Health Law," *The New York Times,* March 9, 2012.

8.3) Peter Schrag, "Dysfunction: Maybe It's What the Voters Want," *The Sacramento Bee,* June 14, 2011.

8.1) The Perils of Polling

Has Polling Killed Democracy Conference, University of Virginia, April 2008

BENJAMIN GINSBERG

In "The Perils of Polling," Benjamin Ginsberg observes that U.S. citizens believe that their government "listen[s] to popular opinion most or at least some of the time." Ginsberg, a self-avowed cynic, is skeptical of the veracity of such beliefs. How does Ginsberg justify his cynicism in the face of such consistency between public policy and public opinion? Ginsberg doesn't deny this connection exists, but he believes that the connection between polling results and public policy is a reflection of an uninformed public being manipulated, rather than an indication that public officials are following public opinion. To support this claim, Ginsberg presents examples of adopted policies that enjoyed wide support from the public even though they benefited only a small portion of the population. Ginsberg sees such widely supported but narrowly beneficial policies as signs that "political forces engineered a shift in opinion" to get their preferred policy adopted. Is Ginsberg onto something, or is he being too cynical? Pay attention to his wide use of polling results to support his arguments, even though he argues that polls are often tools of manipulation. Does his use of polling results mean he thinks polling is sometimes useful?

Politicians, advocacy groups, the media and public officials sponsor thousands of opinion surveys every year to assess public sentiment on issues ranging from abortion to Social Security to war in the Middle East. Some pollsters have argued that opinion surveys provide the most scientific and accurate representation of public opinion. George Gallup, one of the founders of the modern polling industry, asserted that opinion polls, more than any other institution, "bridge the gap between the people and those responsible for making decisions in their name."[1]

Polling, of course, has no official place in the American governmental schema. The Constitution does not require public officials to follow poll results. During the entire Clinton impeachment process, the president's standing in the polls remained high as did Richard Nixon's until the eve of his resignation. Conversely, his declining standing in the polls throughout 2005 and 2006 did not compel George W. Bush to withdraw American forces from Iraq. In fact, Gallup's view notwithstanding, the virtual representation provided by the polls does little to bridge the gap between citizens and decision makers. If anything, the polls render public opinion less disruptive, more permissive and more amenable to government and elite manipulation.

Polling has become so ubiquitous that commentators make little distinction between poll results and public opinion, but they are not the same thing at all. Public opinion can be articulated in ways that present a picture of the public's political thinking very different from the results of sample surveys.[2] Statements from leaders of interest groups, trade unions and religious groups about their adherents' feelings are a common mechanism for expressing public opinion. The hundreds of thousands of letters written each year to newspaper editors and to members of Congress are vehicles for the expression of opinion. Protests, riots and demonstrations express citizens' opinions. Government officials take note of all these manifestations of the public's mood. As corporate executive and political commentator Chester Barnard once noted, before the invention of polling, legislators "read the local newspapers, toured their districts and talked with voters, received letters from the home state and entertained delegations that claimed to speak for large and important blocks of voters."[3] The alternatives to polling survive today. But, when poll results differ from other expressions of public opinion, the polls almost always carry more credibility. The labor leader whose account of rank-and-file sentiment differs from poll results is not likely to be taken seriously. Nor is the politician who claims that his or her policy positions are more popular than the polls show. In 1999, for example, Republican congressional leaders claimed that the public opinion disclosed by letters and phone calls supported their efforts to impeach and convict President Bill Clinton even though national opinion polls indicated that the public opposed Clinton's removal from office. Virtually every commentator took the polls to be correct and accused the GOP of disregarding true public sentiment.

This presumption in favor of the accuracy of the polls stems from their apparent scientific neutrality. Survey analysis is modeled on the methods of the natural sciences and conveys an impression of technical sophistication and objectivity. The polls, moreover, can claim to offer a more reliable and representative view of popular opinion than any alternative. People who claim to speak for groups frequently do not. The distribution of opinion reflected in letters to newspapers and government officials is clearly unrepresentative. Scientific samplings of public opinion provide a corrective for false or biased representations of popular sentiment.

Polling, though, is both more and less than a scientific measure of public opinion. The substitution of polling for other methods of gauging the public's views profoundly affects what is perceived to be public opinion. Polling is what statisticians call an "obtrusive measure."[4] Surveys do not simply record continuities and changes in a naturally-occurring phenomenon. The polls also define how individual opinions are to be aggregated. In opinion surveys, the views of well-informed people usually carry no more weight than those of the clueless.[5] Pollsters also choose the topics for which public opinion will be tested. In other words, the data reported by the polls are not "pure" public opinion but the product of an interaction between the opinion holders and the opinion seekers. As surveys measure opinion, they also form opinion.

In the United States, as in other democracies, citizens expect their government to pay close attention to popular preferences. As we saw earlier, most Americans believe that the government does listen to popular opinion most or at least some of the time. This view is bolstered by a number of scholarly studies that have identified a reasonable correlation between national policy and public opinion over time. Alan D. Monroe, for example, found that in a majority of cases, changes in public policy followed shifts in popular preferences. Conversely, in most cases, if opinion did not change, neither did policy.[6] In a similar vein, Page and Shapiro found that much of the time significant shifts in public opinion were followed by changes in national policy in a direction that seemed to follow opinion.[7] These findings are certainly affirmed by hosts of politicians who not only claim to be guided by the will of the people in all their undertakings, but seem to poll assiduously to find out what that will is.

But, once we accept the notion that there is some measure of congruence or consistency between public opinion and public policy, we should not take this to mean that the public's preferences somehow control the government's conduct. Most citizens do not have strong and autonomous preferences with regard to most public issues. And many lack the basic information that might help them to understand and evaluate policy choices and governmental processes. For example, 40 percent of Americans responding to a recent survey did not know that each state has two senators; 43 percent did not know what an economic recession is; 68 percent did not know that a two-third majority in each house is required for a congressional override of a presidential veto; 70 percent did not know that the term of a U.S. House member is two years; 71 percent could not name their own congressional representative; and 81 percent could not name both of their own state's senators.[8] These findings suggest that many Americans can barely describe, much less control, their government.

When it comes to major public issues, many Americans have too much difficulty grasping the substance of the issue and the potential alternative policies to have any serious or coherent preference. For example, during the 2000 election campaign, reform of the Social Security system became a major issue. George W. Bush had proposed partially "privatizing" the system by allowing individuals to invest some of their payroll taxes in personal retirement accounts whose value would be subject to market fluctuations. Bush made a number of speeches on the topic; the idea was highlighted at the GOP convention; and the news media devoted considerable attention to it. After all the attention Bush's proposal received, however, surveys revealed that most Americans knew little or nothing about it and had no meaningful preferences on the issue. 73 percent of those contacted by Princeton Survey Research Associates after the Republican convention said they knew "little" or "nothing at all" about Bush's proposal.[9] More than half could not say whether Bush's proposed plan would raise taxes or how it might affect their likely Social Security benefits. More than half, however, favored the proposal—whatever it was.[10] The same pattern is apparent in surveys dealing with several other recent political issues.[11]

Many Americans' knowledge of contemporary political issues is limited to some half-remembered fact or claim they saw in an ad or heard on a newscast. And once they acquire some piece of information many individuals will retain it long after it ceases to have any relevance. In a 2005 Harris poll, for example, more than a third of the respondents believed that Iraq possessed weapons of mass destruction at the time of the American invasion—this despite the fact that even President Bush had long since acknowledged that no such weapons had existed. Apparently these respondents hadn't been paying attention.

The unfortunate fact of the matter is that many Americans lack the cognitive tools or basic understanding of political and social realities to understand or to seriously evaluate competing political claims and proposals. Certainly, a minority of affluent, well-educated individuals—perhaps 20 percent of the public according to even the most generous estimates—are knowledgeable about public issues and possess the intellectual tools to evaluate them.[12] The remainder

are essentially what economists call "noise traders," that is, individuals whose actions are based upon faulty information and questionable reasoning. This is, after all, a nation in which, according to a 2004 CBS News survey, 55 percent of all respondents reject the theory of evolution in favor of the idea that God created humans in their present form. This is a nation in which, according to an October 2005 Fox News survey, 84 percent believe in miracles and 79 percent in angels. According to the same survey 37 percent believe in astrology, 24 percent in witches and 27 percent in reincarnation. Perhaps we should be relieved that only 4 percent believe in vampires but, alas, 34 percent believe in ghosts. Some scholars have argued that, on the aggregate, the public can possess wisdom even though many, if not most, individuals are foolish. This argument, though, is based upon rather dubious statistical and logical assumptions.[13]

Americans' lack of information and basic political knowledge and, frankly, lack of a simple capacity to distinguish fact from fable makes many Americans quite vulnerable to manipulation by politicians and advocates wielding the usual instruments of advertising and publicity. And, though they give lip service to the will of the people, politicians and advocates are quite aware of the fact that most of the time many of the people have no particular will or, for that matter, interest in or understanding of public issues. Their goal, as Jacobs and Shapiro note, is to "simulate responsiveness," by developing arguments and ideas that will persuade citizens to agree with their own policy goals.[14] This effort begins with polling. As Clinton pollster Dick Morris affirmed, "You don't use a poll to reshape a program, but to reshape your argumentation for the program so the public supports it."[15] The effort continues with advertising, publicity and propaganda, making use of the information gleaned from the polls.

What do these observations mean for the relationship between opinion and policy identified by Monroe, Page and others? They suggest that opinion and policy are related primarily because of their common underlying origins. Rather than providing evidence that public opinion drives national policy, the correlation between the two derives from the fact that the same political forces seeking to shape national policy often find it useful to create a climate of opinion conducive to their goals.

Thus, for example, a coalition of forces that succeeded in bringing about the elimination of the estate tax in 2001 first made extensive use of polling and publicity over the course of several years to persuade the public that what they labeled the "death tax" was unfair and un-American. This public relations effort was a great success and helped smooth the way for the coalition's lobbying effort in the Congress. As Graetz and Shapiro show, while the federal estate tax actually affected only the wealthiest 2 percent of the populace, the intensive campaign for its repeal seemed to persuade many naive Americans that the tax actually affected them. One poll taken in the wake of the repeal campaign suggested that 77 percent of the populace believed the tax affected all Americans, and several polls indicated that more than one-third of the public believed they themselves would have to pay the tax.[16] When the tax was finally annulled, its elimination was supported by public opinion. But, does this mean that a change in public opinion brought about this change in policy? Hardly. Instead, a particular set of political forces engineered a shift in opinion which helped them to persuade Congress to change national policy. A similar pattern was also observed by Hacker and Pierson when they studied recent changes in tax policy. Citizens, they say, "proved vulnerable to extensive manipulation," as political elites framed a discussion that generated popular support for policy changes that served the interests of a small minority of wealthy Americans.[17]

So much for the primacy of public opinion in the American democratic order. Bryce was far off the mark when he called opinion the "chief and ultimate power" in all nations. Indeed, the notoriously cynical Austrian economist, Joseph Schumpeter, was much closer to the truth when he observed that the will of the people was the "product," not than the "motive power" of the political process.[18]

NOTES

1. George Gallup and Saul Rae, The Pulse of Democracy: The Public Opinion Poll and How It Works (New York: Simon and Schuster, 1940), p. 14.

2. Scott Althaus, Collective Preferences in Democratic Politics (New York: Cambridge, 2003); Benjamin Ginsberg, The Captive Public (New York: Basic Books, 1986); and Susan Herbst, Numbered Voices (Chicago: University of Chicago Press, 1993).

3. Chester Barnard, Public Opinion in a Democracy, pamphlet (Princeton, N.J.: Herbert Baker Foundation, Princeton University, 1939), p. 13.

4. Se Eugene Webb, et al., Unobtrusive Measures: Normative Research in the Social Sciences (Chicago: Rand McNally, 1966).

5. For an excellent discussion of information effects on survey outcomes, see Althaus, chs. 4 and 5.

6. Alan Monroe, "Consistency Between Public Preferences and National Policy Decisions," American Politics Quarterly 7 (1979), pp. 3–18. Also, Alan D. Monroe, "Public Opinion and Public Policy, 1980–1993," Public Opinion Quarterly 62(1), (1998), pp. 6–18.

7. Benjamin Page and Robert Y. Shapiro, "Effects of Public Opinion on Policy," American Political Science Review 77 (1983), pp. 175–190. See also, Jeff Manza, Fay Cook and Benjamin Page (ed.), Navigating Public Opinion (New York: Oxford, 2002), Part I.

8. Carol Glynn, et.al., Public Opinion (Boulder, CO: Westview, 2004), p. 293.

9. George Bishop, The Illusion of Public Opinion (Lanham, MD: Rowman and Littlefield, 2005), ch. 2, p. 35.

10. Bishop, pp. 34–35.

11. For a number of examples, see Bishop, chs. 2 and 7.

12. See for example, Jacob S. Hacker and Paul Pierson, Off Center: The Republican Revolution and the Erosion of American Democracy (New Haven: Yale, 2005), p. 67.

13. Some scholars, to be sure, have argued that although many individuals may lack information or coherent policy preferences, public opinion on aggregate may still be reasonable and sensible. Page and Shapiro, The Rational Public (Chicago: University of Chicago Press, 1992), for example, assert that, "public opinion as a collective phenomenon is . . . meaningful. And indeed rational . . . it is organized in coherent patterns; it is reasonable . . . and it is adaptive to new information" (p. 14). As Althaus, however, has demonstrated, this argument rests upon very shaky statistical foundations. Althaus, ch. 2. Moreover, the notion that aggregate opinion may be reasonable despite the ignorance of individuals assumes that individuals do not communicate with or influence one another. This condition is usually violated in the case of political opinion where the ignorant influence one another and are influenced by politicians and the media. Anyone who doubts this should listen to talk radio. See James Surowiecki, The Wisdom of Crowds (New York: Doubleday, 2004).

14. Jacobs and Shapiro, p. xv.

15. Dick Morris, Behind the Oval Office (Los Angeles: Renaissance, 1999). Quoted in Jacobs and Shapiro, p. xv.

16. Michael Graetz and Ian Shapiro, Death By A Thousand Cuts: The Fight Over Taxing Inherited Wealth (Princeton: Princeton University Press. 2005).

17. Hacker and Pierson, ch. 2.

18. Joseph Schumpeter, Capitalism, Socialism and Democracy, 3rd edition (New York: Harper, 1970), p. 263.

ARTICLE QUESTIONS

1) What specific evidence does Ginsberg provide to support his claim that the "many lack the basic information that might help them to understand and evaluate policy choices"?
2) Assume for a moment that Ginsberg is correct and that elites do manipulate public opinion to get their preferred policies. Does the fact that elites must garner popular support for their policies indicate that public opinion serves as an important check on political action?
3) What is the solution to the problem that Ginsberg identifies?
4) In what ways do you agree with Ginsberg's argument? In what ways do you find his argument unpersuasive?

8.2) White House Works to Shape Debate Over Health Law

The New York Times, March 9, 2012

ROBERT PEAR

Jackie Calmes contributed reporting.

Robert Pear's article "White House Works to Shape Debate Over Health Law" can be interpreted two very different ways. From one perspective Pear's article offers an example of public officials manufacturing public opinion to support their own preferred policies. From this perspective, public opinion isn't something to be heeded but something to be molded. Does this perspective—manipulation by government officials—undermine the entire concept of self-rule? On the other hand, perhaps this interpretation is too cynical: the article can also be interpreted as public officials balancing current public opinion with their best judgment. If the public is woefully uninformed about policy (as Ginsberg argued in the previous article), then perhaps government officials ought to educate the public. Further, if these White House efforts are successful in shaping people's opinions, does that tell us that the public's previous opinions were lightly held and based on limited justification? It could even be argued that the White House's efforts to build support for its positions—rather than just ignoring public opinion and simply substituting its own views—is commendable. Ginsberg's cynical interpretation and this White House effort have something in common: they both show that public opinion is important to public officials; if it were irrelevant, why would they invest so much effort in shaping it?

WASHINGTON—The White House has begun an aggressive campaign to use approaching Supreme Court arguments on the new health care law as a moment to build support for the measure seen as President Obama's signature legislative achievement, hoping to shape public opinion on an issue at the center of the battle for the White House and Congress.

On Wednesday, White House officials summoned dozens of leaders of nonprofit organizations that strongly back the health law to help them coordinate plans for a prayer vigil, press conferences and other events outside the court when justices hear arguments for three days beginning March 26.

The advocates and officials mapped out a strategy to call attention to tangible benefits of the law, like increased insurance coverage for young adults. Sensitive to the idea that they were encouraging demonstrations, White House officials denied that they were trying to gin up support by encouraging rallies outside the Supreme Court, just a stone's throw from Congress on Capitol Hill. They said a main purpose of this week's meeting, in the Eisenhower Executive Office Building adjacent to the White House, was to give the various groups a chance to learn of the plans.

For months, Democrats in Congress and progressive groups have urged the White House to make a more forceful defense of the health care law, which is denounced almost daily by Republican lawmakers and presidential candidates.

Administration officials said that they would much prefer to focus on job creation and the need for clean energy at the moment and that the court arguments were forcing health care to the forefront. But they appear to have decided that they cannot risk allowing the court proceedings to unfold without making sure that backers of the sweeping overhaul will be prominent and outspoken.

Opponents of the law will be active as well and are planning to show their sentiments at a rally on the Capitol grounds on March 27, the second day of Supreme Court arguments. Republican lawmakers, including Senator Patrick J. Toomey of Pennsylvania and Representative Michele Bachmann of Minnesota, are expected to address the rally, being organized by Americans for Prosperity, with support from conservative and free-market groups like the Tea Party Express.

At the White House meeting on Wednesday, a wide range of advocates representing consumers and people with diseases and disabilities—as well as doctors and nurses, labor unions and religious organizations—discussed plans to bolster the landmark law, which is being challenged by 26 states as unconstitutional.

Supporters of the law plan to hold events outside the court on each day of oral argument. The events include speeches by people with medical problems who have benefited or could benefit from the law. In addition, supporters will arrange for radio hosts to interview health care advocates at a "radio row," at the United Methodist Building on Capitol Hill.

People who attended the meeting on Wednesday said the speakers included Jennifer Palmieri, deputy communications director at the White House; Jon Carson, director of the president's

Office of Public Engagement; Jeanne M. Lambrew, deputy assistant to the president for health policy; and Mark B. Childress, a deputy chief of staff at the White House.

"The White House was very encouraging and supportive of our activities," said Ronald F. Pollack, executive director of Families USA, one of more than 60 organizations that sent representatives to the meeting.

Mr. Pollack said the theme of events at the Supreme Court would be, "Protect our health care, protect the law."

Jennifer M. Ng'andu, a health policy specialist at the National Council of La Raza, a Hispanic rights group, said White House officials emphasized that the court case provided "a great opportunity to highlight benefits of the law for real people."

A White House official who attended the session said that at least 100 people were present, but he declined to provide a list of their organizations.

Nicholas Papas, a White House spokesman, confirmed that "outside organizations came together to share with the White House and each other the activities they have planned." In coming weeks, he said, "the administration will continue to implement the law and educate the public about the benefits of health reform."

In the week before the Supreme Court arguments, administration officials will fan out around the country and join local groups in celebrating the second anniversary of the law, signed by Mr. Obama on March 23, 2010.

Just after the law was signed, Senator Charles E. Schumer, Democrat of New York, predicted on the NBC program "Meet the Press" that "those who voted for health care will find it an asset, those who voted against it will find it a liability."

But two years later, public opinion on the law is deeply divided, and polls show significant opposition among Republicans and independent voters in battleground states.

Backers of the law said they would use data supplied by the White House to show how the law had reduced drug costs for older Americans, guaranteed free preventive care for millions of people and allowed many children to stay on their parents' insurance policies.

However, one of the main provisions on which the Supreme Court will focus—a requirement for most Americans to carry health insurance—is not particularly popular, according to opinion polls.

The court is expected to issue its decision in late June, as the presidential campaign enters its crucial final months and Congressional races grow more intense.

Groups working with the White House include the Service Employees International Union; the American Federation of State, County and Municipal Employees; Health Care for America Now, a consumer coalition that fought for passage of the legislation; Protect Your Care, a nonprofit group created last year to defend the 2010 law; and the Center for American Progress, a research and advocacy group with close ties to the White House.

Eddie P. Vale, a spokesman for Protect Your Care, said White House officials at the meeting "sounded pretty excited about the size and scope" of efforts to promote the law this month.

Levi Russell, a spokesman for Americans for Prosperity, said buses would bring people to rally against the health law from Maryland, Michigan, New Jersey, New York, North Carolina, Pennsylvania and Virginia, among other states. The theme is "Hands off my health care."

On its Web site, the Obama re-election campaign describes Americans for Prosperity as a "special-interest front group run by the oil billionaire Koch brothers." In a recent fund-raising appeal, Jim Messina, the campaign manager, said that the oilmen, Charles and David Koch, were "obsessed with making Barack Obama a one-term president."

Mr. Russell said, "The Koch brothers were involved in the founding of Americans for Prosperity and contribute to it, but they are just two out of 90,000 donors."

ARTICLE QUESTIONS

1) According to Pear, what specific activities did While House officials engage in to shape the debate over the health care law? Which activities, if any, do you think were appropriate for White House officials? Which activities, if any, do you think were inappropriate?

2) Does government have a role in educating people on policy matters?

3) When government officials feel it is important to substitute their own judgment for popular opinion, should these officials try to shift public opinion to line up with their own views, or should they simply act without any concern about ignoring public desires? Is this a dichotomous choice or are there other options?

8.3) Dysfunction: Maybe It's What the Voters Want

The Sacramento Bee, June 14, 2011

PETER SCHRAG

The Constitution set up a system of government that filters public opinion in various ways. At the national level, U.S. citizens do not directly vote for public policy, various positions (such as federal judges) are insulated from elections, and public officials are expected to balance public opinion with their own judgment. But many states have removed some of these filters on public opinion. Thirty-eight states have some version of elections for their judges, and more than 25 allow citizens to vote directly on legislation. Direct citizen initiatives were established to get around corrupt government officials who ignored the desires of the people, but these initiatives also remove the ability of government officials to use their best judgment. Consider the example of creating a state budget. When public officials do their job properly, they look at the entire budget before funding a new project or increasing funding for an existing program. Giving funds to one program usually requires reducing funds for others. But when citizens vote to fund a program, it typically is an isolated decision about the merits of that program. In California, voters have required funding of some programs at certain levels—even if these levels are more than these programs need—which sometimes requires other important programs to be cut completely.

Peter Schrag argues in "Dysfunction: Maybe It's What the Voters Want," that direct implementation of public opinion has helped create a dysfunctional government in California. While Californians never directly say they want a dysfunctional government, the responses they give to polling questions and the policies they vote for at the polls indicate that Californians "want a set of incompatible things." For example, they have voted on multiple occasions for policies mandating increased spending on prisons, but polling shows that prisons are the one area where Californians want spending cuts. Californians often say they don't want any new taxes, but they still desire numerous public services. Ultimately, Schrag's article seems to indicate that unfiltered public opinion can lead to outcomes that actually contradict public opinion.

On Sunday, Gov. Jerry Brown pledged once again to "to go back to you, the people, on the fundamental decisions that we have to make as Californians."

But if you read the most recent poll from PPIC, the Public Policy Institute of California, or almost any other recent opinion survey, it's pretty clear that "you, the people" have no clear idea what you want.

Or more accurately, what the people of California want are a set of incompatible things. They want good schools, roads, low university tuition—and they say they're willing to pay more taxes for some of those things—just not any specific tax. No higher vehicle license fees, no higher sales taxes, no higher income tax.

The voters loudly complain about inaction in Sacramento and, if the Legislature fails to agree on a budget by Wednesday's constitutional deadline, they'll dock the politicians' pay. But there isn't the beginning of a clue in the poll data about what voters want done.

Yes, they want to vote on Brown's proposed tax extensions, but they seem to have no intention of voting for them. Don't tax you, don't tax me, tax the man behind the tree.

The voters decreed California's costly "three-strikes" sentencing law in 1994; in 2004, despite the costs both to the state, to families and the unfairness of long sentences for minor crimes, they refused to change it. But the only thing they tell the pollsters they want to cut is prison costs, even as the courts are in effect ordering us either to spend a lot more or unload a quarter of the inmates.

They've voted for a string of other ballot measures that are costing the state billions—stem cell bonds, high-speed rail, children's hospital bonds, after-school programs, park land acquisition—without appropriating one cent to pay for them.

They say they trust their local government more than state government, which is hardly surprising, but of course it's the voters themselves who in passing Proposition 13 in 1978 and a string of other measures in its wake transferred all that power to Sacramento and decimated their own local governments.

Yes, Brown and the Legislature contributed to the confusion by bailing out local governments and schools after Proposition 13 passed, thus reinforcing both the irresponsibility of the locals, who spend most of the money that the state collects in taxes, and the irresponsibility of the voters in freezing property taxes. If they'd felt the pain of the property tax cuts immediately, our fiscal history might have been quite different.

Jerry Brown, in urging a transfer of more authority back to the locals, now seems to have some second thoughts about the old bailout. But does he have any second thoughts about his campaign pledge last year not to raise any taxes unless the people ask for them?

We have a more mature Brown from the one who governed California 30 years ago, but there still seems to be a quirky, go-with-the flow streak in the man. If the polls tell us anything, it's that this is an electorate that deserves—needs—some strong leadership.

Two weeks ago, the voters again told PPIC's pollsters that they trust the initiative process more than their elected representatives, as they have for many years. But it's produced three-plus decades of initiatives—tax cuts, spending limits, legislative term limits, bond issues, the knotty Proposition 98 school spending formula and other ballot-box spending mandates—that have made it so hard for government to function.

Yes, it's true that the anti-tax rigidity of the Sacramento's Republicans, in thrall to Grover Norquist, Washington's rabid "starve-the-beast" anti-taxer, has contributed mightily to the gridlock. But who's to say that they're not doing at least one part of what the voters want?

The state badly needs structural reforms to enable government to function again—on the initiative process, in tax policy, in modifying the super-majority requirements to raise revenues that the voters have imposed on all levels of government.

But it needs even greater changes in its political culture—in the myth that we are over-taxed, in the lack of the communitarian ethic and the optimism that made this a great state in the generation after World War II, in the failure to understand that in starving our schools and universities, letting our parks rot, we are starving our children and destroying our future.

We say we want government to work, but at a time when we ourselves are so ambivalent and divided, and when the electorate is so different socially, economically and ethnically from the population as a whole, is that really what the voters want?

ARTICLE QUESTIONS

1) According to Schrag, what "set of incompatible things" are desired by Californians?

2) Why do you think that public opinion as measured by polls is showing that Californians want incompatible things? How can this problem be solved?

3) If you were an elected official in California who was interested in following public opinion, how would you decide what actions to pursue?

Chapter 9

The Media

Media are all the ways people get information about politics and the wider world: television, radio, newspaper, Internet searches, blogs, Facebook, Twitter, Tumblr, and more. Think about what the word *media*—the plural form of medium—connotes. The very word helps us visualize media as those entities situated between us and events that occur in the world. Without media bridging the gap we would be ignorant of most happenings; our first-hand experiences of politics are limited. Rarely can we attend important sessions of Congress, the Supreme Court, or even our city council. But media don't just provide unfiltered accounts of all world happenings; that would be an impossible task. The intermediary role that media provide grants media outlets selective control over which events to cover and forces them to frame those events. The wider world that we are able to experience through media is by definition a "mediated" presentation filtered through the biases and the structures of media organizations.

Each type of media has its own advantages and limitations. Each change in media—the rise of radio, television, and the Internet—had a profound impact on American politics. Fifty years ago, everyone watched the same newscast and took part in the same debate. Today, each position on the political spectrum tunes in to its own news sources. The readings in this chapter emphasize the newest developments in media. A question that looms above this chapter is the effect of the new media on democracy. In what ways do new media enhance democracy? In what ways do they diminish it?

The first three readings attribute increases in social fragmentation, widening political polarization, and the loss of investigative journalism to the changing media environment. Robert Kaiser, in "The Bad News about the News," laments the loss of the golden era of news when investigative journalists broke the Watergate scandal and reported on the Vietnam War. Kaiser worries that the modern media environment has diminished media organizations' ability to hold public officials accountable. He sees few advantages in the proliferation of freely available news because no one has yet figured out how to make news gathering profitable. The loss of media profitability means that newspapers employ about half as many journalists as they did in the late 1980s and most news organizations no longer have foreign bureaus to do first-hand reporting around the world. Cass Sunstein, in *Republic 2.0*, also emphasizes the potential risks to self-rule posed by the changing media environment. Sunstein, however, approaches these risks from the vantage of consumer choices. He expresses concern that recent media transformations allow people to seek out only media that reinforce their worldviews and can filter out media that challenge their perspectives.

While Sunstein provides a mostly philosophical argument about media-encouraged polarization, the Pew Research Center for the People & the Press released an in-depth empirical study on the topic, titled "Political Polarization and Media Habits." The year-long research project, after marshalling a trove of data on modern media viewing habits, concluded that "when it comes to getting news about politics and government, liberals and conservatives inhabit different worlds."

In "Obama, the Puppet Master," Jim VandeHei and Mike Allen, writing for *Politico*, explore an ominous political repercussion that they see developing. They argue that the altered media environment allows President Obama to be a master of "limiting, shaping, and manipulating media coverage of himself." While previous presidents have used media to their advantage, increases in technology, combined with decreasing media profit margins, have tipped the "balance of power" toward government. In VandeHei and Allen's view, this power shift allows Obama to shape the news in ways previously impossible.

The final two articles in the chapter focus on the power of the media to influence political agendas. Shana Gadarian, a political scientist from Syracuse University, provides some provocative implications of her media research in "How Sensationalist TV Stories on Terrorism Make Americans More Hawkish." Based on her research, conducted in the wake of the 2001 terrorist attacks, she notes that "the more TV [people] watched, the more hawkish . . . their views." She concludes that "media coverage of terrorism with searing images and warnings of more violence . . . is likely to get Americans . . . to line up behind the president's use of force." Justin Wolfers, a professor from the University of Michigan, discusses media effects on crime perceptions in "Perceptions Haven't Caught Up to Decline in Crime." He notes that the violent crime rate "has declined roughly by half since 1993." However, the public is largely unaware of this decline and often thinks crime rates are actually increasing. Because news organizations tend to highlight "newsworthy" and sensational stories, they continue devoting resources to reporting events, such as crime, that are rare. In the end, the public starts to view these rare events as common. The obvious implication of Gadarian's and Wolfers's articles is that distorted perceptions about terrorist attacks or crime rates can establish political agendas that are out of touch with the actual risks.

The media serve as a link between leaders and citizens and the bridge between world events and our living rooms. The national media reflect America itself: raucous, fast-changing, multilingual, multicultural, forceful, rich, loud, and lucrative. Media organizations have immense power to influence our perceptions of the world, and our choices of media can reinforce our own biases. It's important to learn how the media function and how they influence politics.

CHAPTER QUESTIONS

1) In what ways do the media influence politics?
2) Why is a free press important in a democratic country?

3) How does the rise of new media organizations and structures affect democratic self-governance? What aspects of new media are advantageous? What aspects are harmful?

4) What problems for self-governance could result if large portions of the public only view media that reinforce their worldviews?

CHAPTER READINGS

9.1) Robert Kaiser, "The Bad News about the News," *The Brookings Essay*, October 16, 2014.

9.2) Cass Sunstein, *Republic 2.0* [excerpts], Princeton University Press, 2007.

9.3) Amy Mitchell, Jeffrey Gottfried, Jocelyn Kiley, and Katerina Eva Matsa, "Political Polarization and Media Habits," Pew Research Center for the People & the Press, October 21, 2014.

9.4) Jim VandeHei and Mike Allen, "Obama, the Puppet Master," *Politico*, February 18, 2013.

9.5) Shana Gadarian, "How Sensationalist TV Stories on Terrorism Make Americans More Hawkish," *The Monkey Cage Blog*, October 9, 2014.

9.6) Justin Wolfers, "Perceptions Haven't Caught Up to Decline in Crime," *The New York Times*, September 16, 2014.

9.1) The Bad News about the News

The Brookings Essay, October 16, 2014

ROBERT KAISER

The media play an important and powerful role in self-governance: they can inform citizens and hold public officials accountable. For these reasons Robert Kaiser asserts that "journalism . . . provides the lifeblood of a free, democratic society." However, Kaiser worries that current changes in the media environment are stripping the vitality from the media. Based on his experience (he spent more than 50 years as a reporter and editor at *The Washington Post*) he is convinced that "a few distinguished news organizations committed to holding powerful people accountable" would be the best media structure for promoting democracy. The trend, however, is running in exactly the opposite direction. Media upstarts and the proliferation of political blogs have supplanted traditional news organizations, but these displacements have come without replacing the breadth of services provided by their predecessors. Many new-media sources manage to cobble together razor-thin profits because they don't bear the costs of generating the majority of their own news; instead, many media sources rely on "cutting and pasting" stories from traditional news sources and providing commentary on news stories from other sites. In the absence of news-generators, where will these upstarts go find their stories? What content would they comment on? Kaiser traces this problem to the fact that "no one has found a way to make traditional news-gathering sufficiently profitable."

A further concern implicit in Kaiser's argument is that a news environment filled with numerous small media companies lacks sufficient power to hold public officials accountable. A major news organization addresses millions of viewers or readers commands the attention of public officials; in contrast, increasingly smaller media organizations, with increasingly smaller slices of the public's attention, will command little attention from public officials. Kaiser does not assert that our media and our democracy are headed for an unavoidable decline, and he even provides a couple examples of successful new media. Still his assessment about the current changes in media is a somber one.

Obviously, new technologies are radically altering the ways in which we learn, teach, communicate, and are entertained. It is impossible to know today where these upheavals may lead, but where they take us matters profoundly. How the digital revolution plays out over time will be particularly important for journalism, and therefore to the United States, because journalism is the craft that provides the lifeblood of a free, democratic society.

The Founding Fathers knew this. They believed that their experiment in self-governance would require active participation by an informed public, which could only be possible if people had unfettered access to information. James Madison, author of the First Amendment guaranteeing freedom of speech and of the press, summarized the proposition succinctly: "The advancement and diffusion of knowledge is the only guardian of true liberty." Thomas Jefferson explained to his French friend, the Marquis de Lafayette, "The only security of all is in a free press. The force of public opinion cannot be resisted when permitted freely to be expressed." American journalists cherish another of Jefferson's remarks: "Were it left to me to decide whether we should have a government without newspapers or newspapers without a government, I should not hesitate a moment to prefer the latter."

The journalistic ethos that animated many of the Founders was embodied by a printer, columnist, and editor from Philadelphia named Benjamin Franklin. The printing press, which afforded Franklin his livelihood, remained the engine of American democracy for more than two centuries. But then, in the second half of the 20th century, new technologies began to undermine long-established means of sharing information. First television and then the computer and the Internet transformed the way people got their news. Nonetheless, even at the end of the century, the business of providing news and analysis was still a profitable enough undertaking that it could support large organizations of professional reporters and editors in print and broadcast media.

Now, however, in the first years of the 21st century, accelerating technological transformation has undermined the business models that kept American news media afloat, raising the possibility that the great institutions on which we have depended for news of the world around us may not survive.

These are painful words to write for someone who spent 50 years as a reporter and editor at *The Washington Post*. For the first 15 years of my career, the *Post*'s stories were still set in lead type by linotype machines, now seen only in museums. We first began writing on computers in the late 1970s, which seemed like an unequivocally good thing until the rise of the Internet in the 1990s. Then,

gradually, the ground began to shift beneath us. By the time I retired earlier this year, the Graham family had sold the *Post* to Jeff Bezos, the founder of Amazon, for $250 million, a small fraction of its worth just a few years before. Donald Graham, the chief executive at the time, admitted that he did not know how to save the newspaper....

[P]utting newspapers online has not remotely restored their profitability. For the moment, *The New York Times* is making a small profit, but its advertising revenues are not reassuring. *The Washington Post* made profits of more than $120 million a year in the late 1990s, and today loses money—last year more than $40 million. *Newsweek* magazine failed, and *Time* magazine is teetering. Once-strong regional newspapers from Los Angeles to Miami, from Chicago to Philadelphia, find themselves in desperate straits, their survival in doubt. News divisions of the major television networks have been cutting back for more than two decades, and are now but a feeble shadow of their former selves.

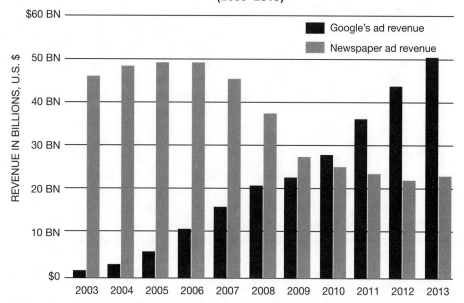

Google's Annual Advertising Revenue (2003–2013)

Sources: Google worldwide, 2001–2013; United States newspapers, 2003–2013.
Newspaper revenue includes online and print advertising and excludes niche publications, direct marketing, and non-daily publication advertising.

Overall the economic devastation would be difficult to exaggerate. One statistic conveys its dimensions: the advertising revenue of all America's newspapers fell from $63.5 billion in 2000 to about $23 billion in 2013, and is still falling. Traditional news organizations' financial well-being depended on the willingness of advertisers to pay to reach the mass audiences they attracted. Advertisers were happy to pay because no other advertising medium was as effective. But in the digital era, which has made it relatively simple to target advertising in very specific ways, a big metropolitan or national newspaper has much less appeal. Internet companies like Google and Facebook are able to sort audiences by the most specific criteria, and thus to offer advertisers the possibility of spending their money only on ads they know will reach only people interested in what they are selling. So Google, the master of targeted advertising, can provide a retailer selling sheets and towels an audience existing exclusively of people who have gone online in the last month to shop for sheets and towels. This explains why even as newspaper revenues have plummeted, the ad revenue of Google has leapt upward year after year—from $70 million in 2001 to an astonishing $50.6 billion in 2013. That is more than two times the combined advertising revenue of every newspaper in America last year.

And the situation for proprietors of newspapers and magazines is likely to get worse. One alarming set of statistics: Americans spend about 5 percent of the time they devote to media of all kinds to magazines and newspapers. But nearly 20 percent of advertising dollars still go to print media. So print media today are getting billions more than they probably deserve from advertisers who, governed by the inertia so common in human affairs, continue to buy space in publications that are steadily losing audience, especially among the young. When those advertisers wake up, revenues will plummet still further.

News organizations have tried to adapt to the new realities. As the Internet became more popular and more important in the first decade of the 21st century, newspaper proprietors dreamed of paying for their newsrooms by mimicking their traditional business model in the online world. Their hope was to create mass followings for their websites that would appeal to advertisers the way their ink-on-paper versions once did. But that's not what happened.

The news organizations with the most popular websites did attract lots of eyeballs, but general advertising on their sites did not produce compelling results for advertisers, so they did not buy as much of it as the papers had hoped. And the price they paid for it steadily declined, because as the Internet grew, the number of sites offering advertising opportunities assured that "supply" outstripped "demand." Advertising revenues for the major news sites never amounted to even a significant fraction of the revenues generated by printed newspapers in the golden age. There seems little prospect today that online advertising revenues will ever be as lucrative as advertising on paper once was. . . .

Despite two decades of trying, no one has found a way to make traditional news-gathering sufficiently profitable to assure its future survival. Serious readers of America's most substantial news media may find this description at odds with their daily experience. After all, *The New York Times*, *The Wall Street Journal*, and *The Washington Post* still provide rich offerings of good journalism every morning, and they have been joined by numerous online providers of both opinion and news—even of classic investigative reporting. Digital publications employ thousands of reporters and editors in new and sometimes promising journalistic enterprises. Is this a disaster?

Of course not—yet. But today's situation is probably misleading. The laws of economics cannot be ignored or repealed. Nor can the actuarial tables. Only about a third of Americans under 35 look at a newspaper even once a week, and the percentage declines every year. A large portion of today's readers of the few remaining good newspapers are much closer to the grave than to high school. Today's young people skitter around the Internet like ice skaters, exercising their short attention spans by looking for fun and, occasionally, seeking out serious information. Audience taste seems to be changing, with the result

How People Get Their News

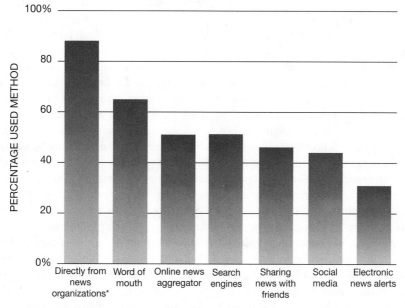

Survey Question: "Did you find news in any of the following ways in the last week, or did you not find news in that way?"
*News organizations include newspapers, TV newcasts, websites, and news wires.
Source: Media Insight Project, 2014.

that among young people particularly there is a declining appetite for the sort of information packages the great newspapers provided, which included national, foreign and local news, business news, cultural news and criticism, editorials and opinion columns, sports and obituaries, lifestyle features, and science news.

Alas for those who continue to want access to that kind of product, there is no right to reliable, intelligent, comprehensive journalism. We only get it when someone provides it. And if it doesn't pay someone a profit, it's not likely to be produced.

Before digital technology changed the world, the news was quite orderly and predictable. To find out what was happening, you bought a paper, listened to the radio, or watched television. Most people relied on one or two sources for all their news—a newspaper and a TV network, for example. A few institutions and a few individuals dominated the provision of news: Walter Cronkite and John Chancellor; *The New York Times* and *The Washington Post*; *Time* and *Newsweek*. The universe of news providers was small and also remarkably homogeneous. David Brinkley could move from NBC to ABC without causing much of a stir. When Roone Arledge, whose first big accomplishment was to make ABC the leading network for sports, was empowered to build a new ABC News, he did it by raiding the staffs of NBC and CBS. Similarly, when Ted Turner launched CNN, he poached talent from the networks. This small, nearly-closed world rarely provided any surprises.

Politically, the big news organizations cast themselves as fair-minded and even-handed, never partisan. *Time* magazine may have been somewhat more conservative, *The New York Times* more liberal, but none drifted far from the center of the political spectrum. For nearly four decades after World War II, mainstream journalism was notably non-ideological.

At the height of their success, all the best news organizations shared two important qualities: a strong sense of responsibility about their roles as providers of news and analysis, and plenty of money to spend on those missions. . . .

The money allowed for an extravagant approach to news. Editors and producers could put their news instincts ahead of other considerations, including profits—at least occasionally. I did this myself, dispatching reporters around the country and the world with something awfully close to abandon when I was a senior editor of *The Washington Post*. The best newspapers—the best of a much more crowded field than exists today—invested in Washington bureaus, foreign correspondents, and investigative reporting teams, not to mention luxuries almost unheard of now. For years, for example, no reporter for the *Los Angeles Times* had to suffer the indignity of flying in coach; business or first class was the norm. The broadcast media enjoyed even more extravagance. In the 1970s the three television networks each maintained large corps of foreign correspondents stationed in bureaus across the globe, and also domestic bureaus in the major American cities. They all did serious documentaries and showed them in prime time.

Editors and producers pursued stories that interested them, without much concern for how readers or viewers might react to the journalism that resulted. Members of this tribe of journalists shared a sense of what "the news" was. The most influential of them were the editors and reporters on the best newspapers, whose decisions were systematically embraced and echoed by other editors and writers, as well as by the producers of television news. As many have noted now that their power has declined, these news executives were gatekeepers of a kind, deciding which stories got the most attention. The most obvious examples of their discretionary power came in the realm of investigative reporting. . . .

The golden era had its shortcomings, to be sure. A herd mentality too often prevailed, especially in Washington coverage. Self-important journalists were too common. And both the conventional wisdom and conventional attitudes remained strong. So, for example, when confronted by a story like the AIDS epidemic, the great news organizations reacted slowly and clumsily. Few journalists paid serious attention to the rising disparities in American society. Toward the end of the era, in the first years of the 21st century, the news media succumbed to the national anxieties produced by the 9/11 attacks and failed to challenge effectively the Bush administration's rush to war in Iraq. Many journalists joined the rush. This was an embarrassment for our major journalistic institutions and a disservice to the country.

Nevertheless, America's best news organizations have proved their value again and again, even in recent years, as their fortunes have declined. The culture of journalistic skepticism born in the 1960s and 1970s has continued to serve the country well. Repeatedly, journalists have broken significant news stories that government officials hoped would never be revealed, from accounts of Americans torturing terror suspects to revelations of the systematic mistreatment of veterans at Walter Reed Hospital; from accounts of the government's eavesdropping programs to descriptions of its vast, post-9/11 intelligence apparatus. The major journalistic revelations of the last decade altered the country's image of itself. They mattered. . . .

The best journalism has most often been produced by those news organizations that have both the resources and the courage to defend their best work when it offends or alarms powerful institutions and individuals. The public may perceive journalism as an individualistic enterprise carried out by lone rangers of rectitude, but this is rarely the case. The best work is usually done by a team that has the backing of an organization committed to maintaining the highest standards of seriousness and integrity, and to nurturing talented reporters and editors. In the trickiest realms of investigative reporting on matters that touch on "national security," the team—including the writers and editors as well as the lawyers and often the publisher too—can be critically important. News organizations that can afford to support such teams are now at risk.

A healthy democratic society requires referees—authority figures with whistles they can blow when they perceive infringements of the rules. Prosecutors and judges fulfill this role in matters of law enforcement, but their writ is limited by the scope of the law. "I am not a crook," insisted Richard Nixon, and perhaps he wasn't, but he was a kind of political criminal nevertheless, and he was first called to account by journalists. Will such whistle blowers be on the job to confront the next Nixon?

Paul Starr, the distinguished Princeton scholar, has put the matter succinctly: "By undermining the economic basis of professional reporting and by fragmenting the public, [the digital revolution] has weakened the ability of the press to act as an effective agent of public accountability. If we take seriously the idea that an independent press serves an essential democratic function, its institutional distress may weaken democracy itself. And that is the danger that confronts us."

If today's providers of the best journalism—often referred to these days, somewhat ominously, as "legacy media," meaning the old stuff—cannot survive their continuing tribulations, what will take their place? Predicting the future is a fool's errand, but some trends are clear. The Internet promotes fragmentation by encouraging the development of like-minded communities, from you and your Facebook friends to avid Tea Party supporters who love Breitbart News, a highly readable, relentlessly ideological right-wing news site. Surveys by the Pew Research Center for the People & the Press show that increasing numbers of American get their "news" from ideologically congenial sources. The news media are fragmenting just as American society is fragmenting—by class, by region, by religious inclination, by generation, by ethnic identity, by politics and more.

The rise of the fragmented news media is quite a recent phenomenon. It really became significant after the inauguration of Barack Obama in

Most Trusted Television News Sources

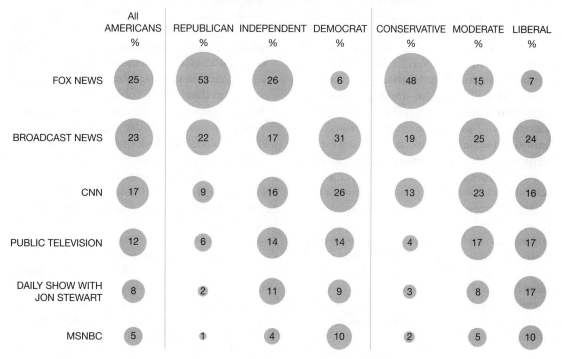

	All AMERICANS %	REPUBLICAN %	INDEPENDENT %	DEMOCRAT %	CONSERVATIVE %	MODERATE %	LIBERAL %
FOX NEWS	25	53	26	6	48	15	7
BROADCAST NEWS	23	22	17	31	19	25	24
CNN	17	9	16	26	13	23	16
PUBLIC TELEVISION	12	6	14	14	4	17	17
DAILY SHOW WITH JON STEWART	8	2	11	9	3	8	17
MSNBC	5	1	4	10	2	5	10

Survey Question: "Which of the following television news sources do you trust the most to provide accurate information about politics and current events?"
Source: PRRI/Brookings, Religion, Values and Immigration Reform Survey Panel Call Back, June 2014.

January 2009. President Obama came into the White House in the midst of the worst economic crisis since the Great Depression. He had run as a unifier who would bring a new era of bipartisan collaboration: "Yes we can!" But no, he couldn't. Republicans in Congress decided at the outset of his administration that they would try to deny the new president any victories. Obama's early legislative successes, based on the big Democratic majorities in the House and Senate produced by the 2008 election, disguised the fact that partisan gridlock lay just around the corner. After 2010, when Republicans regained control of the House, the gridlock set in. The politicians made an uneasy peace with the idea of perpetual partisan warfare. Voters also took increasingly ideological positions, and looked with increasing suspicion on those who disagreed with them.

Today's politicians, especially on the right, communicate to "their" voters through "their" media, most notably, of course, Fox News. Similarly, liberal Democrats like to appear on MSNBC. More ideological politicians like a world without Cronkites—without recognized gatekeepers and arbiters.

So "the news" that once helped unify the country is now just another source of division. Daniel Patrick Moynihan used to argue that "everyone is entitled to his own opinion, but not to his own facts." No longer. Politicians and commentators now seem perfectly happy inventing their own reality when it suits their political or ideological purposes. Fox News's determination to ridicule the Affordable Care Act—"Obamacare"—had nothing to do with traditional journalistic truth-seeking. Rather, it was part of a propaganda campaign. The MSNBC cable network, part of NBC, which used to be a serious news organization, saw a business opportunity in making itself a liberal alternative to Fox, the most profitable cable news network, and now unabashedly propagates a liberal view of the news. Fox and MSNBC have both decided to cater to their audiences not with original reporting of the news (which is expensive), but with commentary on the news interspersed with broadcasts of set-piece events like presidential news conferences. Curiously, or revealingly, there is little outrage in the culture about these

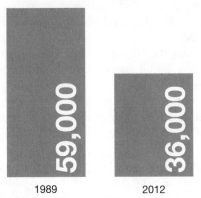

Decline in Newspaper Employees
Number of journalists at U.S. newspapers

1989 — 59,000   2012 — 36,000

Source: "The Bad News About the News," Robert G. Kaiser, October 2014.

developments. We seem to have adapted to the demise of the old expectations about accuracy, fairness, and reporting without much of a fight.

Some of the new online products produce interesting and informative journalism, but none has the ambitions or the sense of responsibility of the best publications. They couldn't afford those luxuries. A great news organization is expensive. The newsroom of *The New York Times* costs about $230 million a year. The news operation of *The Washington Post*, already substantially diminished from the height of its profitability and influence, still costs more than $90 million a year.

Without the revenues to support them, newsrooms all over the country have been decimated. Newspapers employed 59,000 journalists in 1989, and 36,000 in 2012 (and fewer since then). Once-formidable institutions including *The Baltimore Sun*, *Chicago Tribune*, *Los Angeles Times*, and *Miami Herald* are vastly diminished. Others have gone out of business altogether. . . .

Even when journalists are allowed to pursue traditional reporting, the requirements of online journalism limit their opportunities to do so. Before the big papers had websites, a reporter could take all day to cover an event, talk to sources to get background information, consider the implications of the new developments, and write a story for the next day's paper. Today the same reporter has to file multiple versions of the same story as the

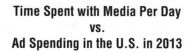

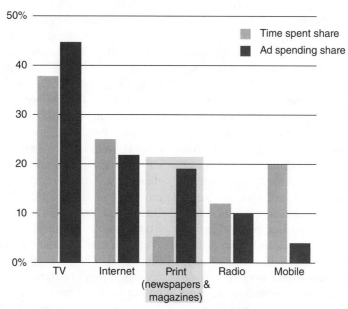

Source: eMarketer, Interactive Advertising Bureau, 2014.

day progresses, adding new tidbits as she acquires them. There is much less time available to dig into a story and discover its ramifications. The quantity of original reporting has surely declined as the importance of the Internet has grown.

One immediate effect of all these changes and cutbacks is that there's no paper in America today that can offer the same coverage of its city, suburbs, and state that it provided 20 or even 10 years ago, and scores of city halls and state legislatures get virtually no coverage by any substantive news organizations. Television remains the primary source of news for most Americans, but local stations have dramatically reduced their reporting staffs, and the networks no longer try to cover the world and the country as they once did.

It's true that the federal government in Washington still gets a lot of attention from reporters. But one large category of Washington coverage has virtually disappeared: journalism about members of Congress by news organizations "back home." A generation ago scores of local newspapers and

television stations employed Washington correspondents who kept an eye on the members of the House and Senate from their cities and states. Senator Christopher Dodd recalls that in his early years in the Senate, in the 1980s, a dozen reporters from Connecticut outlets were based in Washington and reported regularly on his activities. By the time he retired in 2010, that number had fallen to zero. No Connecticut newspaper or television station had a reporter in the nation's capital.

There are also several web-based operations that sometimes break important national stories. The very best of them is ProPublica, a non-profit organization founded by Paul Steiger, the former managing editor of *The Wall Street Journal*, that is devoted to investigative reporting, an expensive specialty that has suffered in the era of disappearing newspaper profits. ProPublica provides *pro bono* journalism of the highest quality, as good as the investigative projects of the major newspapers. Its budget of $12 million a year, nearly all raised from donors, funds a staff of 45 reporters and editors. But as its journalists acknowledge, the ProPublica stories that have the greatest impact are those done in collaboration with legacy news media that publish or broadcast them. Its own excellent website has a relatively small audience.

Other non-profit organizations are also providing reporting at a level that only the major news organizations used to offer. The winner of the 2014 Pulitzer Prize for investigative reporting was Chris Hamby of the Center for Public Integrity in Washington, a non-profit watchdog organization that maintains vast electronic files tracing the flow of money into our politics. Marcus Brauchli, who has served as the senior editor of both *The Wall Street Journal* and *The Washington Post*, observed recently that thanks to Internet offerings, the *quantity* of American journalism has never been greater.

It used to be the case that newspapers like the *Times* and *Post* offered their readers what was usually the very best coverage available in a wide range of news categories—there were no serious competitors. Today there are competitors in every one: ESPN in sports, *Politico* in Washington coverage, BuzzFeed in the world of popular culture, and so on. We at the *Post* used to have a corner on the market in Washington—no competitor could challenge us in any of our major categories. No corners are available now.

If there is some good news, it's hardly enough to be reassuring. Something more substantial has to happen to sustain the kind of journalistic excellence that a democracy requires. Of course there can be technological surprises. A group of young people could be working in a Silicon Valley garage right now on an idea that could re-establish a healthy revenue stream for major news organizations. I certainly hope so. . . .

Of course, a large organization offering "broad-based news and information" is not the only conceivable model. Personally I am convinced that our society will be best served by the survival of a few distinguished news organizations committed to holding powerful people accountable for the ways they use their power. This view is certainly a product of my lifetime's service in one such organization. But there are other possibilities. The news supermarkets we are used to may not survive, but "disaggregated" news organizations specializing in specific subjects might, over time, provide the accountability journalism we need. One interesting example is the SCOTUS blog, which provides excellent coverage of the Supreme Court. It makes no profit, but is supported by Bloomberg. Politico's coverage of Washington and politics, though uneven, is better than that of any but the very best news organizations. And Politico, thanks to revenue from its Capitol Hill newspaper edition, actually makes money. . . .

News as we know it is at risk. So is democratic governance, which depends on an effective watchdog news media. Both have been undermined by changes in society wrought by digital technologies—among the most powerful forces ever unleashed by mankind. We have barely begun the Digital Age, and there is no point in trying to predict just where it will take us. News certainly has a future, but what that will be is unclear. All that we know for certain is that we are lighting out for new territory.

ARTICLE QUESTIONS

1) What evidence does Kaiser provide to justify his argument that there has been a dramatic decline in traditional news sources?

2) Why does Kaiser assert that "journalism is the craft that provides the lifeblood of a free, democratic society"?

3) Why is Kaiser "convinced that . . . a few distinguished news organizations committed to holding powerful people accountable" would represent the best media structure? Do you agree with his assessment?

4) Think of examples of modern media that have positive effects on self-governance. Are these examples likely to be mere exceptions, or can they lead to the next "golden era in journalism"?

9.2) *Republic 2.0* [excerpts]

Princeton University Press, 2007

CASS SUNSTEIN

Cass Sunstein begins *Republic 2.0* with an unlikely depiction of a dystopic world. It is unlikely not because it hard to imagine, but because many would not define it as a dystopia at all. In Sunstein's world people can choose the media that are most pleasing to them: they can listen to music without having to hear songs they despise, they can get news on the topics they most desire, and they can follow the sports teams that elicit their passions. This vision sounds an awful lot like the "brave new world" promised by the newest entertainment devices. It's not hard to envision a CEO of a major company proudly touting filtering technologies capable of providing such a media experience. And while many celebrate the emergence of this new world, Sunstein sees dire repercussions for self-rule. He sees this "personalized" version of the news leading to greater polarization, depriving freedom of speech of its true meaning, and harming the foundations of democratic government. When a people only experience media they individually preselect because it confirms their worldviews, they start to develop entrenched and opposing perspectives that make conciliation nearly impossible. A representative government doesn't require everyone to agree; but, Sunstein argues, self-rule does require people to be aware of competing views, aware of divergent concerns, and engaged with rival arguments.

It is some time in the future. Technology has greatly increased people's ability to "filter" what they want to read, see, and hear. With the aid of the Internet, you are able to design your own newspapers and magazines. You can choose your own programming, with movies, game shows, sports, shopping, and news of your choice. You mix and match.

You need not come across topics and views that you have not sought out. Without any difficulty, you are able to see exactly what you want to see, no more and no less. You can easily find out what "people like you" tend to like and dislike. You avoid what they dislike. You take a close look at what they like.

Maybe you want to focus on sports all the time, and to avoid anything dealing with business or government. It is easy to do exactly that. Maybe you choose replays of your favorite tennis matches in the early evening, live baseball from New York at night, and professional football on the weekends. If you hate sports and want to learn about the Middle East in the evening from the perspective you find most congenial, you can do that too. If you care only about the United States and want to avoid international issues entirely, you can restrict yourself to material involving the United States. So too if you care only about Paris, or London, or

Chicago, or Berlin, or Cape Town, or Beijing, or your hometown.

Perhaps you have no interest at all in "news." Maybe you find "news" impossibly boring. If so, you need not see it at all. Maybe you select programs and stories involving only music and weather. Or perhaps your interests are more specialized still, concentrating on opera, or Beethoven, or Bob Dylan, or modern dance, or some subset of one or more of the above. (Maybe you like early Dylan and hate late Dylan.)

If you are interested in politics, you may want to restrict yourself to certain points of view by hearing only from people with whom you agree. In designing your preferred newspaper, you choose among conservatives, moderates, liberals, vegetarians, the religious right, and socialists. You have your favorite columnists and bloggers; perhaps you want to hear from them and from no one else. Maybe you know that you have a bias, or at least a distinctive set of tastes, and you want to hear from people with that bias or that taste. If so, that is entirely feasible. Or perhaps you are interested in only a few topics. If you believe that the most serious problem is gun control, or climate change, or terrorism, or ethnic and religious tension, or the latest war, you might spend most of your time reading about that problem—if you wish from the point of view that you like best.

Of course everyone else has the same freedom that you do. Many people choose to avoid news altogether. Many people restrict themselves to their own preferred points of view—liberals watching and reading mostly or only liberals; moderates, moderates; conservatives, conservatives; neo-Nazis or terrorist sympathizers, Neo-Nazis or terrorist sympathizers. People in different states and in different countries make predictably different choices. The citizens of Utah see and hear different topics, and different ideas, from the citizens of Massachusetts. The citizens of France see and hear entirely different perspectives from the citizens of China and the United States. And because it is so easy to learn about the choices of "people like you," countless people make the same choices that are made by others like them.

The resulting divisions run along many lines—of religion, ethnicity, nationality, wealth, age, political conviction, and more. People who consider themselves left-of-center make very different selections from those made by people who consider themselves right-of-center. Most whites avoid news and entertainment options designed for African Americans. Many African Americans focus largely on options specifically designed for them. So too with Hispanics. With the reduced importance of the general-interest magazine and newspaper and the flowering of individual programming design, different groups make fundamentally different choices.

The market for news, entertainment, and information has finally been perfected. Consumers are able to see exactly what they want. When the power to filter is unlimited, people can decide, in advance and with perfect accuracy, what they will and will not encounter. They can design something very much like a communications universe of their own choosing. And if they have trouble designing it, it can be designed for them, again with perfect accuracy.

Personalization and Democracy

In many respects, our communications market is rapidly moving in the direction of this apparently utopian picture. As of this writing, many newspapers, including *The Wall Street Journal*, allow readers to create "personalized" electronic editions, containing exactly what they want, and excluding what they do not want.

If you are interested in getting help with the design of an entirely individual paper, you can consult an ever-growing number of sites, including individual.com (helpfully named!) and crayon.com (a less helpful name, but evocative in its own way). Reddit.com "learns what you like as you vote on existing links or submit your own!" Findory.com will help you to personalize not only news, but also blogs, videos, and podcasts. In its own enthusiastic words, "The more articles you click on, the more personalized Findory will look. Our Personalization Technology adapts the website to show you interesting and relevant information based on your reading habits."

If you put the words "personalized news" in any search engine, you will find vivid evidence of what is happening. Google News provides a case in point, with the appealing suggestion, "No one can read all the news that's published every day, so why not set up your page to show you the stories that best represent your interests?" And that is only the tip of the iceberg. Consider TiVo, the television recording system, which is designed to give "you the ultimate control over your TV viewing." TiVo will help you create "your personal TV lineup." It will also learn your tastes, so that it can "suggest other shows that you may want to record and watch based on your preferences." In reality, we are not so very far from complete personalization of the system of communications.

In 1995, MIT technology specialist Nicholas Negroponte prophesied the emergence of "the Daily Me"—a communications package that is personally designed, with each component fully chosen in advance. Negroponte's prophecy was not nearly ambitious enough. As it turns out, you don't need to create a Daily Me. Others can create it for you. If people know a little bit about you, they can discover, and tell you, what "people like you" tend to like—and they can create a Daily Me, just for you, in a matter of seconds.

Many of us are applauding these developments, which obviously increase fun, convenience, and entertainment. But in the midst of the applause, we should insist on asking some questions. How will the increasing power of private control affect democracy? How will the Internet and the explosion of communications options alter the capacity of citizens to govern themselves? What are the social preconditions for a well-functioning system of democratic deliberation, or for individual freedom itself? . . .

[T]he most striking power provided by emerging technologies, *the growing power of consumers to "filter" what they see. . . .*

A large part of my aim is to explore what makes for a well-functioning system of free expression. Above all, I urge that in a diverse society, such a system requires far more than restraints on government censorship and respect for individual choices. For the last decades, this has been the preoccupation of American law and politics, and in fact the law and politics of many other nations as well, including, for example, Germany, France, England, Italy, Russia, and Israel. Censorship is indeed the largest threat to democracy and freedom. But an exclusive focus on government censorship produces serious blind spots. In particular, a well-functioning system of free expression must meet two distinctive requirements.

First, people should be exposed to materials that they would not have chosen in advance. Unplanned, unanticipated encounters are central to democracy itself. Such encounters often involve topics and points of view that people have not sought out and perhaps find quite irritating. They are important partly to ensure against fragmentation and extremism, which are predictable outcomes of any situation in which like-minded people speak only with themselves. I do not suggest that government should force people to see things that they wish to avoid. But I do contend that in a democracy deserving the name, lives should be structured so that people often come across views and topics that they have not specifically selected.

Second, many or most citizens should have a range of common experiences. Without shared experiences, a heterogeneous society will have a much more difficult time in addressing social problems. People may even find it hard to understand one another. Common experiences, emphatically including the common experiences made possible by the media, provide a form of social glue. A system of communications that radically diminishes the number of such experiences will create a number of problems, not least because of the increase in social fragmentation.

As preconditions for a well-functioning democracy, these requirements hold in any large country. They are especially important in a heterogeneous nation, one that faces an occasional risk of fragmentation. They have all the more importance as each nation becomes increasingly global and each citizen becomes, to a greater or lesser degree, a "citizen of the world." Consider, for example, the risks of terrorism, climate change, and avian flu. A sensible perspective on these risks, and others like them, is impossible to obtain if people sort themselves into echo chambers of their own design.

An insistence on these two requirements should not be rooted in nostalgia for some supposedly idyllic past. With respect to communications, the past was hardly idyllic. Compared to any other period in human history, we are in the midst of many extraordinary gains, not least from the standpoint of democracy itself. For us, nostalgia is not only unproductive but also senseless. Things are getting better, not worse. Nor should anything here be taken as a reason for "optimism" or "pessimism," two potential obstacles to clear thinking about new technological developments. If we must choose between them, by all means let us choose optimism. But in view of the many potential gains and losses inevitably associated with massive technological change, any attitude of optimism or pessimism is far too general to be helpful. What I mean to provide is not a basis for pessimism, but a lens through which we might understand, a bit better than before, what makes a system of freedom of expression successful in the first place. That improved understanding will equip us to understand a free nation's own aspirations and thus help in evaluating continuing changes in the system of communications. It will also point the way toward a clearer understanding of the nature of citizenship and of its cultural prerequisites. . . .

[I]t is much too simple to say that any system of communications is desirable if and because it allows individuals to see and hear what they choose. Increased options are certainly good, and the rise of countless "niches" has many advantages. But unanticipated, unchosen exposures and shared experiences are important too.

Precursors and Intermediaries

Unlimited filtering may seem quite strange, perhaps even the stuff of science fiction. But in many ways, it is continuous with what has come before. Filtering is inevitable, a fact of life. It is as old as humanity itself. No one can see, hear, or read everything. In the course of any hour, let alone any day, every one of us engages in massive filtering, simply in order to make life manageable and coherent. Attention is a scarce commodity, and people manage their own attention, sometimes unconsciously and sometimes deliberately, in order to ensure that they are not overwhelmed.

With respect to the world of communications, moreover, a free society gives people a great deal of power to filter out unwanted materials. Only tyrannies force people to read or to watch. In free nations, those who read newspapers do not read the same newspaper; many people do not read any newspaper at all. Every day, people make choices among magazines based on their tastes and their point of view. Sports enthusiasts choose sports magazines, and in many nations they can choose a magazine focused on the sport of their choice—*Basketball Weekly*, say, or the *Practical Horseman*. Conservatives can read *National Review* or the *Weekly Standard*; countless magazines are available for those who like cars; *Dog Fancy* is a popular item for canine enthusiasts; people whose political views are somewhat left of center might like the *American Prospect*; there is even a magazine called *Cigar Aficionado*.

These are simply contemporary illustrations of a longstanding fact of life in democratic countries: a diversity of communications options and a range of possible choices. But the emerging situation does contain large differences, stemming above all from a dramatic increase in available options, a simultaneous increase in individual control over content, and a corresponding decrease in the power of *general-interest intermediaries*. These include newspapers, magazines, and broadcasters. An appreciation of the social functions of general-interest intermediaries will play a large role in this book.

People who rely on such intermediaries have a range of chance encounters, involving shared experiences with diverse others, and also exposure to materials and topics that they did not seek out in advance. You might, for example, read the city newspaper and in the process find a range of stories that you would not have selected if you had the power to do so. Your eyes might come across a story about ethnic tensions in Germany, or crime in Los Angeles, or innovative business practices in Tokyo, or a terrorist attack in India, or a hurricane in New Orleans, and you might read those stories although you would hardly have placed them in your Daily Me. You might watch a particular television channel—perhaps you prefer channel 4—and when your favorite program ends, you might see the beginning of another show, perhaps a drama or news special that you would not have chosen in advance but that somehow catches your eye. Reading *Time* or *Newsweek*, you might come across a discussion of endangered species in Madagascar or genocide in Darfur, and this discussion might interest you, even affect your behavior, maybe even change your life, although you would not have sought it out in the first instance. A system in which individuals lack control over the particular content that they see has a great deal in common with a public street, where you might encounter not only friends, but also a heterogeneous array of people engaged in a wide array of activities (including perhaps bank presidents, political protesters, and panhandlers).

Some people believe that the mass media is dying—that the whole idea of general-interest intermediaries providing shared experiences and exposure to diverse topics and ideas for millions was a short episode in the history of human communications. As a prediction, this view seems overstated; even on the Internet, the mass media continues to have a huge role. But certainly the significance of the mass media has been falling over time. We should not forget that from the stand-point of human history, even in industrialized societies, general-interest intermediaries are relatively new, and far from inevitable. Newspapers, radio stations, and television broadcasters have particular histories with distinctive beginnings and possibly distinctive endings. In fact the twentieth century should be seen as the great era for the general-interest intermediary, which provided similar information and entertainment to millions of people.

The twenty-first century may well be altogether different on this score. Consider one small fact: in 1930, daily newspaper circulation was 1.3 per household, a rate that had fallen to less than 0.50 by 2003—even though the number of years of education, typically correlated with newspaper readership, rose sharply in that period. At the very least, the sheer volume of options and the power to customize are sharply diminishing the social role of the general-interest intermediary. . . .

[T]he unifying issue throughout [is] the various problems, for a democratic society, that might be created by the power of complete filtering. One question, which I answer in the affirmative, is whether individual choices, innocuous and perfectly reasonable in themselves, might produce a large set of social difficulties. Another question, which I also answer in the affirmative, is whether it is important to maintain the equivalent of "street corners" or "commons" where people are exposed to things quite involuntarily. More particularly, I seek to defend a particular conception of democracy—a deliberative conception—and to evaluate, in its terms, the outcome of a system with perfect power of filtering. I also mean to defend a conception of freedom associated with the deliberative conception of democracy and to oppose it to a conception that sees consumption choices by individuals as the very embodiment or soul of freedom.

My claim is emphatically not that street corners and general-interest intermediaries will or would disappear in a world of perfect filtering. To what extent the market will produce them or their equivalents is an empirical issue. Many people like surprises; many of us are curious, and our searches reflect our curiosity. Some people have a strong taste for street corners and for their equivalent on television and the Internet. Indeed, the Internet holds out immense promise for allowing people to be exposed to materials that used to be too hard to find, including new topics and new points of view. If you would like to find out about different forms of cancer and different views about possible treatments, you can do so in less than a minute. If you are interested in learning about the risks associated with different automobiles, a quick search will tell you a great deal. If you would like to know about a particular foreign country, from its customs to its politics to its weather, you can do better with the Internet than you could have done with the best of encyclopedias. (The amazing *Wikipedia*, produced by thousands of volunteers on the Internet, is itself one of the best of encyclopedias.)

Many older people are stunned to see how easy all this is. From the standpoint of those concerned with ensuring access to more opinions and more topics, the new communications technologies can be a terrific boon. But it remains true that many apparent "street corners," on the Internet in particular, are highly specialized, limited as they are to particular views. What I will argue is not that people lack curiosity or that street corners will disappear but instead that there is an insistent need for them, and that a system of freedom of expression should be viewed partly in light of that need. What I will also suggest is that there are serious dangers in a system in which individuals bypass general-interest intermediaries and restrict themselves to opinions and topics of their own choosing. In particular, I will emphasize the risks posed by any situation in which thousands or perhaps millions or even tens of millions of people are mainly listening to louder echoes of their own voices. A situation of this kind is likely to produce far worse than mere fragmentation. . . .

General-Interest Intermediaries as Unacknowledged Public Forums (of the World)

. . . When you read a city newspaper or a national magazine, your eyes will come across a number of articles that you would not have selected in advance. If you are like most people, you will read some of those articles. Perhaps you did not know that you might have an interest in the latest legislative proposal involving national security, or Social Security reform, or Somalia, or recent developments in the Middle East; but a story might catch your attention. What is true for topics is also true for points of view. You might think that you have nothing to learn from someone whose view you abhor. But once you come across the editorial pages, you might well read what they have to say, and you might well benefit from the experience. Perhaps you will be persuaded on one point or another, or informed whether or not you are persuaded. At the same time, the front-page headline, or the cover story in a weekly magazine, is likely to have a high degree of salience for a wide range of people. While shopping at the local grocery store, you might see the cover of *Time* or *Newsweek*, and the story—about a promising politician, a new risk, a surprising development in Europe—might catch your attention, so you might pick up the issue and learn something even if you had no interest in advance.

Unplanned and unchosen encounters often turn out to do a great deal of good, for individuals and society at large. In some cases, they even change people's lives. The same is true, though in a different way, for unwanted encounters. In some cases, you might be irritated by seeing an editorial from your least favorite writer. You might wish that the editorial weren't there. But despite yourself, your curiosity might be piqued, and you might read it. Perhaps this isn't a lot of fun. But it might prompt you to reassess your own view and even to revise it. At the very least, you will have learned what many of your fellow citizens think and why they think it. What is true for arguments is also true for topics, as when you encounter, with some displeasure, a series of stories on crime or global warming or Iraq or same-sex marriage or alcohol abuse, but find yourself learning a bit, or more than a bit, from what those stories have to say.

Television broadcasters have similar functions. Maybe the best example is what has become an institution in many nations: the evening news. If you tune into the evening news, you will learn about a number of topics that you would not have chosen

in advance. Because of the speed and immediacy of television, broadcasters perform these public-forum-type functions even more than general-interest intermediaries in the print media. The "lead story" on the networks is likely to have a great deal of public salience, helping to define central issues and creating a kind of shared focus of attention for many millions of people. And what happens after the lead story—the coverage of a menu of topics both domestic and international—creates something like a speakers' corner beyond anything ever imagined in Hyde Park.

None of these claims depends on a judgment that general-interest intermediaries always do an excellent—or even a good—job. Sometimes such intermediaries fail to provide even a minimal understanding of topics or opinions. Sometimes they offer a watered-down version of what most people already think. Sometimes they suffer from prejudices and biases of their own. Sometimes they deal little with substance and veer toward sound bites and sensationalism, properly deplored trends in the last decades.

What matters for present purposes is that in their best forms, general-interest intermediaries expose people to a range of topics and views at the same time that they provide shared experiences for a heterogeneous public. Indeed, general-interest intermediaries of this sort have large advantages over streets and parks precisely because most of them tend to be so much less local and so much more national, even international. Typically they expose people to questions and problems in other areas, even other nations. They even provide a form of modest, backdoor cosmopolitanism, ensuring that many people will learn something about diverse areas of the planet, regardless of whether they are much interested, initially or ever, in doing so.

Of course general-interest intermediaries are not public forums in the technical sense that the law recognizes. These are private rather than public institutions. Most important, members of the public do not have a legal right of access to them. Individual citizens are not allowed to override the editorial and economic judgments and choices of private owners. In the 1970s, a sharp constitutional debate on precisely this issue resulted in a resounding defeat for those who claimed a constitutionally guaranteed access right. But the question of legal compulsion is really incidental to my central claim here. Society's general-interest intermediaries, even without legal compulsion, serve many of the functions of public forums. They promote shared experiences; they expose people to information and views that would not have been selected in advance. . . .

I will identify three problems in the hypothesized world of perfect filtering. These difficulties might well beset any system in which individuals had complete control over their communications universe and exercised that control so as to create echo chambers or information cocoons.

The first difficulty involves *fragmentation*. The problem here comes from the creation of diverse speech communities whose members talk and listen mostly to one another. A possible consequence is considerable difficulty in mutual understanding. When society is fragmented in this way, diverse groups will tend to *polarize* in a way that can breed extremism and even hatred and violence. New technologies, emphatically including the Internet, are dramatically increasing people's ability to hear echoes of their own voices and to wall themselves off from others. An important result is the existence of *cybercascades*—processes of information exchange in which a certain fact or point of view becomes widespread, simply because so many people seem to believe it.

The second difficulty involves a distinctive characteristic of information. Information is a public good in the technical sense that once one person knows something, other people are likely to benefit as well. If you learn about crime in the neighborhood or about the problem of climate change, you might well tell other people too, and they will benefit from what you have learned. In a system in which each person can "customize" his own communications universe, there is a risk that people will make choices that generate too little information. An advantage of a system with general-interest intermediaries and with public forums—with broad access by speakers to diverse publics—is that it ensures a kind of social

spreading of information. At the same time, an individually filtered speech universe is likely to produce too few of what I will call *solidarity goods*—goods whose value increases with the number of people who are consuming them. A presidential debate is a classic example of a solidarity good.

The third and final difficulty has to do with the proper understanding of freedom and the relationship between consumers and citizens. If we believe in consumer sovereignty, and if we celebrate the power to filter, we are likely to think that freedom consists in the satisfaction of private preferences—in an absence of restrictions on individual choices. This is a widely held view about freedom. Indeed, it is a view that underlies much current thinking about free speech. But it is badly misconceived. Of course free choice is important. But freedom properly understood consists not simply in the satisfaction of whatever preferences people have, but also in the chance to have preferences and beliefs formed under decent conditions—in the ability to have preferences formed after exposure to a sufficient amount of information and also to an appropriately wide and diverse range of options. There can be no assurance of freedom in a system committed to the Daily Me. . . .

In the face of dramatic recent increases in communications options, there is an omnipresent risk of information overload—too many options, too many topics, too many opinions, a cacophony of voices. Indeed the risk of overload and the need for filtering go hand in hand. Bruce Springsteen's music may be timeless, but his hit from the 1990s, "57 Channels and Nothing On," is hopelessly out of date in light of the number of current programming options, certainly if we take account of the Internet. (Contradicting Springsteen, TiVo exclaims, "There's always something on TV that you'll like!") Filtering, often in the form of narrowing, is inevitable in order to avoid overload, to impose some order on an overwhelming number of sources of information.

By itself this is not a problem. But when options are so plentiful, many people will take the opportunity to listen to those points of view that they find most agreeable. For many of us, of course, what matters is that we enjoy what we see or read, or learn from it, and it is not necessary that we are comforted by it. But there is a natural human tendency to make choices with respect to entertainment and news that do not disturb our preexisting view of the world.

I am not suggesting that the Internet is a lonely or antisocial domain. In contrast to television, many of the emerging technologies are extraordinarily social, increasing people's capacity to form bonds with individuals and groups that would otherwise have been entirely inaccessible. Email, instant messaging, texting, and Internet discussion groups provide increasingly remarkable opportunities, not for isolation, but for the creation of new groups and connections. This is the foundation for the concern about the risk of fragmentation.

Consider in this regard a lovely little experiment. Members of a nationally representative group of Americans were asked whether they would like to read news stories from one of four sources: Fox (known to be conservative), *National Public Radio* (known to be liberal), CNN (often thought to be liberal), and the British Broadcasting Network (whose politics are not widely known to Americans). The stories came in different news categories: American politics, the war in Iraq, "race in America," crime, travel, and sports. It turns out that for the first four categories, Republicans chose Fox by an overwhelming margin. By contrast, Democrats split their "votes" among *National Public Radio* and CNN—and showed a general aversion to Fox. For travel and sports, the divide between Republicans and Democrats was much smaller. By contrast, independents showed no preference for any particular source.

There was another finding, perhaps a more striking one: *people's level of interest in the same news stories was greatly affected by the network label.* For Republicans, the identical headline became far more interesting, and the story became far more attractive, if it carried the Fox label. In fact the Republican "hit rate" for the same news stories was three times higher when it was labeled "Fox'! (Interestingly, the hit rate was doubled when sports

and travel stories were so labeled.) Democrats showed a real aversion to stories labeled "Fox," and the CNN and NPR labels created a modest increase in their interest. The overall conclusion is that Fox attracts substantial Republican support and that Democratic viewers and readers take pains to avoid Fox—while CNN and *National Public Radio* have noticeable but weak brand loyalty among Democrats. This is only one experiment, to be sure, but there is every reason to suspect that the result would generalize—that people with identifiable leanings are consulting sources including websites, that match their predilections, and are avoiding sources that do not cater to those predilections.

All this is just the tip of the iceberg. "Because the Internet makes it easier to find like-minded individuals, it can facilitate and strengthen fringe communities that have a common ideology but are dispersed geographically. Thus, particle physicists, Star Trek fans, and members of militia group have used the Internet to find each other, swap information and stoke each others' passions. In many cases, their heated dialogues might never have reached critical mass as long as geographical separation diluted them to a few parts per million." It is worth underlining the idea that people are working to "stoke each others' passions," because that idea will play a large role in the discussion to follow. Of course many of those with committed views on one or another topic—gun control, abortion, affirmative action—are speaking mostly with each other. Linking behavior follows a similar pattern.

My own study, conducted with Lesley Wexler in 2000, found the same basic picture. Of a random study of 60 political sites, only 9, or 15 percent, provided links to sites of those with opposing views, whereas 35, or almost 60 percent, provided links to like-minded sites. . . . In November 2006, Spencer Short and I did a follow-up study, which found a similar basic picture. Of a random study of 50 political sites, only 17, or 34 percent, provide links to sites of those with opposing views, whereas 41, or almost 82 percent, provide links to like-minded sites. . . .

One of the most striking facts here is that when links to opposing sites are provided, it is often to show how dangerous, dumb, or contemptible the views of the adversary really are. Even more striking is the extent to which sites are providing links to like-minded sites. show the number of sites that have one or more such link, but in a way they greatly understate what is happening. Several organizations, for example, offer links to dozens or even hundreds of like-minded sites.

All this is perfectly natural, even reasonable. Those who visit certain sites are probably more likely to want to visit similar sites, and people who create a site with one point of view are unlikely to want to promote their adversaries. (Recall that collaborative filtering works because people tend to like what people like them tend to like.) And of course it is true that many people who consult sites with one point of view do not restrict themselves to like-minded sources of information. But what we now know about both links and individual behavior supports the general view that many people are mostly hearing more and louder echoes of their own voices. To say the least, this is undesirable from the democratic standpoint.

I do not mean to deny the obvious fact that any system that allows for freedom of choice will create some balkanization of opinion. Long before the advent of the Internet, and in an era of a handful of television stations, people made self-conscious choices among newspapers and radio stations. In any era, many people want to be comforted rather than challenged. Magazines and newspapers, for example, often cater to people with definite interests in certain points of view. Since the early nineteenth century, African American newspapers have been widely read by African Americans, and these newspapers offer significantly different coverage of common issues than white-oriented newspapers and also make dramatically different choices about what issues are important. Whites rarely read such newspapers.

But what is emerging nonetheless counts as a significant change. With a dramatic increase in options, and a greater power to customize, comes a corresponding increase in the range of actual choices, and those choices are likely, in many cases, to match demographic characteristics, preexisting political convictions, or both. Of course this has many advantages; among other things, it will greatly increase the aggregate amount of information, the entertainment value of choices, and the sheer fun of the options. But there are problems as well. If diverse groups are seeing and hearing quite different points of view, or focusing on quite different topics, mutual understanding might be difficult, and it might be increasingly hard for people to solve problems that society faces together.

Take some extreme examples. Many Americans fear that certain environmental problems—abandoned hazardous waste sites, genetic engineering of food, climate change—are extremely serious and require immediate government action. But others believe that the same problems are imaginative fictions, generated by zealots and self-serving politicians. Many Americans think that most welfare recipients are indolent and content to live off of the work of others. On this view, "welfare reform," to be worthy of the name, consists of reduced handouts, a step necessary to encourage people to fend for themselves. But many other Americans believe that welfare recipients generally face severe disadvantages and would be entirely willing to work if decent jobs were available. On this view, welfare reform, understood as reductions in benefits, is an act of official cruelty. Many people believe that the largest threat to American security remains terrorism, and that if terrorism is not a top priority, catastrophic attacks are likely to ensue. Many others believe that while terrorism presents serious risks, the threat has been overblown, and that other problems, including climate change, deserve at least equal attention.

To say the least, it will be difficult for people armed with such opposing perspectives to reach anything like common ground or to make progress on the underlying questions. Consider how these difficulties will increase if people do not know the competing view, consistently avoid speaking with one another, and are unaware how to address divergent concerns of fellow citizens.

ARTICLE QUESTIONS

1) Sunstein identifies some specific repercussions that occur when people narrow their sources of information to those they preselect because they reinforce their worldviews. Name three.

2) If Sunstein is correct that our individual media choices have a profound effect on self-governance, would it be prudent to control people's media choices? What role should government play in solving the problems that Sunstein identifies?

3) Think about the times you have "stumbled upon" news stories you didn't seek out. Did these experiences come from news sources that express opinions that differ from yours? Have any of these unplanned media exposures changed how you viewed an issue? Have they informed you about something you didn't know you would be interested in?

4) In the modern media environment, how do people get exposed to news they don't seek out? Should these exposures be encouraged and promoted?

9.3) Political Polarization and Media Habits

Pew Research Center for the People & the Press, October 21, 2014

AMY MITCHELL, JEFFREY GOTTFRIED, JOCELYN KILEY, AND KATERINA EVA MATSA

Not all media cover the same events, and not all events are covered the same way. It is entirely possible for two people to watch two different media sources and see two different presentations of the world. People experiencing widely different media presentations are likely to express widely different views, perhaps views so widely different they could be considered polarized. To better understand political polarization in the United States, the Pew Research Center for the People & the Press examined how people get information about government and politics. Their findings indicated that those expressing the most consistently conservative and the most consistently liberal views inform themselves in strikingly different ways. In fact, there is little overlap in the news sources used or trusted by those inhabiting these polarized ideological groups. It is very important to note that Pew's study does not tell us if exposure to different news sources drives people's political views; it is possible that people's divergent political views cause them to seek out different news sources. But even if people's already established views drive which news sources they seek out, the constant exposure to divergent news presentations can exacerbate political polarization. According to this study from the Pew Research Center, the percentage of the American population expressing consistently conservative or consistently liberal views is small, but this small slice of the public possesses a disproportionate influence on political discourse: those on the extremes are the most likely to vote, most likely to donate to campaigns, and most likely to be sought out by others for political information.

When it comes to getting news about politics and government, liberals and conservatives inhabit different worlds. There is little overlap in the news sources they turn to and trust. And whether discussing politics online or with friends, they are more likely than others to interact with like-minded individuals, according to a new Pew Research Center study.

The project—part of a year-long effort to shed light on political polarization in America—looks at the ways people get information about government and politics in three different settings: the news media, social media and the way people talk about politics with friends and family. In all three areas, the study finds that those with the most consistent ideological views on the left and right have information streams that are distinct from those of individuals with more mixed political views—and very distinct from each other.

These cleavages can be overstated. The study also suggests that in America today, it is virtually impossible to live in an ideological bubble. Most Americans rely on an array of outlets—with varying audience profiles—for political news. And many consistent conservatives and liberals hear dissenting political views in their everyday lives.

Yet as our major report on political polarization found, those at both the left and right ends of the spectrum, who together comprise about 20% of the public overall, have a greater impact on the political process than do those with more mixed ideological views. They are the most likely to vote, donate to campaigns and participate directly in politics. The five ideological groups in this analysis (consistent liberals, mostly liberals, mixed, mostly conservatives and consistent conservatives) are based on responses to 10 questions about a range of political values. That those who express consistently conservative or consistently liberal opinions have different ways of informing themselves about politics and government is not surprising. But the depth of these divisions—and the differences between those who have strong ideological views and those who do not—are striking.

Overall, the study finds that consistent conservatives:

- Are tightly clustered around a single news source, far more than any other group in the survey, with 47% citing Fox News as their main source for news about government and politics.
- Express greater distrust than trust of 24 of the 36 news sources measured in the survey. At the same time, fully 88% of consistent conservatives trust Fox News.
- Are, when on Facebook, more likely than those in other ideological groups to hear political opinions that are in line with their own views.
- Are more likely to have friends who share their own political views. Two-thirds (66%) say most of their close friends share their views on government and politics.

By contrast, those with consistently liberal views:

- Are less unified in their media loyalty; they rely on a greater range of news outlets, including some—like NPR and *The New York Times*—that others use far less.
- Express more trust than distrust of 28 of the 36 news outlets in the survey. NPR, PBS and the BBC are the most trusted news sources for consistent liberals.
- Are more likely than those in other ideological groups to block or "defriend" someone on a social network—as well as to end a personal friendship—because of politics.
- Are more likely to follow issue-based groups, rather than political parties or candidates, in their Facebook feeds.

Those with down-the-line conservative and liberal views do share some common ground; they are much more likely than others to closely follow government and political news. This carries over to their discussions of politics and government. Nearly four-in-ten consistent conservatives (39%) and 30% of consistent liberals tend to drive political discussions—that is, they talk about politics often, say others tend to turn to them for information rather than the reverse, and describe themselves as leaders rather than listeners in these kinds of conversations. Among those with mixed ideological views, just 12% play a similar role. . . .

This report is based on a follow-up survey, about where people get political news and information, conducted among the 88% of panel members with online access. While the picture drawn might be slightly different if those without internet access had been included, this report provides a thorough look at political information consumption by the large online population. It is important to note, though, that those at either end of the ideological spectrum are not isolated from dissenting views about politics. Nearly half (47%) of across-the-board conservatives—and 59% of across-the-board liberals—say they at least sometimes disagree with one of their closest political discussion partners.

For those closer to the middle of the ideological spectrum, learning about politics, or discussing it with friends and family, is a less of a focus. When they do follow politics, their main news sources include CNN, local TV and Fox News, along with Yahoo News and Google News, which aggregate stories from a wide assortment of outlets; these U.S. adults see more of a mix of views in social media and are less likely to be aware of their friends' political leanings.

This study, the latest in a series of reports on political polarization, is based on an online survey conducted March 19–April 29, 2014 with 2,901 members of the Pew Research Center's new American Trends Panel—a panel recruited from a telephone survey of 10,013 adults conducted earlier this year.

Among the key findings:

Media Sources: Nearly Half of Consistent Conservatives Cite Fox News

When it comes to choosing a media source for political news, conservatives orient strongly around Fox News. Nearly half of consistent conservatives (47%) name it as their main source for government and political news, as do almost a third (31%) of those with mostly conservative views. No other sources come close.

Consistent liberals, on the other hand, volunteer a wider range of main sources for political news—no source is named by more than 15% of consistent liberals and 20% of those who are mostly liberal. Still, consistent liberals are more than twice as likely as web-using adults overall to name NPR (13% vs. 5%), MSNBC (12% vs. 4%) and *The New York Times* (10% vs. 3%) as their top source for political news.

Main Source of Government and Political News

% whose main source for news about gov't and politics is...

Total	Consistently liberal	Mostly liberal	Mixed	Mostly conservative	Consistently conservative
CNN 16%	CNN 15%	CNN 20%	CNN 20%	Fox News 31%	Fox News 47%
Fox News 14	NPR 13	Local TV 11	Local TV 16	CNN 9	Local radio 11
Local TV 10	MSNBC 12	NPR 9	Fox News 8	Local TV 6	Local TV 5
NPR 5	New York Times 10	Fox News 5	Yahoo News 7	Local radio 6	Local newspaper 3
Local radio 4	Local TV 5	MSNBC 5	Google News 6	Yahoo News 6	Google News 3

American Trends Panel (wave 1). Survey conducted March 19–April 29, 2014. Q19-Q19d. Based on web respondents. Ideological consistency based on a scale of 10 political values questions (see About the Survey for more details). Respondents were first asked what platform (TV, radio, etc.) they most use for news about government and politics, and then were asked to name the outlet they most turn to. Up to three answer were accepted.

Source: PEW RESEARCH CENTER

Among the large group of respondents with mixed ideological views, CNN (20%) and local TV (16%) are top sources; Fox News (8%), Yahoo News (7%) and Google News (6%) round out their top five sources.

Trust and Distrust: Liberals Trust Many, Conservatives Trust Few

At least as important as *where* people turn for news is *whose* news they trust. And here, the ideological differences are especially stark.

Trust Levels of News Sources by Ideological Group

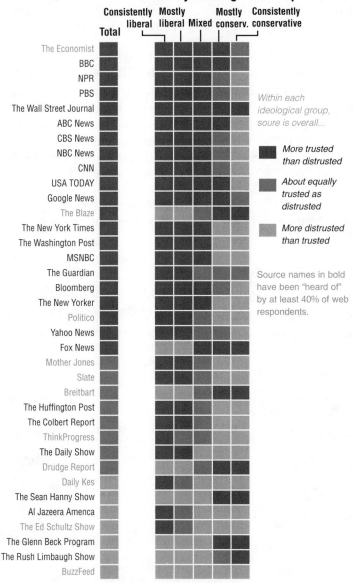

Within each ideological group, soure is overall...

■ More trusted than distrusted

■ About equally trusted as distrusted

■ More distrusted than trusted

Source names in bold have been "heard of" by at least 40% of web respondents.

American Trends Panel (wave 1). Survey conducted March 19–April 29, 2014. Q21a-21b. Based on web respondents. Ideological consistency based on a scale of 10 political values questions (see about the survey). Grouping of outlets is determined by whether the percent who trust each source is significantly different from the percent who distrust each source. Outlets are then ranked by the proportion of those who trust more than distrust each.

Source: PEW RESEARCH CENTER

Respondents were asked whether they had heard of each of the 36 outlets listed in the accompanying graphic. For those they had heard of, they were asked about their trust—or distrust—in each source.

Liberals, overall, trust a much larger mix of news outlets than others do. Of the 36 different outlets considered, 28 are more trusted than distrusted by consistent liberals. Just eight earn higher shares of distrust than trust. Still, among those eight, the levels of distrust can be high: fully 81% of consistent liberals distrust Fox News, and 75% distrust the Rush Limbaugh Show. Among consistent conservatives, by contrast, there are 24 sources that draw more distrust than trust. The same is true for 15 sources among those with *mostly* conservative views. And, of the eight outlets more trusted than distrusted by consistent conservatives, all but one, on balance, are distrusted by consistent liberals.

Also at play here is the degree to which people are more familiar with certain news sources than others. Some outlets such as CNN, ABC News and Fox News, are recognized by at least nine-in-ten respondents, meaning that more respondents offer a view of these outlets one way or the other. Outlets currently occupying more niche markets, such as Politico, the Economist or BuzzFeed, are known by only about a third of respondents. Thus, while they may elicit strong views in one direction, the share of respondents weighing in is relatively small. . . .

Social Media: Conservatives More Likely to Have Like-Minded Friends

In the growing social media space, most users encounter a mix of political views. But consistent conservatives are twice as likely as the typical Facebook user to see political opinions on Facebook that are mostly in line with their own views (47% vs. 23%). Consistent liberals, on average, hear a somewhat wider range of views than consistent conservatives—about a third (32%) mainly see posts in line with their own opinions.

Consistent Conservatives See More Facebook Posts in Line With Their Views

% who say posts about politics on Facebook are mostly or always in line with their own views...

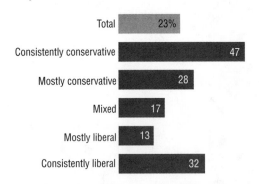

American Trends Panel (wave 1). Survey conducted March 19–April 29, 2014. Q33e. Based on Facebook users who see at least some posts about government and politics on Facebook and pay at least some attention to them (N=1,627). Ideological consistency based on a scale of 10 political values questions (see About the Survey for more details).

Source: PEW RESEARCH CENTER

Consistent Liberals More Likely to Block Others Because of Politics

% of Facebook users who have hidden, blocked, defriended or stopped following someone because they disagreed with something that person posted about politics...

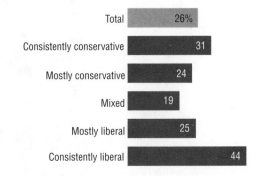

American Trends Panel (wave 1). Survey conducted March 19–April 29, 2014. Q35. Based on web respondents who are Facebook users (N=2,153). Ideological consistency based on a scale of 10 political values questions (see About the Survey for more details).

But that doesn't mean consistent liberals necessarily embrace contrasting views. Roughly four-in-ten consistent liberals on Facebook (44%) say they have blocked or defriended someone on social media because they disagreed with something that person posted about politics. This compares with 31% of consistent conservatives and just 26% of all Facebook users who have done the same.

Consistent liberals who pay attention to politics on Facebook are also more likely than others to "like" or follow issue-based groups: 60% do this, compared with 46% of consistent conservatives and just a third (33%) of those with mixed views. And both the left and the right are more likely than others to follow political parties or elected officials: 49% of consistent conservatives and 42% of consistent liberals do so, compared with 29% of Facebook users overall.

Talking Politics: Dissenting Views Penetrate, but Less Frequently for the Ideologically Consistent

In personal conversations about politics, those on the right and left are more likely to largely hear views in line with their own thinking.

While only a quarter (25%) of respondents with mixed ideological views say most of their close friends share their own political views, that is true of roughly half (52%) of consistent liberals and two-thirds (66%) of consistent conservatives. And, when those who talk about politics are asked to name up to three people they most often talk to about politics, half (50%) of consistent conservatives name only individuals they describe as also being conservative—outpacing the 31% of consistent liberals who name only liberals.

At the same time, consistent liberals are more likely to stop talking to someone because of politics. Roughly a quarter (24%) have done so, compared with 16% of consistent conservatives and around 10% of those with more mixed political views.

Still, a solid portion of even the most ideologically-aligned respondents encounter some political disagreement with their close discussion partners. Nearly half (47%) of consistent conservatives who talk about politics name one or more discussion partners with whom they disagree at least some of the time. This figure rises to more than half (59%) of consistent liberals and even larger shares of those with mostly liberal and ideologically-mixed political views (79% each).

Consistent Conservatives More Likely to Have Close Friends Who Share Their Political Views

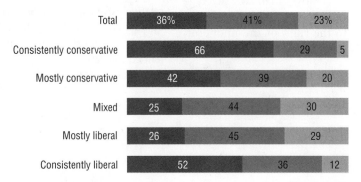

% who say...

■ Most close friends share my views on govt and politics
■ Some close friends share my views, but many don't
▪ I don't really know what most close friends think

	Most close friends share	Some close friends share, but many don't	Don't really know
Total	36%	41%	23%
Consistently conservative	66	29	5
Mostly conservative	42	39	20
Mixed	25	44	30
Mostly liberal	26	45	29
Consistently liberal	52	36	12

But Consistent Liberals More Likely to Drop a Friend

% who stopped talking to/being friends with someone because of politics...

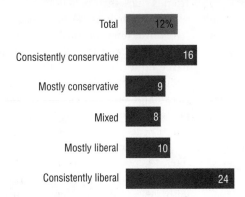

American Trends Panel (wave 1). Survey conducted March 19–April 29, 2014. Q44, Q46. Based on web respondents. Ideological consistency based on a scale of 10 political values questions (see About the Survey for more details).

Source: PEW RESEARCH CENTER

Media Outlets by the Ideological Composition of Their Audience

Ideological differences in media source preferences result in distinct audience profiles for many media outlets. Many sources, such as *The Wall Street Journal*, *USA TODAY*, ABC News, CBS News and NBC News have audiences that are, on average, ideologically similar to the average web respondent.

Reflecting liberals' use of a greater number of media sources, there are more outlets whose readers, watchers and listeners fall to the left of the average web respondent than to the right. At the same time, a handful of outlets have audiences that are more conservative than the average respondent.

Fox News sits to the right of the midpoint, but is not nearly as far right as several other sources, such as the radio shows of Rush Limbaugh or Glenn Beck. A closer look at the audience breakdowns reveals why: While consistent conservatives get news from Fox News at very high rates, many of those with less conservative views also use Fox News. By contrast, the audiences for Limbaugh and Beck are overwhelmingly conservative.

By comparison, the average consumer of *The Wall Street Journal* sits very close to the typical survey respondent, but the range of Journal readers is far broader because it appeals to people on both the left and the right. As a result, while respondents overall cluster toward the center of the ideological spectrum, the Journal's audience is relatively evenly distributed across the continuum: 20% are consistent liberals, 21% mostly liberal, 24% mixed, 22% mostly conservative and 13% consistent conservative. . . .

Ideological Placement of Each Source's Audience

Average ideological placement on a 10=point scale of ideological consistency of those who got news from each source in the past week...

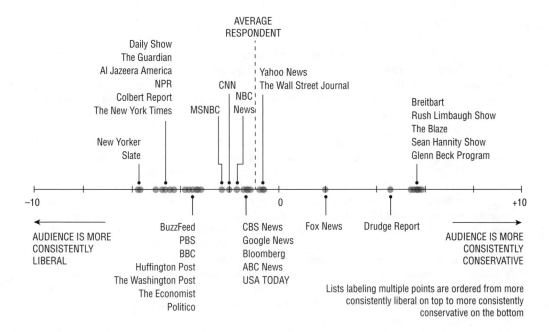

AVERAGE
RESPONDENT

Daily Show
The Guardian
Al Jazeera America
NPR
Colbert Report
The New York Times

Yahoo News
The Wall Street Journal

CNN
NBC
News

MSNBC

Breitbart
Rush Limbaugh Show
The Blaze
Sean Hannity Show
Glenn Beck Program

New Yorker
Slate

−10   0   +10

AUDIENCE IS MORE
CONSISTENTLY
LIBERAL

BuzzFeed
PBS
BBC
Huffington Post
The Washington Post
The Economist
Politico

CBS News
Google News
Bloomberg
ABC News
USA TODAY

Fox News

Drudge Report

AUDIENCE IS MORE
CONSISTENTLY
CONSERVATIVE

Lists labeling multiple points are ordered from more
consistently liberal on top to more consistently
conservative on the bottom

American Trends Panel (wave 1). Survey conducted March 19–April 29, 2014. Q22. Based on all web respondents. Ideological consistency based on a scale of 10 political values questions (see About the Survey for more details). ThinkProgress, DailyKos, Mother Jones, and The Ed Schultz Show are not included in this graphic because audience sample sizes are too small to analyze.

Source: PEW RESEARCH CENTER

ARTICLE QUESTIONS

1) What were the three different settings where people get political information that are included in this study?

2) What contrasts in the behavior of the consistently conservative and the consistently liberal did the study identify?

3) Is political polarization a concern for politics? Why?

4) Do any of the trends identified in the study make you concerned about increasing polarization? Do any of the trends provide you with hope? Why?

9.4) Obama, the Puppet Master

Politico, February 18, 2013

JIM VANDEHEI AND MIKE ALLEN

Katie Glueck contributed to this report.

> Every change in media has profound effects on politics. Presidents and other political actors have employed new media developments to promote their political aims. Franklin Roosevelt used radio in his "fireside chats" to directly communicate with the public. John Kennedy used the expansion of television to emphasize his charisma and on-camera personality. Former movie star Ronald Regan masterfully arranged imagery to elicit emotions in ways that outshined the spoken and printed word.
>
> Placed in the context of constant media changes, Jim VandeHei and Mike Allen's article for *Politico*, "Obama, the Puppet Master," could be seen as a new twist on an old story. But VandeHei and Allen argue that the changes occurring in today's media environment are something more profound. They assert that today we have an environment where news organizations are dependent on the White House for access to information, but the White House is less dependent on news organizations for dissemination. Advances in technology allow the White House to craft its own video, snap its own photographs, and draft its own stories to directly disseminate the president's message. The stories tied to these video and photos are instantly released to the public through social media. And due to their lack of resources, most media organizations are forced to present these government-issued news releases as "the news." As VandeHei and Allen argue, budget restrictions and access limitations often mean that media organizations must choose between reposting the "spin" from government-sponsored press releases or forgoing While House coverage.

President Barack Obama is a master at limiting, shaping and manipulating media coverage of himself and his White House.

Not for the reason that conservatives suspect: namely, that a liberal press willingly and eagerly allows itself to get manipulated. Instead, the mastery mostly flows from a White House that has taken old tricks for shaping coverage (staged leaks, friendly interviews) and put them on steroids using new ones (social media, content creation, precision targeting). And it's an equal opportunity strategy: Media across the ideological spectrum are left scrambling for access.

The results are transformational. With more technology, and fewer resources at many media companies, the balance of power between the White House and press has tipped unmistakably toward the government. This is an arguably dangerous development, and one that the Obama White House—fluent in digital media and no fan of the mainstream press—has exploited cleverly and ruthlessly. And future presidents from both parties will undoubtedly copy and expand on this approach.

"The balance of power used to be much more in favor of the mainstream press," said Mike McCurry, who was press secretary to President Bill Clinton during the Monica Lewinsky scandal. Nowadays, he said, "The White House gets away with stuff I would never have dreamed of doing. When I talk to White House reporters now, they say it's really tough to do business with people who don't see the need to be cooperative."

McCurry and his colleagues in the Clinton White House were hardly above putting their boss in front of gentle questions: Clinton and Vice President Al Gore often preferred the safety of "Larry King Live" to the rhetorical combat of the briefing room. But Obama and his aides have raised it to an art form: The president has shut down interviews with many of the White House reporters who know the most and ask the toughest questions. Instead, he spends way more time talking directly to voters via friendly shows and media personalities. Why bother with *The New York Times* beat reporter when Obama can go on "The View"?

At the same time, this White House has greatly curtailed impromptu moments where reporters can ask tough questions after a staged event—or snap a picture of the president that was not shot by government-paid photographers.

The frustrated Obama press corps neared rebellion this past holiday weekend when reporters and photographers were not even allowed onto the Floridian National Golf Club, where Obama was golfing. That breached the tradition of the pool "holding" in the clubhouse and often covering—and even questioning—the president on the first and last holes.

Obama boasted Thursday during a Google+ Hangout from the White House: "This is the most transparent administration in history." The people who cover him day to day see it very differently.

"The way the president's availability to the press has shrunk in the last two years is a disgrace," said ABC News White House reporter Ann Compton, who has covered every president back to Gerald R. Ford. "The president's day-to-day policy development—on immigration, on guns—is almost totally opaque to the reporters trying to do a responsible job of covering it. There are no readouts from big meetings he has with people from the outside, and many of them aren't even on his schedule. This is different from every president I covered. This White House goes to extreme lengths to keep the press away."

One authentically new technique pioneered by the Obama White House is extensive government creation of content (photos of the president, videos of White House officials, blog posts written by Obama aides), which can then be instantly released to the masses through social media. They often include footage unavailable to the press.

Brooks Kraft, a contributing photographer to Time, said White House officials "have a willing and able and hungry press that eats this stuff up, partly because the news organizations are cash-strapped."

"White House handout photos used to be reserved for historically important events—9/11, or deliberations about war," Kraft said. "This White House regularly releases [day-in-the-life] images of the president . . . a nice picture of the president looking pensive . . . from events that could have

been covered by the press pool. But I don't blame the White House for doing it, because networks and newspapers use them. So the White House has built its own content distribution network."

When Obama nominated Elena Kagan for the Supreme Court, she gave one interview—to White House TV, produced by Obama aides.

"There's no question that technology has significantly altered the playing field of competitive journalism," said Josh Earnest, principal deputy White House press secretary—and the voice of "West Wing Week," produced by the administration.

"Our ongoing challenge is to engage media outlets with audiences large and small—occasionally harnessing technology to find new ways to do so."

By no means does Obama escape tough scrutiny or altogether avoid improvisational moments. And by no means is Obama unique in wanting to control his public image and message—every president pushes this to the outer limits. His 2012 opponent, Mitt Romney, was equally adept at substance-free encounters with reporters.

But something is different with this White House. Obama's aides are better at using technology and exploiting the president's "brand." They are more disciplined about cracking down on staff that leak, or reporters who write things they don't like. And they are obsessed with taking advantage of Twitter, Facebook, YouTube and every other social media forums, not just for campaigns, but governing.

"They use every technique anyone has ever thought of, and some no one ever had," *New York Times* White House reporter Peter Baker told us. "They can be very responsive and very helpful at pulling back the curtain at times while keeping you at bay at others. And they're not at all shy about making clear when they don't like your stories, which is quite often."

Conservatives assume a cozy relationship between this White House and the reporters who cover it. Wrong. Many reporters find Obama himself strangely fearful of talking with them and often aloof and cocky when he does. They find his staff needlessly stingy with information and thin-skinned about any tough coverage. He gets more-favorable-than-not coverage because many staffers are fearful of talking to reporters, even anonymously, and some reporters inevitably worry access or the chance of a presidential interview will decrease if they get in the face of this White House.

Obama himself sees little upside to wide-ranging interviews with the beat reporters for the big newspapers—hence, the stiffing of even *The New York Times* since 2010. The president's staff often finds Washington reporters whiny, needy and too enamored with trivial matters or their own self-importance.

So the White House has escalated the use of several media manipulation techniques:

• The super-safe, softball interview is an Obama specialty. The kid glove interview of Obama and outgoing Secretary of State Hillary Clinton by Steve Kroft of CBS's "60 Minutes" is simply the latest in a long line of these. Obama gives frequent interviews (an astonishing 674 in his first term, compared with 217 for President George W. Bush, according to statistics compiled by Martha Joynt Kumar, a political scientist at Towson University), but they are often with network anchors or local TV stations, and rarely with the reporters who cover the White House day to day.

"This administration loves to boast about how transparent they are, but they're transparent about things they want to be transparent about," said Mark Knoller, the veteran CBS News reporter. "He gives interviews not for our benefit, but to achieve his objective." Knoller last talked to Obama in 2010—and that was when Knoller was in then-press secretary Robert Gibbs's office, and the president walked in.

• There's the classic weekend document dump to avoid negative coverage. By our count, the White House has done this nearly two dozen times, and almost always to minimize attention to embarrassing or messy facts. "What you guys call a document dump, we call transparency," the White House's Earnest shot back. If that's the case, the White House was exceptionally transparent during the Solyndra controversy, releasing details three times on a Friday.

• There is the iron-fisted control of access to White House information and officials. Top officials recently discouraged Cabinet secretaries from talking about sequestration. And even top officials privately gripe about the muzzle put on them by the White House.

• They are also masters of scrutiny avoidance. The president has not granted an interview to print reporters at *The New York Times*, *The Washington Post*, *The Wall Street Journal*, *POLITICO* and others in years. These are the reporters who are often most likely to ask tough, unpredictable questions.

Kumar, who works out of the White House press room and tallies every question a journalist asks the president, has found that in his first term Obama held brief press availabilities after photos ops or announcements one-third as often as George W. Bush did in his first term—107 to Bush's 355.

• While White House officials deny it is intentional, this administration—like its predecessors—does some good old-fashioned bullying of reporters: making clear there will be no interviews, or even questions at press conferences, if aides are displeased with their coverage.

Still, the most unique twist by this White House has been the government's generating and distributing of content.

A number of these techniques were on vivid display two weekends ago, when the White House released a six-month-old photo of the president shooting skeet, buttressing his claim in a New Republic interview that he fires at clay pigeons "all the time" at Camp David.

Obama and his team, especially newly promoted senior adviser Dan Pfeiffer, often bemoan the media's endless chase of superficial and distracting storylines. So how did the president's inner circle handle the silly dust-up about whether the president really did shoot skeet?

Pfeiffer and White House press secretary Jay Carney tweeted a link to the photo, with Pfeiffer writing that it was "[f]or all the skeeters" (doubters, or "skeet birthers"). Longtime adviser David

Plouffe then taunted critics on Twitter: "Attn skeet birthers. Make our day—let the photoshop conspiracies begin!" Plouffe soon followed up with: "Day made. The skeet birthers are out in full force in response to POTUS pic. Makes for most excellent, delusional reading."

The controversy started with an interview coconducted by Chris Hughes, a former Obama supporter and now publisher of The New Republic. The government created the content (the photo), released it on its terms (Twitter) and then used Twitter again to stoke stories about conservatives who didn't believe Obama ever shot a gun in the first place.

"The people you need to participate in the process are not always the people hitting 'refresh' on news websites," said Jen Psaki, the Obama campaign's traveling press secretary, who last week was appointed the State Department spokeswoman. "The goal is not to satisfy the requester, but doing what is necessary to get into people's homes and communicate your agenda to the American people."

ARTICLE QUESTIONS

1) According to VandeHei and Allen, what recent changes in the media environment have tipped the balance of power toward the government?

2) What specific strategies do VandeHei and Allen claim that Obama's staff have developed and perfected for controlling Obama's image and handling the press?

3) VandeHei and Allen focus on the negative repercussions of technological advances for press access to the president. Are there any ways that the recent changes in technology and media can be used to pull back the White House's control over the information available to the public?

9.5) How Sensationalist TV Stories on Terrorism Make Americans More Hawkish

The Monkey Cage Blog, October 9, 2014

SHANA GADARIAN

Shana Gadarian is assistant professor of political science at Syracuse University's Maxwell School.

Media have the power to influence opinions; however, this influence is often indirect. According to one theory of media influence, media exposure rarely changes what we think about issues (especially about issues where we have strongly held beliefs); rather, the media have influence because they tell us what issues to think about. The ability of media coverage to drive debate toward particular topics is often referred to as the media's power to set an agenda. On any given day there are multiple important events occurring, any number of which could command media attention. But given time restrictions, budget constraints, and the need to maintain an audience, only certain events are covered—and those events are the ones we think about.

Shana Gadarian, a political scientist from Syracuse University writing for *The Monkey Cage Blog* (a media acquisition of *The Washington Post* that allows political science research to be quickly disseminated and publically debated), provides a great example of the potential effects of the media's agenda setting role in her post "How Sensationalist TV Stories on Terrorism Make Americans More Hawkish." As Gadarian notes, media coverage doesn't need to directly argue that more money should be spent fighting terrorism to influence our opinions. Her research indicates that merely seeing "images and warnings of more violence to come" increases Americans' concerns about terrorism and makes them more likely to support presidential action. Terrorism or rare disease outbreaks like Ebola tend to get much more coverage than car accidents or the flu, both of which kill many more people. When news coverage focuses on certain events, such as terrorism, it focuses the political agenda on these issues and subtly changes our opinions.

Television news in the last several weeks has seemed eerily reminiscent of the period after September 11 2001, flooding the airwaves with frightening, violent imagery, and a sense that terrorism is likely. According to the media monitoring service TVEyes, CNN mentioned the Islamic State more than 3,800 times in the past several weeks. The Islamic State itself utilizes the media to spread its message and recruit followers through gruesome videos of attacks and beheadings, creating fear in publics targeted for attacks. Americans are paying attention to this news and are increasingly concerned about the Islamic State. In a recent Wall Street Journal/NBC poll, 94 percent of respondents were familiar with the murders of two U.S. journalists by ISIS, and 47 percent think that the country is less safe than before the 9/11 attacks. Again, just like the period after September 11, Americans seem to support military action in the Middle East. They are increasingly in favor of military strikes against the Islamic State. In a September 20 Gallup Poll, 60 percent of respondents supported air strikes, up from 39 percent support in June, at the beginning of Islamic state sieges on Mosul, Tikrit, and Sinjar.

Political and media observers, particularly on the left, worry that media coverage of the Islamic State is terrifying Americans and persuading them to support foreign policies and candidates that they would otherwise not support. Political science suggests that their fears are warranted. My own research—conducted in the wake of 9/11— provides strong evidence that both the amount and tone of media coverage of terrorism can significantly influence foreign policy attitudes. Americans who were already worried about future terrorism after 9/11, were more likely to support the use of military force abroad and increased spending on security at home after seeing news

stories about terrorism with images like the World Trade Center on fire.

My research used two statistical approaches (OLS regression and an instrumental variables approach) to analyze data from an American National Election Studies 2000–2002–2004 panel that interviewed the same respondents both before and after the 9/11 attacks, asking how TV viewing changed public attitudes to security policy [see Figure 9.1]. TV news viewing didn't much change the views of respondents who thought that future terrorist attacks in the United States were unlikely in the short term. However, as the graphs below show it *did* appear to change the views of the two-thirds of respondents who thought that future attacks were likely or very likely. The more TV they watched, the more hawkish were their views. Democrats were especially affected by televised images of terrorism. Democrats who had watched the World Trade Center fall were more likely to have warm feelings toward President George W. Bush than Democrats who had not seen this image.

Even five years after 9/11, seeing televised images of terrorism made people more likely to support the types of hawkish counterterrorism policies advocated by the Bush administration. In 2006, I worked together with YouGov/Polimetrix to create an experiment involving a representative sample of 1,220 Americans. Some of these 1,220 were picked at random to watch a TV story unrelated to terrorism, some to watch a TV story about terrorism with neutral images and no emotional commentary, and some a TV story about terrorism with scary visuals chosen to emphasize the threat of terrorism, such as the burning World Trade Center and bloodied victims of the 2005 London transit bombings. After watching one of the three news stories, respondents answered a series of questions on U.S. foreign policy.

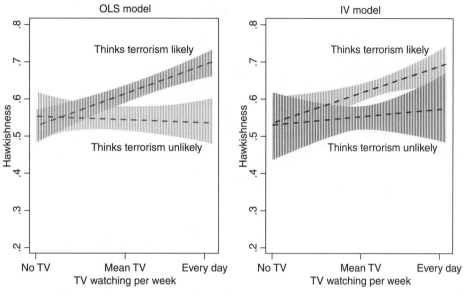

Foreign Policy Attitudes 2002

Source: 2000–2004 NES
Predicated values and 95% CI

Figure 9.1 TV News Exposure Increases Support for Hawkishness for Americans Concerned about Terrorism

The graphic on the next page shows that scary visuals have a big effect on people who think that terrorism is likely or very likely in the near future [see Figure 9.2]. The black circles represent the differences in attitudes between respondents who saw the neutral story about terrorism and respondents who saw the story that was unrelated to terrorism. This tells us about the consequences of watching TV news items with threatening *information* about terrorism. The white open diamonds represent the differences in attitudes between people who saw the TV news item with scary visuals about terrorism, and people who saw the TV news item with neutral visuals about terrorism. This tells about the consequences of watching TV news items with *frightening imagery*. When people's foreign policy views move in a hawkish direction, they are shown on the right of the vertical dotted line and when they move toward the dovish end appear to the left of the line.

Not only did the scary visual condition increase support for hawkish policy by about 6 percent compared to the news story which did not talk about terrorism, but the TV news item with scary visuals increased support for militaristic policies more than the TV news item with neutral visuals, even though they provided the exact same information. Respondents who saw the news item with scary visuals were more likely than those who watched the version with non-emotional imagery to support military solutions to international problems and higher spending on areas such as defense and border security, and to have more favorable views on the government's handling of terrorism. Although not all of the differences between the neutral and scary visuals conditions reach conventional levels of statistical significance, the overall pattern of findings is very clear. Threatening news makes people more hawkish even on its own, but it is most influential when it is presented in a sensationalistic way.

Terrorism is newsworthy because it is inherently dramatic and threatening. Media competition means that journalists and editors have incentives to use emotionally powerful visuals and story lines

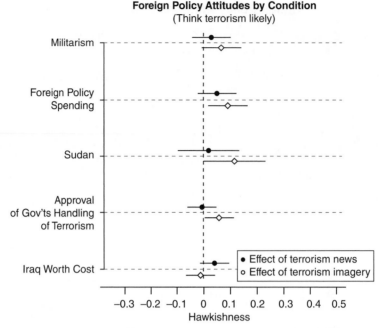

Figure 9.2   Scary Terrorism Imagery Increases Support for Hawkish Policy

to gain and maintain ever-shrinking news audiences. During the years after 9/11, this sensationalistic news coverage increased support for the hawkish foreign policy advocated by the president.

For sure, graphic news imagery does not always move the public toward hawkishness. Disturbing images of chemical attacks on Syrian civilians were not enough to convince a majority of Americans to support military action there in 2013. Where media images of terrorism enhance a sense of fear and political leaders agree on a set of policies to counter threats, the American public is likely to support those policies. During times of crisis, the political spectrum shrinks, leaving the president as the dominant voice on foreign policy, and making a frightened public more likely to endorse the president's policies. However, when opposition voices return, Americans are likely to support the foreign policy advocated by their party leaders even when frightened.

All this suggests that frightening media images of the Islamic State will probably make the public more hawkish. The September Gallup Poll tells us that Republicans and Democrats supported air strikes on ISIS at equally high rates (65 percent of Republicans; 64 percent of Democrats), reflecting growing hawkishness among Democrats. Only 34 percent of Democrats supported military strikes in June. As President Obama made the case for military strikes, Democrats in the public, many of whom were probably concerned about future terrorism, adopted the president's position. Congress approved of President Obama's plan to arm moderate Syrian rebels in September and approval ratings of the president's handling of foreign policy are on the rise, again making hawkish policy dominant. No president wants to seem indifferent to or flatly wrong about the risk of terrorism, making it more likely that presidents will see military action as necessary to protect the United States. My research tells us that media coverage of terrorism with searing images and warnings of more violence to come is likely to get Americans who are worried about terrorism to line up behind the president's use of force.

ARTICLE QUESTIONS

1) What evidence does Gadarian provide to linking news coverage and public support for military action?
2) Based on the evidence provided by Gadarian's studies, do you think that your opinions about terrorism and the need for military actions are influenced by broadcast news? Why or why not?

9.6) Perceptions Haven't Caught Up to Decline in Crime

The New York Times, September 16, 2014

JUSTIN WOLFERS

Justin Wolfers is a senior fellow at the Peterson Institute for International Economics and professor of economics and public policy at the University of Michigan.

Perhaps the biggest biases of any news organization in the United States are (1) to make a profit and (2) to be newsworthy. Because of these biases, the events that are the most sensational and unusual tend to get the most news coverage. The word "news" is derived from the word "new." It makes sense that people aren't inclined to pay attention to "the olds"—they want to hear "the news." A standing parable in the news industry is the "man bites dog" story. Most people will tell you that it is more common for a dog to bite a person than for a person to bite a dog. But which of these two events is more likely to be "newsworthy"? If the news only presents stories of people biting dogs, will people eventually start to assume that this is more common than the reverse?

Justin Wolfers, a political scientist writing for *The New York Times* blog The Upshot, provides an example of how the media bias for the sensational can affect people's perceptions. In his article "Perceptions Haven't Caught Up to Decline in Crime," he notes that even though the violent crime rate "has declined roughly by half since 1993," people's perceptions are that crime rates have increased. Because the media focus on the sensational and unusual, even when crime rates fall, crime is still reported on at similar levels. Most people experience crime, not first hand but through media reports. Interestingly enough, even if media stories explain that crime rates are declining, the very depiction of specific crimes focuses people's attention and shifts their perceptions. If crime reporting takes up a similar or increased amount of media space, people often perceive that as indicating that crime is up.

Here's a narrative you rarely hear: Our lives are safer. This message is so rarely heard that half of all respondents to a recent YouGov poll suggested that the violent crime rate had risen over the past two decades. The reality, of course, is that it has fallen enormously.

The decline in violent crime is one of the most striking trends over recent decades; the rate has declined roughly by half since 1993.

To be precise, the F.B.I.'s count of violent crimes reported to law enforcement has declined from a rate of 747 violent incidents per 100,000 people in 1993 to 387 incidents per 100,000 people in 2012, which is the most recent year for which it has published complete data. This reflects the fact that over this period, the homicide rate has fallen by 51 percent; forcible rapes have declined by 35 percent; robberies have decreased by 56 percent; and the rate of aggravated assault has been cut by 45 percent. Property crime rates are also sharply down.

These trends aren't caused by changes in our willingness to report crime to the police. We see an even more significant decline in violent crime in data derived from surveys asking people whether they've been the victims of certain crimes over the past year. The National Crime Victimization Survey reports that the rate of violent victimizations has declined by 67 percent since 1993. This reflects a 70 percent decline in rape and sexual assault; a 66 percent decline in robbery; a 77 percent decline in aggravated assault; and a 64 percent decline in simple assault. This survey has nothing to say about the decline in homicide, for obvious reasons.

The gap between perception and reality is particularly large when it comes to New York City. The same YouGov survey also asked people to assess the relative safety of 10 large cities. New York was, after Chicago, the city most likely to be rated as "fairly unsafe," or "very unsafe," while Dallas/Fort Worth and Houston were most likely to be rated as "very safe," or "fairly safe." The reality, of course, is that the actual violent crime rate in New York is around half that in either Dallas or Houston, and lower than that in other big cities.

It's an unfortunate fact that media reporting on individual crimes yields a relentlessly dismal drumbeat of downbeat news. But even as each reported crime yields a story that is terrifying enough to shape our perceptions, the truth is that none of them tells us much about the broader trends. Far better to ignore the anecdotes and focus instead on the big picture, and the hard data tells us: There's been a remarkable decline in crime.

ARTICLE QUESTIONS

1) Prior to reading this article, were you aware of the sharp decline in crime statistics from 1993 to 2012? Why do people rarely hear this narrative?
2) What are the implications of people perceiving that crime rates are higher than they actually are?
3) When you seek out news, do you seek out the sensational and unusual?
4) How should media organizations deal with the bias for covering the sensational? Should they not report the "news"?

Chapter 10

Campaigns and Elections

Americans vote more often, for more offices, than the people of any of other nation. Presidents and members of Congress, governors, and mayors, school board leaders, city council members, and even many judges all owe their position to the will of the people. There are over 520,000 elected offices at the local, state, and national level, which is about 1 for every 420 Americans eligible to vote. This hyper-focus on elections is part of what it means to be an American, and it highlights a distrust of unaccountable power: Americans are often uncomfortable with appointed positions, preferring to vote for numerous offices. In fact, there were times during U.S. history when some jurisdictions elected people to be the dog catcher. However, elections provide more than the ability to check a box next to the candidate or proposition of your choice. When they function well, elections involve a process of public debate and citizen deliberation, they help hold elected officials accountable, and they help determine public policy.

One of the first steps in the electoral process is determining who is eligible to participate. The commonly told story surrounding voting rights in America includes a narrative of constant expansion, but the real story is more complex: voting rights have both expanded and contracted throughout U.S. history. For example, New Jersey allowed women and blacks to vote as early as 1776 but then stopped in 1807; it wasn't until 1920 that women could vote again in New Jersey. The Fifteenth Amendment, adopted in 1870, made disenfranchisement because of race unconstitutional; however, federal voting protections were later rolled back, and by 1908 every state in the Deep South had adopted a constitution explicitly denying blacks the franchise. In Clarke Canfield's 2010 article "Portland, Maine, Weighs Letting Noncitizens Vote," he discusses a ballot measure to grant noncitizens the right to vote in local elections. This may seem like a foreign idea today, but as the article notes, noncitizens were able to vote during much of U.S. history. In a similar story of contracting voting rights, disenfranchising felons become more common after the Civil War. As this article and the debates over felony disenfranchisement highlight, voting rights both expand and contract over time.

Voting rights are largely set at the state and local level. The national government, and especially the courts, frame state and local decisions with basic Constitutional rights—which are often highly contested. In "Justice Department Blocks Texas on Photo ID for Voting," Charlie Savage explores a particular conflict between the national government and the state of Texas over requiring photo identification to vote, but the story reflects controversies over federalism and civil rights. Jamelle Bouie argues in "Making Voting Constitutional" that the state-versus-national conflict over who has the authority to make electoral laws can be traced to the lack of an explicit right to vote in the Constitution. As it emerged in 1789, the Constitution granted nearly exclusive authority to the states to determine voter eligibility. As amendments were added, the federal government acquired increased authority to regulate states' electoral procedures. Still, these amendments only establish limits on *denying* voting rights; no provision in the Constitution grants a positive right to vote. As these articles show, elections are a product of both state and national policies. In fact, in the United States there is no such thing as a national election; rather, there are 50 state elections, each with different rules and procedures.

Most election coverage focuses on the roles of candidates, voters, campaign strategy, and public opinion in determining the outcomes. What often gets left out of this coverage is the importance of the "rules of the game." The next two readings show how electoral rules often determine electoral outcomes. *The Los Angeles Times* editorial "President, by Popular Vote," shows the importance of electoral rules by detailing an alternative to the current Electoral College system for selecting the president. Four times in U.S. history the winner of the presidential election lost the popular vote to another candidate. With different rules the outcomes of those elections would have changed without a single voter behaving differently. Similarly, *The New York Times* editorial, "How to Expand the Voter Rolls," shows the importance of registration processes for determining who votes, which in turn can change who gets elected. The United States has one of the lowest voter turnout rates in the developed world: only 53.6% of the voting-age population cast ballots in the 2012 presidential election. News articles often blame the apathy of the American public for this low turnout, but the rules that govern voting and registration also dictate voter turnout. As an extreme example, Australia routinely has a turnout of greater than 95%—then again, Australia has compulsory voting, meaning people can face fines for failing to cast a ballot. Adopting a similar rule in the United States would likely increase turnout, although it might run counter to U.S. notions of liberty. These two articles underscore that elections are as much the product of electoral rules as they are the results of voter choices, candidate selections, and campaign strategies.

Trying to predict the outcomes of elections is a deeply ingrained part of America's electoral system. Based on careful analysis of elections, social scientists have developed sophisticated models for predicting electoral outcomes by identifying trends in voting behavior. Here's one trend you can incorporate into your predictions that will have you accurately predicting elections, at least most of the time: incumbents almost always win. In 2012, 90% of House incumbents who sought reelection were successful; so were 91% of senators. A reelection rate hovering around 90% has held consistent for decades. Peter Baker and Eric Lipton's article "In a Tight Race, Obama Draws on the Levers of His Power" provides some insight into why incumbents are a "safe bet." The article focuses on Obama using his incumbency advantage, but many of the particulars can be generalized to any incumbent. Incumbency advantage is just one of many electoral trends that have been identified. Measures of the economy also help to predict whether the party in control of Congress and the presidency will retain or lose seats. There are limits to what models can tell us, but when social scientists look at the rules of the game and the historic trends, they can often predict the outcome of elections with a high level of accuracy long before campaigning has begun.

Another important theme runs through this chapter's readings: are U.S. elections democratic enough? The rules determine who can vote and influence who will win. Knowing the current rules, and the resulting outcomes, helps us evaluate U.S. elections. As you engage the readings in this chapter, ask yourself what aspects of U.S. elections promote the ideals we desire? What should we change?

CHAPTER QUESTIONS

1) Are U.S. elections democratic enough? What, if anything, should change to make them more or less democratic?
2) What are some unique aspects of U.S. elections compared to elections conducted in other countries?
3) What are some changes that have occurred to the rules governing U.S. elections over the past 200 years?
4) Why was the Electoral College system of selecting the president established? What would be required to eliminate the Electoral College? What are the implications of making such a change?

CHAPTER READINGS

10.1) Clarke Canfield, "Portland, Maine, Weighs Letting Noncitizens Vote," Associated Press, October 23, 2010.
10.2) Charlie Savage, "Justice Department Blocks Texas on Photo ID for Voting," *The New York Times*, March 13, 2012.
10.3) Jamelle Bouie, "Making Voting Constitutional," *The American Prospect*, January 30, 2013.
10.4) "President, by Popular Vote," *The Los Angeles Times*, November 12, 2012.
10.5) "How to Expand the Voter Rolls," *The New York Times*, April 6, 2012.
10.6) Peter Baker and Eric Lipton, "In a Tight Race, Obama Draws on the Levers of His Power," *The New York Times*, September 19, 2012.

10.1) Portland, Maine, Weighs Letting Noncitizens Vote

Associated Press, October 23, 2010

CLARKE CANFIELD

PORTLAND, Maine—Throughout U.S. history, states have labeled categories of citizens as "undesirable" voters and denied the franchise to people from these objectionable groups. Initially those without large amounts of property were viewed as unreliable; at other times women, slaves, blacks, those under 21 years old, Native Americans, Mexican-Americans, Chinese-Americans, those belonging to certain religions, and various other groups were denied voting rights. Few would argue that five-year-olds make desirable voters, but other categories remain contentious. Overall the number of categories of people deemed undesirable has been reduced, but states still go through the same process. In almost all states, those under 18 are excluded from voting (although there are a few exceptions). People currently incarcerated for crimes are barred from voting in all but two states, and 13 states deny those convicted of certain crimes from ever voting again. In many states there are mental competency requirements to vote. People living in Washington, D.C., do not get to elect a voting member of Congress (despite having a population almost 10% greater than Wyoming). Citizens in the U.S. territories, such as Puerto Rico, Guam, the U.S. Virgin Islands, American Samoa, and the Northern Mariana Islands, do get to vote for president or for voting members of Congress. Puerto Rico even has a population larger than Connecticut, a state with seven Electoral College votes in 2012.

In Clarke Canfield's 2010 article "Portland, Maine, Weighs Letting Noncitizens Vote," he discusses a ballot measure to allow noncitizens to vote in local elections. Denying legal resident noncitizens the vote is more common today than it was 100 years ago. In fact, 1928 marked the first year that no state allowed noncitizens to vote. This shows how rights contract as well as expand. The idea of noncitizen voting remains contentious. Since this article was published, a bill was introduced in the New York City Council to allow noncitizens to vote in local elections. It garnered lots of support in both 2013 and 2014 but has yet to be adopted. As this reading shows, a few other cities allow noncitizens to vote in local elections.

Another connected issue to both noncitizen voting and felony disenfranchisement is the fact that noncitizens and felons count as part of a local and state population. Thus the people who can vote in these states and cities get an increased number of representatives based on having a population of people who can't vote. For example in upstate New York nearly one-third of the people credited with moving to the area between the 1990 and 2000 census were incarcerated. This added to the representation of the non-incarcerated residents. California's noncitizen population of 5.5 million adds five extra House seats and five Electoral College votes for the portion of the population of people that are eligible to vote.

Like his neighbors, Claude Rwaganje pays taxes on his income and taxes on his cars. His children have gone to Portland's public schools. He's interested in the workings of Maine's largest city, which he has called home for 13 years.

There's one vital difference, though: Rwaganje isn't a U.S. citizen and isn't allowed to vote on those taxes or on school issues. That may soon change.

Portland residents will vote November 2 on a proposal to give legal residents who are not U.S. citizens the right to vote in local elections, joining places like San Francisco and Chicago that have already loosened the rules or are considering it.

Noncitizens hold down jobs, pay taxes, own businesses, volunteer in the community and serve in the military, and it's only fair they be allowed to vote, Rwaganje said.

"We have immigrants who are playing key roles in different issues of this country, but they don't get the right to vote," said Rwaganje, 40, who moved to the U.S. because of political strife in his native Congo and runs a nonprofit that offers financial advice to immigrants.

Opponents of the measure say immigrants already have an avenue to cast ballots—by becoming citizens. Allowing noncitizens to vote dilutes the meaning of citizenship, they say, adding that it could lead to fraud and unfairly sway elections.

"My primary objection is I don't think it is right, I don't think it is just, I don't think it is fair," Portland resident Barbara Campbell Harvey said.

In San Francisco, a ballot question November 2 will ask voters whether they want to allow noncitizens to vote in school board elections if they are the parents, legal guardians or caregivers of children in the school system.

Noncitizens are allowed to vote in school board elections in Chicago and in municipal elections in half a dozen towns in Maryland, said Ron Hayduk, a professor at the City University of New York and author of "Democracy for All: Restoring Immigrant Voting Rights in the United States."

New York City allowed noncitizens to vote in community school board elections until 2003, when the school board system was reorganized, and several municipalities in Massachusetts have approved allowing it but don't yet have the required approval from the Legislature, he said.

The Maine ballot questions asks whether legal immigrants who are city residents but not U.S. citizens should be allowed to vote in municipal elections. If the measure passes, noncitizens would be able to cast ballots in school board, city council and school budget elections, as well as other local issues, but not on federal or statewide matters.

The Maine League of Young Voters, which spearheaded the drive to force the question on the ballot, estimates there are 5,000 to 7,500 immigrants in Portland, roughly half of whom are not U.S. citizens. They come from more than 100 countries, with the two largest groups from Somalia and Latin America.

On a recent day in a small lunchroom at the Al-Amin Halal Market, a group of Somali men ate lunch and talked in their native language. A sign advertised the day's offerings, including hilib ari (goat), bariis (rice) and baasto (spaghetti).

Abdirizak Daud, 40, moved to Minneapolis 18 years ago before coming to Portland in 2006. He hasn't been able to find a job. Some of his nine children have attended Portland schools, and he'd like to have a say in who's looking over the school system and the city, he said.

But between his limited English and the financial demands, Daud hasn't been able to become a citizen.

"I like the Democrats. I want to vote for Democrats, but I don't have citizenship," he said.

To become a citizen, immigrants must be a lawful permanent resident for at least five years, pass tests on English and U.S. history and government, and swear allegiance to the United States.

Supporters of Portland's ballot measure say the process is cumbersome, time-consuming and costly. The filing fee and fingerprinting costs alone are $675, and many immigrants spend hundreds of dollars more on English and civics classes and for a lawyer to help them through the process.

Allowing noncitizens to vote fits with basic democratic principles, Hayduk said.

Historically, 40 states allowed noncitizens to vote going back to 1776, but an anti-immigrant backlash in the late 1800s and early 1900s resulted in laws that eliminated their voting rights by 1926, Hayduk said.

"We look back in history and we say that was a bad thing that we didn't allow African-Americans to vote, or we didn't allow half the population, women, to vote, or we didn't allow younger people to vote," he said. "We've modified our election laws to become more inclusive to incorporate more members of society."

The Federation for American Immigration Reform, a Washington, D.C., group that advocates tougher immigration enforcement, says voting is a privilege and should be limited to citizens.

"People who are legal immigrants to the United States after a five-year waiting period can become citizens and become enfranchised," spokesman Ira Mehlman said. "But until then, being here as a legal immigrant is a conditional agreement, sort of like a trial period. You have to demonstrate you are the type of person we would want to have as a citizen, then you can become a citizen and vote."

ARTICLE QUESTIONS

1) Identify two arguments made in the article for why legal resident noncitizens should be allowed to vote in local elections in Portland, Maine. Identify two arguments for why noncitizens should not be able to participate.

2) What groups of people used to be excluded from the electorate because they were seen as "undesirable" voters? What groups are still excluded today?

3) A basic tenet of democratic theory is that those affected by a decision should have a role in making that decision, but there are obvious limits as to how far this maxim can be carried. Where should the line be drawn for who should be included and who should be excluded from being able to vote?

10.2) Justice Department Blocks Texas on Photo ID for Voting

The New York Times, March 13, 2012

CHARLIE SAVAGE

Despite the Constitution's celebration of representative government, it failed to grant anyone the right to vote. The first time the phrase "right to vote" appeared in the Constitution was in the Fourteenth Amendment, nearly 80 years after the Constitutional Convention. Voting rights and electoral procedures are largely established at the state and local level, with some constraints imposed by the elections clause of the Constitution in Article I, Section 4, some amendments added to the Constitution, some federal court decisions, and a few congressional statutes. U.S. electoral policy clearly highlights the complexity of the U.S. federal system. Charlie Savage's article "Justice Department Blocks Texas on Photo ID for Voting" is a few years old—and much has occurred since its publication—but the article provides one of the best introductions to the contemporary controversy over voting rights.

Starting in 1965, states with a history of discrimination were required to have all changes to their electoral laws preapproved by the federal government. This preapproval process (known as preclearance) prevented Texas from adopting a voter identification law because the Department of Justice (DOJ), and later a federal court, determined the law would impair the voting rights of minority groups. But only some states were subject to preclearance; thus, Indiana and several other states were able to adopt voter identification laws without seeking preclearance (although all states could be sued after the laws were adopted if people felt they infringed on their voting rights). In 2013 the Supreme Court struck down the formula for determining which states faced preclearance, so no states were subject to the provision. Within two hours of the Court's decision, Texas officials said they would go forward with the law that was previously prevented by preclearance. Citizens in Texas and the DOJ sued after the law went into effect, and a federal district court ruled that the law imposed unconstitutional discrimination. Texas appealed the decision, and the federal appeals court allowed the law to be implemented during the 2014 midterm elections while the case is awaiting appeal.

This article brings up numerous issues. One, of course, is whether voter identification laws are an effective means of protecting the integrity of elections. But another important question is this: Who should have the authority to make this determination? Should each state get to decide? Should Congress be able to set up a regulatory process, or should it be up to the federal courts? Also, if the courts get to decide, does that mean that the decisions will almost always come after a discriminatory election law was used and the election has been conducted? These questions are all on shifting ground; whatever the answer is today is unlikely to be the answer tomorrow.

WASHINGTON—The Justice Department's civil rights division on Monday blocked Texas from enforcing a new law requiring voters to present photo identification at the polls, contending that the law would disproportionately suppress turnout among eligible Hispanic voters.

The decision, which follows a similar move in December blocking a law in South Carolina, brought the Obama administration deeper into the politically and racially charged fight over a wave of new voting restrictions, enacted largely by Republicans in the name of combating voter fraud.

In a letter to the Texas state government, Thomas E. Perez, the assistant attorney general for civil rights, said the state had failed to meet its requirement, under the Voting Rights Act, to show that the measure would not disproportionately disenfranchise registered minority voters.

"Even using the data most favorable to the state, Hispanics disproportionately lack either a driver's license or a personal identification card," Mr. Perez wrote, "and that disparity is statistically significant."

Texas has roughly 12.8 million registered voters, of whom about 2.8 million are Hispanic. The state had supplied two sets of data comparing its voter rolls with a list of people who had valid state-issued photo identification cards—one from September and the other from January—showing that Hispanic voters were 46.5 percent to 120 percent more likely to lack such identification than were non-Hispanics.

Under the Voting Rights Act, jurisdictions that have a history of suppressing minority voting—like Texas—must show that any proposed change to voting rules would not have a disproportionate effect on minority voters, even if there is no evidence of discriminatory intent. Such "preclearance" can be granted either by the Justice Department or by a panel of federal judges.

Texas officials had argued that they would take sufficient steps to mitigate any impact of the law, including giving free identification cards to voters who lacked them. But the department said the proposed efforts were not enough, citing the bureaucratic difficulties and cost of obtaining birth certificates or other documents necessary to get the cards.

In anticipation that the administration might not clear the law, Texas officials had already asked a panel of judges to allow them to enforce the law. A hearing in that case is scheduled for this week.

Benjamin Todd Jealous, the president of the National Association for the Advancement of Colored People, praised the decision, saying the state law "would have blocked hundreds of thousands of Hispanic voters from the polls just because they lack a state-issued photo ID."

But Gov. Rick Perry called the decision "yet another example of the Obama administration's continuing and pervasive federal overreach." He argued that there was "no valid reason" for rejecting the law since it required "nothing more extensive than the type of photo identification necessary to receive a library card or board an airplane."

Under the state's existing system, voters are issued certificates when they register that enable them to vote. But last year, Mr. Perry signed a law that would replace that system with one requiring voters to present one of several photographic cards at their polling station.

The approved documents include a state-issued driver's license or identification, a license to carry a concealed gun, or several forms of federal identification. Student identification cards would not count.

The measure was part of a wave of new voting restrictions passed around the country, mostly by Republicans, after their sweeping victories in the 2010 elections. More than a dozen states tightened election rules, including eight that passed variations of a photo identification rule.

Supporters argue that such restrictions are necessary to prevent fraud. In a statement, Greg Abbott, the Texas attorney general, said state prosecutors had won about 50 convictions related to various kinds of election fraud over the past decade, and he listed several that appeared to involve in-person voter impersonation—the kind addressed by photo ID requirements.

Critics say there is no evidence of significant amounts of in-person voter impersonation fraud and contend the restrictions are a veiled effort to suppress turnout by legitimate voters who tend to vote for Democrats, including students, the indigent and minorities.

"We note that the state's submission did not include evidence of significant in-person voter impersonation not already addressed by the state's existing laws," Mr. Perez wrote.

The analysis of the Texas law was complicated because the state submitted two sets of data that had conflicting numbers, showing that either 603,892 or 795,955 registered voters lacked a driver's license or state-issued identification card.

But the Justice Department concluded that there was a statistically significant disparity either way: in the first data set, 4.3 percent of non-Hispanic voters lacked the required identification, versus 6.3 of Hispanic voters.

In the second set, 4.9 percent of non-Hispanic voters lacked it, as compared with 10.8 percent of Hispanic voters.

The section of the Voting Rights Act at issue does not apply to jurisdictions that do not have a discriminatory past, giving the Justice Department less power to intervene in some states that have enacted such laws.

In 2008, the Supreme Court ruled that a similar Indiana law did not violate the United States Constitution, but that case did not involve the higher standards of the Voting Rights Act or presentation of statistical evidence about any disparate impact.

Still, on Monday, a judge in Dane County, Wis., blocked that state's new photo identification voting law, ruling that it was unconstitutional under Wisconsin's charter.

ARTICLE QUESTIONS

1) What was the Justice Department's reasoning for blocking the Texas law?
2) Why did Texas Governor Rick Perry and Texas Attorney General Greg Abbott argue the photo identification law was justified?
3) Should states be free to adopt voter identification laws? What role should the federal government have in overseeing state elections?

10.3) Making Voting Constitutional

The American Prospect, January 30, 2013

JAMELLE BOUIE

If you want to shock someone, tell them, "There's no right to vote in the U.S. Constitution." The phrase "the right to vote" first appears in the Constitution in the Fourteenth Amendment. It also appears in the Fifteenth, Nineteenth, Twenty-fourth, and Twenty-sixth amendments. But, as Jamelle Bouie argues in "Making Voting Constitutional," the right as established by these amendments is a "negative liberty establishing" the reasons that cannot be used to deny the right. Theoretically, a state could decide to deny voting rights to everyone and conform to the requirements of these amendments. A blanket denial of the right to vote would not be denying the right to vote based on age, sex, or race and it would not establish a poll tax, which is what these amendments prohibit. But what would be different if a right to vote existed? Bouie argues that ensuring such a right would have both symbolic and practical importance. Amending the Constitution is a herculean task; does Bouie convince you that such an effort is warranted?

Early last year, when Attorney General Eric Holder took a strong stand against voter-identification laws, he emphasized how much they violate core American ideals. "What we are talking here is a constitutional right," he said. "This is not a privilege. The right to vote is something that is fundamental to who we are as Americans. We have people who have given their lives—people have sacrificed a great deal in order for people to have the right to vote. It's what distinguishes the United States from most other countries."

The problem is Eric Holder is wrong. Unlike citizens in every other advanced democracy—and many other developing ones—Americans don't have a right to vote. Popular perception notwithstanding, the Constitution provides no explicit guarantee of voting rights. Instead, it outlines a few broad parameters. Article 1, Section 2, stipulates that the House of Representatives "shall be composed of Members chosen every second Year by the People of the several States," while Article 1, Section 4, reserves the conduct of elections to the states. The Constitution does, however, detail the ways in which groups of people cannot be denied the vote. The 15th Amendment says you can't prevent African American men from voting. The 19th Amendment says you can't keep women from voting. Nor can you keep citizens of Washington, D.C., (23rd Amendment) or 18-year-olds (26th Amendment) from exercising the franchise. If you can vote for the most "numerous" branch of your state legislature, then you can also vote for U.S. Senate (17th Amendment).

These amendments were passed in different circumstances, but they share one quality—they're statements of negative liberty, establishing whom the government can't restrict when it comes to voting. Beyond these guidelines, states have wide leeway in how they construct voting systems. Some, like California, have opted to make voting as easy as possible, with early-voting periods, widely available absentee ballots, and online registration. Others, like Virginia, have made voting difficult, with strict ID laws and no early voting. Throughout American history, some lawmakers and officials have seen the federal government's hands-off approach as an opportunity to tighten their grip on power and suppress opposition. At the end of Reconstruction, states passed laws to restrict African American voting. Governments led by the Democratic Party throughout the country—not just the South—had passed poll taxes, literacy requirements, and grandfather clauses, all

designed to keep blacks away from the polls. When those weren't enough, vigilantes resorted to violence, with the tacit (or outright) approval of local authorities.

It wasn't until the Voting Rights Act of 1965 that the federal government made a proactive move to secure the voting rights of all citizens, and of African Americans in particular. But that didn't put an end to the states' suppressive shenanigans. During the 2000 election, to cite one unforgettable example, Florida officials made an active effort to remove voters from the rolls (in the interest of "protecting the vote") and keep former felons from voting. In 2004, Ohio's secretary of state, Republican Kenneth Blackwell, pushed strict measures that would disqualify provisional ballots submitted to the wrong precinct, even if they came from registered voters (and even if poll workers, not voters, were at fault). In 2011 and 2012, Republicans in state legislatures across the country passed "voter integrity" laws that instituted draconian ID requirements for voters and made it difficult for millions of Americans—disproportionately black and Latino—to vote. "Voter fraud" was the stated reason for these measures, but independent experts have found no evidence of the kind of fraud—voter impersonation—that would be stopped by requiring photo IDs.

In our large, polarized democracy, voting has been an issue fraught with partisanship and ideology. But the ability of states to restrict participation stems from the peculiar fact that Americans don't enjoy the right to vote. We came close once. Following the end of the Civil War, an early draft of the 15th Amendment featured a blanket right to vote (excluding women); this was rejected in favor of limited suffrage for freedmen. The reason? Southern Republicans didn't want to enfranchise former Confederates, Western politicians feared that Chinese would participate, and Northern states worried that they would have to abandon their own restrictions on voting.

There have been periodic attempts to revive the right-to-vote idea. In 2005, for example, Representative Jesse Jackson Jr. introduced a right-to-vote amendment that won meager support from other House members. But the recent attempts to block voters and make voting cumbersome—dramatized by the long lines of the 2012 presidential election—could act as a catalyst for a new movement to codify, in the Constitution, a right to vote.

Proponents say that an affirmative constitutional right would, at the very least, force state lawmakers and election administrators to think twice about measures and election procedures that harm voters. "A constitutional amendment for the right to vote is needed to make it explicit," says Judith Browne Dianis, co-director of the Advancement Project, a civil-rights organization. "Making it explicit will send a signal to state legislatures and courts that any barriers to our democracy must be carefully devised so that they don't disenfranchise people." The Supreme Court, she notes, has been happy to defer to states' laws on voting, even if the result is to keep some people from exercising the franchise. In 2008, the Court upheld Indiana's voter-identification law, declaring that it wasn't unconstitutional to require photo identification at the polls because the state had a "valid interest" in deterring fraud. That ruling was made despite Indiana's inability to produce a single example of in-person voter fraud.

A right-to-vote amendment would raise the standard of constitutional review for voter-identification laws and other measures that deplete the pool of voters. Currently states have to show only a "compelling interest" for their laws to pass muster. An affirmative right to vote would compel courts to apply "strict scrutiny," the standard used to review laws that operate on the basis of race and other characteristics. The burden would then be on a state like Indiana to prove voter fraud and to show that IDs or other requirements are needed to prevent further problems.

"One way to read the Constitution is as a narrative, and that narrative is one of ever-increasing inclusion and participation for people," says Jamie Raskin, a Maryland state senator and professor of law at American University in Washington, D.C. Raskin believes that a right-to-vote amendment could be used to settle a question that has always been at the center of our political disputes: Who participates in our democracy?

The founders were preoccupied with what they called "republican virtue." As they saw it, a democratic society couldn't function without a virtuous citizenry participating in public life, with virtue defined by one's economic independence. If you owned your land, the founders believed, you had the ability to reason free of self-interest, and thus you possessed virtue. If you were a lowly worker, or dependent on others for your livelihood, you were too compromised to make political choices, and thus you lacked virtue. Of course, it's no accident that the only people who had republican virtue—white male landowners—were also the people who defined it. They were, in their estimation, the only people to possess the independence, control, and faculties to govern the country and protect it from mob rule.

Even though we've expanded the Constitution to protect voting rights for women, minorities, and young adults, the idea that some people have virtue and others don't is still embedded in our political thought. . . .

The same idea is at work in felon-disenfranchisement laws: Committing a crime robs you of your virtue, the thinking goes, and it is up to the virtuous political leaders to determine whether you can return from prison as a full member of society.

The call for a right-to-vote amendment is an attempt to redefine virtue away from exclusion and toward a broader and more inclusive view. James Savage, a professor of political theory at the University of Virginia, points out that this concept is also rooted in the founders' views. "A fundamental characteristic of republican virtue is citizen participation in political life," he says. "Virtuous citizens are obligated to engage in political life, minimally by voting. As part of its purpose, the state should encourage this virtuous participation, not impede it."

An affirmative right to vote would create a more democratic society. It would also help shift power back to everyday citizens. A country in which more people vote is one where wealth and corporate influence are a little less powerful. Almost every progressive change of the past century, from the original Progressive Era to the Great Society, was pushed along by efforts to expand the electorate and bring more people into the process. The 17th Amendment, by allowing for direct election of senators, took power away from the corporations who influenced state legislatures and gave it to ordinary people. Women, empowered by the 19th Amendment, helped elect Franklin Roosevelt, Harry Truman, and other liberal politicians. A right-to-vote amendment would further that legacy.

The odds of passing an amendment—any amendment—are long. Only 27 have made the cut, and the most important ones came during times of great national turmoil. Even something as commonsensical as the Equal Rights Amendment, which would constitutionally guarantee the equality of women, is unlikely to pass. This has much to do with the arduous process for amending the Constitution. First, Congress has to pass the proposed amendment by a two-thirds majority (it doesn't need presidential approval). Then three-quarters of the states have to approve the amendment. Given overwhelming GOP support for voter identification and other exclusionary measures, it's hard to imagine a sufficient number of Republican lawmakers voting to affirm the right to vote. The chances in states are perhaps even slimmer than in Congress: If you divide the country into states with voter-identification laws and those without, and assume the voter-ID states would oppose the amendment, you would be 17 states short of the necessary number even if all the non-ID states ratified it. Then again, as Raskin notes, "every constitutional amendment seems impossible up to the point it becomes inevitable." . . .

Most Americans already believe that the vote is sacrosanct. The least we can do is enshrine it in our laws. By making the right to vote a rallying point, progressives would show their commitment to expanding democracy. "We've taken a defensive posture," Ellison says, "and it's a bad way to organize. It's also not a way to inspire people. If you want to inspire people, you have to lift sights, and I think a constitutional amendment is the way to do that."

ARTICLE QUESTIONS

1) According to the article, what is the difference between the Constitution protecting a right to vote and what the Constitution currently protects?

2) What does the article claim would change if the Constitution protected a right to vote?

3) Were you surprised to read that the Constitution doesn't include a right to vote? Would you support amending the Constitution to include a right to vote? Why or why not?

10.4) President, by Popular Vote

The Los Angeles Times, November 12, 2012

The Electoral College system offends modern sensibilities and should be replaced.

Presidential elections garner the most public attention and the greatest voter turnout. Under the Electoral College system each state is allotted a number of electors who vote for president; each state establishes its own procedures for selecting electors. Four times in U.S. history the Electoral College picked a winner who had lost the popular vote. To keep the loser from winning once again, many observers wish to abolish the Electoral College and let the public directly elect the president (although political scientists support the Electoral College for keeping down costs, suppressing fraud and minimizing third parties).

To abolish the Electoral College the Constitution would have to be amended, and a constitutional amendment requires approval from two thirds of both houses of Congress and three quarters of the states. Based on the structure of the Electoral College, "swing states" and less-populated states have increased influence in selecting the president: a citizen in a small state like Wyoming gets almost four times more voting power than a citizen from California. The added voting power in small states might discourage its representatives from supporting an amendment to abolish the Electoral College. If all small states refused, no amendment could pass. Is there really no way to abolish the Electoral College even if a significant majority of the country desires such a change? *The Los Angeles Times* editorial "President, by Popular Vote" details a strategy to get around this conundrum.

By a fairly solid margin, Tuesday's presidential election spared Americans the hand-wringing that would have accompanied a split decision like that of 2000. George W. Bush, of course, won the electoral college that year but fell just short in the popular vote. This year, Barack Obama cruised to victory in the electoral college and won the electorate by about 3 million votes.

When a presidential candidate wins the electoral college but loses the popular vote—as Bush, Benjamin Harrison and Rutherford B. Hayes did—it does not diminish the legitimacy of the election. Each of those candidates won by the rules and went on to serve as president. Nevertheless, few Americans would deny that it is troubling and fundamentally undemocratic to be governed by a president who was opposed by more than half of his countrymen.

The electoral college, as it came to be known, was specifically designed to thwart the democratic impulses that alarmed the founders of the republic. Rather than permit a direct vote of the people—remember that "the people" in that era did not include women, blacks or the poor—the Constitution provided that the president would be picked by electors. Those electors would be chosen by the states and allocated according to how many congressional representatives were assigned to each state. The preferences of the people mattered not at all.

Happily, the expansion of the franchise is one of the noblest aspects of America's political evolution. Today, many of those groups disenfranchised at the outset join in what Walt Whitman evocatively extolled as "choosing day." And yet the electoral college remains. There are efforts to replace it, and the 2012 election should once again propel those efforts forward, not to favor one party or the other but to broaden and deepen democracy for all.

There are at least two ways to accomplish that. One would be to abolish the electoral college altogether. But that would require a constitutional amendment, which would mean securing the approval of two-thirds of Congress as well as ratification by three-quarters of the states. In today's political climate, it's difficult to imagine that kind of consensus being achievable.

The other route is more clever. It requires states to pass legislation awarding their electoral votes for president to the winner of the national popular vote. That legislation, however, would take effect only when states with combined electoral votes of 270 or more—the winning margin in the electoral college—sign on to the system. The practical effect would be to ensure that the winner of the popular vote also would win the electoral college, and thus become president. As of today, nine states, including California, with a combined 132 electoral votes have approved the idea.

That system would change the way presidential races are run. Had it been in place this year, for instance, Mitt Romney might have stumped in interior California to boost his popular vote there. Instead, he and Obama bypassed California because Romney knew he could not win it and Obama knew he could not lose it.

Meanwhile, they poured more than $200 million into Ohio, spending so much time there that one election-night commentator remarked that it looked more like a race for governor of that state than for president of all the states. That's the practical effect of the current system: It drives candidates and money to the handful of closely contested states, and encourages them to ignore the larger numbers of voters in California, New York, Texas and other populous states where the balance of power is so squarely on one side or the other that no amount of campaigning is likely to affect it.

That once may have conformed with a crimped view of voting and those permitted to influence the outcome. However, it offends modern sensibilities, and should be replaced by a system in which the winner of the popular vote becomes president of the United States.

ARTICLE QUESTIONS

1) According to the editorial, why was the Electoral College system established?
2) Explain the Electoral College reform that California and eight other states have approved. How would presidential campaigns change if such a reform were implemented?
3) Should the United States move to a system of electing the president by a popular vote? What are the advantages and disadvantages of the Electoral College?
4) Does the existence of the Electoral College challenge the democratic nature of U.S. elections?

10.5) How to Expand the Voter Rolls

The New York Times, April 6, 2012

U.S. voter turnout is among the lowest in the developed world. In the 2014 midterm elections, just 36.4% of the voting eligible population cast ballots. Presidential elections have higher turnout, but it still hovers around 50%. *The New York Times* editorial "How to Expand the Voter Rolls" explains the importance of the registration process for determining electoral turnout. As the article notes, only 68% of all eligible voters are even registered. In some states this requires registering weeks in advance of the election, as well as reregistering every time you move. In countries with high voter turnout, there are no "personal registration requirements." For example, Canada automatically registers voters, resulting in 93% of its population being registered.

While no state automatically registers its voters, there is still wide diversity in the registration processes. Ten states allowed same-day registration for the 2014 midterm elections—people could both register and cast a ballot on election day. Of the nine states with the highest voter turnout in 2014, seven allowed same-day registration. For the 2012 presidential election, states with same-day registration had 71% turnout compared to 59% turnout for states without same-day registration. In the end, voter turnout is not simply the result of voter apathy or voter engagement; the rules governing elections matter significantly.

A country that should be encouraging more people to vote is still using an archaic voter registration system that creates barriers to getting a ballot. In 2008, 75 million eligible people did not vote in the presidential election, and 80 percent of them were not registered.

The vast majority of states rely on a 19th-century registration method: requiring people to fill out a paper form when they become eligible to vote, often at a government office, and to repeat the process every time they move. This is a significant reason why the United States has a low voter participation rate.

The persistence of the paper system is all the more frustrating because a growing number of states have shown that technology can get more people on voter rolls. There's no reason why every state cannot automatically register eligible voters when they have contact with a government agency. The most common method, now used in 17 states, electronically sends data from motor vehicle departments to election offices.

Ten states allow people to register online, and others, including California, are preparing to do so. In Washington State, for example, anyone with a driver's license or state ID can register over the Internet. The paperless systems are much cheaper than the old forms and far more accurate. A recent study by the Pew Center on the States found that 24 million voter registrations (about 12 percent) are significantly inaccurate because they had not been updated or were erroneous to start with.

The Brennan Center for Justice reports that paperless systems have doubled the number of registrations through motor vehicle departments in Kansas and Washington State. In South Dakota, seven times as many people registered to vote at motor vehicle offices after an automated system began in 2006. Online registration is particularly appealing to young voters; in Arizona, a new system has increased the registration of voters ages 18 to 24 from 29 percent in 2000 to 53 percent in 2008.

The obsolete paper system has resulted in an overall registration rate of only 68 percent in the United States. Canada, by contrast, registers 93 percent of its population, using a computerized system that automatically gathers records from tax forms, the military and vital statistics agencies, as well as motor vehicle offices.

This country has a long and terrible tradition of erecting barriers to participation. In earlier eras, the obstacles were overt, like literacy tests to keep minorities and poor people off the rolls. Recent methods are subtler but still harmful. In 2004, Ohio briefly banned registration forms not printed on 80-pound paper to make it easier to invalidate minority voter drives without access to the forms. Even now, many Republican lawmakers are doing everything they can to maintain intimidating requirements.

Florida, for example, has put stringent restrictions on voter registration drives, imposing fines and even criminal penalties for the slightest infraction of complex rules. Groups like the League of Women Voters and Rock the Vote say they won't participate in such a system. Election officials say the rules limiting these drives are a significant reason that new registrations are lower than they were four years ago.

Since President Obama was elected with help from a surge of support from new voters, similar laws have been passed or introduced in South Carolina, Michigan, Illinois, and several other states as part of a Republican effort to restrict voting by groups that tend to vote Democratic.

It should be self-evident that the country benefits when more citizens are engaged in the electoral process, but too many lawmakers are trying to reduce participation for short-term political gain. Given the progress some states have achieved with new registration methods, it's time for Congress to step in and require that all states bring their systems into the digital age.

ARTICLE QUESTIONS

1) What percentage of the population that didn't vote in the 2008 presidential election were not registered to vote?

2) What examples of ways to increase voter registration does the article cite?

3) If people are failing to vote, what is the advantage in making it easier for them to do so?

4) Why is high voter turnout viewed positively? Are there good reasons for people to choose not to vote?

10.6 In a Tight Race, Obama Draws on the Levers of His Power

The New York Times, September 19, 2012

PETER BAKER AND ERIC LIPTON

In U.S. elections, incumbents almost always win: a reelection rate hovering around 90% has held consistent for decades. In 2014, 96% of House incumbents who sought reelection were successful, as were 95% of senators. This reelection rate occurred despite a Congressional approval rate of 14%. The disconnect between congressional approval and reelection rates is partially because people rate their own members of Congress more highly than they rate Congress as a body. But the other part of the answer is that incumbents have a huge advantage when it comes to campaigning. Peter Baker and Eric Lipton's article "In a Tight Race, Obama Draws on the Levers of His Power" focuses on Obama using his advantage as an incumbent in 2012, but many of the particulars from the article can be generalized to the concept of "incumbency advantage." As Baker and Lipton note, "every president lives at the intersection of policy and politics." This intersection is especially true for members of the House, who face reelection every two years. Every action a congressmember takes in office must be evaluated for its effects on his or her reelection chances. Of course, this was the constitutional Framers' intention; if government officials are concerned about getting reelected, it will keep them connected to the desires of the people.

Incumbents have the advantage of touting their "day job" in their campaign efforts. If a major bill is passed or a speech is delivered on the floor of Congress, the resulting news serves as a free campaign advertisement. In fact, almost everything an incumbent does is news, just because he or she is an elected official. And news coverage of government officials results in a tremendous campaign advantage: name recognition. The very fact that an incumbent is already serving in the office makes it easier for the voters to visualize him or her as electable. Because Barack Obama was the president during the 2012 campaign, he was depicted as "presidential" in news coverage. This made it easier for people to visualize voting for him. Incumbency advantage is one of the biggest concerns for people opposed to restrictions on campaign donations. Because incumbents are well known, they have less need for expensive campaign ads. A challenger may need to outspend the incumbent just to pull even in name recognition.

For months, government lawyers and economists worked behind the scenes to develop a trade case against China. Then last month came a eureka moment: They confirmed the existence of a Chinese subsidy program for automobiles and parts that in their view violated international trade rules. They finished a complaint, circulated it among agencies and proposed a time frame for filing.

That's when President Obama's political team took over, providing a textbook example of how an incumbent can harness the power of the office to bolster the case for re-election. Rather than leave it to the trade office to announce the complaint, Mr. Obama decided to do it himself. Aides scheduled it for a campaign swing to the auto-dependent battleground state of Ohio, leaked it to the state's largest newspaper, then sent other journalists a link to the resulting story plus voter-friendly talking points.

Every president lives at the intersection of policy and politics, never more so than during a campaign season. Locked in a tight race with Mitt Romney, Mr. Obama and his team have been pulling every lever of the federal government within reach, announcing initiatives aimed at critical constituencies, dispatching cabinet secretaries to competitive areas, coordinating campaign events to match popular government actions and forestalling or even reversing other government decisions that could hurt the president's chances of a second term.

On Friday, Mr. Obama will designate Chimney Rock in Colorado a national monument, preserving thousands of acres and aiding tourism in another swing state, a decision shared Wednesday with a Denver newspaper. When he flew to Iowa last month, Mr. Obama arrived just as his administration announced drought relief for farmers and released a report promoting his support for wind power. After critics attacked him for inhibiting oil and gas production by considering an obscure lizard for the endangered species list, the administration decided it wasn't so endangered after all.

Some of the most significant policy announcements of recent months were keyed to important voter blocs. Mr. Obama reversed position to endorse same-sex marriage before attending a big-dollar fund-raiser with gay and lesbian leaders. Just before addressing a national Latino organization, he used executive power to allow illegal immigrants to remain in the country if they had come as children.

White House officials acknowledged that they calibrate announcements and trips to maximize the advantages of incumbency but said the policy decisions themselves were made on substance. They also noted that while cabinet secretaries travel to swing states, they also travel to states that are not competitive. And they said that on some level it is impossible to separate the candidate from the president.

"The president is not going to put off what he believes are important actions, such as protecting jobs for American workers, until after the election," said Eric Schultz, a White House spokesman. "These decisions are made on the merits by professionals with the relevant policy expertise, are often months in the making and always reflect the president's longstanding positions."

Republicans, naturally, see it differently. "He looks like he is aiding his re-election with the power of the Oval Office," said Matt Schlapp, who was White House political director for President George W. Bush. "He looks worried, reactive. It's fair to ask that if this China decision was for policy issues alone then why wait until right before the first debate to announce it?"

Each White House tests the boundaries. President Bill Clinton used the Lincoln Bedroom to entertain financial donors. Mr. Bush's strategist, Karl Rove, oversaw an "asset deployment team" that managed trips and grant announcements. Both got in trouble. Mr. Clinton's fund-raising triggered Congressional investigations while the Office of Special Counsel, an independent agency, concluded that the Bush White House violated federal law by creating a "political boiler room" coordinating campaign activities.

The same agency determined last week that Kathleen Sebelius, the health and human services secretary, violated the law by advocating Mr. Obama's re-election during an official trip to North Carolina. The trip was reclassified to political and the cost reimbursed. "Keeping the roles straight can be a difficult task, particularly on mixed trips that involve both campaign and official stops on the same day," Ms. Sebelius wrote investigators.

Other cabinet secretaries have had active travel schedules to important electoral states. Since July, Interior Secretary Ken Salazar has traveled to at least 15 states for public events, according to his schedule, including Wisconsin, Nevada, Pennsylvania, Florida and Colorado. During the same period in 2010, he traveled to 10 states, according to agency records. At various stops, Mr. Salazar promoted Mr. Obama's energy and conservation policies.

Mr. Salazar took an airboat tour of the Everglades in Florida days after Agriculture Secretary Tom Vilsack visited to announce $80 million for an Everglades protection program. Mr. Vilsack hinted at why that small chunk of Florida had received so much attention when he appeared at the opening of Mr. Obama's campaign office in Port St. Lucie. "You win Florida and you win the presidency," Mr. Vilsack said at the event. "And I have been told you win this region, you win Florida."

While announcing new initiatives during campaign season is standard practice, Mr. Obama's team also seems focused on stopping policies that may be politically hazardous. In June, the Interior Department rejected their own plans to designate a lizard known as the dunes sagebrush as endangered by oil and gas activities. After analysis, the department declared that "the lizard is no longer in danger of extinction."

"The administration did not want to face criticism from the oil and gas industry during an election year," said Taylor McKinnon, a public lands advocate at the Center for Biological Diversity.

Blake Androff, an Interior Department spokesman, said the decision was "based entirely on the best available science and in accordance with the law," not politics, and came only after industry and state officials agreed to voluntary conservation measures.

He added that Mr. Salazar's travel was also extensive in non-election years, reflecting the job of overseeing hundreds of millions of acres of public land. A spokesman for Mr. Vilsack said his Florida trip was planned so he could spend one day on official business and another stumping for Mr. Obama on his own time. But on Tuesday, the same day a reporter inquired about the mixing of politics and policy on the trip, the Obama campaign sent a check for $1,606.24 to reimburse taxpayers for airfare and hotel—timing that Agriculture Department officials said was a coincidence.

When it came to the China case, officials said it was in the works for much of the year but took months to find evidence of unfair trading practices. They went down a number of blind alleys before getting the first indication of the Chinese subsidy program over the summer. Then last month, they determined it was real and deemed it a violation. At that point, officials said, there was no justification to delay filing.

And if it happened to help the campaign, Josh Earnest, a White House spokesman, told reporters, "I'll let our opponents and all you guys assess whether or not there's a political benefit for the president."

ARTICLE QUESTIONS

1) What advantages did Obama have in the 2012 campaign because he was the incumbent?

2) What are the implications for democratic elections when incumbents win more than 90% of the time?

Chapter 11

Political Parties

Political parties have evolved through the years, but their essential purpose remains the same: a party is an organization, with a public following, established to win elections, generally by promoting a set of principles. Political parties organize American government around competing ideas. As the vote expanded to include more Americans, political parties rose up to organize the armies of new voters. By the middle of the nineteenth century political parties were the largest and most influential political organizations in the nation.

Americans have always had a love/hate relationship with parties. The country's Founders provided strongly worded warnings about the evils of political parties. Thomas Jefferson wrote to a friend, "if I could not go to heaven but with a party, I would not go there at all." Despite this damning statement, Jefferson exhibited the classic love/hate relationship with political parties; he is widely considered the founder of the modern-day political party the Democratic-Republicans (also known as the Jeffersonian Republicans), which he used to get elected to the presidency in 1800.

Despite the disdain that many Americans have for political parties, parties perform essential democratic functions. In fact, no modern democracy has existed without them, and in many emerging democracies the lack of strong parties has stalled democratization. In countries where political party affiliations haven't solidified, politics often resort to clashes over clan and tribal identities; parties channel social clashes into struggles over political ideas.

In *Better Parties, Better Government*, Peter Wallison and Joel Gora argue that strengthening U.S. political parties would provide numerous benefits to voters, such as improved mechanisms for holding representatives accountable. They also suggest that augmented political party strength would decrease the power of special interests, facilitate voter choice, create more stable policies, better educate the electorate, and improve voter mobilization. While Wallison and Gora advocate for stronger political party organizations, Alan Greenblatt, in "Why Partisans Can't Kick the Hypocrisy Habit," notes that party loyalties and party identification are already strong and are intensifying. Greenblatt reports that Americans are now more likely to switch their religion than their political party. Even more important to political debates is Greenblatt's observation that Americans are often more inclined to trade in their political opinions than their party preference. As Greenblatt notes, there are many cases where party identification pushes people to judge similar events very differently. A recent example of this concerns people's opinions over the National Security Agency's (NSA) monitoring of phone traffic. When Republican George W. Bush was president, Republicans were more likely than Democrats to support NSA monitoring. Once Barack Obama, a Democrat, became president, the same program found more support among Democrats than Republicans.

A defining aspect of the political party system in the United States: There are only two parties. Most democracies operate a multiparty system. Third party candidates rarely win in the United States. In "Can Activists Win by Losing?" Ambreen Ali focuses on candidates, particularly third-party candidates, running for office with a unique conception of winning. Many third-party candidates know they are unlikely to garner the most votes, but for many "winning" is beside the point; their primary objective is using the electoral system as a platform to promote their ideas and to push for policy reforms. Many political scientists argue that third-party organizations have historically influenced American policy. If third parties have significant impacts on the two-party system and are often successful at getting their policies enacted, does this mean we should stop viewing the United States as a rigid two-party system?

In sum, political parties play an essential role in American politics. At the same time, Americans right back to the founding have been uneasy about parties and partisanship. These doubts lead to calls for reform. But as with all debates on reform, it is important to consider the positive attributes provided by existing systems.

CHAPTER QUESTIONS

1) What important roles do political parties play in a democracy?
2) How can the ultimate goal of winning elections compromise political parties' benefits to democracy?
3) What are the advantages and disadvantages of having a two-party system? Why do we have a two-party system?
4) What reforms should be made to the U.S. party system?

CHAPTER READINGS

11.1) Peter J. Wallison and Joel M. Gora, "*Better Parties, Better Government: A Realistic Program for Campaign Finance Reform*" [excerpts]. Washington, DC: AEI Press, 2009.

11.2) Alan Greenblatt, "Why Partisans Can't Kick the Hypocrisy Habit," *National Public Radio*, June 14, 2013.

11.3) Ambreen Ali, "Can Activists Win by Losing?" Congress.org, August 12, 2008.

11.1) Better Parties, Better Government: A Realistic Program for Campaign Finance Reform [excerpts]

Washington, DC: The AEI Press, 2009

PETER J. WALLISON AND JOEL M. GORA

Political parties are an essential part of American politics, yet many Americans remain leery of organizations focused on winning elections. These concerns have led many states to adopt reforms limiting the influence of political parties. Many of these reforms include adopting nonpartisan elections, preventing parties from endorsing candidates, and implementing direct voter nominations of candidates. But there may be unintended consequences from these changes. Political parties recruit candidates to run for office; when states turn to nonpartisan local elections, they often find there are no candidates running for the post. Nonpartisan local elections generally see lower voter turnout than partisan ones. Voters often rely on a candidate's party identification as a cue for how to vote (conservatives can vote for the Republican candidate, liberals for the Democrat). Shut out the parties, and the voters have a more difficult time making choices. One more unintended consequence of restraining parties: Interest groups often step in to fill the void. Which would do a better job informing voters: Interest groups (for example, Pro-life groups, Pro-choice organizations, environmental groups, the National Rifle Association) or political parties? Or are there other choices?

In *Better Parties, Better Government*, Peter Wallison and Joel Gora focus on the benefits that political parties provide to a representative government. They argue that "in a well-functioning party system, the parties would offer a program. If they gain a legislative majority . . . they bear the responsibility . . . if they fail . . . they risk being turned out of power at the next election." But is the vision they lay out too idealized? Wallison and Gora note that their plan will likely be met with skepticism because of "the traditional American fear of concentrations of power." Are there reasons besides traditional fears to be skeptical of increasing the power of parties?

[T]here is nothing in our Constitution that is inconsistent with strong parties that . . . exert some influence over the policy positions of their candidates and officeholders. . . . [W]e outline the benefits more powerful parties will bring, in general, to the functioning of government, and thus what benefits would flow from parties taking a greater role in policy formulation.

Continuity in policy. The erosion of party financial power that culminated in the 1960s not only placed incumbents in a stronger position vis-à-vis their challengersbut also left the U.S. political process without any institution that could maintain a continuity of purpose or policy beyond a single president's administration. Although parties were never strongly programmatic institutions, they saw themselves as standing for something. As long as they had a significant role in the choice of the presidential nominee, the policies of the

president and the party were hard to distinguish. But as primaries and local caucuses became more important, parties gradually lost their ability to choose their presidential candidate and they also ceded their policy role to the presidential candidate chosen for them by the voters.

Thus the policies of the president became the policies of his party, and if a party did not control the White House it simply had no policymaking apparatus and no coherent policies. Even in cases where a party had elected a president, the policies that were the reason for his election, and that had animated his administration, were simply packed off with his files at the end of his term in office. The next president, even of the same party, started with a clean slate. The absence of parties from the policy field also affected Congress, which—without any institutionalized system for the development of a program to take to the American people before an election—was unable to serve as a policy counterweight to the president. This was especially true if the majority party in one or both houses of Congress did not also control the White House; the only viable strategy for a house of Congress that had no coherent program of its own was to oppose or frustrate the president's program. Mann and Ornstein make this point: "The presidency gained enormous power during much of the twentieth century, particularly over national security, and public expectations about what the occupant of the White House could and should accomplish soared. Congress in turn was increasingly judged by whether it facilitated or frustrated the president's agenda."

Because parties are the only informal national political institutions that survive from presidential administration to presidential administration, the loss of any party role in policy meant the loss of policy continuity. This loss in turn made change far more difficult to achieve. The Constitution sets up a system of checks and balances that permits change to occur, but only slowly over time. It's a brilliantly conceived structure for protecting the individual against government encroachment, but moving the system to accommodate change seems to require steady pressure over many years. With the president the only source of policy initiatives, and without political parties to carry forward ideas beyond a single presidency, it becomes difficult to accommodate government policies to major changes in economic conditions or technology.

Without some strong source of party discipline, it is impossible for a political party to create a program on which its candidates can run. The inclination of candidates will always be to preserve their independence and their ability to choose the terms on which they will stake their election. This is understandable, and in most cases unexceptionable, but candidate independence is a prescription for continued weakness in congressional policymaking, and that in turn promises a continued lack of a policy mandate for elected officials. Thus, to the extent that permitting political parties to fund the campaigns of their candidates will enable them to create and enforce party discipline, one

clear benefit will be to provide continuity in political party positions from administration to administration. This continuity will make change easier to achieve in the American constitutional system.

Choice in public policy. Despite the ambivalence of the population at large, political parties have always had supporters outside politics itself, especially in the academic community. The strongest advocates of party government have frequently been political scientists and professional students of government. One such student, Woodrow Wilson, wrote in his doctoral thesis in 1885 that "parties should act in distinct organizations, in accordance with avowed principles, under easily recognized leaders, in order that the voters might be able to declare by their ballots, not only their condemnation of any past policy, by withdrawing all support from the party responsible for it; but also and particularly their will as to the future administration of the government, by bringing into power a party pledged to the adoption of acceptable policy."

Wilson was arguing that parties should be far more powerful than they have ever been in the United States, but he was also pointing to one of the key benefits of political parties: providing voters with a choice. In 1950, a committee of the American Political Science Association issued a report entitled *Toward a More Responsible Two-Party System*. The committee, made up of some of the most respected political scientists of the day, called parties "indispensable instruments of government," and went on to affirm that "popular government in a nation of 150 million people requires political parties which provide the electorate with a proper range of choice between alternatives of action.... The crux of public affairs lies in the necessity for more effective formulation of general policies and programs and for better integration of all of the far-flung activities of modern government."

This statement concisely summarizes the potential role of a party in providing the electorate with a choice, and is known to political scientists as the "responsible party doctrine." The role envisioned for the party cannot of course be performed by a single senator or representative, who can tell his constituents what he will support but not promise them that it will be accomplished if he's elected. The president can come closest to making this promise, but even he must negotiate his program with Congress after his election, and in many cases the president's program is not enacted or, if enacted, comes out in a barely recognizable form.

How, then, without parties that offer a choice, does the public make its will known? The answer is: with difficulty. Every four years, the American people elect a president, and if his majority is large enough, and he has been clear enough about his intentions, he is said to have a mandate. But unless the new president is seen as responsible for his party achieving a majority in Congress, he must contend with the fact that most of the members of Congress owe him nothing and are more concerned about the needs of their own constituencies than his success. Since they are the ones who have to raise the funds for their reelection, they must also keep in mind the fact that their constituents and financial supporters may have different views than they about the president's program; and for members of Congress, constituent and financial support is likely to be more persuasive than the ties of party loyalty.

Thus, with each candidate running independently, even though under a party label, it is difficult to tell what an election means. One party may have acquired a majority in the House, Senate, or both, but what does this victory mean? What have the people really voted for, and what kind of mandate have they provided? These ambiguities are among the most significant reasons that our government moves so slowly—or not at all—to address pressing problems. In reality, when the American people vote, they send a very mixed message. They elect a president who may have a personal program, but they also elect a Congress that is fractionalized along numerous lines and that has many different ideas about the national welfare. How can anyone determine in such a system what the American people have voted for? How can a majority for action be developed in this political environment?

Strong political parties can bring clarity to this question. Parties have always been capable of developing a set of programs and policies as a platform for a presidential campaign. Despite the widespread view that these documents are filled with meaningless generalities, that is not the case. As Sabato and Larson note in comparing the Democratic and Republican platforms in 2000, "On a host of issues, the two parties could not have taken more divergent substantive positions—and there is nothing mushy or tepid about the rhetoric employed, either." They add that "the 2000 platforms were not exceptional in this regard," and they cite a study showing that between 1944 and 1976, the parties' platforms "were consistently and significantly different."

Admittedly, the platforms are aspirational in nature rather than true programs for action. But a comprehensible and comprehensive party program, drawing upon the aspirational elements of its platform, could impose a great deal of order on the chaotic system that now prevails in U.S. government policymaking. Unfortunately, within the current candidate-centered campaign finance system, the political parties do not have sufficient leverage with their own candidates to induce their support for either the quadrennial platform or any other set of policies and programs.

In a well-functioning party system, the parties would offer a program. If they gain a legislative majority, they have been given a mandate to enact their program. If their program fails to meet the objectives they set out for it, they bear the responsibility, just as they must if they fail to enact their program at all. In both cases, they risk being turned out of power at the next election.

It should be clear that parties can adopt programs and get them enacted. So too can party members working in concert, such as we saw when the House Republicans promoted and passed their Contract with America. It would have been just as easy for the Republican Party outside Congress to adopt the Contract with America, but the party has not for nearly a century seen itself as a policy-formulating institution, and its effort to adopt a program probably would have been opposed by elected officials. Nevertheless, the Contract presented the voters with a clear choice, and it shows that a multifaceted program can be formulated by, and form the base of an election campaign for, a group with the power to enact it. Certainly a party with the power to finance its own candidates would have the necessary leverage to gain the support of its candidates for such a program.

Fostering of accountability. Developing programs that provide a choice for voters is one thing; taking responsibility for enacting a program and for its success is another. As Sabato and Larson note: "Accountability without parties is impossible in a system as multifaceted as America's. After all, under the separation of powers arrangement, no one—not even the president—can individually be held responsible for fixing a major problem because no one alone has the power to do so. Collective responsibility by means of a common party label is the only way for voters to ensure that officials are held accountable for the performance of the government."

The current electoral system in the United States makes it very difficult for voters to hold politicians accountable and assign responsibility for political failure. In federal elections, the voters elect representatives and senators, but the connection between the policies of these lawmakers and actions by Congress is highly attenuated. This is because the power of an individual lawmaker is very small, and the ability to get legislation adopted singlehandedly is virtually nonexistent. Accordingly, how is a voter to know whom to hold accountable if, despite the election of the person he voted for, nothing happens in Washington? The senator or representative elected with the support of a majority of voters can easily point out that he is only a single lawmaker, and unable, without the support of a majority of the Senate and House, to get legislation adopted. Anyone who has ever heard a member of Congress denounce the failings of Congress in a speech to his constituents knows exactly what is going on. Under these circumstances, responsibility is diminished or lost. As Aldrich notes: "No one person either can or should be held accountable for actions taken by the House, Senate, and president together. The political party as a collective enterprise, organizing competition for the full range of offices, provides the only means for holding elected officials responsible for what they do collectively."

This failure of accountability will never be resolved until political parties begin to develop their own programs and go before the American voters with a promise to adopt certain legislation if the party is given a legislative majority. As Woodrow Wilson suggested, the parties—and only the parties—are in a position to offer the voters a meaningful choice in what they want Congress to do. The choice of a president is binary—that is, there are generally two candidates, and the voters have an opportunity to choose between them along the dimensions of policy, personality, and background. When a president is elected, voters have a reasonably good idea of where he wants to take the country. The choice for the Senate or the House of Representatives is far more complicated; the voters have no idea, when they elect a representative or senator, what Congress as a whole will ultimately do, or they have only the most general idea of how their votes will produce a particular result. There is no effective way, in other words, for voters to hold individual senators and representatives accountable for the failure to enact the legislative program that the candidate offered to the voters during the election process.

This is a significant problem in the U.S. constitutional system, because the system works effectively with only two parties and thus, unlike parliamentary systems, does not create a significant voice or bargaining unit for the voter who is strongly interested in a particular policy. In multiparty systems, the necessity for party coalitions gives voters a much more clearly articulated and effective way to affect national policy than is true of a two-party system. This deficiency, however, can be corrected by elections in which the parties themselves are held accountable. Thus, strengthened political parties—parties that promise the voters a series of programmatic results if they are given power, and that can be defeated if the results are not forthcoming—provide the electorate with a meaningful choice. Voters would then have a better idea of what to expect if they vote for the candidates of a party. And they could hold the party accountable far more easily than their representative or senator, who obviously does not have the power by himself to enact needed legislation.

Nor would stronger parties necessarily diminish the power of the presidency. In our constitutional system the president is a major player in the policy process, and can be of a different party than the one that controls Congress. In that case, there is further bargaining, and the president and his party will have to take their chances on opposing the programs of a party that has won a legislative majority. In reality, as occurs today, the outcome is likely to be a compromise, with both sides—the president and Congress—claiming to have fulfilled the mandate received from the voters. But at the next election, the voters will have an opportunity to decide whether this was true from their all-important perspective.

If the president is of the same party as the congressional majority, that will ease the process of getting his legislative package adopted. His window for success will not be limited to the "first hundred days," before the drama of his election and inauguration is exhausted and Congress begins to fracture again along traditional lines. The president's program, of course, will have been vetted with his party—will become the program of the party—before the election, so there will be little question about who is responsible if the program is not adopted. And yet, if the program ultimately adopted is not satisfactory to the voters, there will be another congressional election two years later, where the opposition party will be able to present its contrasting set of initiatives.

Aggregation of special interests. Stronger political parties would have an important role in aggregating a wide variety of special interests into a coalition. If our government functions effectively with only two parties, then each of them has to include within it a huge number of special interests that demand representation at the national level.

The American Political Science Association report on the party system was prompted by what was seen, even then, as a decline in the role of parties in the American political system. Addressing the question of integrating special interests into a broader program for the nation as a whole, the committee recognized the crucial role parties play: "By themselves, the interest groups cannot attempt to define public policy democratically. Coherent public policies do not emerge as the mathematical result of the claims of all the pressure groups. The integration of the interest groups into the political system is a function of the parties. Any tendency in the direction of a strengthened party system encourages the interest groups to align themselves with one or the other of the major parties."

This suggests that strengthened parties will reduce the tendency of special interests to capture officeholders. To the extent that these interests believe that their priorities can be enacted through the parties, they will not press their views as aggressively on individual officeholders. Correlatively, if a successful party can enact its program, the special interests will not be able to gain much traction in Congress for policies and programs that have not been adopted by one of the parties. Thus increasing the power of the parties by giving them a stronger campaign finance role will help focus special interests on the political parties rather than on the candidates and officeholders. Subsuming special interests within the larger national coalition of interests represented by the parties will make the adoption of legislation much easier; Congress will not appear—as it often does today—incapable of resolving difficult issues of policy. If the president's program is different from that of the party that controls Congress, bargaining will ensue, but in this case there is a greater likelihood that an agreement reached between the leaders of Congress and the president will actually be implemented in legislation.

Some might worry that with campaign contributions increasingly going to the parties, parties are at risk of being corrupted. But as we suggested in the previous chapter, there are great and important differences between the influence that can be brought to bear on a party through a campaign contribution and one that can be brought to bear on a particular lawmaker. The position of the party as a broad-based institution that is raising substantial amounts of money for a national campaign immediately attenuates the influence of any single contribution. Any contribution is likely to be lost in the huge sums that the parties will be able to raise from many different constituencies. In addition, the party, unlike the individual candidate, has an interest in winning nationally, and to do so must assemble a broad coalition of interests. Tilting toward any particular special interest will impair this balancing process. In other words, if political parties are given the power to develop policy and programs, they will be able to reduce the power of special interests, not be swayed by it, and be more likely to develop a broad national program of legislative action.

Support for governmental initiatives. Of necessity, a program advanced by a party will be skeletal in nature. The devil, as they say, will be in the details, and these will come to light and be worked out through hearings and informal consultations with affected interests. Indeed, even party initiatives that attracted considerable support in a past election can easily lose support as the compromises required for legislation in a pluralistic society are stitched together.

In the end, however, if a legislative initiative emerges, the American people will have to be able to see it as a fulfillment of the mandate they gave. If the president is on board, a substantial proportion of this task will have been accomplished, but even with the support of the president it may be difficult to build the consensus among major groups that controversial legislation requires. A unified position by the sponsoring party and its members will be essential in that effort. The members are a ready-made core coalition around which the necessary national support can be organized. Stronger parties—parties which the American people understand to have some direct relationship to policies, programs, and governance—will be able to enlist far more interest from the electorate. Sidney Milkis notes that in the past, "political parties . . . played a critical part in linking private and public concerns, as well as local loyalties and national purpose." If sufficiently strengthened through the ability to finance the campaigns of their candidates, this is the role they could play once again.

Conclusion

We have shown . . . the benefits that would flow to our democracy if political parties were able to finance and exert more influence over their candidates and officeholders. The most important of these is to provide a mechanism with which the electorate can hold their representatives accountable and fix responsibility for failure. But other benefits would be almost as important: the power of special interests would be diminished; the voters would have a clearer sense of what the parties would do if they gained a majority; and the parties, by carrying their policy focus over a longer period than simply a single presidency, would be able to provide a more stable and consistent set of programs. In addition, the parties would have a continuing and institutional interest in educating the American electorate on the benefits of the programs they are advancing, and thus mobilizing support for initiatives that would otherwise lie dormant.

Weighed against these advantages is, at bottom, the traditional American fear of concentrations of power. Many Americans will reject the idea of more powerful parties because of concern that this will give unelected party bosses great power over the government's policies. But this is like saying that unelected CEOs, rather than consumers, determine whether a product is successful in the market. The central fact associated with political parties is that they are interested in only one thing—gaining and holding political power. In a vigorous democratic system, competition between the parties for the support of the voters should ensure that the parties' influence over their candidates and officeholders will advance the voters' interests.

ARTICLE QUESTIONS

1) What are the five categories of benefits that Wallison and Gora argue more powerful political parties could bring to the functioning of government?
2) Why do Wallison and Gora argue that stronger political parties would provide the electorate with a meaningful choice? Do you agree?
3) Do you think partisanship should be reduced in government? Why? How does your answer reinforce and reject the arguments made by Wallison and Gora?

11.2) Why Partisans Can't Kick the Hypocrisy Habit

National Public Radio, June 14, 2013

ALAN GREENBLATT

Even though the United States has weak political parties compared to those in other democratic countries, Americans are more likely to express a strong party preference. This powerful attachment to one party is called party identification. Party identification often begins in childhood, and many of us retain a party allegiance the same way we retain loyalty to a sports team. The party identification of one's parents is often shown to be the best predictor of people's party identification. Party identification is also correlated with racial and ethnic backgrounds. African-Americans, Mexican-Americans, Puerto Ricans, and women tend to vote Democratic. Whites, men, Cubans, and evangelical voters tend to be Republicans. The political events that are occurring at the national level when a voter forms a political attachment also matter. The only mass shift in political identification occurring over the past 25 years or so is an increasing trend for people to refuse party labels and identify as independents. Recent polls place the proportion of independents at about 38 percent, but many students of politics observe that if you ask independents a few follow-up questions, they respond exactly like people who identify as Republicans or Democrats.

In "Why Partisans Can't Kick the Hypocrisy Habit," Alan Greenblatt, reporting for *National Public Radio*, observes one of the implications of strong party identification. He notes that Americans are more likely to switch their religion or change their political opinions than they are to switch their political party. This means Democrats who currently oppose the actions of a Republican president will often flip to support these same actions if taken by a Democratic president (and of course, Republicans make these same opinion switches to support Republicans). Greenblatt focuses on the potential hypocrisy of such switches of opinion, but his story also highlights one of the important roles that political parties play: they facilitate voter choice by providing shortcuts for understanding complex policy. The "cues" provided by party elites help voters know which policies to support. When people see elites they identify with supporting a policy, they are likely to support it as well. Taking shortcuts may seem problematic, but imagine trying to form an opinion on all public policies and on all political candidates in the absence of any party cues. The need for these shortcuts means that party identification is often the best predictor of people's voting behavior.

American politics has become like a big square dance. When the music stops after an election, people switch to the other side on a number of issues, depending on whether their party remains in power.

That was pretty clear this week, when polls revealed more Democrats than Republicans support tracking of phone traffic by the National Security Agency—the exact opposite of where things stood under President George W. Bush.

A *Washington Post*-Pew Research Center poll released Monday showed that 64 percent of Democrats support such efforts, up from just 36 percent in 2006. Republican support, meanwhile, had dropped from 75 percent to 52 percent.

It's not just a question of whether you trust the current president to carry out data mining in a way that targets terrorists and not innocent Americans. Partisans hold malleable positions in a number of areas—foreign policy, the economy and even presidential appointees who continue to serve under a new administration.

"People change their views depending on which party is in power, and not based on objective conditions on the ground," says George Washington University political scientist John Sides.

My President, Right or Wrong

It's not surprising that partisans are more willing to give one of their own a break, particularly when it comes to matters like scandals.

But the president—any president—has become like the New York Yankees. You either love him and root for his success, or you hate him.

Political scientists talk about a "perceptual screen" through which many voters view the world, tending to support certain policy stances based on where their party stands. Studies over the years have consistently shown that partisans tend to have a rosier view of the economy if someone they support is in the White House.

"Democrats support [military] interventions where Democratic presidents lead them," says James Stimson, a political scientist at the University of North Carolina. "Republicans support them when Republican presidents lead."

This isn't just blind faith. Most people don't spend their time reading position papers, so they look to their party's leaders for cues. If I'm with them on tax cuts and education, the thinking goes, I'll probably like their approach to immigration.

That's an increasingly safe bet in an era where the parties are almost perfectly sorted ideologically. There are few conservative Democrats left, certainly compared with 50 years ago, and practically no liberal Republicans.

So people can feel pretty secure that their party's position on a given issue is not going to be far out of line with how they think on other issues.

"Especially on a new issue, people are not very informed about the details of the policy, so they tend to accept the position of the political elites they trust, on the assumption they share the same interests," says Sunshine Hillygus, a political scientist at Duke.

An Important Identity

People aren't willing to flip-flop on every issue. Most people hold firm views on matters such as abortion and gun rights that won't change with new occupants in the White House or the speaker's chair.

But because opinion within parties tends to be so uniform—and gets reinforced by supportive media and social media circles—sometimes people's opinions do shift so that they line up better with their partisan brethren.

That may be the case, for instance, with gay marriage, support for which has become almost an article of faith among Democrats. A Fox News poll released Thursday found that 65 percent of Democrats support gay marriage, while 69 percent of Republicans oppose it.

Although many people like to describe themselves as independent, partisanship has become an important aspect of identity. Some are more loyal to their partisan leanings than their own church, says University of Notre Dame political scientist David Campbell.

"Our findings indicate that for many but not all Americans, when they're faced with this choice between their politics and religion, they hold fast to their politics and switch religion, or more often switch out of their religion," he says.

A recent Stanford University study found that people are more likely to have hostile feelings toward people of the other party than members of another race.

"People are more likely to see their party as in the right, no matter what, and the other party as wrong," says Shanto Iyengar, the Stanford study's lead author. "People get more upset if they are asked to contemplate the prospect of their son or daughter marrying outside the party than outside their religion."

Hating the Other Guy

Indeed, over the past 50 years, the percentage of people who said they would disapprove if their children married someone from the other party has spiked from 5 percent to 40 percent.

This is the flip side of tending to support the position of your own party: Many people today not only disagree with but despise the other party and its adherents.

Republican opposition to policies President Obama has proposed has been a hallmark of his entire administration. When Bush was in office, conversely, Democrats made no secret of their disdain or even hatred of him.

Voters have an intuitive sense this is going on. How many times over the past four years have you heard the phrase, "Imagine the outrage if Bush had done X?"

"The other side is not just your opponent, but bad and evil," says Lara Brown, an independent political analyst. "Everyone flips positions based on who's in power."

All this makes it more difficult to achieve lasting consensus. If politics is a matter of partisan loyalty and personality, it's difficult to convince the broad majority of the country that an idea is right, no matter what.

"When issues were uncoupled from parties, one could make an appeal on the merits," says Jack Pitney, a government professor at Claremont McKenna College. "But to the extent issues are associated with the party, you win by mobilizing the party."

ARTICLE QUESTIONS

1) Why do people look to the position held by a party or party elites when forming an opinion?

2) Is there a political party you most align with? Why do you think you align with that party? Do your parents align with the same party?

3) Do you know anyone who has switched his or her opinion on a policy based on which political party was endorsing the policy?

11.3) Can Activists Win by Losing?

Congress.org, August 12, 2008

AMBREEN ALI

Even if they don't win, challengers can sway incumbents to rethink policies.

Since Democrats and Republicans compete to win "swing votes" in the political center, the two major parties often drift to the middle of the political spectrum. Third-party movements can inject strong and controversial views into the major parties' platforms. If the dominant parties continue to ignore third-party issues that gain enough public support, then the party risks losing supporters. In many cases, once a third-party issue gains enough popularity, either the Democrats or Republicans will adopt it, hoping to draw the support of the third-party voters. This process of engulfing third parties has led to numerous political reforms, such as the direct election of senators, voting rights for women, the elimination of child labor, prohibitions on drinking, worker safety protections, desegregation, the income tax, and limits on immigrants.

The list of reforms first advocated by third parties is so extensive that many political scientists argue that third-party organizations have influenced policy well beyond their levels of support. But just because many issues first advocated by third parties were later adopted doesn't necessarily tell us if running for office to promote an idea is effective. This is the question that Ambreen Ali asks in his article, "Can Activists Win by Losing?" Ali focuses on candidates who run for office so they can gain a platform to promote their ideas. Such candidates are often called "issue candidates" because they care more about an issue than actually winning office. Some of the people quoted in Ali's article support issue candidates; others argue that the money and effort directed to an electoral campaign could be better used by directly promoting the issue. What do you think?

Many West Virginians saw the late Sen. Robert Byrd as their champion, a Democratic incumbent who was willing to resist the coal industry's strong grasp over the state.

So when West Virginia's governor—who has called coal a "cornerstone fuel of the future"—made a bid for the Senate vacancy, Ken Hechler decided to step up.

"I don't think any one individual should anoint himself without competition to take the seat which Sen. Byrd occupied," said Hechler, a former congressman and secretary of state.

He told the *Charleston Daily Mail* that he didn't care if he actually won. Rather, his campaign would ensure that mountaintop removal mining—which many of the state's environmentalists and community advocates oppose—would be part of the electoral debate.

"A vote for me is not a vote for Ken Hechler," he said. "It's tantamount to a vote against mountain removal."

The 95-year-old challenger isn't the only activist-turn-politician in this year's elections. Many advocacy groups have endorsed candidates with a long shot of winning with the hope that they will force incumbents to address certain policy issues.

In South Carolina, environmentalist Tom Clements has been running as a third-party alternative to Republican Sen. Jim DeMint with a similar purpose.

"I'm gonna have fun doing this, and I want to raise some issues that I don't think would be raised if I weren't in the race," he told *The State* newspaper, mentioning concerns about coastal drilling, government spending, and fossil fuels.

Tea party groups have also embraced the strategy, picking fiscal conservatives to challenge incumbent Republicans and Democrats.

They have tried to make this election about limited government, free enterprise, and individual liberties—the tea-party trinity—instead of social issues like abortion or immigration.

"Our presence has caused candidates to return to talking about those core values," said Julianne Thompson, Georgia coordinator for Tea Party Patriots.

That happened in places like Alabama, where Republican Martha Roby defeated tea-party challenger Rick Barber. Though he lost, his bid may have influenced Roby to endorse tea-party ideas like requiring bills be posted for 72 hours before a vote can take place.

Of course, lawmakers aren't simply responding to the tea parties when they suggest lowering taxes and reducing government spending. Many voters share those concerns as the unemployment rate remains high and the economy recovers slowly.

But tea party leaders have been strategizing since last fall on how to use electoral politics to draw attention to their concerns.

"Two years ago, I don't think you could have predicted that the majority of the debate would be focused on these issues," said Mark Meckler, a national coordinator for the Patriots.

While Meckler believes they have been successful, others question whether a costly election bid is the best way to help a cause.

Candidates often have to spend a lot of money on advertising and campaigning before citizens and the media pay attention.

West Virginia's Hechler may be the most prominent mountaintop removal candidate, but he is not the first.

The Mountain Party has been running gubernatorial candidates for years without notice, according to local strategist Curtis Wilkerson. They usually poll in the single digits and lack sufficient funds for their campaigns.

"Far too often people don't know they're running," Wilkerson, who owns the consultancy Orion Strategies, said. In news stories, he said "they're listed in the et cetera of the story."

He also questioned Hechler's plan, saying that his election bid may actually be distracting voters from the coal-mining issue. Wilkerson believes Hechler's campaign money could have been better spent on issue-focused ads.

"The general public can't see beyond a 95-year-old candidate for the U.S. Senate," Wilkerson said. "That's defeating the purpose of him running."

Hechler defended his bid, saying he believes now that he could win.

"I've decided to abandon my humility and say that, my gosh, I'm going to go for it," he said.

If he doesn't win, Hechler still believes he will have pressured the new senator to reconsider how mining affects West Virginians.

"We will register thousands of voters to show their opposition to mountaintop removal on the ballot," he said.

ARTICLE QUESTIONS

1) What are the advantages and disadvantages with having "issue candidates" run for office? Do you think it is an effective strategy to promote policy reforms?

2) Would you vote for a candidate even if you know that he or she has no chance of winning the election? Why?

3) Should political structures should be changed to give third parties a better chance to win office? Why?

Chapter 12

Interest Groups

Interest groups are so central to American government that it is difficult to imagine our system without them. An *interest group is an organization dedicated to influencing government.* We often criticize interest groups for being selfish. But the average American belongs to two interest groups, donates to five, and is represented by dozens. Even if you don't join or donate to an interest group, you still benefit from many groups. In fact, interest groups and the lobbyists they employ advocate for almost everything you care about. They represent schools, hospitals, churches, the environment, the homeless, the elderly, gun owners, businesses and industries, and professions. Your college or university and your city or town probably has a lobby group paid to represent your interests. Even political science has a lobbyist in Washington!

Political scientists starting with James Madison and Alexis de Tocqueville have theorized about the role of interest groups in U.S. politics. This theorizing has produced competing concepts. Some scholars emphasize pluralism. Pluralists argue that the American political process is open to a diversity of interests; as long as open competition among groups continues, no single set of interests dominates. Pluralists view this open competition as allowing the collective good to ultimately prevail. In contrast, scholars sympathetic to power elite theory emphasize the dominance of some interests at the expense of others. These scholars contend that even though interest groups represent a wide spectrum of societal interests, they may not represent all interests equally well. From this perspective, the interests of the richest and most powerful carry disproportionate influence. Reflecting on the competing concepts of pluralism and power elite theory will help you better understand the readings in this chapter and many of the debates about U.S. politics you will encounter.

The first two readings in this chapter underscore a key conundrum in interest groups politics: interest groups provide an avenue to political power for underrepresented groups, but they often provide the best representation to the most privileged segments of society. Dara Strolovitch's *Affirmative Advocacy: Race, Class, and Gender in Interest Group Politics* clearly articulates this conundrum by employing components of both pluralism and power elite theory. She notes that groups excluded from the political process can—and often must—use interest groups to further their interests. At the same time, she observes that sustaining an interest group requires resources; therefore, those with the greatest resources—and the most political power—are often the best represented by interest groups.

Jonathan Salant and Lizzie O'Leary, in "Six Lobbyists per Lawmaker Work on Health Overhaul," provide an example of the interest group bias toward representing those with the greatest resources. Their article reports on the massive lobbying effort during the 2009 healthcare overhaul. They write that lobbyists were paid to "ensure that whatever measure eventually [became] law [didn't] cripple the industry they represent." The ability of those with the greatest resources and power to support the most powerful interest groups—which can further entrench their interests—creates a situation where the societal groups that most need interest group advocacy are often underrepresented.

In her article "Ready for a Surprise? Money Does Equal Access in Washington," Matea Gold reports on an experiment designed to test the assumption that money influences political outcomes. The results supported the assumption that those able to donate money are afforded greater access to elected officials and their staff. This finding may offer some evidence for power elite theory. While Gold's article supports an assumption about money and the influence of well-funded interest groups, *The New York Times* article "Hiring Federal Lobbyists, Towns Learn Money Talks," challenges another assumption. The article discusses the incredible financial resources that towns and cities have been able to acquire by hiring lobbyists. Americans often think of interest groups and the lobbyists they employ as entities representing interests they oppose. But—as pluralists assert and this article shows—interest groups and lobbyists don't just work on behalf of the rich and powerful.

A central puzzle in this chapter is whether interest groups' influence enhances American democracy or reinforces inequities. Pluralists emphasize the role of interest groups in providing an avenue to political power for underrepresented groups. Power elite theory focuses on interest groups' enhanced ability to represent elite interests. One of the most important challenges in U.S. politics is to figure out how interest group politics can expand access to political power to all societal groups (as pluralists hope) without allowing interest groups to reinforce elite dominance (as supporters of power elite theory fear).

CHAPTER QUESTIONS

1) What interest groups do you, your friends, and your family members belong to or support?
2) Why do people form interest groups?
3) What important role do interest groups play in a democracy? How might interest groups hinder democracy?
4) What segments of society are the most likely to form and benefit from interest groups?
5) In what ways do you think pluralism and power elite theory most accurately describe the role of interest groups in U.S. politics?

CHAPTER READINGS

12.1) Dara Strolovitch, *Affirmative Advocacy: Race, Class, and Gender in Interest Group Politics* [excerpts]. Chicago: University of Chicago Press, 2007.

12.2) Jonathan D. Salant and Lizzie O'Leary, "Six Lobbyists per Lawmaker Work on Health Overhaul," *Bloomberg News*, August 14, 2009.

12.3) Matea Gold, "Ready for a Surprise? Money Does Equal Access in Washington," *The Monkey Cage Blog*, March 11, 2014.

12.4) Jodi Rudoren and Aron Pilhofer, "Hiring Federal Lobbyists, Towns Learn Money Talks," *The New York Times*, July 2, 2006.

12.1) Affirmative Advocacy: Race, Class, and Gender in Interest Group Politics [excerpts]

Chicago: University of Chicago Press, 2007

DARA STROLOVITCH

> In *Affirmative Advocacy: Race, Class, and Gender in Interest Group Politics* Dara Strolovitch argues that national-level advocacy organizations—a particular type of interest group—are "a crucial conduit for the articulation and representation of disadvantaged interests in U.S. politics." She observes that interest groups provide one of the few avenues to political power for those excluded from the political process. In support of this observation she notes that before women gained the right to vote, and when African-Americans were denied access to the ballot, interest groups were formed to promote these groups' interests. Up to this point Strolovitch's argument is consistent with the concept of pluralism: the numerous access points for competing interests promote the collective good. However, Strolovitch's full argument is more consistent with power elite theory. She notes that even though "advocacy organizations often were the only voice for these [disadvantaged] groups, they were nonetheless comparatively weak and greatly outnumbered and out-resourced by business, financial, and professional interest groups."
>
> The biggest contribution of Strolovitch's research is based on her review of interest groups dedicated to advancing the interests of disadvantaged groups. Based on this review, she found that even groups dedicated to representing disadvantaged segments of society typically place more emphasis on advancing the interests of their most advantaged members. For example, interest groups promoting women's rights often do a better job of advancing the interests of economically privileged women. Strolovitch employs the term "intersectionally disadvantaged" to describe people who are part of a disadvantaged subgroup within a disadvantaged group. Strolovitch notes that interest groups often devote the least attention to the most disadvantaged subgroups among their constituents. Despite this finding, Strolovitch sees the results of her research as positive. As part of her research, she identified specific strategies used by organizations that do the best job of advocating for the intersectionally disadvantaged.

Writers since Alexis de Tocqueville have recognized that American civic organizations are a key component of a healthy democratic society and citizenry. Tocqueville and his intellectual descendants argue that civil-society organizations, including everything from unions to bowling leagues, promote democratic values such as freedom of speech and association, social capital, civic participation, leadership skills, trust in government, and cross-class alliances.

One form of civic organization—national-level advocacy or social movement organizations—has historically been a crucial conduit for the articulation and representation of disadvantaged interests in U.S. politics, particularly for groups that are ill served by the two major political parties. Advocacy organizations have presented historically marginalized groups with an alternative mode of representation within an electoral system that provides insufficient means for transmitting the preferences and interests of those citizens. For many years, these organizations often were the sole political voice afforded groups such as southern blacks and women of all races, who were denied formal voting rights until well into the twentieth century. Long before women won the right to vote in 1920, for example, organizations such as the National American Woman Suffrage Association (formed in 1890) and the National Woman's Party (formed in 1913) mobilized women and lobbied legislators on their behalf, providing some insider access for the mass movements with which they were associated. Similarly, the National Association for the Advancement of Colored People (NAACP, formed in 1909) provided political and legal representation for African Americans in the

South who, after a brief period of voting following Reconstruction and the passage of the Fifteenth Amendment in 1870, were largely disenfranchised and denied formal representation until the passage and enforcement of the Voting Rights Act of 1965.

While advocacy organizations often were the only voice for these groups, they were nonetheless comparatively weak, greatly outnumbered and out-resourced by business, financial, and professional interest groups.The 1960s and 1970s, however, witnessed an explosion in the number of movements and organizations speaking on behalf of disadvantaged populations. Mass mobilization and increased representation led to greater opportunity and mobility for many women, members of racial minority groups, and low-income people. . . . Organizations advocating on their behalf pursued lawsuits, regulations, and legislation aimed at ending de jure racial and sex-based discrimination and increasing resources and opportunities for those groups, and many of their efforts bore fruit.

In 1963, for example, the Equal Pay Act prohibited sex-based wage discrimination. The following year saw the passage of the 1964 Civil Rights Act, which barred discrimination in public accommodations, in government, and in employment, and established the Equal Employment Opportunity Commission (EEOC) to investigate complaints of discrimination and impose penalties on offenders. That same year, the United States Congress passed the Economic Opportunity Act, the centerpiece of President Lyndon Johnson's War on Poverty, creating programs to attack poverty and unemployment through, for example, job training, education, legal services, and community health centers. In 1965, the Voting Rights Act prohibited racial discrimination in voting, amendments to the Immigration and Nationality Act liberalized national-origins quotas in immigration, and the Social Security Act established Medicare and Medicaid, providing health care for elderly and low-income people. That was also the year that President Johnson signed Executive Order 11246, calling on federal government contractors to "take affirmative action" against discrimination based

on "race, creed, color, or national origin." Two years later, in 1967, this order was extended by Executive Order 11375 to include sex-based discrimination. Title IX of the Education Amendments of 1972 banned sex discrimination in schools. In 1973, the Supreme Court struck down the restrictive abortion laws that were on the books in most states at that time and upheld a 1968 EEOC ruling prohibiting sex-segregated "help wanted" ads in newspapers. Also in 1973, Congress passed the Equal Credit Opportunity Act, prohibiting discrimination on the basis of sex, race, marital status, religion, national origin, age, or receipt of public assistance in consumer credit practices.

With these developments came increased resources, newly fortified rights, more political power, and greater levels of mobilization than ever before for groups such as women, racial minorities, and low-income people.

. . . As James Q. Wilson observes in the introduction to the revised version of his 1974 classic *Political Organizations*. "Since roughly 1970 we have entered a new era. Groups once excluded are now included. Pluralism that once was a distant promise is now a baffling reality." However, he continues, "we are all represented by groups, and yet we all feel we all feel unrepresented. A thousand voices are heard in Washington, but none sounds like our own."

. . . It is, in fact, less and less the case that once excluded groups such as women, racial minorities, and low-income people simply have no representation in national politics and policy making. Indeed, there are many organizations (and increasing numbers of elected representatives) that advocate on their behalf in the policy process. However, the nature and extent of this advocacy is extremely uneven, and its net result is to privilege advantaged subgroups of those constituencies and to marginalize the interests of disadvantaged ones. Organizations are simply far less active when it comes to issues affecting intersectionally marginalized groups. They compensate somewhat for these low levels of activity by engaging in coalitions that address disadvantaged-subgroup issues and by making relatively generous use of court tactics when it comes to such issues (at least when compared with majority issues). Nonetheless, activities in these two realms more often reinforce rather rectify the biases against intersectionally disadvantaged subgroups that are present in the broader political environment in which the relative power of organizations that speak for marginalized groups remains far less than that of the multitude of other organizations that represent advantaged constituencies.

Although these findings might seem logical from a strategic point of view, especially in light of concerns about organizational maintenance and in the context of a hostile political climate and limited resources, they are cause for concern. It may indeed be reasonable for organizations to focus their energies on the issues that they believe hold the greatest interest or have the broadest impact on their constituency or on issues that demand immediate attention, but I have shown that neither of these logics governs how organizations actually allocate their time and resources or explains their low levels of attention to disadvantaged constituents. Instead, organizations employ a double standard that determines the level of energy they devote to issues affecting subgroups of their broader constituency, a double standard based on the status of the subgroup affected rather than on the breadth or depth of the impact of the policy issue in question. As a consequence, the issues affecting advantaged subgroups receive disproportionately high levels of attention and resources, while issues affecting marginalized and disadvantaged subgroups, with some important exceptions, receive disproportionately *low* levels. This imbalance persists even in cases where the disadvantaged-subgroup issues affect a substantial portion of a constituency and when they are on the legislative, administrative, or judicial agenda.

Even if it were true that low levels of activity on disadvantaged-subgroup issues were the result of calculated decisions to focus on salient issues that have a broad impact, it would nonetheless be neither logical nor fair to sacrifice the interests of intersectionally disadvantaged groups to those of the majority. Asking weak constituencies to subsume their interests to those of privileged subgroups is even more troubling. Moreover, it is clear from the survey and interview data that the dedicated and well-intentioned officers at these organizations do not *want* to underserve intersectionally marginalized subgroups of their constituencies. In fact, the evidence shows just the opposite: The advocacy groups in this study position themselves as advocates for the weak and voiceless and lay claim to the egalitarian goals of the social movements with which they are affiliated. With the political legitimacy and power that derive from these claims comes the expectation that they will represent all members of their constituencies, using their positions to mediate among these constituencies as well as between their constituents and the constituents of other marginalized groups.

Not every organization can represent every constituent or potential constituent at all times, nor can organizations flout the exigencies of organizational maintenance or focus exclusively on disadvantaged subgroups to the exclusion of majorities and advantaged subgroups. Advocacy organizations must walk a fine line as they negotiate the task of using insider tactics to fight for outsider groups in national politics, balancing the need for legitimacy with both grassroots constituencies and affluent donors and policy-making elites. However, an intersectional approach helps us appreciate that neglecting the inequalities within marginalized groups widens the gaps among differently situated members of these groups and privileges those subgroups within their constituencies that are already the most advantaged. For organizations that charge themselves with narrowing the gaps among racial, gender, and economic groups within politics and society, the expectation that they will represent multiply marginalized constituents becomes increasingly important under conditions of advanced marginalization, as levels of political access rise and the status and living conditions of relatively privileged members of once excluded groups improve. Even, and perhaps especially, when these improvements are under siege, defending them ought to be accompanied by attempts to pursue changes that benefit members of marginalized groups who have benefited least from those previous victories.

In this context, many of the findings presented throughout this book raise red flags about the quality of representation afforded intersectionally disadvantaged subgroups by the organizations on which they rely to compensate for their relative lack of political power and formal representation. As such, the results reinforce the claims of scholars . . . who have drawn our attention to a wide range of significant limitations to interest groups and other national-level staff-led organizations when it comes to improving conditions for disadvantaged populations. The patterns I have described reveal that the overall level and tenor of advocacy on issues affecting intersectionally disadvantaged subgroups is lower and less rigorous than it is when it comes to other issue types. In addition, organizations pass up crucial opportunities to act as mediators for disadvantaged subgroups among the differently situated groups that make up their constituencies and between these constituencies and the larger polity. Instead, much of the mediating that they do *compounds* the problems faced by intersectionally disadvantaged groups. Rather than inspiring feelings of intersectionally linked fate by asking their *more*-advantaged constituents to help their less-advantaged ones, they are more likely to ask less-advantaged constituents to make do with those benefits that eventually trickle down to them. Failing to make the case for these multiply marginalized subgroups within their constituencies and within the broader community of organizations representing marginalized groups limits the possibility that they will do so effectively to the larger polity. This limitation reinforces rather than alleviates the marginalization of intersectionally disadvantaged constituents. In spite of sincere ambitions to advocate on behalf of their least advantaged constituents, then, the organizations that claim to speak for intersectionally disadvantaged subgroups are not effectively representing them in national politics. Instead, the voices and concerns of these groups are drowned out and marginalized by the majority and especially by advantaged subgroups. As a consequence, for intersectionally marginalized groups, the quality of representation is inferior to that received by advantaged subgroups.

The implications of this state of affairs are even more profound when considered in light of the modest proportion of the larger interest group universe that continues to be constituted by organizations that represent marginalized groups. Using data collected by Kay Lehman Schlozman, Sidney Verba, and Henry Brady as part of the Project on Political Equality, Scholzman and Traci Burch show that of the nearly 12,000 organizations listed in the 2001 edition of *Washington Representatives,* 35 percent represent corporations, 13 percent represent trade and other business associations, and 7 percent represent occupational groups. Less than 5 percent are public interest groups, less than 4 percent are identity-based organizations representing groups such as women, racial minorities, and LGBT people, and only 1 percent are labor unions. Only a fraction of 1 percent of the organizations are social welfare organizations or organizations that represent poor and low-income people, a proportion that remains almost identical to the proportion that Schlozman and Tierney found almost twenty years earlier.

Considered together, the small proportion of social and economic justice organizations within the overall interest group system and the biases within these organizations themselves powerfully demonstrate the tremendous hurdles and disadvantages faced by groups such as women, racial minorities, and low-income people in their quest for representation in national politics.

Story of Possibility

Despite this rather dreary picture, the data also reveal that advocacy organizations play a crucial role in combating a broader mobilization of bias in politics and public opinion. Consequently, these organizations offer an alternative conception of representation that foregrounds the importance of advocacy, redistribution, and the pursuit of social justice as some of its central goals. A wide array of evidence demonstrates that advocacy organizations *want to* represent intersectionally disadvantaged subgroups of their constituencies, and there are circumstances and conditions under which they do so. Consequently, in spite of the current shortcomings, such organizations serve as some of the best possibilities that marginal groups have for gaining an institutionalized voice in American politics. Conceived in this way, interest groups are an underused and undervalued democratic form of the sort that Young suggests we look to in order to improve representation for marginalized groups, building on and working within the structure and strictures of the American electoral system while simultaneously working to transform it.

ARTICLE QUESTIONS

1) Strolovitch credits organizations advocating on the behalf of "women, members of racial minority groups, and low-income people" with achieving what specific policy successes?

2) Do you agree with Strolovitch's conclusion that "interest groups are an underused and undervalued democratic form" that can "improve representation of marginalized groups"?

3) How can interest groups be structured to better represent disadvantaged groups?

12.2) Six Lobbyists per Lawmaker Work on Health Overhaul

Bloomberg News, August 14, 2009

JONATHAN D. SALANT AND LIZZIE O'LEARY

Interest groups large and small spend an estimated $8 billion a year attempting to influence Washington policymaking. The fact that the largest amount of spending on lobbyists comes from groups representing multibillion-dollar businesses, financial interests, and professional organizations could indicate support for power elite theory. Obviously, economically disadvantaged groups have fewer resources to spend on lobbyists. Still, the facts that lobbyists are employed by a wide spectrum of interests and that business interests often lose on issues they spend heavily to influence could be viewed as adding some support for the theory of pluralism.

Jonathan Salant and Lizzie O'Leary, in "Six Lobbyists per Lawmaker Work on Health Overhaul," report on the massive lobbying effort during the 2009 healthcare overhaul. The article continues the debate between pluralism and elite power theory. On the one hand, the article notes that the lobbyists working on the healthcare legislation represented views "on all sides of the issue." This supports the pluralist idea of competing interests canceling each other out. On the other hand, the article notes that the volume of money invested in the healthcare overhaul is potentially "drowning out the voices of citizens and the groups that speak for them."

If there is any doubt that President Barack Obama's plan to overhaul U.S. health care is the hottest topic in Congress, just ask the 3,300 lobbyists who have lined up to work on the issue.

That's six lobbyists for each of the 535 members of the House and Senate, according to Senate records, and three times the number of people registered to lobby on defense. More than 1,500 organizations have health-care lobbyists, and about three more are signing up each day. Every one of the 10 biggest lobbying firms by revenue is involved in an effort that could affect 17 percent of the U.S. economy.

These groups spent $263.4 million on lobbying during the first six months of 2009, according to the Center for Responsive Politics, a Washington-based research group, more than any other industry. They spent $241.4 million during the same period of

2008. Drugmakers alone spent $134.5 million, 64 percent more than the next biggest spenders, oil and gas companies.

"Whenever you have a big piece of legislation like this, it's like ringing the dinner bell for K Street," said Bill Allison, a senior fellow at the Sunlight Foundation, a Washington-based watchdog group, referring to the street in the capital where many lobbying firms have offices.

Stock Prices

Health-insurer and managed-care stocks have gained this year, led by WellCare Health Plans Inc., based in Tampa, Florida; Cigna Corp., based in Philadelphia; and Coventry Health Care Inc., a Bethesda, Maryland, company. The three paced a 13 percent increase in the Standard & Poor's Supercomposite Managed Health Care Index since Jan. 1. Drugmaker shares have stagnated.

Health-care lobbyists said their efforts are the biggest since the successful 1986 effort to overhaul the tax code. The result is a debate involving thousands of disparate voices, forcing Congress to pick winners and losers.

"There's a lot of money at stake and there are a lot of special interests who don't want their ox gored," Allison said.

The lobbyists are on all sides of the issue. Pharmaceutical Research and Manufacturers of America, the Washington-based trade group for drug companies such as Thousand Oaks, California-based Amgen Inc. and New York-based Pfizer Inc., has embraced a health-care overhaul.

Amgen, Pfizer

Lobbying by Amgen, the world's largest biotechnology company, is intended to "effectively shape health-care policy," said Kelley Davenport, a spokeswoman. Pfizer, the world's largest drugmaker, is "dedicated to insuring that our voice is heard," said spokesman Ray Kerins.

The Washington-based U.S. Chamber of Commerce, the nation's largest business lobby, is opposing efforts to offer government-run health insurance to compete with private companies. The chamber spent $26 million in the first six months of 2009 to lobby, more than any other group.

For lobbyists, the goal is to ensure that whatever measure eventually becomes law doesn't cripple the industry they represent.

"They assume health-care reform is going to happen and they want to be protected," said John Jonas, a partner with the lobbying firm of Patton Boggs LLP in Washington.

Patton Boggs, the top lobbying firm in terms of revenue, has three dozen clients in the health-care debate, including New York-based Bristol-Myers Squibb Co., and Bentonville, Arkansas-based Wal-Mart Stores Inc., more than any other lobbying firm.

Bristol-Myers, Walmart

Brian Henry, a spokesman for Bristol-Myers, maker of the world's No. 2 best-selling drug Plavix, said the company wants to ensure any legislation preserves incentives for innovation. "We believe the health-care system needs to be reformed and we've specifically supported an employer mandate and cost-containment measures," said Greg Rossiter, a spokesman for Walmart, the largest U.S. employer.

The lobbyists fill the appointment books of lawmakers, and line up at House and Senate office buildings. The staff of Senate Finance Committee Chairman Max Baucus, a Montana Democrat, rotates weekly meetings among the various groups in the health-care debate, providers one week, purchasers a second, consumers a third.

"We hear from lobbyists all the time," said Representative Frank Pallone, a New Jersey Democrat who heads the House Energy and Commerce health subcommittee.

The blitz by lobbyists carries a risk for the public, said Larry McNeely, a health-care advocate with the Boston-based U.S. Public Interest Research Group.

'Drowning Out'

"The sheer quantity of money that's sloshed around Washington is drowning out the voices of citizens and the groups that speak up for them," said McNeely, whose group backs a public health plan, which Obama and many Democrats consider a centerpiece of any proposal and most Republicans oppose.

The lobbying push also risks delaying legislation, said Rogan Kersh, associate dean at New York University's Wagner School of Public Service.

"That amount of activity is inevitably going to slow down the process," Kersh said.

The quest for influence isn't limited to lobbying. Health-care advocates have spent $53 million on commercials, according to Arlington, Virginia-based TNS Media Intelligence/Campaign Media Analysis, which tracks advertising spending.

The health-care industry also contributed $20.5 million to federal candidates and the political parties during the first six months of the year, according to the Center for Responsive Politics. Senate Majority Leader Harry Reid, a Nevada Democrat who is up for re-election next year, received $382,400, more than any other lawmaker.

"There is a cacophony going on with so much money and so many individuals hoping to shape the legislation," said Sheila Krumholz, executive director of the Center for Responsive Politics, a Washington-based research group.

The number of lobbyists could grow once Congress returns next month and resumes efforts to enact legislation by the end of the year.

"They have just decided this is serious enough and more fully understand the impact it's going to have," Jonas said.

ARTICLE QUESTIONS

1) According to the article, what group spent the most on lobbying on healthcare in the first six months of 2009? What position did the organization take?
2) In what ways beyond lobbying does the article cite interest groups spending money to influence healthcare legislation?
3) Do you think this article provides more support for the pluralist or the power elite theory of interest group politics?
4) What would be the advantages and disadvantages of preventing lobbying on healthcare reform?

12.3) Ready for a Surprise? Money Does Equal Access in Washington

The Monkey Cage Blog, March 11, 2014

MATEA GOLD

It is often assumed that money and lobbying carry influence. In fact, elite power theory is in part supported by citing the massive campaign and lobbyist spending by wealthy, corporate, and financial interests. But can the influence of money on politics be proven? Matea Gold, in her *Monkey Cage Blog* article "Ready for a Surprise? Money Does Equal Access in Washington," reports on an experiment designed by two political science graduate students who were attempting to answer this very question. The experiment consisted of sending two sets of emails. In one set "a donor" sought a meeting with a member of Congress, while in the other set "a constituent" did so. "Donors" were significantly more likely than "constituents" to get a meeting with a member of Congress or a high-level staffers. This is an important finding because it shows an instance of money affording access. However, the results do not show what donating money (or having the ability to donate money) provides beyond access; it is still an open question whether someone's potential to donate money increases the influence of his or her views. Randomized field studies like this one are increasingly being used by political scientists to better understand important political questions. Can you think of a field study that could help prove that someone's potential to donate money increases the influence of his or her views?

It's a widely accepted truism in Washington: Campaign donations buy access. While that belief governs much about the way politics operate, there's a surprising lack of scientific evidence to bolster that assumption, which is the subject of substantial academic debate.

Two political science graduate students are now seeking to bring some precision to that discussion through the kind of randomized, controlled study used to test the impact of pharmaceuticals.

Joshua Kalla at Yale University and David Broockman at the University of California, Berkeley, are out today with the results of a novel field experiment that measured how campaign donations—even the prospect of them—alter the behavior of members of Congress and their staff. To do so, they recruited the help of a real political group, the liberal organization CREDO Action, and embedded the experiment into a real lobbying effort during last summer's August recess, when the group sought to secure co-sponsors for a chemical-banning bill.

Here's how it worked: Last summer, a group of CREDO fellows e-mailed congressional offices seeking meetings to discuss the measure, sending one of two different form letters.

The first e-mail had the subject line: "Meeting with local campaign donors about cosponsoring bill." The body of the e-mail said that about a dozen CREDO members "who are active political donors" were interested in meeting with the member of Congress in his or her home district to discuss the legislation.

The second e-mail stripped out the donor references and instead said "local constituents" were looking to meet the member of Congress.

In both cases, CREDO organizers noted that if a House member was not available, the group sought to meet with the most senior staffer available.

The e-mails went out to 191 members of Congress—all members of the same political party—who had not already co-sponsored the bill.

(The study's authors do not disclose which party the members represented, but it's safe to assume they were Democrats, considering CREDO's political orientation.) Each office was randomly assigned one of the two e-mails, with about two-thirds getting the request from constituents and one-third getting the request from donors.

It's worth noting that all those who met with congressional offices were real CREDO members or political donors, none of whom knew they were part of an experiment.

The results: Only 2.4 percent of the offices made the member of Congress or chief of staff available when they believed those attending were just constituents, but 12.5 percent did when they were told the attendees were political donors.

Also, nearly one in five of the donor groups got access to a senior staffer, while just 5.5 percent of the constituent groups did. That means the donors had more than three times the access to top staffers than the constituents.

Broockman said he was surprised by the size of the difference, and noted that the study may actually underestimate the access of political donors, since none of the offices were told ahead of time the identities of the contributors, how much they had given—or even whether they had donated to that member of Congress.

That was done to address a question raised in the Supreme Court's *Citizens United* decision, which argued that lawmakers are not influenced by political money that does not go directly to their campaigns.

"That was a really key piece," Broockman said. "It gets very far away from the quid pro quos that the court suggested are the only ways influence operates."

The study, currently under consideration for publication, drew praise from Donald P. Green, a professor of political science at Columbia University and expert in the use of field experimentation to study politics, who reviewed the results and said they showed a small but clear pattern.

"It's convincing, but not overwhelming," said Green, adding that he is eager to see others attempt to replicate the study in other arenas.

He praised the rigor of the experiment, saying such a randomized field study was long overdue.

"What is interesting is that it was done on the left, so it cannot be dismissed as a cheap shot at the right-of-center donors who are so often in the news," said Green, who taught both Kalla and Broockman as undergraduates at Yale.

Becky Bond, political director for CREDO, which frequently participates in social science experiments, said she is not worried that the group will now have a harder time getting access to members of Congress who might be put off by being used as guinea pigs.

"We are really committed to having science have an impact on all of these discussions," she said. "I have concerns that we don't have more of these experiments that help tell us the impact of money and politics."

ARTICLE QUESTIONS

1) How much more likely did the study find that a member of Congress or their chief of staff would be available when they believed they were meeting with political donors rather than constituents?

2) Why do you think "there's a surprising lack of scientific evidence" that campaign donations buy access?

3) How important are the findings of this experiment? What do we know based on this information? What remains unknown based on the findings of this experiment?

4) Design an experiment that would further our knowledge about the influence of money on political outcomes.

12.4) Hiring Federal Lobbyists, Towns Learn Money Talks

The New York Times, July 2, 2006

JODI RUDOREN AND ARON PILHOFER

Most of us enjoy the benefits of a lobbyist—without even knowing about it. The name *lobbyist* was originally given to someone who hung around the Capitol lobby waiting to grab the attention of a congressmember to advocate for a particular policy. Today a lobbyist is defined as someone who contacts government officials (even outside of the Capitol lobby) on behalf of a particular cause or issue.

In "Hiring Federal Lobbyists, Towns Learn Money Talks," Jodi Rudoren and Aron Pilhofer provide an example of lobbyists advocating for resources that benefit people even without their knowledge. As the article notes, "cities and towns—and school districts and transit authorities and utility agencies—across the country are increasingly . . . putting lobbyists on retainer to leverage their local tax dollars into federal tax dollars." As Rudoren and Pilhofer report, when a local government agency is faced with raising taxes, increasing fees, or cutting services, it is often a better investment to hire a lobbyist to get money from the federal government. The article provides numerous examples. For example, Treasure Island, a small town in Florida, "yielded $285.83 in federal money" for every dollar it paid to its lobbyist organization. A potential problem with this strategy is that this advocacy rarely increases the total money spent on local government; it just redirects where the money is going. This can mean that local governments that hire lobbyists are flooded with cash while equally needy governments see their revenue streams dry up.

The article notes that many of the federal dollars directed to local governments came in the form of earmarks, which are funds appropriated to a particular project. Congress banned earmarks in 2011. But there are loopholes in what counts as an earmark, and there are many sources of revenue that can pay for local projects. Lobbyists discover many ways to direct funds to local projects—even if the money is directed through procedures not labeled "earmarks."

TREASURE ISLAND, Fla.—Rebuffed on several requests for state and federal financing to help rebuild its crumbling bridge, this small resort town was all but resigned to raising the money by doubling the 50-cent bridge toll, increasing property taxes and issuing bonds.

But in a last-ditch gambit, city officials hired a federal lobbyist who had known the local congressman for four decades. Within weeks, the congressman, Representative C. W. Bill Young, called the mayor to say he had slipped a special $50 million appropriation, known as an earmark, into an omnibus bill.

The city had originally sought $15 million. But Mr. Young—a Republican who was then the all-powerful chairman of the Appropriations Committee and, as his lobbyist friend knew, believes public roads should be free—raised it to eliminate the toll.

Since that windfall three years ago, Treasure Island has continued to pay $5,000 a month to the lobbying firm, Alcalde & Fay, and has continued to reap earmarks: $500,000 to fix a sewer plant, $625,000 to repair wooden walkways over the dunes, $450,000 for pedestrian crosswalks.

"They're worth every penny they get," said Mayor Mary Maloof, who led a parade of antique cars to open the new bridge on June 10. "When we started talking about it, there were plenty of eyebrows raised that we would be doing such a thing. But it's turned out to be a valuable tool for helping us cover costs."

Cities and towns—and school districts and transit authorities and utility agencies—across the country are increasingly reaching for that same toolbox, putting lobbyists on retainer to leverage their local tax dollars into federal tax dollars.

Since 1998, the number of public entities hiring private firms to represent them in Washington has nearly doubled to 1,421 from 763, as places like Treasure Island, population 7,514, have jumped

onboard with behemoths like Miami that have long had lobbyists.

Most of these new clients had never sought earmarks—some had never even heard of them—before someone knocked on their door, essentially offering big pots for a pittance. Others had read in the newspaper about neighbors with lobbyists building bridges or beach walks and felt pressure to keep up with the municipal Joneses.

"We're all in competition for the same dollars, and you want all the advantages you can have," said John Litton, city manager in Lake Mary, Fla., about 20 miles north of Orlando.

The collective bill over eight years has topped $640 million.

Enlisted almost exclusively to land earmarks, lobbyists for local governments have boomed alongside a broader explosion in such appropriations, to 12,852 items worth $64 billion last year from 4,219 pet projects totaling $27.7 billion in 1998. The prolific earmarking does not change the overall budget's bottom line, but how the pie is cut: dollars are doled out, often in secret, at the whim of a lone legislator—often under the influence of a lobbyist—rather than through a competitive process.

It is against the law to use federal money to hire lobbyists. Yet local officials' near-unanimous justification is that the lobbyists pay for themselves many times over through the infusion of federal funds.

Ronald D. Utt, a senior fellow at the Heritage Foundation and a frequent critic of earmarks, said he was most troubled at seeing firms solicit public clients with virtual guarantees that they could deliver "dollars for pennies" (or billions for millions).

"The mystery to me is the way they are able to promise returns," Mr. Utt said, pointing to the revolving door between Congressional appropriators' payrolls and lobby shops, as well as to lobbyists' generous campaign contributions. "It goes beyond mere influence peddling to just out-right, classic third-world corruption."

The most vivid case of earmark-related corruption came with the conviction this year of Jack Abramoff for trading huge fees from Indian tribes for influence with lawmakers. Public entities have also played a prominent role in the current federal investigation of the links between Representative Jerry Lewis, the current Appropriations Committee chairman, and the lobbying firm Copeland Lowery Jacquez Denton & White, leading to sub-poenas of several of the firm's government clients in Mr. Lewis's Southern California district.

Lobbyists say there is nothing improper in their political activity. In fact, they use it as a sell-ing point. In a 2002 proposal to the City of Pembroke Pines, an Alcalde lobbyist pointed to monthly fund-raisers the firm held at its offices in Arlington, Va., and said attending events "very frequently" for Republicans and Democrats alike "does allow us to better our local government clients."

Although local officials are rarely active in the campaign-contribution race that accompanies the earmarks derby, the firm's employees have given upward of $200,000 to more than 100 politicians since 1997, nearly half in Florida and in other states where it has clusters of public clients.

"Because we enjoy a considerable clientele from the private sector," the Alcalde proposal read, "we are able to significantly participate in the political and fund-raising process that might at times better enable us to access public policy makers on behalf of all the firm's clients."

Beyond any question of quid pro quo, however, some critics say the new ubiquity of private lobby-ists paid with public money perverts basic demo-cratic tenets. Of the 250 top-grossing firms in Washington, 48 have state, local and tribal govern-ments as their leading source of revenue, far more than any other sector, according to the Center for Public Integrity, which monitors lobbying.

Tim Phillips, president of Americans for Pros-perity, one of several Washington watchdog groups critical of earmarks, said it was local politi-cians' mandate to make their needs known—and the job of members of Congress to look out for them.

"If you're a mayor or a city councilman and you have to hire a lobbyist, what a gross admission of failure on your part," Mr. Phillips said. "I would think they have a fiduciary responsibility to not put taxpayer dollars into lobbyists when they're elected to be, really, the lobbyist for the people."

The mayors and city council members, though, point to the special appropriations as proof of their fiscal prudence.

Alcalde & Fay is one of three firms—along with Patton Boggs and the Ferguson Group—that col-lected $25 million from public clients in the past eight years, much more than any other lobbyists. A close look at Alcalde & Fay's 44 public clients in Florida alone shows that, since 2001, $9.8 million in lobbying fees translated into $173 million in ear-marks, or a return of $18.41 on every dollar spent.

In Treasure Island, each dollar to Alcalde & Fay yielded $285.83 in federal money.

A Game Changed

To understand how the game has changed, con-sider the visit of West Virginia University leaders to Senator Robert C. Byrd's office one day in 1989.

They went to see Mr. Byrd—a Democrat long known as the "prince of pork" for pumping money into hometown projects, and then the chairman of the Appropriations Committee—about a research center. When the senator learned the delegation included several lobbyists, he directed them to wait in the lobby.

Mr. Byrd asked for an $18 million earmark, then withdrew the request after an article in *The Washington Post* revealed that the lobbying firm, Cassidy & Associates, was the origin of the univer-sity's idea for where to seek the money.

"I'm on the Appropriations Committee—if I can't do it, nobody can," The Post quoted Mr. Byrd as saying. "Why do you waste your money on a lobbyist when I'm being paid to be your senator?"

These days, such comments seem quaint.

Some lawmakers still insist that lobbyists are unnecessary for local governments, but far from being kicked out of meetings on Capitol Hill, the lobbyists typically arrange them.

When Ms. Maloof, the Treasure Island mayor, makes her annual pilgrimage to Washington to press her case, her lobbyist, L. A. Bafalis—a former Republican Congressman from Florida—picks her up at the airport and escorts her through the day's meetings, paying for lunch in the Capitol's members-only dining room.

A typical monthly retainer is $5,000, with raises over time—and success. For that, according to interviews with more than a dozen Alcalde & Fay clients, the firm sends weekly e-mail messages detailing available federal grants and arranges once-a-year visits to Washington. In between, some clients speak to their lobbyists weekly, while others go a month or more without a phone call.

The Municipalities Practice Group at Alcalde, which accounts for about half the firm's client roster and a third of its $12 million annual revenue, was born with the firm, in 1973. Hector Alcalde had been chief of staff to a congressman from Tampa for a dozen years, and his first client was the Tampa Port Authority, which still pays the firm about $80,000 a year, according to Senate reports.

The City of Tampa eventually signed on, too. And the surrounding county, Hillsborough. Then the neighboring county, Pinellas. The City of Clearwater, 23 miles west of Tampa, became a client in the 1990's, and it was Alcalde & Fay's success in getting Clearwater $22 million in 2000 to replace its own bridge that got Treasure Island's attention.

And so on.

In the 2002 pitch to Pembroke Pines, Alcalde & Fay boasted of having 35 public clients on its roster, including many of the town's neighbors. Now it has 85.

"All of them say, 'We're paying taxes, this is a way for us to get back our fair share of what we're paying into,'" said Andy Wahlquist, a partner who handles several of the firm's public clients in Florida.

Noting the proliferation of earmarks, Kevin Fay, the firm's president, said, "They're compelled to try to get some of that money if the programs are out there."

A snapshot analysis shows that hiring a lobbyist seems to help.

Looking at the 10 Florida cities with populations closest to Treasure Island's, none have lobbyists registered with the Senate; the only earmark among them was $25,000 last year for a veterans' memorial at Alachua City Hall.

North Miami Beach and Homestead, Alcalde & Fay clients with about 40,000 residents each, got a combined $13 million in earmarks in the past five years, while six cities of similar size got none. (Dunedin, population 35,691, lacked a lobbyist but got three earmarks totaling $2.7 million while its congressman, Mr. Young, ran the Appropriations Committee.)

Local leaders say they lack both the knowledge of bureaucratic procedures and the political contacts to navigate the complex world of federal appropriations. Besides, they are thousands of miles from Washington, picking up garbage and running recreation programs and putting police officers on beats.

Cyndie Goudeau, the Clearwater city clerk, said she could comfortably approach her own congressman, Mr. Young, "but if I walk into a representative or a senator's office that's not from this area, they don't know me from a man on the moon."

"But they know Danielle, they know Hector Alcalde, they know that firm," Ms. Goudeau said, referring to Danielle McBeth, the Alcalde partner who handles Clearwater's account. "If we didn't have one, we wouldn't be getting the funding we're getting."

In the past five years, Clearwater has collected 37 earmarks totaling some $30 million, or $26.25 for each dollar paid to Alcalde & Fay. Besides the sleek, curvaceous bridge leading from downtown to the city's island beaches, the city collected $4 million to transform the streetscape along the water, $1.5 million for a homeless shelter, $1 million for police technology and more.

"In a perfect world, you wouldn't need them," Ms. Goudeau said as she showed off the bridge one recent morning. "But the world's not perfect."

Flying to Washington in February, Joe A. Martinez, chairman of the Miami-Dade County Commission, studied biographies of members of the transportation committee he hoped to persuade to finance a new commuter rail line. He noticed one, Representative Corinne Brown, from Florida, but she is a Democrat—he is not—and from Jacksonville, the other end of the state.

So he called Mr. Alcalde. It turns out that Ms. Brown's daughter, Shantrel Brown Fields, is an associate at the firm.

"I had a meeting with her the next day," Mr. Martinez said of Representative Brown. "I got results."

Last year, Miami-Dade spent more than any other government entity on lobbying, $1.36 million. Totaling fees for the past eight years, it ranks sixth, with $6.7 million; topping the charts are the Metropolitan Water District of Southern California and the Gila River Indian Community, which each spent more than $10 million.

Spreading the Wealth

In general, the largest states had the most public entities with lobbyists—and the biggest fees—but there are notable exceptions: Louisiana ranks fifth, for example, with its government agencies spending nearly $24 million from 1998 to 2005, and Puerto Rico ranks ninth, with $19 million, about the same as Michigan, Illinois and Pennsylvania, which have two or three times Puerto Rico's 3.8 million people.

Mr. Martinez said that after taking over as Miami-Dade chairman last year, he decided to slash the lobbying budget in half, fire 8 of the 11 firms on contract and send his own employee to open a Washington office. But that employee does not have the contacts, Mr. Martinez said: "He doesn't have access to all these people."

Large governments like Miami-Dade—along with ports, airports and public utilities—have long had people in Washington looking out for their interests. What has changed in the past few years is the number of smaller entities looking to get in on the action.

The number of cities with lobbyists, for example, has grown to 511 from 234 in 1998, and the number of counties has also doubled, to 186 from 85. Fifty-nine public school districts had lobbyists last year, up from 19 in 1998, while the number of police and fire departments with their own paid representatives jumped to 16, from just 2.

In Florida, Lake Mary, population 13,922, signed up for $5,000 a month in 2002, joining the two nearby county governments, the local airport, the wastewater authority and the nearby towns of Sanford (population 49,252) and Oviedo (population 30,800) on Alcalde & Fay's client list. But after three years, $220,000 and half a dozen requests for money, all Lake Mary got was a $100,000 clock tower that plays Christmas and wedding music. So the City Council terminated the contract last year, then promptly hired another lobbyist, based in Orlando.

"We felt that if we were going to invest that kind of money, we wanted to attempt to try to get more return on our investment," Mr. Litton said. "Sometimes in the bigger firms you kind of envision yourself as just a number."

Of Alcalde's 44 Florida government clients, half a dozen got no earmarks in the past five years; five more got less than a dollar back in earmarks for every dollar spent on lobbying. The City of Tampa and Orange County also recently fired Alcalde & Fay upon changes in their elected leadership.

"If there's a long list of clients that have something in common with Orange County, i.e., being a local government in central Florida or the state of Florida, then it would occur to me that there's the potential, at least, to dilute your effectiveness," said the county's new mayor, Richard T. Crotty. "There's only so much money to go around, and if you cut the pie 40 ways instead of two ways, that's not as good a deal."

If Alcalde & Fay has cornered the Florida market, Bradley Arant Rose & White dominates Alabama, its home state. Robertson, Monagle & Eastaugh, an Anchorage firm, represents nearly half the public entities in Alaska with lobbyists. Then there are firms like Marlowe & Company, in Washington, which sells itself as an expert in getting money to prevent beach erosion.

Rather than creating a conflict of interest, partners of Alcalde & Fay said that having a geographic cluster of clients allowed them to concentrate on a certain Congressional delegation. They said they were careful to present each client's priorities and, as Mr. Wahlquist put it, never "go to the Hill with more than one client in mind."

A Need for Professionals

The four-lane, 1.4-mile bridge connecting this spit of land with St. Petersburg was built in 1939, when Treasure Island was unincorporated and had just a handful of homes. By 2003, it rated 3.3 out of 100 on a standard bridge rating. "At zero, you're in the water," said Don Hambidge, the public works director.

Chuck Coward, the former city manager, said the city planned to issue $25 million in bonds backed by toll revenue, and to seek $15 million from the federal government and $10 million from the state. But, he said: "Treasure Island's a very small city. It's not savvy in federal politics."

"We thought we had a worthy project, we thought there were a lot of attributes to it, but we were not skilled in presenting those," Mr. Coward said, recalling several years of requests without results. "After talking with Clearwater, we thought very certainly some professional assistance would be appropriate."

Mr. Bafalis, the lobbyist assigned to Treasure Island, had served in the State Legislature and in Congress with Mr. Young before a failed bid for the governor's nomination in 1982. He mentioned Mr. Young's aversion to tolls when he first met with Mr. Coward on September 23, the day before Mr. Coward met with Mr. Young about the bridge.

Like Mr. Bafalis, Mr. Young declined to be interviewed for this article. But his chief of staff, Harry Glenn, said the removal of the toll had been key to obtaining the earmark, not hiring the congressman's old friend.

"When asked the question whether a city or county needs to hire a lobbyist, he has always told them they don't need to hire a lobbyist to work with their own congressman," Mr. Glenn said. "That's his job. Those are the people he was elected to represent. He doesn't need to work through somebody else to schedule a meeting with a mayor or a city council member."

At the bridge ceremony, where residents nibbled "no toll house cookies," it was Mr. Young who got thanked, not Mr. Bafalis. A 1927 fire engine was the first vehicle to roll across, followed by a forest green Ford Tudor Deluxe as old as the original bridge and two dozen more classics, like a 1959 turquoise Impala and a 1967 cherry Camaro convertible, both complete with fuzzy dice.

Though only one lane flowed in each direction—the two other lanes should be done by next summer—residents were relieved to have their evacuation route reopened in time for hurricane season, and to be able to cut as much as 40 minutes from their commute into town.

The City Council, meanwhile, may yet consider raising property taxes this summer. Without the toll, they would otherwise have no money for maintenance of the new bridge. Unless Alcalde & Fay helps find another earmark.

ARTICLE QUESTIONS

1) What specific benefits did Treasure Island receive from hiring a lobbyist?
2) Do you think the residents of these towns are aware of the direct benefits they receive from lobbyists who working on behalf of their local governments? Can you think of lobbyists employed to work for your benefit?
3) What drawbacks do you see with local governments using lobbyists to secure state and federal funds?
4) If you were elected to a local government agency, would you hire a lobbyist to advocate for your citizens' needs?

Chapter 13

Congress

The Constitution put Congress at the center of American government. The first article of the Constitution focuses on Congress and provides it with more powers than any other branch of government. As Federalist 51 put it, "in republican government, the legislative authority necessarily predominates." Perhaps it is a logical necessity that the representative branch predominates in a representative government. Still, many of the Framers were fearful of legislative power. Despite the checking powers given to each of the branches, Federalist 51 explained it was impossible "to give to each department an equal power of self-defense"; therefore the legislative power was divided once more to establish a bicameral Congress. This bicameral structure—which is relatively unusual in other nations—is perhaps the most defining feature of the U.S. Congress.

The Connecticut Compromise (which established the bicameral Congress) split the legislative power. House seats are allocated by population; Texas has 36 seats, Vermont has one. In the Senate, each state has two seats regardless of size. In 1790 the Senate consisted of 26 members representing the interests of 13 states and a 65-member House representing a population of about 4 million. Today, Congress consists of 100 senators representing 50 states, and a 435-member House representing about 310 million. Based on the unequal distribution of the population, it is now possible for the representatives of less than 15% of the country to block legislation desired by the representatives of the other 85%.

In 2013, Congress passed fewer public laws than in any year since *Vital Statistics on Congress* began tracking this in 1947. Public opinion polling revealed a record low (just 7%) approval rating for Congress in 2014. Some polls even presented Congress as less popular than root canals, head lice, traffic jams, and cockroaches. Yet in 2012, 90% of House incumbents who sought reelection were successful, as were 91% of senators. A reelection rate hovering around 90% has held consistent for decades, and most congressional scholars argue this will continue despite the public's apparent contempt for Congress. The lack of equal representation, the public disdain, and the inability to legislate have left scholars wondering whether the branch, purposely divided into two chambers, has reached a point where it can simply be described as "the broken branch."

The five readings in this chapter reflect some modern critiques of Congress. Ari Shapiro, reporting for *National Public Radio* (NPR), notes in "Would the U.S. Be Better Off with a Parliament?" that separating the legislative and executive authority into different branches is unusual among European democracies. Shapiro quotes several prominent political scientists who argue this unusual structure might generate an unusually high level of gridlock. Adam Liptak, in "Smaller States Find Outsize Clout Growing in Senate," laments the disproportionate power afforded senators from sparsely populated states. Liptak reports on the amplified levels of federal aid given to low-population states and traces this to the overrepresentation in the Senate of these states. In "What If Senators Represented People by Income or Race, Not by State?" Annie Lowrey also notes the unrepresentative nature of the Senate, but she shifts her focus to the lack of representation of racial minorities, the economically disadvantaged, the young, and women. She proposes some hypothetical representative structures to exhibit the disproportionate representation of some groups in the United States, but her larger point is that representative structures drive legislative outcomes.

The last two readings discuss what many scholars argue is the primary motivation of congressmembers: getting reelected. The Framers saw the desire to get reelected as an important check on the tyranny; in order to get reelected, congressmembers would need to convince their constituents that they were serving the public's interest. But getting reelected may not be as direct as pleasing the public. In his *Washington Post* article "People Hate Congress, but Most Incumbents Get Re-elected. What Gives?" Chris Cillizza provides a modern-day examination of Fenno's paradox. The paradox, articulated by congressional scholar Richard Fenno, illuminates why the American public continues to reelect the same congressional representatives despite their dislike of Congress as a whole. Jake Sherman's *Politico* article "Defense Cuts Hit Home for John Boehner, Eric Cantor" provides an important follow-up to Cillizza's piece. Where Cillizza focuses on the behavior of voters, Sherman focuses on how Fenno's paradox might direct the behavior of members of Congress.

E pluribus unum, a Latin phrase meaning "out of many, one," has long been considered the de facto motto of the United States. It is in Congress that the divergent interests of the population are supposed to be distilled into national policy. But, there is an inherent tension in making one policy out of many interests: it involves compromise. This is messy work, and it is part of the reason why Congress might remain the least popular branch of the federal government. The articles in this chapter point to ways that Congress might better achieve its responsibility to represent the public; however, reforms to make Congress popular remain elusive. While the public often say they want members of Congress to work together and to be less divisive, the public is often divided on important issues. Congress may simply be reflecting a divided people.

CHAPTER QUESTIONS

1) Why does the reelection rate for members of Congress remain so high when the public's opinion of Congress is so low?
2) Does the Senate still perform the function the Framers intended?

3) What reforms, if any, should be made to Congress's representative structure?

4) Is it accurate to label Congress "the broken branch"?

CHAPTER READINGS

13.1) Ari Shapiro, "Would the U.S. Be Better Off with a Parliament?" *National Public Radio*, October 12, 2013.

13.2) Adam Liptak, "Smaller States Find Outsize Clout Growing in Senate," *The New York Times*, March 11, 2013.

13.3) Annie Lowrey, "What If Senators Represented People by Income or Race, Not by State?" *The Washington Post*, February 7, 2011.

13.4) Chris Cillizza, "People Hate Congress, but Most Incumbents Get Re-elected. What Gives?" *The Washington Post*, May 9, 2013.

13.5) Jake Sherman, "Defense Cuts Hit Home for John Boehner, Eric Cantor," *Politico*, February 28, 2011.

13.1) Would the U.S. Be Better Off with a Parliament?

National Public Radio, October 12, 2013

ARI SHAPIRO

> In "Would the U.S. Be Better Off with a Parliament?," Ari Shapiro, reporting for *National Public Radio*, underscores the heightened level of political gridlock experienced in the United States compared to European democracies. The article cites three main differences between the United States and most European democracies. The United States has (1) a strong system of separated powers, (2) lax rules on campaign donations, and (3) more political meetings held in public. Many people recognize these characteristics as core commitments of the U.S. political system: separation of powers was established to reduce tyranny, protection of individual liberties may conflict with laws that restrict political donations, and public meetings permit people to monitor their government officials. Given these core commitments of the U.S. political system, the article unsurprisingly ends on the somewhat pessimistic note that these structures are unlikely to change.

There are many reasons for the gridlock in Washington. Some are recent developments, as the U.S. becomes more politically polarized. Others are structural, built into the American political system.

Regardless, the extreme paralysis that has recently become the norm in D.C. almost never happens in Western European democracies.

"You're asking: Do other democracies have this problem? And the answer is: Not many," says Jane Mansbridge, a professor at the Harvard Kennedy School.

Mansbridge just finished her term as president of the American Political Science Association. While in that position, she appointed a task force to spend the past year studying how agreements are negotiated in American politics. The group looked at why there's so much stalemate in the U.S. right now.

One question they asked was whether this country can learn lessons from European democracies where there's less paralysis.

"We tried to think about why it is that other countries have had less difficulty in negotiating agreements," says Boston University's Cathie Jo Martin, who was co-chairwoman of the task force. "You don't see these kinds of stalemates happening elsewhere."

One reason for the U.S. tendency toward gridlock is that this country has what Mansbridge describes as "a very strong separation of powers."

The separation of powers is essential to the American political system. The president needs Congress to pass bills; Congress needs the president to sign bills into law; the courts can declare laws unconstitutional.

In most of Europe, things work differently, says Thomas Risse of the Free University in Berlin.

"In most European parliamentary democracies, the prime ministers or the chancellors are not directly elected by the people," Risse says, "but they're elected by the parliament itself, as a result of which they usually have a stable majority."

It would be as if the American president's party always controlled Congress.

Of course, America will never become a parliamentary system. But even setting that aside, political scientists say there are other lessons the U.S. can take from Europe.

Martin has concluded that money shapes the American political system in powerful and unique ways.

"I think the campaign finance issue is probably the single most important difference between America and the rest of the world," she says.

When asked how many other countries with highly functioning democracies have lax donation rules, she replies, "I can't think of any . . . almost all countries control finance."

Today in the U.S., if lawmakers don't toe the line, outside groups can threaten to bankroll challengers. President Obama expressed concern about that phenomenon at his most recent White House news conference, while acknowledging that he's not entirely innocent either.

"You have some ideological extremist who has a big bankroll, and they can entirely skew our politics," Obama said.

The political scientists on this project found other ways that European democracies avoid gridlock, too. For example, Mansbridge says Europeans more often hold key meetings in private.

"When you've made a decision, like the Supreme Court, you explain it, but you don't necessarily let the public see everything you do," Mansbridge says.

Republican Rep. Paul Ryan of Wisconsin seemed to take that lesson to heart Thursday, when reporters tried to question him after a White House meeting.

"Can you be more specific about [Obama's] concerns?" a reporter asked.

"I'd rather not, because we're negotiating right now. No offense, we're not going to negotiate through the media. We're going to negotiate straight with the White House," Ryan said.

While many political scientists agree on changes that could help lessen the chances of gridlock in the U.S., they also agree on the likelihood that these changes will happen:

"I have to admit to a fair amount of pessimism," says Martin of Boston University.

"The honest answer is I'm pretty pessimistic," says Alan Jacobs of the University of British Columbia.

Asked how all of this looks from Europe, Risse in Berlin replies, "Pretty dysfunctional, I have to say."

At least on this point, the U.S. and Europe see things exactly the same way.

ARTICLE QUESTIONS

1) How does the article claim European parliamentary democracies are different from the U.S. system of separation of powers?
2) Is it worth putting up with gridlock to maintain our commitment to separation of powers? Why or why not?
3) What do you think it would take for U.S. residents to decide to modify their commitment to the system of separation of powers, lax campaign rules, and open government meetings?

13.2) Smaller States Find Outsize Clout Growing in Senate

The New York Times, March 11, 2013

ADAM LIPTAK

The disproportionate power enjoyed in the Senate by small states is playing a growing role in the political dynamic on issues as varied as gun control, immigration and campaign finance.

Adam Liptak, in "Smaller States Find Outsize Clout Growing in Senate," critiques the "malapportioned" Senate for providing disproportionate resources to less-populated states and for preventing policies favored by senators representing the majority of the population. If we define democracy based on the principle of "one person, one vote," then the Senate misses widely. Liptak argues that the difference in representation between a citizen in the least populated state (Wyoming) and one in the most populated state (California) is so extreme that the Senate could statistically be defined as "the least democratic legislative chamber in any developed nation."

Liptak's analysis must be tempered by the historical knowledge that the original objective of the Senate was to frustrate majoritarian government and to provide representation to the states. But does the Senate still perform these duties? The Connecticut Compromise granted senators six-year terms and allowed states to appoint their senators (rather than having them elected). Thus, the House would represent the people and the Senate the states. In 1913 the Seventeenth Amendment was ratified, requiring the direct election of senators. Now that senators are elected by, and answerable to, the citizens of their state, do they represent the interests of their states in a way that differs from the representation provided by the House?

Big State, Small State

RUTLAND, Vt.—In the four years after the financial crisis struck, a great wave of federal stimulus money washed over Rutland County. It helped pay for bridges, roads, preschool programs, a community health center, buses and fire trucks, water mains and tanks, even a project to make sure fish could still swim down the river while a bridge was being rebuilt.

Just down Route 4, at the New York border, the landscape abruptly turns from spiffy to scruffy. Washington County, N.Y., which is home to about 60,000 people—just as Rutland is—saw only a quarter as much money.

"We didn't receive a lot," said Peter Aust, the president of the local chamber of commerce on the New York side. "We never saw any of the positive impact of the stimulus funds."

Vermont's 625,000 residents have two United States senators, and so do New York's 19 million. That means that a Vermonter has 30 times the voting power in the Senate of a New Yorker just over the state line—the biggest inequality between two adjacent states. The nation's largest gap, between Wyoming and California, is more than double that.

The difference in the fortunes of Rutland and Washington Counties reflects the growing disparity in their citizens' voting power, and it is not an anomaly. The Constitution has always given residents of states with small populations a lift, but the size and importance of the gap has grown markedly in recent decades, in ways the framers probably never anticipated. It affects the political dynamic of issues as varied as gun control, immigration and campaign finance.

In response, lawmakers, lawyers and watchdog groups have begun pushing for change. A lawsuit to curb the small-state advantage in the Senate's rules is moving through the courts. The Senate has already made modest changes to rules concerning the filibuster, which has particularly benefited senators from small states. And eight states and the District of Columbia have endorsed a proposal to reduce the chances that the small-state advantage in the Electoral College will allow a loser of the popular vote to win the presidency.

To be sure, some scholars and members of Congress view the small-state advantage as a vital part of the constitutional structure and say the growth of that advantage is no cause for worry. Others say it is an authentic but insoluble problem.

What is certain is that the power of the smaller states is large and growing. Political scientists call it a striking exception to the democratic principle of "one person, one vote." Indeed, they say, the Senate may be the least democratic legislative chamber in any developed nation.

Behind the growth of the advantage is an increase in population gap between large and small states, with large states adding many more people than small ones in the last half-century. There is a widening demographic split, too, with the larger states becoming more urban and liberal, and the smaller ones remaining rural and conservative, which lends a new significance to the disparity in their political power.

The threat of the filibuster in the Senate, which has become far more common than in past decades, plays a role, too. Research by two political scientists, Lauren C. Bell and L. Marvin Overby, has found that small-state senators, often in leadership positions, have amplified their power by using the filibuster more often than their large-state counterparts.

Beyond influencing government spending, these shifts generally benefit conservative causes and hurt liberal ones. When small states block or shape legislation backed by senators representing a majority of Americans, most of the senators on the winning side tend to be Republicans, because Republicans disproportionately live in small states and Democrats, especially African-Americans and Latinos, are more likely to live in large states like California, New York, Florida and Illinois. Among the nation's five smallest states, only Vermont tilts liberal, while Alaska, Wyoming and the Dakotas have each voted Republican in every presidential election since 1968.

Recent bills to overhaul the immigration system and increase disclosure of campaign spending have won the support of senators representing a majority of the population but have not yet passed. A sweeping climate bill, meant to raise the cost of carbon emissions, passed the House, where seats are allocated by population, but not the Senate.

Each of those bills is a major Democratic Party priority. Throughout his second term, President Obama is likely to be lining up with a majority of large-state Congress members on his biggest goals and against a majority of small-state lawmakers.

It is easiest to measure the small-state advantage in dollars. Over the past few years, as the federal government has spent hundreds of billions to respond to the financial crisis, it has done much more to assist the residents of small states than large ones. The top five per capita recipients of federal stimulus grants were states so small that they have only a single House member.

"From highway bills to homeland security," said Sarah A. Binder, a political scientist at George Washington University, "small states make out like bandits."

Here in Rutland, the federal government has spent $2,500 per person since early 2009, compared with $600 per person across the state border in Washington County.

As the money started arriving, Senator Bernard Sanders, the Vermont independent, took credit for having delivered a "hefty share of the national funding." Senator Kirsten Gillibrand, a New York Democrat, vowed to fight for her state's "fair share."

As a matter of constitutional design, small states have punched above their weight politically for as long as the United States has existed. The founding of the country depended in part on the Great Compromise, which created a legislative chamber—the Senate—in which every state had the same political voice, regardless of population. The advantage small states enjoy in the Senate is echoed in the Electoral College, where each state is allocated votes not only for its House members (reflecting the state's population) but also for its senators (a two-vote bonus).

No one expects the small-state advantage to disappear, given its constitutional roots. But its growing importance has caused some large-state policy makers and advocates for giving all citizens an equal voice in democracy to begin exploring ways to counteract it. Those pushing for change tend to be Democrats.

One plan, enacted into law by eight states and the District of Columbia, would effectively cancel the small states' Electoral College edge. The nine jurisdictions have pledged to allocate their 132 electoral votes to the winner of the national popular vote—if they can persuade states with 138 more votes to make the same commitment. (That would represent the bare majority of the 538 electoral votes needed for a presidential candidate to prevail.)

The states that have agreed to the arrangement range in size from Vermont to California, and they are dominated by Democrats. But support for changing the Electoral College cuts across party lines. In a recent Gallup Poll, 61 percent of Republicans, 63 percent of independents and 66 percent of Democrats said they favored abolishing the system and awarding the presidency to the winner of the popular vote.

In 2000, had electoral votes been allocated by population, without the two-vote bonuses, Al Gore would have prevailed over George W. Bush. Alexander Keyssar, a historian of democracy at Harvard, said he would not be surprised if another Republican candidate won the presidency while losing the popular vote in coming decades, given the structure of the Electoral College.

Critics of the outsize power of small states have also turned to the courts. In December, four House members and the advocacy group Common Cause filed an appeal in a lawsuit challenging the Senate's filibuster rule on the ground that it "upsets the balance in the Great Compromise" that created the Senate.

The filibuster "has significantly increased the underrepresentation of people living in the most populous states," the suit said. But for the rule, it said, the Dream Act, which would have given some immigrants who arrived illegally as children a path to legalization, and the Disclose Act, requiring greater reporting of political spending, would be law.

A federal judge in Washington dismissed the suit, saying he was "powerless to address" what he acknowledged was an "important and controversial issue." The judge instead sided with lawyers for the Senate, who said that the challengers lacked standing to sue and that the courts lacked power to rule on the internal workings of another branch of the government.

However these individual efforts fare, the basic disparity between large and small states is wired into the constitutional framework. Some scholars say that this is as it should be and that the advantages enjoyed by small states are necessary to prevent them from becoming a voiceless minority.

"Without it, wealth and power would tend to flow to the prosperous coasts and cities and away from less-populated rural areas," said Stephen Macedo, a political scientist at Princeton.

Gary L. Gregg II, a political scientist who holds the Mitch McConnell Chair in Leadership at the University of Louisville, similarly argued that urban areas already have enough power, as the home of most major government agencies, news media organizations, companies and universities. "A simple, direct democracy will centralize all power," he wrote recently, "in urban areas to the detriment of the rest of the nation."

Others say the country needs to make changes to preserve its democratic vitality. They have called for an overhaul of the Constitution, as far-fetched an idea as that may be.

"The Senate constitutes a threat to the vitality of the American political system in the 21st century," said Sanford Levinson, a law professor at the University of Texas, "and it warrants a constitutional convention to rectify it."

Frances E. Lee, a political scientist at the University of Maryland, said the problem was as real as the solution elusive, adding that she and other scholars have tried without success to find a contemporary reason to exempt the Senate from the usual rules of granting citizens an equal voice in their government. "I can't think of any way to justify it based on democratic principles," Professor Lee said.

The Biggest Gap of All

Fresno, Calif., is a city of a half-million people with a long list of problems, including 14 percent unemployment, the aftermath of a foreclosure crisis, homeless encampments that dot the sun-blasted landscape and worries about the safety of the surrounding county's drinking water.

A thousand miles away, a roughly comparable number of people inhabit the entire state of Wyoming. Like Fresno and its environs, Wyoming is rural, with an economy largely based on agriculture. It is also in much better shape than Fresno, with an unemployment rate around 5 percent.

Even so, Wyoming receives far more assistance from the federal government than Fresno does. The half-million residents of Wyoming also have much more sway over federal policy than the half-million residents of Fresno. The vote people in Fresno remember best was taken in 2007, when an immigration overhaul bill that included a guest worker program failed in the Senate. Both agricultural businesses and leaders of Fresno's large Hispanic population supported the bill, much as polls suggested a majority of Americans did.

But the immigration bill died in the Senate after a 53-46 vote rejecting a bid to move the bill forward to final passage. Wyoming's two senators were in the majority and California's two senators on the losing side.

Had the votes been allocated by population, the result would have been lopsided in the other direction, with 57 votes in favor and 43 against.

Even 57 votes would not have been enough to overcome a filibuster, which requires 60. In the last few years, 41 senators representing as little as a third of the nation's population have frequently blocked legislation, as the filibuster (or the threat of it) has become a routine part of Senate business.

Beyond the filibuster, senators from Wyoming and other small states regularly oppose and often thwart programs popular in states with vastly bigger populations. The 38 million people who live in the nation's 22 smallest states, including Wyoming, are represented by 44 senators. The 38 million residents of California are represented by two senators.

In one of every 10 especially consequential votes in the Senate over the two decades ending in 2010, as chosen by *Congressional Quarterly*, the winning side would have lost had voting been allocated by population. And in 24 of the 27 such votes, the majority of the senators on the winning side were Republicans.

David Mayhew, a political scientist at Yale, cautioned that the political benefit to Republicans is "quite small as well as quite stable," adding that it is important not to lose sight of small blue states like Delaware, Hawaii, Rhode Island and Vermont. But he acknowledged that small states of both political stripes receive disproportionate federal benefits. Professor Lee, an author of "Sizing Up the Senate: The Unequal Consequences of Equal Representation," argues that the partisan impact of the small-state advantage is larger. "There is a Republican tilt in the Senate," she said.

"The way Republicans are distributed across the nation is more efficient," she added, referring to the more even allocation of Republican voters, allowing them to form majorities in small-population states. Democrats are more tightly clustered, especially in large metropolitan areas.

Born of a Compromise

Equal representation of the states in the Senate is a consequence of the Great Compromise, the 1787 deal that resolved a seemingly intractable dispute between the smaller states and a handful of large ones like Massachusetts, Pennsylvania and Virginia. But the country was very different then. The population was about four million, and the maximum disparity in voting power between states was perhaps 11 to 1. It is now six times greater than that. Even scholars who criticize how voting

power is allocated in the Senate agree that parts of its design play an important role in the constitutional structure. With its longer terms and fewer members, the Senate can, in theory, be more collegial, take the long view and be insulated from passing passions.

But those qualities do not depend on unequal representation among people who live in different states. The current allocation of power in the Senate, many legal scholars and political scientists say, does not protect minorities with distinctive characteristics, much less disadvantaged ones.

To the contrary, the disproportionate voting power of small states is a sort of happenstance that has on occasion left a stain on the nation's history.

Robert A. Dahl, the Yale political scientist, who is 97 and has been studying American government for more than 70 years, has argued that slavery survived thanks to the disproportionate influence of small-population Southern states. The House passed eight antislavery measures between 1800 and 1860; all died in the Senate. The civil rights movement of the mid-20th century, he added, was slowed by senators representing small-population states.

As the population of the United States has grown a hundredfold since the founding, to more than 310 million, the Supreme Court has swept away most instances of unequal representation beyond the Senate. In a series of seminal cases in the 1960s, the court forbade states to give small-population counties or districts a larger voice than ones with more people, in both state legislatures and the House.

"The conception of political equality from the Declaration of Independence, to Lincoln's Gettysburg Address, to the Fifteenth, Seventeenth, and Nineteenth Amendments can mean only one thing—one person, one vote," Justice William O. Douglas wrote for the court in 1963, referring to the amendments that extended the franchise to blacks and women and required the popular election of the Senate.

The rulings revolutionized American politics— everywhere but in the Senate, which the

Constitution protected from change and where the disparities in voting power have instead become more extreme.

A Barrier to Change

In his memoirs, Chief Justice Earl Warren described the cases from the 1960s establishing the equality of each citizen's vote as the most important achievement of the court he led for 16 years. That made them more important in his view than *Brown v. Board of Education*, which ordered the desegregation of public schools, and *Gideon v. Wainwright*, which guaranteed lawyers for poor people accused of serious crimes.

"Legislators represent people, not trees or acres," Chief Justice Warren wrote for the court in 1964, rejecting the argument that state senators, like federal ones, could represent geographic areas with varying populations. "Legislators are elected by voters, not farms or cities or economic interests."

Applying that principle to the Senate would be very hard. Even an ordinary constitutional amendment would not do the trick, as the framers of the Constitution went out of their way to require states to agree before their power is diminished. Article V of the Constitution sets out the procedure for amendments and requires a two-thirds vote of both houses of Congress or action by two-thirds of state legislatures to get things started. But the article makes an exception for the Senate. "No state, without its consent, shall be deprived of its equal suffrage in the Senate," the article concludes.

The United States Senate is hardly the only legislature that does not stick strictly to the principle of equal representation. Political scientists use the term "malapportioned" to describe the phenomenon, and it is common around the world.

But the Senate is in contention for the least democratic legislative chamber. In some other countries with federal systems, in which states or provinces have independent political power, a malapportioned upper house may have only a weak or advisory role. In the United States, the Senate is at least equal in power to the House, and it possesses some distinctive responsibilities, like treaty ratification and the approval of presidential appointments. A recent appeals court decision severely limiting the president's power to make recess appointments, if it stands, will further increase the Senate's power.

Professor Dahl has calculated the difference between the local government unit with the most voting power and that with the least. The smallest ratio, 1.5, was in Austria, while in Belgium, Spain, India, Germany, Australia and Canada the ratio was never higher than 21 to 1.

In this country, the ratio between Wyoming's representation and California's is 66 to 1. By that measure, Professor Dahl found, only Brazil, Argentina and Russia had less democratic chambers. A separate analysis, by David Samuels and Richard Snyder, similarly found that geographically large countries with federal systems tend to overrepresent sparsely populated areas.

This pattern has policy consequences, notably ones concerning the environment. "Nations with malapportioned political systems have lower gasoline taxes (and lower pump prices) than nations with more equitable representation of urban constituencies," two political scientists, J. Lawrence Broz and Daniel Maliniak, wrote in a recent study. Such countries also took longer to ratify the Kyoto Protocol on climate change, if they ratified it at all. These differences were, they wrote, a consequence of the fact that "rural voters in industrialized countries rely more heavily on fossil fuels than urban voters."

In 2009, the House of Representatives narrowly approved a bill to address climate change, but only after months of horse-trading that granted concessions and money to rural states. That was an example, Mr. Broz and Mr. Maliniak said, of compensating rural residents for the burdens of reducing greenhouse-gas emissions.

But it was not enough. The bill died in the Senate.

Overrepresentation in the Senate is among the reasons why the smallest states (and their local governments) received more federal aid per capita in 2010.

	People per Senator	Aid per Capita
Wyoming	290,000	$4,180
Vermont	310,000	3,270
North Dakota	350,000	3,220
Alaska	370,000	4,680
South Dakota	420,000	2,640
Delaware	460,000	3,700
Montana	500,000	2,840
Rhode Island	530,000	2,800
New Hampshire	660,000	1,790
Maine	660,000	2,700
Hawaii	700,000	1,850
Idaho	800,000	1,950
West Virginia	930,000	2,610
Nebraska	930,000	1,710
New Mexico	1,040,000	3,310
Nevada	1,380,000	1,340
Utah	1,430,000	1,520
Kansas	1,440,000	1,750

	People per Senator	Aid per Capita
Arkansas	1,470,000	2,200
Mississippi	1,490,000	2,900
Iowa	1,540,000	1,930
Connecticut	1,800,000	2,150
Oklahoma	1,910,000	2,140
Oregon	1,950,000	2,050
Kentucky	2,190,000	2,250
Louisiana	2,300,000	2,960
South Carolina	2,360,000	1,790
Alabama	2,410,000	1,800
Colorado	2,590,000	1,520
Minnesota	2,690,000	2,050
Wisconsin	2,860,000	1,880
New York*	9,790,000	3,170
Texas	13,030,000	1,740
California	19,020,000	1,790

*New York voluntarily expanded its Medicaid program, qualifying it for a large federal match in 2010.

ARTICLE QUESTIONS

1) What argument presented in the article did you find the most persuasive for describing why it is important to reform the Senate to represent all U.S. residents more equally? What argument did you find the strongest for why it is important to maintain extra representation for residents of less-populated states?

2) Does the Senate's deviation from the democratic principle of "one person, one vote" mean that the Senate is anti-democratic?

3) Liptak reports that "in a series of seminal cases in the 1960s, the [Supreme] Court forbade states to give small-population counties or districts" equal representation with more populated counties or districts because the practice violates the principle of "one person, one vote." Is there a good reason to forbid states from adopting a representational style that mirrors that of the U.S. Senate?

13.3) What If Senators Represented People by Income or Race, Not by State?

The Washington Post, February 7, 2010

ANNIE LOWREY

In "What If Senators Represented People by Income or Race, Not by State?" Annie Lowrey explores the representational structure of the Senate. The Senate was partially established to provide geographical representation; two senators are selected from each state regardless of the state's population. As Lowrey illustrates with the account of Senator Ben Nelson—who almost negotiated a particularly beneficial arrangement for the state of Nebraska before agreeing to vote for the Affordable Care Act—the need for senators to please their constituents often drives their behavior. However, unlike many journalists, Lowrey does not take an overly critical view of Senator Nelson's actions. She writes: "you can't blame Nelson for doing exactly what the founders asked him to do."

The lesson contained in Lowrey's article is that representational structures drive outcomes. To demonstrate this concept she proposes some hypothetical representative structures. The styles of representation she proposes reflect *descriptive representation*, the idea that representatives should share some descriptive characteristics (like race or gender) with their constituents. She argues that each of these proposed styles of descriptive representation would change the deals brokered and legislative outcomes reached. For example, she argues that if the number of women in the Senate reflected women's percentage of the population (more than 50%) then "the horrible dearth of child-care options for working mothers would seem untenable." It is important not to get too caught up in Lowrey's specific proposals for new representative structures. These proposals are really just thought experiments employed to illustrate two points: (1) the Senate is unrepresentative of the public and (2) representative structures drive legislative outcomes.

On Wednesday, President Obama joined Senate Democrats at their retreat, urging them to "finish the job" on health-care reform "even though it's hard."

That crowd knows how hard it can be. To get the 60 votes needed to pass the health-care bill last Christmas Eve, Senate Majority Leader Harry Reid worked furiously. The final holdout was Ben Nelson, a centrist Democrat from Nebraska. With time running out, Reid offered to have the federal government pay for the expansion of the state's Medicaid program in perpetuity—and Nelson signed on to the bill.

Members of both parties were vociferous in criticizing the "Cornhusker kickback," as it came to be known. "That's not change we can believe in!" crowed Lindsey Graham (R-S.C.). "That is the worst in politics."

He's right about one thing: That wasn't change. It was a type of deal as old as the Senate itself. Back in the summer of 1787, the founders debated how to structure the legislature. James Madison, of the large state of Virginia, drafted a plan for a bicameral parliament, with both chambers apportioned by population. William Paterson, of the smaller state of New Jersey, called for a single house. In July, they compromised: two houses, one proportionate to population and one with two representatives per state.

The Great Compromise was intended to make sure the big states didn't trample the little guys. But today, with 37 more states on the scene, the little ones wield disproportionate power. "Half of the population of the nation lives in 10 states, which have 20 senators. The other half lives in 40 states that have 80 senators," says the official Senate historian, Donald Ritchie. Small states and states whose representatives might tip the balance on a key vote make out like bandits, as their senators demand outsize appropriations in return for their support. The Nelson fracas was nothing other than the Senate working exactly as it was designed to.

But what if the 100-member Senate were designed to mirror the overall U.S. population—and were based on statistics rather than state lines?

Imagine a chamber in which senators were elected by different income brackets—with two senators representing the poorest 2 percent of the electorate, two senators representing the richest 2 percent and so on.

Based on Census Bureau data, five senators would represent Americans earning between $100,000 and $1 million individually per year, with a single senator working on behalf of the millionaires (technically, it would be two-tenths of a senator). Eight senators would represent Americans with no income. Sixteen would represent Americans who make less than $10,000 a year, an amount well below the federal poverty line for families. The bulk of the senators would work on behalf of the middle class, with 34 representing Americans making $30,000 to $80,000 per year.

Imagine trying to convince someone—Michael Bloomberg, perhaps?—to be the lonely senator representing the richest percentile. And what if the senators were apportioned according to jobs figures? This year, the unemployed would have gained two seats. Think of the deals that would be made to attract that bloc!

Or how about if senators represented particular demographic groups, based on gender and race? White women would elect the biggest group of senators—37 of them, though only 38 women have ever served in the Senate, with 17 currently in office. White men would have 36 seats. Black women, Hispanic women and Hispanic men would have six each; black men five; and Asian women and men two each. Women voters would control a steady and permanent majority—making, say, discriminatory health-care measures such as the Stupak Amendment and the horrible dearth of child-care options for working mothers seem untenable.

What about a Senate in which voters cast ballots for candidates campaigning to win over a certain age group? Thirteen senators would vie for 18-to-24-year-olds, who strongly support measures such as the cap-and-trade climate bill and marriage rights for gays. Nearly all of these senators would be Democrats. Americans over 65 would control 16 seats—and would be mostly Republicans interested in protecting Medicare and the broader status quo. The baby boomer bubble would be largely in the eldest category, though its stragglers would round out the segment of voters, probably split between the parties, that is edging up on retirement. Thirty-six senators would serve 25-to-44-year-olds, and 35 senators 45-to-64-year-olds—and would be likely to push the very issues now on the table, including health care, entitlement viability and tax breaks for the middle class.

However you slice it (or us), a new voting model would shake up the Senate's agenda. A senator vying for the $60,000 bracket—filled with working parents concerned with putting children through school—might need to promise Pell Grant reform and improved school lunches. One can imagine a coalition of senators for the elderly and senators for 20-somethings working to loosen federal laws around medical marijuana.

These deals, of course, would be very different from the deal Ben Nelson cut for Nebraska. But they highlight a truth so obvious it isn't often examined: Senators represent states. And states' priorities can seem strange when viewed in a national light. The Great Compromise promised just the kind of last-minute deal that Nelson struck, ensuring that the needs of his small state were recognized in the nationwide initiative.

These days, people don't much like the anti-democratic structure of the Senate and the bring-home-the-bacon politics it begets. Recent polls have shown that Americans despise the upper chamber—more than the House, more than the White House. But you can't blame Nelson for doing exactly what the founders asked him to do.

ARTICLE QUESTIONS

1) What are the three representative structures Lowrey proposes? How does she suggest legislative outcomes might change for each?

2) Lowrey asserts that senators like Ben Nelson are incorrectly being blamed for a *structure* that drives their behavior. Is Lowrey correct to absolve individual senators for causing Americans to dislike the way the Senate functions?

3) The standard belief is that senators represent the interests of their states, but do all state residents have the same desires? For example, California has two liberal Democrats representing the state in the Senate. Does it seem likely that California residents who belong to the Republican Party think the Democratic senators from California are representing their interests? Is it possible that California Republicans have more in common with the Republican senators representing Texas? If so, does it make sense to argue that senators represent the interests of their states?

13.4) People Hate Congress, but Most Incumbents Get Re-elected. What Gives?

The Washington Post, May 9, 2013

CHRIS CILLIZZA

Every two years at election time, it is common to read of an impending anti-incumbent wave that will "wash the bums" out of Congress. And with every election cycle, about 90 percent of the incumbents who seek reelection are returned to office. In this *Washington Post* article "People Hate Congress, but Most Incumbents Get Re-elected. What Gives?" Chris Cillizza offers two explanations. First: it is easier to hate an institution (like Congress) than a person (like your representative). Two: the people paying the most attention (those who are most likely to vote) approve of their representatives at the highest rate.

Cillizza's article provides a modern-day example of Fenno's paradox. Congressional scholar Richard Fenno wanted to understand how Americans could simultaneously love their congressional representatives while loathing Congress. If everyone loves his or her representative, shouldn't we also love a Congress composed of these beloved representatives? One of the arguments that Fenno emphasized for this paradox (which Cillizza omits from his article) is the ability of members of Congress to "bring home the bacon": they often win praise for channeling federal money and services to their district. People usually know all about the goods and services—the bridges and Veteran's hospitals—that their members procured for the district. While "bringing home the bacon" endears representatives to their constituents, it often enrages the rest of the American public. Since the only representatives we elect bring our district goods and services, we approve of them— while we are resigned to complaining about all the representatives elected from other districts.

In 2012, Congressional approval averaged 15 percent, the lowest in nearly four decades of Gallup polling. And yet, 90 percent of House Members and 91 percent of Senators who sought re-election won last November.

The seeming paradox between the low regard with which people hold Congress and the high rate of re-election of incumbents is explained well by new data released by Gallup on Thursday that points to a simple reality: People hate

Congress but (generally) like their Member of Congress.

Gallup found that 46 percent of respondents said they approved of "the way the representative from your congressional district is handling his or her job" while 41 percent disapproved. That's in spite of the fact that overall Congressional approval was at just 16 percent in the same survey and hasn't been higher than 24 percent since the start of 2011.

Even more fascinating, Gallup asked a different set of respondents if they could name their Congressman and his/her party and then followed up with a question on whether they approved of the person.

Roughly one in three people (35 percent) could name their Member of Congress—that was surprisingly high, at least to us—and, of that group, 62 percent approve of how their Member of Congress is going about their job while 32 percent disapprove. "Americans who say they can name their congressional representative skew older, more highly educated and somewhat Republican," writes Gallup's Elizabeth Mendes.

The numbers tell a fascinating story.

First, they make clear that it's far easier to hate an institution—like, say, FIFA—than an individual, particularly an individual you sort-of, kind-of think you know. There's a natural tendency to assume your guy or gal isn't like everyone else—how could they be bad since you voted for them?—and they are doing everything they can to make things better up there/down there/out there in Washington.

Second, it's clear that the voters paying the most attention—as in those who can, you know, name who represents them—are far more positive about their Members' service than the average person in the district. Voters paying more attention are, of course, much more likely to vote and, therefore, the sample of people actually turning out on election day tends to be favorably inclined toward their Member. That, in turn, makes the incumbent's re-election much more likely.

Those two factors help explain why Congressional approval is at record lows but re-election rates remain near or above 90 percent. Bloomberg's Greg Giroux notes that in 2010 84 percent of Senators and 85 percent of House members won re-election. But that appears to be the exception not the rule with 95 percent (or more) of House members typically winning re-election dating back four decades. (The last time—aside from 2010—where less than 90 percent of House incumbents seeking re-election won was in 1974 when 89.6 percent did so.)

The message from voters to Congress? Throw the bums out. But not my bum.

ARTICLE QUESTIONS

1) What percentage of Americans, according to the Gallup poll results cited in the article, approved of "the way the representative from your congressional district is handling his or her job"? What percentage approved of the performance of Congress overall?

2) Why does Cillizza find it significant that people who can name their representative "are far more positive about their Members' service than the average person in the district"?

3) What do you think it would take to cause a majority of congressional incumbents to lose in an election cycle?

13.5) Defense Cuts Hit Home for John Boehner, Eric Cantor

Politico, February 28, 2011

JAKE SHERMAN

Jake Sherman's *Politico* article "Defense Cuts Hit Home for John Boehner, Eric Cantor" recounts a dilemma faced by Republican leaders in the House: should they "cut federal spending or protect jobs at home"? As self-avowed fiscal conservatives, Speaker of the House John Boehner and House Majority Leader Eric Cantor promote cutting federal spending, but as elected representatives from districts in Ohio and Virginia, they want to serve their constituents (which can lead to reelection). As Sherman explains, when a spending bill was proposed in the House that would cut federal spending, partly by cutting programs in Ohio and Virginia, Boehner and Cantor found themselves in a conundrum. Should they remain true to their fiscal conservative beliefs, or should they protect the interests of their districts? As Sherman reports, the bicameral structure of the U.S. Congress allowed Boehner and Cantor to pull off a "political twofer" that maintained their reputation as fiscal conservatives while keeping federal spending in their districts.

Cut federal spending or protect jobs at home, that's the quandary for House Speaker John Boehner and Majority Leader Eric Cantor as House Republicans take on one of the most contentious issues in their party: cutting military programs.

So far, the message the two House leaders have tried to convey to their eager budget-cutters is that they are willing to take hits on their home-state projects if that's the path to smaller deficits.

But it's unclear if the cuts will get through the Senate, and that could provide them both with a political twofer: enhanced reputations as fiscal conservatives but no real job loss or reduction of federal cash flow to their constituents.

It's a political tightrope so risky that Cantor's staff won't even talk about it except in the broadest of terms, while Boehner offers measured remarks.

Their first test came earlier this month, when an amendment stripping $450 million in 2010 funding for a second engine for the F-35 Joint Strike Fighter was offered to the short-term continuing resolution that will keep the government running through September.

The engine is partly built at General Electric plants in Ohio, Boehner's home state. Another piece of the engine is built by Rolls-Royce, which has employees in Cantor's Virginia.

The engine program is one that the Obama administration and the Pentagon oppose. But Boehner and Cantor support it, saying that spending money now to nurture competition in the engine-building program will save the government money down the road.

Still, Boehner and Cantor allowed the amendment—offered by second-term Rep. Tom Rooney (R-Fla.)—to come to the floor for a public vote, knowing it would pass. They easily could have stopped the amendment from being offered, using the leadership-appointed members of the Rules Committee.

Instead, it became the first amendment to the floor, and it sailed through the House by 35 votes, garnering Republican and Democratic support. When asked about it, Boehner said he is "committed to the House working its will.... This is not about me, this is not about my district, this ought to be about the U.S. House speaking on behalf of all Americans, both Democrats and Republicans."

But the House action doesn't ensure the death of the program. Sen. Rob Portman (R-Ohio), a former House colleague of Boehner's, and Sen. Sherrod Brown (D-Ohio) both favor the project. When asked if Boehner would urge them to restore funding, the speaker said: "I have no comment."

The engine amendment was just the start of what will be a protracted, two-year debate on spending in Washington, and Ohio and Virginia will have a lot at stake when the focus turns to the military.

Near Boehner's western Ohio district sits Wright-Patterson Air Force Base—one of the largest in the country, and the largest single-site employer in the Buckeye State with 27,000 in active duty, civilians and contractors.

A large-scale program based out of Wright-Patterson was spared in the House debate on the continuing resolution: a roughly $539 million 2010 allocation for a program to acquire and develop a new generation of air tankers. The bid for the program, called KC-X, was awarded to Boeing.

Other than that, officials at the base don't know how cuts in Boehner's House will affect them.

"There are overall efforts to become more efficient, and we know the Air Force has looked across the board to identify $3.4 billion in efficiencies in FY12," said base spokesman Daryl Mayer. "That certainly affects us."

Michael Steel, a spokesman for Boehner, said that the speaker "promised the people of the 8th District of Ohio that he will work for a secure America and a smaller, more accountable government."

"That is how he will approach all issues relating to the federal budget," Steel told POLITICO.

While Ohioans may be unsure of the impact on jobs there, that's not the case in Virginia, where one of the largest military bases—U.S. Joint Forces Command in Norfolk—is slated to be shut down.

President Barack Obama, along with the Defense Department, has ordered the shuttering of what's known as JFCOM in a bid for more efficiency. Not all the jobs would be lost, since the administration has signaled they would try to keep some in the state.

Cantor, when he was in the minority, spoke out loudly against the closure—as did nearly all Virginia politicians. Virginia Republicans—including Cantor—sent a letter to Defense Secretary Robert Gates saying that they were "alarmed" at Gates's "lack of analytical rigor" in supporting the base's shuttering.

During the House budget debate, GOP leadership allowed Rep. Randy Forbes (R-Va.) to offer an amendment blocking the Defense Department from spending any money to shut down the Norfolk facility. It passed by voice vote, allowing members to avoid a recorded vote on the issue.

Anger with Cantor over military cuts extends even to some of the most unlikely of places: funding of the Metrorail system.

Recent base closures across the country have funneled scores of new military personnel to Fort Belvoir and Quantico, adding to the population of Fairfax County and other localities. Local officials are leaning on their congressional delegation to secure funding for road and transit improvements to ease expected congestion problems.

But the House budget measure zeroed out funding for Metro. "I thought we were all for one, one for all," said Rep. Gerry Connolly (D-Va.), who thought Cantor should take a tougher stance on keeping Metro funding.

Cantor aides declined to say how he'll balance military cuts in Virginia with cutting budgets. They also wouldn't reveal whether their boss shouted out "aye" or "nay" to the Forbes amendment that protected the Norfolk military facility. And they won't share his thoughts on cuts to Metro or whether he would support funding the controversial GE engine if that comes back from the Senate.

"Eric has made clear that he is committed to cutting government spending so that we can begin to live within our means, while ensuring the safety and security of our country," press secretary Laena Fallon said in response to a list of detailed questions.

With 9.6 percent unemployment in Ohio and 6.7 in Virginia, the leadership pair hardly would like to see more people without jobs. But the cuts to military personnel could keep coming. The 2012 budgets and beyond are expected to include even deeper cuts to a variety of departments—including military offices.

That is likely to incite debate from yet another Republican corner, those who oppose significant military cuts for national security reasons.

Earlier this month, as the House was finishing its work on the budget measure, The Heritage Foundation released a memo with a blaring headline: "Defense Cuts in FY 2011 Would Hurt Troops."

"Clearly, defense spending is not 'out of control,' nor is it the cause of our rapidly ballooning debt," Heritage Vice President Kim Murphy wrote elsewhere on the group's website. "And yet lawmakers insist our security take a hit."

ARTICLE QUESTIONS

1) What does Sherman mean by a "political twofer"?
2) How does the bicameral structure of the U.S. Congress allow Boehner to pull off this twofer?
3) How do you think Boehner would have behaved if he couldn't rely on the Senate to kill the bill he allowed to pass in the House? Can we ever know for sure?
4) Based on Boehner's action in the article, do you think the bicameral nature of the U.S. Congress harms Americans' ability to hold their elected officials accountable?

Chapter 14

The Presidency

Many in the United States view the president as the most powerful person in the world. But how powerful is the constitutionally created presidency? Some scholars argue it is a weak office with few explicit powers that is further circumscribed by abundant congressional checks. Other scholars argue the United States has an imperial presidency capable of acting unilaterally in the face of congressional and judicial resistance. How can scholars' perceptions diverge so widely? As we will see, it is not always clear what powers the president may exercise. Further, it is also possible that the powers of the presidency vary based on circumstances. Since the power of the president partially relies on powers delegated by Congress, and Congress possesses numerous checks on presidential power, Congress's inclination to control presidential actions may determine the extent of presidential power.

If the president were confined to exercising the powers clearly expressed by the Constitution—typically termed the expressed powers—the office appears very weak. (Article II, which lays out the powers of the president, is both brief and vague.) But this hasn't prevented presidents, starting with George Washington, from asserting the prerogative to act where the Constitution is silent. Asserting this prerogative alters the brevity of Article II from a constraint to an expansion of executive authority. Supporters of a strong presidency claim that there are vast inherent powers that come with being president, even if the Constitution doesn't explicitly list them. There are also powers delegated to the president from Congress, and then there are informal powers possessed by the president (which derive from being a celebrity and being able to appeal directly to the people). When one considers the modern expressed, inherent, delegated, and informal powers, perhaps the presidency has transformed from a weak office into an imperial one.

All of the readings in this chapter confront (and try to clarify) the powers of the presidency. George Will, a Pulitzer Prize–winning writer known for his conservative journalism, argues that the Constitution places significant restraints on presidential war powers in "Congress's Unused War Powers." To accentuate his argument, Will provides examples "of Congress restraining executive war-making." Ultimately, his point is that Congress has the constitutional duty and power to restrain the presidency in the area of war powers, but all too often the institution allows itself to be marginalized by the president. While Will argues that Congress needs to assert its authority, Anita Kumar, in "Obama Turning to Executive Power to Get What He Wants," provides examples of President Obama asserting presidential authority in the face of congressional inaction. This article reflects the protracted debate about the appropriate use and limits of unilateral executive action. The article also hints at an important theme in the debate about presidential power: when a president takes unilateral actions one supports, these actions are often justified, but when the president takes similar actions one finds objectionable, they are often denounced as executive overreach. After all the debate about the proper role of the presidency in a democratic government, is it possible that an "imperial presidency" is simply one that takes actions we personally oppose?

The next two articles argue that Americans place unrealistic expectations on the president. Allen Greenblatt, reporting for *National Public Radio* in "Why Obama (And Any President) Fails to Meet Expectations," reemphasizes "that presidents are at the mercy of Congress." Greenblatt acknowledges that this is something that many people know, but he asserts that this critically important point often "gets overlooked in the rush to assume that what a president wants, a president can get." Greenblatt also suggests that presidential power may not be the same at all times. He notes that when divided government, polarized political parties, and split public approval ratings of the president exist, it is doubtful that any president will be able to realize his or her agenda. These restraints may expose the popular restraint placed on the presidency. If the president's power peaks when a large majority of the population, and Congress, supports them, then the ability to take unilateral presidential action may expand and contract based on popular support. Political scientist Norm Ornstein writes in his *National Journal* article "The Most Enduring Myth about the Presidency" that the environment surrounding a president determines presidential success. Orenstein is critical of arguments that attribute presidential success to a president's persuasive abilities. As he sees it, a president's success hinges on the number in Congress who are support the president's goals rather than the number of congressmembers the president can persuade.

So which is it? Is the presidency a weak office or is there an imperial presidency? If we focus on the formally expressed powers, the presidency may seem weak. If we view how the presidency has functioned with these powers, perhaps the office appears mighty. It is also possible we have both types of presidencies. Perhaps some conditions allow a president to take advantage of expressed, inherent, delegated, and informal powers while other conditions restrain the use of these powers.

CHAPTER QUESTIONS

1) What powers does the presidency now have that are not explicitly expressed in the Constitution?
2) How does the power of the presidency relate to the powers of the other two branches?
3) What conditions allow a president to be powerful?
4) What role does a president's personality play in his or her ability to achieve their agenda?
5) What is the proper role of the presidency in a democracy?

CHAPTER READINGS

14.1) George Will, "Congress's Unused War Powers," *The Washington Post*, November 4, 2007.

14.2) Anita Kumar, "Obama Turning to Executive Power to Get What He Wants," *McClatchy Newspapers*, March 19, 2013.

14.3) Allen Greenblatt, "Why Obama (And Any President) Fails to Meet Expectations," *National Public Radio*, March 12, 2013.

14.4) Norm Ornstein, "The Most Enduring Myth about the Presidency," *National Journal*, April 22, 2014.

14.1) Congress's Unused War Powers

The Washington Post, November 4, 2007

GEORGE WILL

The Constitution grants few exclusive powers to the president; almost all of the president's powers are shared with Congress. Yet, every president since Harry Truman has claimed that inherent in being commander in chief is the exclusive authority to deploy troops whenever and wherever the president chooses. While it is true that the president is "Commander in Chief of the Army and Navy," the Constitution charges Congress with raising an Army and Navy, declaring war, and authorizing funding for war. The Constitution appears to split war powers more than most presidents admit, and more than most people realize. As George Will points out in "Congress's Unused War Powers," Congress sometimes neglects its constitutional war powers. Will fears that when Congress does, it delegates even more authority to the president.

Will observes that "American history is replete with examples of Congress restraining executive war-making." But he also asserts that members of Congress are more likely to challenge presidential war making when the president is in the opposing party. Partisan views of presidential power are not confined to Congress; many journalists and citizens use a partisan lens when critiquing a president for going beyond his or her constitutional authority. The fact that this is often the case makes this article even more interesting. Will is a well-known conservative intellectual and journalist, but he wrote this critique of presidential overreach in 2007, when Republican George Bush was president. Will even critiques other Republicans, like former New York Governor Rudy Giuliani, for misreading the extent of presidential power.

Americans are wondering, with the lassitude of uninvolved spectators, whether the president will initiate a war with Iran. Some Democratic presidential candidates worry, or purport to, that he might claim an authorization for war in a Senate resolution labeling an Iranian Revolutionary Guard unit a terrorist organization. Some Democratic representatives oppose the president's request for $88 million to equip B-2 stealth bombers to carry huge "bunker-buster" bombs, hoping to thereby impede a presidential decision to attack Iran's hardened nuclear facilities.

While legislators try to leash a president by tinkering with a weapon, they are ignoring a sufficient leash—the Constitution. They are derelict in their sworn duty to uphold it. Regarding the most momentous thing government does, make war, the constitutional system of checks and balances is broken.

Congress can, however, put the Constitution's bridle back on the presidency. Congress can end unfettered executive war-making by *deciding* to. That might not require, but would be facilitated by, enacting the Constitutional War Powers Resolution. Introduced last week by Rep. Walter B. Jones, a North Carolina Republican, it technically amends but essentially would supplant the existing War Powers Resolution, which has been a nullity ever since it was passed in 1973 over President Richard Nixon's veto.

Jones's measure is designed to ensure that deciding to go to war is, as the Founders insisted it be, a "collective judgment." It would prohibit presidents from initiating military actions except to repel or retaliate for sudden attacks on America or American troops abroad, or to protect and evacuate U.S. citizens abroad. It would provide for expedited judicial review to enforce compliance with the resolution and would permit the use of federal funds only for military actions taken in compliance with the resolution.

It reflects conclusions reached by the War Powers Initiative of the Constitution Project. That nonpartisan organization's 2005 study notes that Congress's appropriation power augments the requirement of advance authorization by Congress before the nation goes to war. It enables Congress to stop the use of force by cutting off its funding. That check is augmented by the Antideficiency Act, which prohibits any expenditure or obligation of funds not appropriated by Congress, and by legislation that criminalizes violations of the act.

All this refutes Rudy Giuliani's recent suggestion that the president might have "the inherent authority to support the troops" even if funding were cut off. Besides, American history is replete with examples of Congress restraining executive warmaking. (See "Congress at War: The Politics of Conflict Since 1789," a book by Charles A. Stevenson.) Congress has forbidden: Sending draftees outside this hemisphere (1940–41); introduction of combat troops into Laos or Thailand (1969); reintroduction of troops into Cambodia (1970); combat operations in Southeast Asia (1973); military operations in Angola (1976); use of force in Lebanon other than for self-defense (1983); military activities in Nicaragua (1980s). In 1993 and 1994, Congress mandated the withdrawal of troops from Somalia and forbade military actions in Rwanda.

When Congress authorized the president "to use all necessary and appropriate force" against those complicit in the September 11, 2001, attacks, Congress *refused* to adopt administration language authorizing force "to deter and preempt any future" terrorism or aggression. The wonder is that the administration bothered to seek this language.

The administration's "presidentialists"—including the president—believe presidents are constitutionally emancipated from all restraints regarding core executive functions, particularly those concerning defense and waging war. Clearly they think the rejected language would have added nothing to the president's inherent powers.

Congress's powers were most dramatically abandoned and ignored regarding Korea. Although President Harry S. Truman came from a Congress controlled by his party and friends, he never sought congressional authorization to send troops into massive and sustained conflict. Instead, he asserted broad authority to "execute" treaties such as the U.N. Charter.

For today's Democrats, resistance to unilateral presidential war-making reflects not principled constitutionalism but petulance about the current president. Democrats were supine when President Bill Clinton launched a sustained air war against Serbia without congressional authorization. Instead, he cited NATO's authorization—as though that were an adequate substitute for the collective judgment that the Constitution mandates. Republicans, supposed defenders of limited government, actually are enablers of an unlimited presidency. Their belief in strict construction of the Constitution evaporates, and they become, in behavior if not in thought, adherents of the woolly idea of a "living Constitution." They endorse, by their passivity, the idea that new threats justify ignoring the Framers' text and logic about shared responsibility for war-making.

Unless and until Congress stops prattling about presidential "usurpation" of power and asserts its own, it will remain derelict regarding its duty of mutual participation in war-making. And it will merit its current marginalization.

ARTICLE QUESTIONS

1) According to Will, how did the Framers insist the decision to go to war should be made?

2) What are two examples of Congress restraining executive war making included in the article?

3) Even if Will is correct in his assertion that the Constitution assigns Congress the "duty of mutual participation in war-making," is this still a desirable division of powers? Why or why not?

4) What should be done when a president usurps congressional war powers?

14.2) Obama Turning to Executive Power to Get What He Wants

McClatchy Newspapers, March 19, 2013

ANITA KUMAR

Anita Kumar, in "Obama Turning to Executive Power to Get What He Wants," provides examples of President Obama asserting unilateral executive authority in the face of congressional inaction. Executive orders are directives given by the president to executive agencies that have the force of law but do not go through Congress. Some executive orders cover minuscule details for organizing executive branch operations such as setting up a new council or office, or for defining how the U.S. flag is to be designed. Others, such as the examples provided in the article, have gone so far as to "delay the deportation of young illegal immigrants when Congress wouldn't agree . . . or required the Centers for Disease Control and Prevention to research gun violence, which Congress halted nearly 15 years ago." Executive orders like these two are especially controversial when they are used to maneuver around Congress because Congress refuses, or is unable, to take action. Still, executive orders are more limited than legislation, and they can be replaced by the next president. For example, an executive order by President Obama to increase the minimum wage for federal contract workers from $7.25 to $10.10 will likely affect about 500,000 workers, but only federal legislation passed by Congress could apply this wage increase to all workers, and the following president could rescind this pay raise with a conflicting executive order.

It is very rare for Congress or the Supreme Court to put the brakes on an executive order. Of the nearly 14,000 executive orders issued in U.S. history, only two have been struck down by the Court. Congress can refuse to fund an executive order or pass legislation that directly conflicts with the presidential directive, but that legislation is subject to a presidential veto. However, while the article quotes some groups lamenting President Obama's use of executive authority, it also cites other groups encouraging him to take bolder actions. This might show that many Americans aren't as fearful of unilateral presidential action as they are of policies they don't like.

WASHINGTON—President Barack Obama came into office four years ago skeptical of pushing the power of the White House to the limit, especially if it appeared to be circumventing Congress.

Now, as he launches his second term, Obama has grown more comfortable wielding power to try to move his own agenda forward, particularly when a deeply fractured, often-hostile Congress gets in his way.

He's done it with a package of tools, some of which date to George Washington and some invented in the modern era of an increasingly powerful presidency. And he's done it with a frequency that belies his original campaign criticisms of predecessor George W. Bush, invites criticisms that he's bypassing the checks and balances of Congress and the courts, and whets the appetite of liberal activists who want him to do even more to advance their goals.

While his decision to send drones to kill U.S. citizens suspected of terrorism has garnered a torrent of criticism, his use of executive orders and other powers at home is deeper and wider.

He delayed the deportation of young illegal immigrants when Congress wouldn't agree. He ordered the Centers for Disease Control and Prevention to research gun violence, which Congress halted nearly 15 years ago. He told the Justice Department to stop defending the Defense of Marriage Act, deciding that the 1996 law defining marriage as between a man and a woman was unconstitutional. He's vowed to act on his own if Congress didn't pass policies to prepare for climate change.

Arguably more than any other president in modern history, he's using executive actions, primarily orders, to bypass or pressure a Congress where the opposition Republicans can block any proposal.

"It's gridlocked and dysfunctional. The place is a mess," said Rena Steinzor, a law professor at the University of Maryland. "I think (executive action) is an inevitable tool given what's happened."

Now that Obama has showed a willingness to use those tactics, advocacy groups, supporters and even members of Congress are lobbying him to do so more and more.

The Center for Progressive Reform, a liberal advocacy group composed of law professors, including Steinzor, has pressed Obama to sign seven executive orders on health, safety and the environment during his second term.

Seventy environmental groups wrote a letter urging the president to restrict emissions at existing power plants.

Sen. Barbara Mikulski, D-Md., the chairwoman of the Appropriations Committee, sent a letter to the White House asking Obama to ban federal contractors from retaliating against employees who share salary information.

Gay rights organizations recently demonstrated in front of the White House to encourage the president to sign an executive order to bar discrimination based on sexual orientation or gender identity by companies that have federal contracts, eager for Obama to act after nearly two decades of failed attempts to get Congress to pass a similar bill.

"It's ridiculous that we're having to push this hard for the president to simply pick up a pen," said Heather Cronk, the managing director of the gay rights group GetEQUAL. "It's reprehensible that, after signing orders on gun control, cybersecurity and all manner of other topics, the president is still laboring over this decision."

The White House didn't respond to repeated requests for comment.

In January, Obama said he continued to believe that legislation was "sturdier and more stable" than executive actions, but that sometimes they were necessary, such as his January directive for the federal government to research gun violence.

"There are certain issues where a judicious use of executive power can move the argument forward or solve problems that are of immediate-enough import that we can't afford not to do it," the former constitutional professor told *The New Republic* magazine.

Presidents since George Washington have signed executive orders, an oft-overlooked power not explicitly defined in the Constitution. More than half of all executive orders in the nation's history—nearly 14,000—have been issued since 1933.

Many serve symbolic purposes, from lowering flags to creating a new military medal. Some are used to form commissions or give federal employees a day off. Still others are more serious, and contentious: Abraham Lincoln releasing political prisoners, Franklin D. Roosevelt creating internment camps for Japanese-Americans, Dwight Eisenhower desegregating schools.

"Starting in the 20th century, we have seen more and more that have lawlike functions," said Gene Healy, a vice president of the Cato Institute, a libertarian research center, who's the author of "The Cult of the Presidency: America's Dangerous Devotion to Executive Power."

Most presidents in recent history generally have issued a few hundred orders, and hundreds more memorandums and directives.

Jimmy Carter initiated a program designed to end discrimination at colleges. Ronald Reagan overturned price controls on domestic oil production. George H. W. Bush stopped imports of some semi-automatic firearms. Bill Clinton set aside large tracts of land as national monuments. George W. Bush made it easier for religious groups to receive federal dollars.

"The expectation is that they all do this," said Ken Mayer, a political science professor at the University of Wisconsin-Madison who wrote "With the Stroke of a Pen: Executive Orders and Presidential Power." "That is the typical way of doing things."

But, experts say, Obama's actions are more noticeable because as a candidate he was critical of Bush's use of power. In particular, he singled out his predecessor's use of signing statements, documents issued when a president signs a bill that clarifies his understanding of the law.

"These last few years we've seen an unacceptable abuse of power at home," Obama said in an October 2007 speech. "We've paid a heavy price for having a president whose priority is expanding his own power."

Yet Obama's use of power echoes that of his predecessors. For example, he signed 145 executive orders in his first term, putting him on track to issue as many as the 291 that Bush did in two terms.

John Yoo, who wrote the legal opinions that supported an expansion of presidential power after the 2001 terrorist attacks, including harsh interrogation methods that some called torture, said he thought that executive orders were sometimes appropriate—when conducting internal management and implementing power given to the president by Congress or the Constitution—but he thinks that Obama has gone too far.

"I think President Obama has been as equally aggressive as President Bush, and in fact he has sometimes used the very same language to suggest that he would not obey congressional laws that intrude on his commander-in-chief power," said Yoo, who's now a law professor at the University of California at Berkeley. "This is utterly hypocritical, both when compared to his campaign stances and the position of his supporters in Congress, who have suddenly discovered the virtues of silence."

Most of Obama's actions are written statements aimed at federal agencies that are published everywhere from the White House website to the Federal Register. Some are classified and hidden from public view.

"It seems to be more calculated to prod Congress," said Phillip J. Cooper, the author of "By Order of the President: The Use and Abuse of Executive Direct Action." "I can't remember a president being that consistent, direct and public."

Bush was criticized for many of his actions on surveillance and interrogation techniques, but attention has focused on Obama's use of actions mostly about domestic issues.

In his first two years in the White House, when fellow Democrats controlled Capitol Hill, Obama largely worked through the regular legislative process to try to achieve his domestic agenda. His biggest achievements—including a federal health care overhaul and a stimulus package designed to boost the economy—came about with little or no Republican support.

But Republicans took control of the House of Representatives in 2010, making the task of passing legislation all the more difficult for a man with a detached personality who doesn't relish schmoozing with lawmakers. By the next year, Obama wasn't shy about his reasons for flexing his presidential power.

In fall 2011, he launched the "We Can't Wait" campaign, unveiling dozens of policies through executive orders—creating jobs for veterans, adopting fuel efficiency standards and stopping drug shortages—that came straight from his jobs bills that faltered in Congress.

"We're not waiting for Congress," Obama said in Denver that year when he announced a plan to reduce college costs. "I intend to do everything in my power right now to act on behalf of the American people, with or without Congress. We can't wait for Congress to do its job. So where they won't act, I will."

When Congress killed legislation aimed at curbing the emissions that cause global warming, Obama directed the Environmental Protection Agency to write regulations on its own incorporating some parts of the bill.

When Congress defeated pro-union legislation, he had the National Labor Relations Board and the Labor Department issue rules incorporating some parts of the bill.

"The president looks more and more like a king that the Constitution was designed to replace," Sen. Charles Grassley, R-Iowa, said on the Senate floor last year.

While Republicans complain that Obama's actions cross a line, experts say some of them are less aggressive than they appear.

After the mass shooting in Newtown, Conn., in December, the White House boasted of implementing 23 executive actions to curb gun control. In reality, Obama issued a trio of modest directives that instructed federal agencies to trace guns and send information for background checks to a database.

In his State of the Union address last month, Obama instructed businesses to improve the security of computers to help prevent hacking. But he doesn't have the legal authority to force private companies to act.

"The executive order can be a useful tool but there are only certain things he can do," said Melanie Teplinsky, an American University law professor who's spoken extensively on cyber-law.

Executive actions often are fleeting. They generally don't settle a political debate, and the next president, Congress or a court may overturn them.

Consider the so-called Mexico City policy. With it, Reagan banned federal money from going to international family-planning groups that provide abortions. Clinton rescinded the policy. George W. Bush reinstated it, and Obama reversed course again.

But congressional and legal action are rare. In 1952, the Supreme Court threw out Harry Truman's order authorizing the seizure of steel mills during a series of strikes. In 1996, the District of Columbia Court of Appeals dismissed an order by Clinton that banned the government from contracting with companies that hire workers despite an ongoing strike.

Obama has seen some pushback.

Congress prohibited him from spending money to move inmates from the Guantanamo Bay U.S. naval base in Cuba after he signed an order that said it would close. A Chinese company sued Obama for killing its wind farm projects by executive order after he said they were too close to a military training site. A federal appeals court recently ruled that he'd exceeded his constitutional powers when he named several people to the National Labor Relations Board while the Senate was in recess.

But Obama appears to be undaunted.

"If Congress won't act soon to protect future generations," he told Congress last month, "I will."

ARTICLE QUESTIONS

1) Name four executive actions taken by President Obama that are listed in the article.
2) What executive actions does the article list "advocacy groups, supporters and even members of Congress are lobbying" President Obama to adopt?
3) How does President Obama's use of executive orders rate compared to previous presidents?
4) Under what conditions (if any) should a president act unilaterally if Congress is failing to take action?

14.3) Why Obama (And Any President) Fails to Meet Expectations

National Public Radio, March 12, 2013

ALAN GREENBLATT

Allen Greenblatt, reporting for *National Public Radio*, argues in "Why Obama (And Any President) Fails to Meet Expectations" that the "perceived failings [of modern presidents] may be the result of an inflated expectations game." We can summarize Greenblatt's explanation of the game like this: people's expectations of the president are widely unrealistic, and as a result presidents overpromise—which further increases our expectations. In the end, the public feels the president failed to deliver on these expectations, no matter how unrealistic they were.

Despite the fact that "presidents are at the mercy of Congress," Greenblatt highlights that the United States tends to be a very "president-centric" country. He emphasizes this presidential focus by pointing to monuments like Mt. Rushmore and the portraits of presidents hanging in many elementary school classrooms. Think about these additional examples not in Greenblatt's article: we have become accustomed to referring to "the Bush era tax cuts," which ignores Congress's control of the budget, and we refer to "Bush's War in Iraq" without acknowledging that Congress authorized the funding. Abraham Lincoln is referred to as the Great Emancipator (despite the fact that the Emancipation Proclamation allowed slavery to continue in at least three states), but the 38th Congress that drafted the Thirteenth Amendment (which is what abolished legalized slavery throughout the United States) is largely forgotten.

Greenblatt sees the level of presidential power as fluctuating. When there is divided government (when at least one house of Congress is controlled by a different party from the president's), when political parties are polarized, and when nearly half the country doesn't approve of the president, it is even more difficult for a president to accomplish his or her agenda. On the other hand, popular presidents with a large majority from their own party in Congress can accomplish a great deal. In short, public opinion and separation of powers might produce a powerful president at some times and a weak one at others.

As with other recent presidents, Barack Obama is disliked and distrusted by roughly half the public. But some of his perceived failings may be the result of an inflated expectations game that all modern presidents must play.

Whether President Obama attacks members of Congress, takes them out to dinner or pays them visits on Capitol Hill, he needs their support in order to achieve major parts of his agenda.

That presidents are at the mercy of Congress when it comes to budgets and legislation is an obvious point, and one deeply embedded in the U.S. constitutional system.

But it's a truism that often gets overlooked in the rush to assume that what a president wants, a president can get.

"We are taught that presidents are the center of government, and great presidents can make things happen," says Matthew Eshbaugh-Soha, a political scientist at the University of North Texas. "There's this Rushmore view, and it's a myth."

Obama has made mistakes, and, naturally, many Americans think his policies on issues such as tax rates and health care were wrongheaded to begin with. However, some of his perceived failings may be the result of an inflated expectations game that all modern presidents must play.

"Expectations tend to be wildly unrealistic," says Thomas Mann, a senior fellow at the Brookings Institution. "Presidents can be important, but their scope for solving problems that are the source of substantial disagreement [is] exceedingly limited within our constitutional system."

Given the constraints of divided government and the current polarized landscape, not many presidents would be able to accomplish more than Obama has, says Lara Brown, a political scientist at Pennsylvania's Villanova University.

Still, all presidents are dealt tough cards. Obama has not always played his well, Brown argues, because he tends to promise more than he can deliver and then attempt to lay the blame elsewhere, typically on congressional Republicans.

"I don't imagine history will forgive him for his self-constructed victimhood to the House GOP," she says. "Successful leaders control the political definition of their actions."

Majesty of the Office

Walk into an elementary-school classroom, and chances are still pretty good that you'll see mini-portraits of all of the presidents lining the wall.

Schoolchildren, however, are not taught the names of Thomas B. Reed or Nelson W. Aldrich or any other bygone congressional leaders.

"My 6-year-old daughter, when she was asked what she would do as president, said she'd lower taxes and bring peace to the world," says Jack Pitney, a government professor at Claremont McKenna College in California. "That's the way children think of the world—that presidents actually do these things."

That sense of the majesty and centrality of the presidency tends to stay with Americans as adults. Books such as *The Age of Reagan* and *The Age of Jackson* argue through their very titles that presidents can dominate and define their eras.

"The modern presidency is in fact that notion that the president is in some sense front and center," says Bill Connelly, a political scientist at Washington and Lee University in Virginia.

Less Potential to Persuade

But in order to achieve great things, a president has to bend Congress and the country to his will.

"It's tough governing," says Mann, the Brookings scholar. "It's especially tough now, given the differences between the parties."

Mann faults congressional Republicans for being unyielding. He notes that many 1960s-era members of the GOP were willing to support Lyndon B. Johnson's civil rights agenda. Conversely, conservative Democrats backed Ronald Reagan's tax cuts in 1981, even as their party controlled the House.

But liberal Republicans and conservative Democrats are few and far between these days. Old-fashioned aisle-crossing seldom happens, making life difficult for a president facing a divided Congress.

In addition, the public has become more polarized. As with other recent presidents, Obama is disliked and distrusted by roughly half the public.

"If you're looking at half the population that disagrees with you already, it's not like the president can put pressure on Congress by making people agree with him," says Eshbaugh-Soha of the University of North Texas. "If a president once had real potential to influence the public through speeches, that really isn't possible anymore."

Can't Control the Economy

There's some research to suggest that presidents who talk optimistically about the economy can help boost consumer confidence, Eshbaugh-Soha notes. But even if a president can convince the nation and Congress that his economic ideas are the way to go, he'll still have a limited ability to shape the economy.

As Pitney notes, a president is only one part of a government that controls only some aspects of the economy. The political branches set fiscal policy (tax and spending rates), yet have limited influence over what the Federal Reserve decides regarding monetary policy (interest rates and the size of the money supply).

All of these governmental actors in total may help set conditions, but they can't make a market economy boom on their own—especially in an era of global finance. While presidential fortunes may rise and fall with the economy, expectations that a president can create jobs or make the economy grow are generally overblown.

"That expectation, that presidents have the wherewithal to manage the economy, has led the economy to control any number of presidents, Republicans and Democrats," says Connelly, the Washington and Lee political scientist. "The economy goes down, and we blame presidents. It sets presidents up for failure."

What Have You Done Lately?

All presidents may nod with recognition when reminded of Abraham Lincoln's words from 1864: "I claim not to have controlled events, but confess plainly that events have controlled me."

For certain, all presidents have the same set of powers granted to them by the Constitution to make appointments and veto legislation. How they combine those enunciated powers with less formal ones, such as their command of the bully pulpit, in order to respond to the events of their time is what separates the great ones from the mediocre.

"Obama's dilemma was also Bush's dilemma, and Clinton's, etc.," Connelly says.

It's impossible to judge presidential success in midterm. Connelly notes that many presidents regarded as failures still managed to achieve some real victories.

Americans empower presidents when they need to, he says, whether it was Lincoln during the Civil War or George W. Bush following the attacks of September 11, 2001. "Then we immediately start pushing back and trying to humble these individuals," Connelly says.

That might be the perverse upside to the expectations game. Hoping for so much from the White

House, Americans tend to denigrate presidents who disappoint—a mood swing that keeps our awe of the office in check.

"We use these people and we throw them out," Connelly says. "Madison would say it's a good thing, that as a democratic people we are impatient."

ARTICLE QUESTIONS

1) What do you think are the ultimate repercussions of the American public's unrealistic expectations of the president?
2) Do you think a candidate for president could get elected if he or she didn't "overpromise" what he or she could accomplish?

14.4) The Most Enduring Myth about the Presidency

National Journal, April 22, 2014

NORM ORNSTEIN

The Green Lantern theory just won't go away.

In "The Most Enduring Myth about the Presidency" political scientist Norm Ornstein seeks to dispel the myth of an all-powerful presidency possessed with heroic powers. Ornstein claims it is the environment surrounding a president, not the president's persuasive powers, that determines success.

Ornstein argues that for a president to accomplish his or her agenda the president must have the support of Congress and the public. But the ability to get members of Congress on the president's side is not determined by the president's persuasive competency. Orenstein argues that a president needs a Congress staffed with a sufficient number of members from his or her political party, and Congress must contain members of the opposing party willing to work with the president. Based on this calculation, a president achieves his or her agenda not because the president can "bully" (or persuade) others, but because the president's goals are in sync with those of other elected officials.

The LBJ Library recently held a multiday program to commemorate the 50th anniversary of the Civil Rights Act, and by all accounts, the program was stirring and stimulating, up to and including President Obama's speech.

But there was one downside: the reactivation of one of the most enduring memes and myths about the presidency, and especially the Obama presidency. Like Rasputin (or Whac-A-Mole), it keeps coming back even after it has been bludgeoned and obliterated by facts and logic. I feel compelled to whack this mole once more.

The meme is what Matthew Yglesias, writing in 2006, referred to as "the Green Lantern Theory of Geopolitics," and has been refined by Greg Sargent

and Brendan Nyhan into the Green Lantern Theory of the presidency. In a nutshell, it attributes heroic powers to a president—if only he would use them. And the holders of this theory have turned it into the meme that if only Obama used his power of persuasion, he could have the kind of success that LBJ enjoyed with the Great Society, that Bill Clinton enjoyed in his alliance with Newt Gingrich that gave us welfare reform and fiscal success, that Ronald Reagan had with Dan Rostenkowski and Bill Bradley to get tax reform, and so on.

If only Obama had dealt with Congress the way LBJ did—persuading, cajoling, threatening, and sweet-talking members to attain his goals—his presidency would not be on the ropes and he would be a hero. If only Obama would schmooze with lawmakers the way Bill Clinton did, he would have much greater success. If only Obama would work with Republicans and not try to steamroll them, he could be a hero and have a fiscal deal that would solve the long-term debt problem.

If only the proponents of this theory would step back and look at the realities of all these presidencies (or would read or reread the Richard Neustadt classic, *Presidential Power*).

I do understand the sentiment here and the frustration over the deep dysfunction that has taken over our politics. It is tempting to believe that a president could overcome the tribalism, polarization, and challenges of the permanent campaign, by doing what other presidents did to overcome their challenges. It is not as if passing legislation and making policy was easy in the old days.

But here is the reality, starting with the Johnson presidency. I do not want to denigrate LBJ or downplay his remarkable accomplishments and the courage he displayed in taking on his own base, Southern Democrats, to enact landmark civil-rights and voting-rights laws that have done more to transform America in a positive way than almost anything else in our lifetimes. And it is a fact that the 89th Congress, that of the Great Society, can make the case for having more sweeping accomplishments, from voting rights to Medicare to elementary and secondary education reform, than any other.

LBJ had a lot to do with the agenda, and the accomplishments. But his drive for civil rights was aided in 1964 by having the momentum following John F. Kennedy's assassination, and the partnership of Republicans Everett Dirksen and Bill McCullough, detailed beautifully in new books by Clay Risen and Todd Purdum. And Johnson was aided substantially in 1965–66 by having swollen majorities of his own party in both chambers of Congress—68 of 100 senators, and 295 House members, more than 2-to-1 margins. While Johnson needed, and got, substantial Republican support on civil rights and voting rights to overcome Southern Democrats' opposition, he did not get a lot of Republicans supporting the rest of his domestic agenda. He had enough Democrats supporting those policies to ensure passage, and he got enough GOP votes on final passage of key bills to ensure the legitimacy of the actions.

Johnson deserves credit for horse-trading (for example, finding concessions to give to Democrat Wilbur Mills, chairman of the House Ways and Means Committee, to get his support for Medicare), but it was the numbers that made the difference. Consider what happened in the next two years, after the 1966 midterm elections depleted Democratic ranks and enlarged Republican ones. LBJ was still the great master of Congress—but without the votes, the record was anything but robust. All the cajoling and persuading and horse-trading in the world did not matter.

Now briefly consider other presidents. Ronald Reagan was a master negotiator, and he has the distinction of having two major pieces of legislation, tax reform and immigration reform, enacted in his second term, without the overwhelming numbers that Johnson enjoyed in 1965–66. What Reagan did have, just like Johnson had on civil rights, was active and eager partners from the other party. The drive for tax reform did not start with Reagan, but with Democrats Bill Bradley and Dick Gephardt, whose reform bill became the template for the law that ultimately passed. They, and Ways and Means Chairman Dan Rostenkowski, were delighted to make their mark in history (and for Bradley and Gephardt, to advance their presidential ambitions) by working with the lame-duck Republican president. The same desire to craft transformative policy was there for both Alan Simpson and Ron Mazzoli, a Senate Republican and a House Democrat, who put together immigration legislation with limited involvement by the White House.

As for Bill Clinton, he was as politically adept as any president in modern times, and as charismatic and compelling as anyone. But the reality is that these great talents did not convince a single Republican to support his economic plan in 1993, nor enough Democrats to pass the plan for a crucial seven-plus months; did not stop the Republicans under Speaker Newt Gingrich from shutting down the government twice; and did not stop the House toward the end of his presidency from impeaching him on shaky grounds, with no chance of conviction in the Senate. The brief windows of close cooperation in 1996, after Gingrich's humiliation following the second shutdown, were opened for pragmatic, tactical reasons by Republicans eager to win a second consecutive term in the majority, and ended shortly after they had accomplished that goal.

When Obama had the numbers, not as robust as LBJ's but robust enough, he had a terrific record of legislative accomplishments. The 111th Congress ranks just below the 89th in terms of significant and far-reaching enactments, from the components of the economic stimulus plan to the health care bill to Dodd/Frank and credit-card reform. But all were done with either no or minimal Republican support. LBJ and Reagan had willing partners from the opposite party; Obama has had

none. Nothing that he could have done would have changed the clear, deliberate policy of Republicans uniting to oppose and obstruct his agenda, that altered long-standing Senate norms to use the filibuster in ways it had never been employed before, including in the LBJ, Reagan, and Clinton eras, that drew sharp lines of total opposition on policies like health reform and raising taxes as part of a broad budget deal.

Could Obama have done more to bond with lawmakers? Sure, especially with members of his own party, which would help more now, when he is in the throes of second-term blues, than it would have when he achieved remarkable party unity in his first two years. But the brutal reality, in today's politics, is that LBJ, if he were here now, could not be the LBJ of the Great Society years in this environment. Nobody can, and to demand otherwise is both futile and foolish.

ARTICLE QUESTIONS

1) How does Ornstein explain the "Green Lantern Theory of the presidency"?
2) What conditions does Ornstein claim were necessary for President Johnson to accomplish so much of his agenda?
3) Based on what Ornstein wrote in this article, do you think he would view President Obama as a successful president?

Chapter 15

Bureaucracy

Bureaucracies perform a wide range of jobs—managing the nation's defense, overseeing the economy, forecasting the weather, providing food stamps, monitoring viruses, managing the borders, and much more. Our representative government is only as good as the bureaucracy that puts public policy into effect. Despite all the important functions performed by the federal bureaucracy, politicians from all sides take shots at bureaucrats: they freeze their pay, downsize departments, and disparage millions of individuals. The general public is also critical: our executive bureaucracy costs too much, say some, while others argue that bureaucratic inertia makes it difficult to respond to policy crises. Amidst all the criticisms it is sometimes hard to remember the reason why bureaucracies are created and the important functions they perform.

The national bureaucracy is specifically charged with implementing the laws passed by Congress and signed by the president. But this process culminates in a political tension; it is not readily apparent who is in charge of managing the unelected public servants in the federal bureaucracy. Many different players have a role, including the public, the president, Congress, and interest groups. Even with—or perhaps because of—all those masters, bureaucrats have considerable discretion in how they carry out their work. This freedom poses the threat, of an essential but unelected—and often unaccountable—workforce of civil servants.

Matthew Spalding's article in the *National Review*, "A Republic If You Want It," reflects some of the critiques of bureaucracy. He warns about the expanding role of the federal bureaucracy. However, this reading is more than just an example of the vigorous assaults often leveled at the federal bureaucracy; it also provides an example of the potential tension between preserving representative accountability and expanding the role of unelected administrators.

Douglas Amy, a professor of politics at Mount Holyoke College who publishes the Government is Good website, provides a counterpoint to the types of arguments offered by Spalding. In an essay titled "The Case for Bureaucracy" Amy argues that attacks on bureaucracy are "based more on mythology than reality" and are intentionally "exaggerated" to legitimize appeals for deregulation and privatization. To counter these "myths" he considers "the case *for* bureaucracy" by highlighting numerous studies emphasizing the "valuable and indispensable roles" bureaucracy plays.

The third reading is an excerpt from Robert Reich's 1997 book *Locked in the Cabinet*. Reich's book provides an insider's account of the federal bureaucracy, presented as a series of his diary entries during his tenure as Secretary of Labor (1993–1997). The entries offer deep insights into the complexities of the United States's unusual bureaucratic structure. As you read this excerpt you will join Reich in marveling at the bureaucratic structures that have evolved in the United States to implement legislation and mange government services.

It is difficult to imagine a military, a highway system, or an infrastructure capable of supporting commerce, education, or other public goods in the absence of the federal bureaucracy. While some level of federal bureaucracy is essential to basic notions of good government, this question remains: Is the modern federal bureaucracy compatible with ideals of democratic governance? The readings in this chapter offer the criticisms, praises, and tensions inherent in the ongoing debates over the federal bureaucracy.

CHAPTER QUESTIONS

1) In what ways does bureaucracy challenge representative government?
2) In what ways does bureaucracy support representative government?
3) What are some of the competing arguments that explain the growth of the federal bureaucracy over the past hundred years?
4) Do you think that the federal bureaucracy will continue to expand? Why?

CHAPTER READINGS

15.1) Matthew Spalding, "A Republic If You Want It," *National Review*, February 8, 2010.
15.2) Douglas Amy, "The Case for Bureaucracy," *Government Is Good Blog*, 2007.
15.3) Robert Reich, *Locked in the Cabinet*, selections on Congressional Hearings and Hiring Subordinates. Knopf; First edition, 1997, pp. 37–9, 41–4, 51–2, 108–110.

15.1) A Republic, If You Want It

National Review, February 8, 2010

MATTHEW SPALDING

The Left's overreach invites the Founders' return.

> As a modern-day conservative, Matthew Spalding harkens back to an original vision of the Constitution. He worries that the vision of the Founders is being supplanted by an expanding federal bureaucracy. His article "A Republic If You Want It," from *National Review* (a popular conservative magazine), traces the historic buildup of the federal bureaucracy to depict how the once limited-role of the U.S. government has expanded. He deplores this progression for infringing on individual liberties, the ideals of representative government, and the power of state governments.
>
> One of Spalding's primary complaints is that "many policy decisions that were previously the constitutional responsibility of elected legislators are delegated to faceless bureaucrats." He sees this shift as relegating Congress to a mere "supervisory body overseeing a vast array of administrative policymakers and rulemaking agencies." In addition to Congress being sidelined by the expansion of bureaucracy, Spalding asserts that "this bureaucracy has become so overwhelming that it's not clear how modern presidents can fulfill their constitutional obligation" to faithfully execute the laws. He paints a bleak picture of the federal bureaucracy, where he sees "the real decisions and details of governing" being carried out by "bureaucrats who are mostly unaccountable and invisible to the public."

Our federal government, once limited to certain core functions, now dominates virtually every area of American life. Its authority is all but unquestioned, seemingly restricted only by expediency and the occasional budget constraint.

Congress passes massive pieces of legislation with little serious deliberation, bills that are written in secret and generally unread before the vote. The national legislature is increasingly a supervisory body overseeing a vast array of administrative policymakers and rulemaking agencies. Although the Constitution vests legislative powers in Congress, the majority of "laws" are promulgated in the guise of "regulations" by bureaucrats who are mostly unaccountable and invisible to the public.

Americans are wrapped in an intricate web of government policies and procedures. States, localities, and private institutions are submerged by national programs. The states, which increasingly administer policies emanating from Washington, act like supplicants seeking relief from the federal government. Growing streams of money flow from Washington to every congressional district and municipality, as well as to businesses, organizations, and individuals that are subject to escalating federal regulations.

This bureaucracy has become so overwhelming that it's not clear how modern presidents can fulfill their constitutional obligation to "take care that the laws be faithfully executed." President Obama, like his recent predecessors, has appointed a swarm of policy "czars"—*über*-bureaucrats operating outside the cabinet structure and perhaps the Constitution—to promote political objectives in an administration supposedly under executive control.

Is this the outcome of the greatest experiment in self-government mankind ever has attempted?

We can trace the concept of the modern state back to the theories of Thomas Hobbes, who wanted to replace the old order with an all-powerful "Leviathan" that would impose a new order, and Jean-Jacques Rousseau, who, to achieve absolute equality, favored an absolute state that would rule over the people through a vaguely defined concept called the "general will." It was Alexis de Tocqueville who first pointed out the potential for a new form of despotism in such a centralized, egalitarian state: It might not tyrannize, but it would enervate and extinguish liberty by reducing self-governing people "to being nothing more than a herd of timid and industrious animals of which the government is the shepherd."

The Americanized version of the modern state was born in the early 20th century. American "progressives," under the spell of German thinkers, decided that advances in science and history had opened the possibility of a new, more efficient form of democratic government, which they called the "administrative state." Thus began the most revolutionary change of the last hundred years: the massive shift of power from institutions of constitutional government to a labyrinthine network of unelected, unaccountable experts who would rule in the name of the people.

The great challenge of democracy, as the Founders understood it, was to restrict and structure the government to secure the rights articulated in the Declaration of Independence—preventing tyranny while preserving liberty. The solution was to create a strong, energetic government of limited authority. Its powers were enumerated in a written constitution, separated into functions and responsibilities and further divided between national and state governments in a system of federalism. The result was a framework of limited government and a vast sphere of freedom, leaving ample room for republican self-government.

Progressives viewed the Constitution as a dusty 18th-century plan unsuited for the modern day. Its basic mechanisms were obsolete and inefficient; it was a reactionary document, designed to stifle change. They believed that just as science and reason had brought technological changes and new methods of study to the physical world, they would also bring great improvements to politics and society. For this to be possible, however, government could not be restricted to securing a few natural rights or exercising certain limited powers. Instead, government must become dynamic, constantly changing and growing to pursue the ceaseless objective of *progress*.

The progressive movement—under a Republican president, Theodore Roosevelt, and then a Democratic one, Woodrow Wilson—set forth a platform for modern liberalism to refound America according to ideas that were alien to the original Founders. "Some citizens of this country have never got beyond the Declaration of Independence," Wilson wrote in 1912. "All that progressives ask or desire is permission—in an era when 'development,' 'evolution,' is the scientific word— to interpret the Constitution according to the Darwinian principle; all they ask is recognition of the fact that a nation is a living thing and not a machine."

While the Founders went to great lengths to moderate democracy and limit government, the progressives believed that barriers to change had to be removed or circumvented, and government expanded. To encourage democratic change while directing and controlling it, the progressives posited a sharp distinction between politics and what they called "administration." Politics would remain the realm of expressing opinions, but the real decisions and details of governing would be handled by administrators, separate and immune from the influence of politics.

This permanent class of bureaucrats would address the particulars of accomplishing the broad objectives of reform, making decisions, most of them unseen and beyond public scrutiny, on the basis of scientific facts and statistical data rather than political opinions. The ruling class would reside in the recesses of a host of alphabet agencies such as the FTC (the Federal Trade Commission, created in 1914) and the SEC (the Securities and Exchange Commission, created in 1934). As "objective" and "neutral" experts, the theory went, these administrators would act above petty partisanship and faction.

The progressives emphasized not a *separation* of powers, which divided and checked the government, but rather a *combination* of powers, which would concentrate its authority and direct its actions. While seeming to advocate more democracy, the progressives of a century ago, like their descendants today, actually wanted the opposite: more centralized government *control*.

So it is that today, many policy decisions that were previously the constitutional responsibility of elected legislators are delegated to faceless bureaucrats whose "rules" have the full force and effect of laws passed by Congress. In writing legislation, Congress uses broad language that essentially hands legislative power over to agencies, along with the authority to execute rules and adjudicate violations.

The objective of progressive thinking, which remains a major force in modern-day liberalism, was to transform America from a decentralized, self-governing society into a centralized, progressive society focused on *national* ideals and the achievement of "social justice." Sociological conditions would be changed through government regulation of society and the economy; socioeconomic problems would be solved by redistributing wealth and benefits.

Liberty no longer would be a condition based on human nature and the exercise of God-given natural rights, but a changing concept whose evolution was guided by government. And since the progressives could not get rid of the "old" Constitution—this was seen as neither desirable nor possible, given its elevated status and historic significance in American political life—they invented the idea of a "living" Constitution that would be flexible and pliable, capable of "growth" and adaptation in changing times.

In this view, government must be ever more actively involved in day-to-day American life. Given the goal of boundless social progress, government by definition must itself be boundless. "It is denied that any limit can be set to governmental activity," prominent scholar (and later FDR adviser) Charles Merriam wrote, summarizing the views of his fellow progressive theorists. "The modern idea as to what is the purpose of the state has radically changed since the days of the 'Fathers,'" he continued, because

> the exigencies of modern industrial and urban life have forced the state to intervene at so many points where an immediate individual interest is difficult to show, that the old doctrine has been given up for the theory that the state acts for the general welfare. It is not admitted that there are no limits to the action of the state, but on the other hand it is fully conceded that

there are no 'natural rights' which bar the way. The question is now one of expediency rather than of principle.

This intellectual construct began to attain political expression with targeted legislation, such as the Pure Food and Drug Act under TR and the Clayton Anti-Trust Act under President Wilson. These efforts were augmented by constitutional amendments that allowed the collection of a federal income tax to fund the national government and required the direct election of senators (thus undermining the federal character of the national legislature).

The trend continued under the New Deal. "The day of the great promoter or the financial Titan, to whom we granted everything if only he would build, or develop, is over," Franklin D. Roosevelt pronounced in 1932. "The day of enlightened administration has come." Although most of FDR's programs were temporary and experimental, they represented an expansion of government unprecedented in American society—as did the Supreme Court's late-1930s endorsement of the new "living" Constitution.

It was FDR who called for a "Second Bill of Rights" that would "assure us equality in the pursuit of happiness." Roosevelt held that the primary task of modern government is to alleviate citizens' want by guaranteeing their economic security. The implications of this redefinition are incalculable, since the list of economic "rights" is unlimited. It requires more and more government programs and regulation of the economy—hence the welfare state—to achieve higher and higher levels of happiness and well-being.

The administrative state took off in the mid-1960s with Lyndon Johnson's Great Society. By creating a truly national bureaucracy of open-ended social programs in housing, education, the environment, and urban renewal (most of which, such as the "War on Poverty," failed to achieve their goals), the Great Society and its progeny effected the greatest expansion of the administrative state in American history.

The Great Society also took the progressive argument one step farther, by asserting that the purpose of government no longer was "to secure these rights," as the Declaration of Independence says, but "to fulfill these rights." That was the title of Johnson's 1965 commencement address at Howard University, in which he laid out the shift from securing equality of opportunity to guaranteeing equality of outcome.

"It is not enough just to open the gates of opportunity. All our citizens must have the ability to walk through those gates," Johnson proclaimed. "We seek not just freedom but opportunity. We seek not just legal equity but human ability, not just equality as a right and a theory but equality as a fact and equality as a result."

And now progressive reformism is back. We're witnessing huge increases in government spending, regulations, and programs. And as the national government becomes more centralized and bureaucratic, it will also become less democratic, and more despotic, than ever.

The tangled legislation supposedly intended to "reform" health care is a perfect example. It would regulate a significant segment of society that has been in progressives' crosshairs for over a hundred years. Nationalized health care was first proposed in 1904, modeled on German social insurance. It was in the Progressive party's platform of 1912. It came back under FDR and Truman, then Johnson, then Clinton, and now Obama. And the goal all along has had little to do with the quality of health care. The objective is rather to remove about a sixth of the economy from private control and bring it under the thumb of the state, whose "experts" will choose and ration its goods and services.

President Obama and the Democratic leadership prescribe a government-run health plan, burdensome mandates on employers, and massive new regulatory authority over health-care markets. Their requirement for individuals to buy insurance is unprecedented and unconstitutional: If the Commerce Clause can be used to regulate inactivity, then the government is truly without limit. They would transfer most decision-making to a collection of federal agencies, bureaus, and commissions such as the ominous-sounding "Health Choices Administration." And their legislation is packed with enough pork projects and corrupt deals to make even the hardest Tammany Hall operative blush.

It would be easier, of course, just to skip the legislative process, and when it comes to climate change that's exactly what the progressives are doing. In declaring carbon dioxide to be a dangerous pollutant, the Environmental Protection Agency essentially granted itself authority to regulate every aspect of American life—without any accountability to those pesky voters.

The Left has long maintained that the administrative state is inevitable, permanent, and ever-expanding—the final form of "democratic" governance. The rise of progressive liberalism, they say, has finally gotten us over our love affair with the Founding and its archaic canons of natural rights and limited constitutionalism. The New Deal and the fruits of centralized authority brought most Democrats around to this view, and over time, many Republicans came to accept the progressive argument as well. Seeing responsible stewardship of the modern state and incremental reforms around its edges as the only viable option, these Republicans tried to make government more efficient, more frugal, and more compassionate—but never questioned its direction.

As a result, politics came to be seen as the ebb and flow between periods of "progress" and "change," on one hand, and brief interregnums to defend and consolidate the status quo, on the other. Other than the aberration of Ronald Reagan and a few unruly conservatives, there seemed to be no real challenge to the liberal project itself, so all the Democrats thought they had to do was wait for the bursting forth of the next great era of reformism. Was it to be launched by Jimmy Carter? Bill Clinton? At long last came the watershed election of Barack Obama.

But a funny thing happened on the way to the next revolution.

The Left's over-reading of the 2008 election gave rise to a vastly overreaching agenda that is deeply unpopular. Large numbers of citizens, many never before engaged in politics, are protesting in the streets and challenging their elected officials in town-hall meetings and on talk-radio shows. Forty percent of Americans now self-identify as conservatives—double the amount of liberals—largely because independents are beginning to take sides. Almost 60 percent believe the nation is on the wrong track.

Voters are deeply impassioned about a new cluster of issues—spending, debt, the role of government, the loss of liberty—that heretofore lacked a focal point to concentrate the public's anger. *The Washington Post* reports that "by 58 percent to 38 percent, Americans prefer smaller government and fewer services to larger government with more services. In the last year and a half, the margin between those favoring smaller over larger government has moved from five points to 20 points." Is it possible that Americans are waking up to the modern state's long train of abuses and usurpations?

There is something about a nation founded on principles, something unique in its politics that often gets shoved to the background but never disappears. Most of the time, American politics is about local issues and the small handful of policy questions that top the national agenda. But once in a while, it is instead about voters' stepping back and taking a longer view as they evaluate the present in the light of our founding principles. That is why all the great turning-point elections in U.S. history ultimately came down to a debate about the meaning and trajectory of America.

In our era of big government and the administrative state, the conventional wisdom has been that serious political realignment—bringing politics and government back into harmony with the principles of the Declaration of Independence and the Constitution—is no longer possible. Yet we are seeing early indications that we may be entering a period of just such realignment. Perhaps the progressive transformation is incomplete, and the form of the modern state not yet settled—at least not by the American people.

This creates a historic opening for conservatives.

Growing opposition to runaway spending and debt, and to a looming government takeover of health care, doesn't necessarily mean that voters want to scrap Social Security or close down the Department of Education. But it may mean that they are ready to reembrace clear, enforceable limits on the state. The opportunity and the challenge for those who seek to conserve America's liberating principles is to turn the healthy public sentiment of the moment, which stands against a partisan agenda to revive an activist state, into a settled and enduring political opinion about the nature and purpose of constitutional government.

To do that, conservatives must make a compelling argument that shifts the narrative of American politics and defines a new direction for the country. We must present a clear choice: stay the course of progressive liberalism, which moves away from popular consent, the rule of law, and constitutional government, and toward a failed, undemocratic, and illiberal form of statism; or correct course in an effort to restore the conditions of liberty and renew the bedrock principles and constitutional wisdom that are the roots of America's continuing greatness.

The American people are poised to make the right decision. The strength and clarity of the Founders' argument, if given contemporary expression and brought to a decision, might well establish a governing conservative consensus and undermine the very foundation of the unlimited administrative state. It would be a monumental step on the long path back to republican self-government.

ARTICLE QUESTIONS

1) Name three of Spalding's criticisms about the increase of the federal bureaucracy.

2) How does Spalding argue that ideals endorsed by American progressives in the twentieth century led to the modern "administrative state"?

3) How does Spalding see the vision of the Founders in conflict with the vision of progressives, Franklin D. Roosevelt's call for a "Second Bill of Rights," and Lyndon Johnson's Great Society?

4) In what ways do you find Spalding's argument convincing? In what ways do you find it unpersuasive? Why?

15.2) The Case for Bureaucracy

Government Is Good Blog, 2007

DOUGLAS AMY

A web project of Douglas J. Amy, Professor of Politics at Mount Holyoke College.

> Douglas Amy, argues that many attacks on bureaucracy are myths perpetuated by "anti-government" activists to delegitimize the federal bureaucracy. He asserts that these "negative stereotypes" of bureaucracy help legitimize appeals for deregulation and privatization and sees these attacks as "highly exaggerated and often simply mistaken."
>
> The thrust of Amy's article is to debunk the popular critiques of bureaucracy. He claims that "studies show bureaucracy and bureaucrats are not nearly as bad as we usually think they are." Amy has a definite perspective and does not try to be unbiased. His goal is to "consider the case *for* bureaucracy," which he argues plays "many valuable and indispensable roles in our society." He supports his argument with numerous studies. His openness about his bias, his research citations, and the detailed presentation of his argument helps the reader evaluate his claims. After reading Amy's arguments you may not agree with his case for bureaucracy, but you should be able to better reflect upon your own biases and generate some informed theories about the role of modern-day bureaucracies.

> Most criticisms of government bureaucracy are based more on myth than reality. These agencies actually play a valuable and indispensable role in making our society a better place to live.

We all know the case *against* bureaucracy. Just say the word to yourself and consider the images it evokes. Massive waste. Inefficiency. Poor service. Ever-growing organizations. Mindless rules. Reams of useless forms. The term "bureaucrat" also comes loaded with a whole host of negative connotations: lazy, hostile, overpaid, imperious, and inflexible. In short, bureaucracy and bureaucrats are unmitigated bad things—with absolutely no redeeming qualities.

Conservatives like to play on this popular prejudice by constantly equating government with bureaucracy. The comments of Charlton Heston are typical: "Of course, government is the problem. The armies of bureaucrats proliferating like gerbils, scurrying like lemmings in pursuit of the ever-expanding federal agenda testify to that amply."[1] Once government is thought of as "bureaucracy," the case for reducing it becomes obvious. Who could complain if Republicans want to reduce these "armies of bureaucrats"? Everyone knows that we would all be better off with less bureaucracy and fewer bureaucrats in our lives. So when conservatives want to make shrinking government sound attractive, they say they are cutting "bureaucracy"—not "programs." Most people value government programs—especially in the areas of education, health and the environment—and do not want to see them reduced; but everyone hates bureaucracy. Using the term "bureaucracy" in this way is a rhetorical sleight-of-hand that obscures the real costs of cutting back on government programs.

But while disparaging and attacking government bureaucracy has become a very effective tactic for anti-government activists, it is based more on mythology than reality. Much of what we think is wrong with bureaucracy—and what conservatives keep telling us—is highly exaggerated and often simply mistaken. This article takes a careful look at bureaucracy and finds that there is little evidence to support most of the common criticisms of these administrative agencies. Studies show that bureaucracy and bureaucrats are not nearly as bad as we usually think they are. We will also consider the case *for* bureaucracy—that these much-maligned organizations and the public servants that work in them are actually playing many valuable and indispensable roles in our society. Many of the significant achievements of modern democratic government would in fact not be possible without the large bureaucracies that oversee and implement them. It turns out that government bureaucracies are actually good.

Myth No. 1: Bureaucracies Are Immensely Wasteful

A few years ago, local officials in my town were holding a public meeting to promote a referendum that would raise taxes to pay for vital city services. A man in the audience rose to object to the tax increase, arguing that instead the city should first get rid of all the waste in the city bureaucracy. The mayor explained that after years of cutbacks in city government, there really was no "fat" left to cut from the budget, and then asked the man what specific cuts he was suggesting. The man said that he didn't know much about the city budget, but that he "knew" that there "had to be" some waste that could be cut out instead of raising taxes.

Such is the strength of the notion that government bureaucracies are inherently wasteful. Even if we don't know much about government, we are absolutely certain that government agencies are wasteful. In fact, waste is the number one citizen complaint about government—and bureaucracy usually takes most of the blame for this. Seventy percent of Americans agree that when something is run by government, it is usually wasteful and inefficient.[2] And conservatives never tire of taking advantage of this view to lambaste the government. As two conservative economists have explained: "As every taxpayer knows, government is wasteful and inefficient; it always has been and always will be." Cutting bureaucratic waste has become a constant theme of conservatives, and it has become a major rationale for cutting taxes. They argue that we can have the best of both worlds: we can reduce taxes and also not cut back on needed government programs. How? By simply cutting out all the "fat" in government. . . .

People tend to think there is a large amount of waste in government in part because of the loose way this term is used. For instance, some conservative critics of government count as waste those programs they simply don't like—such as the Legal Services Corporation, the National Endowment for the Arts, AmeriCorps, and subsidies for public television. But to use the term "waste" in this way makes it entirely a political judgment and renders it essentially meaningless. Normally the term "government waste" refers to the inefficient use of funds because of overstaffing, poor productivity, etc. But conservatives are not opposed to the National Endowment for the Arts because that agency is inefficient; they oppose it on ideological grounds. They wouldn't support the NEA no matter how "lean and mean" it was. It is a misleading, then, to use the term "waste" in this way. . . .

Myth No. 2: Business Is Always Better Than Bureaucracy

Another of the more persistent myths about bureaucracy is that "business is better"—that businesses are always more efficient than government efforts. Since government bureaucracies don't have to produce a profit and they are not subject to market competition, it is argued, they have much less incentive to be cost-efficient in their management and delivery of services. The assumed superiority of business has become so commonsensical that it is hardly ever questioned at all. This notion has also become an important argument for conservatives in their effort to reduce government and to privatize many of its functions. But are public agencies always less efficient than businesses? A careful look at this issue casts doubt on this common belief.

There have been many empirical studies examining the efficiency of government bureaucracies versus business in a variety of areas, including refuse collection, electrical utilities, public transportation, water supply systems, and hospital administration. The findings have been mixed. Some studies of electric utilities have found that publicly owned ones were more efficient and charged lower prices than privately owned utilities. Several other studies found the opposite, and yet others found no significant differences.[6] Studies of other services produced similar kinds of mixed results. Charles Goodsell is a professor of Public Administration and Public Affairs at Virginia Polytechnic

Institute and State University who has spent much of his life studying bureaucracy. After examining these efficiency studies, he concluded: "In short, there is much evidence that is ambivalent. The assumption that business always does better than government is not upheld. . . . When you add up all these study results, the basis for the mantra that business is always better evaporates. . . ."[7]

Myth No. 3: We Want the Government to Act Like a Business

The astronaut John Glenn tells a story about his first trip into space. As he sat in the capsule, waiting nervously on the launching pad, he couldn't stop thinking about the fact that NASA had given the contract for the rocket to the lowest bidder. This raises another important point about government bureaucracies: we don't always want them to act like businesses. Conservatives are constantly saying that we would all be better off if government were run like a business. But would we? Businesses are obsessed with their bottom lines and are always looking for the cheapest way to make a product or deliver a service. But in many cases, we don't want government services to be as cheap as possible. Often, with government, the main concern is the quality of the service, not its costs. For example, do we really want to spend the least amount of money possible on our air traffic control system? Obviously not—the main goal should be maximizing the safety of the aviation system. Also, do we want the cheapest possible workforce in charge of security at our airports? Again, of course not—and this point was even acknowledged by Republicans when they agreed to abandon private security companies in favor of a federalized system in the wake of the 9/11 tragedy. Private security had certainly cost less, but it is clearly better to have a federal program that spends more money on training personnel and pays higher salaries to attract employees who are more capable.

Similarly, we don't really want the cheapest system for dispensing justice in our society. We could certainly save a lot on court costs if we didn't pay for lawyers for those who can't afford them and if we got rid of jury trials and lengthy appeal processes. But this would undermine the main goal of providing justice. The point here is clear: unlike businesses, public agencies are not just concerned with the bottom line. We expect our government organizations to pursue a wide variety of important goals, and often cost is not the most important consideration. In this sense, it is unfair to expect many government bureaucracies to be as cheap to run as businesses.

Myth No. 4: Bureaucracy Is a Major Cause of Government Growth

Conservatives also like to charge that bureaucracy is one of the main causes of government growth. They argue that government bureaucracies have an inherent tendency to expand. The reason is this: agency officials bent on their own career advancement are always pushing to increase their power and their budgets. Thus, bureaucracies—like cancer—inevitably become ever-growing entities with ever-increasing destructive effects. Bureaucracies are constantly eating up more tax-payer dollars and imposing more and more rules on American citizens.

This criticism of bureaucracy seems plausible, but is it really true? The evidence suggests that it is not. Consider, for example, the assumption that we are plagued by an ever-growing federal bureaucracy. Figures show that federal agencies have not been growing at an alarming rate. If we go back to 1970, we find that 2,997,000 civilians worked for the federal government at that time. By 2009, that figure had actually gone down—to 2,804,000.[16] So much for the constantly expanding federal bureaucracy.

Second, it is not clear at all that bureaucrats are always seeking to expand their agencies and their budgets. This budget-maximizing thesis was directly contradicted by a study conducted by Julie Dolan.[17] She compared the views of members of the federal senior civil service to those of the general public when it came to whether we should be spending more or less in a wide variety of policy areas, including education, healthcare, defense, welfare, environment, college financial aid, AIDS research, homelessness, etc. She found that in most areas the public was willing to support increased spending much more than the agency administrators. And in most cases, a majority of these administrators did not support increased budgets. This was due, she believed, to administrators having a more realistic and sophisticated knowledge of these issues and programs. Her conclusion: "In sum, the budget-*minimizing* tendencies of federal administrators reported here suggest that self-interest is not as powerful a motivator as previously believed, and they suggest we should revise our theories about self-interested bureaucrats inflating government budgets for their own gain."[18]

Another theory of bureaucratic expansion suggests that the government grows because once an administrative agency is established, it will stick around even when its program is no longer needed. In short, the bureaucracy never shrinks, it only grows. However, studies have shown that the conservatives are just plain wrong when they claim that outmoded programs are rarely purged from government. Robert Stein and Kenneth Bikers completed a study in which they examined the number of federal programs that were eliminated between 1971 and 1990. During that twenty-year span, an average of thirty-six federal programs were terminated each year.[19] A pretty amazing figure. The commonly held notion that bureaucracies never die is clearly false. . . .

Myth No. 5: Bureaucracies Usually Provide Poor Service

Yet another common criticism of government bureaucracies is that they routinely provide very poor service to the public. Unlike businesses, where the rule is "the customer is always right," public agencies seemed to adhere to the rule that "it's my way or the highway." Many people have stories of at least one frustrating encounter with a government worker where they received rude or inadequate service.

But how frequent are these bad experiences? How widespread is dissatisfaction with government workers and the services they provide? Studies show that negative experiences are not nearly as common as many think and that most people's encounters with government workers actually turn out well. For example, when a survey was done in Virginia about the quality of the services provided by local government workers, the results were surprisingly positive. Over 80 percent of citizens said that the services they receive from the fire department, EMS service, police department, public library, and parks and recreation were either "excellent" or "good." An average of a mere 2.7 percent of citizens rated these public services as "poor."[23] Pretty impressive figures for any organization.

Perhaps more surprisingly, surveys show high citizen evaluations for most large *federal* agencies as well. The Pew Research Center conducted a survey in 2000 of citizens and businesspeople who used the services of the Social Security Administration, the Environmental Protection Agency, the Food and Drug Administration, the Internal Revenue Service, and the Federal Aviation Administration. Predictably, only 47.6 percent had a favorable view of the IRS. But 84.5 percent had favorable views of the FDA. For the Social Security Administration that figure was 72.0; for the FAA, 69.3; and for the EPA, 68.0. What makes these strong favorable ratings all the more impressive is that they include the views of people from businesses being regulated by these agencies—respondents who are going to naturally feel some hostility toward these bureaucracies. . . .

This is not to suggest that people don't sometimes have bad encounters with government bureaucracies—we all have. The point here is that these encounters are not the rule, and we usually get pretty good service from our public agencies. It is also worth keeping in mind that bad encounters with bureaucrats are not limited to the public sector. Who hasn't had a horrible time trying to get approval for a drug or a medical procedure from the rigid bureaucrats in private health insurance companies? And who hasn't wandered through seemingly endless phone trees and spent hours on hold just trying to get some technical help from large computer and software companies? Instances of poor service are hardly confined to government bureaucracies.

Myth No. 6: Agencies Should Treat Us as Individuals

People are sometimes frustrated because government administrators do not treat them as individuals. Instead, they are treated like a "number"—simply one case among many others—without any seeming sensitivity to the distinctiveness of their particular situation. Why must bureaucrats slavishly follow the rules, and not treat each person uniquely depending on his or her circumstances? Why can't that police officer see that we were speeding because we were late in picking up our child at school, not because we were being irresponsible? Why can't that city official simply wave the zoning rules so that we can run our new business out of our home?

It is true that bureaucrats' treatment of us *is* often based on general rules and policies, rather than who we are as individuals. But what we fail to see is that this is actually a good thing. We should *want* bureaucrats to not treat people as individuals. Treating everyone the same is in the public interest—and often in our own interest as well. It is what ensures that government agencies treat everyone fairly and impartially. Dealing with us impersonally is what guarantees that our treatment is not arbitrary, discriminatory, or abusive. It is what discourages police officers from handing out tickets based on your race or the political bumper stickers on your car. It is what helps to ensure that government contracts are given to the lowest bidders, not those companies that give the most in campaign contributions.

If government workers had the ability to ignore procedures and treat us as individuals, this would also give them enormous power over us—which is exactly what we don't want to happen. Imagine that you had been waiting in a long line at the Department of Motor Vehicles. A clerk recognizes a friend at the end of the line and decides to serve them next. It is unlikely that you would praise this "bending" of the rules for this individual—you would undoubtedly be mad about the unfairness of this action. You would be upset about the lack of impersonal, rule-based treatment by officials. . . .

Bureaucracy Is Good

So far, we've seen that government bureaucracies are not nearly as bad as conservative critics and popular mythology make them out to be. However, there is a much more *positive* case that can be made here—the case for bureaucracies actually being a good thing. It is not a difficult case to make. It begins with a simple fact: the modern state as we know it cannot exist without large bureaucratic agencies to implement its programs. Modern democratic governments are necessarily bureaucratic entities. And if this is true, then the successes of modern government have to also be considered the successes of government bureaucracies as well. The fact that Social Security has dramatically reduced poverty among the elderly should be counted as an achievement of this agency's bureaucracy. The Environmental Protection Agency should also get much of the credit for our being able to breathe cleaner air and drink safer water.

In short, if government is good, then government bureaucracies are good. If government programs have had many enormously positive impacts on the lives of every Americans, some of the credit for this has to go to the agencies that make these programs work. Without bureaucracy, modern democratic governments could not possibly fulfill all the crucial roles it plays in society—including creating more economic security, curing diseases, caring for the environment, dispensing justice, educating our children, and protecting us from a variety of harms. . . .

So if you feel that America is a good place to live, at least part of the credit for that must be given to government bureaucracies. Literally, the good life as we know it in the United States could not exist without the numerous and various essential tasks being performed by these public agencies on all levels of government.

NOTES

1. Charlton Heston, in a speech given at Hillsdale College.
http://www.libertyhaven.com/politicsandcurrentevents/governmentreformitsrealrole/reaganright.shtml

2. Jacob Weisberg, *In Defense of Government* (New York: Scribner, 1996), p. 32.

6. Charles Goodsell, *The Case for Bureaucracy: A Public Administration Polemic,* 4th ed. (Washington, D.C.: CQ Press, 2004), p. 52. This excellent and much underappreciated book is the basis for most of the arguments made in this article—and for its title.

7. Goodsell, p. 54.

16. U.S. Government, *Statistical Abstract of the United States* (Washington D.C.: U.S. Government Printing Office, 2009) Table 478.

17. Julie Dolan, "The Budget-Minimizing Bureaucrat? Empirical Evidence from the Senior Executive Service," *Public Administration* 62, no. 1 (January/February 2002).

18. Dolan, p. 47.

19. Cited in Goodsell, p. 123.

23. Goodsell, p. 25.

ARTICLE QUESTIONS

1) What are the six myths about bureaucracy Amy explores?
2) Why does Amy argue we don't want government to act like a business?
3) Why does Amy argue it is "actually a good thing" that government agencies don't treat us like individuals?
4) In what ways do you find Amy's argument convincing? In what ways do you find it unpersuasive? Why?

15.3) *Locked in the Cabinet*, Selections on Congressional Hearings and Hiring Subordinates

Knopf; First Edition, 1997, pp. 37–9, 41–4, 51–2, 108–110

ROBERT REICH

Robert Reich, Secretary of Labor from 1993 to 1997, published his experiences working in the Clinton administration in his 1997 book *Locked in the Cabinet*. The book is written as a series of diary entries, making it a quick and entertaining read. Despite Reich's insider status, he manages to critique America's unusual bureaucratic structure. As Reich notes, every new president gets 3,000 high-level appointments, who are then responsible for overseeing more than 2 million federal employees. These appointed managers are not required to possess any special qualifications (other than an ability to be confirmed by a majority of the Senate). At the top of this appointment hierarchy are the Cabinet positions. Today the Cabinet consists of the heads of 15 executive departments, including the Secretary of State, Secretary of Defense, Attorney General, and—the position that Reich held—Secretary of Labor.

One of the primary ways Congress engages in oversight of the executive branch is by providing "advice and consent" on presidential nominations. The modern-day version of advice and consent is most visible during televised confirmation hearings, where senators question the nominee. As Reich's humorous confirmation experience highlights, it is difficult for the Senate to provide meaningful oversight when nominees are tutored to display deceitful deference to the senators and are coached to avoid answering the senators' questions. Reich notes that the strange bureaucratic structure does not end with the confirmation process: once the nominee is confirmed, there is no formalized transition from one Secretary to the next, and there is no training manual for how to do the job.

The United States developed this process of political appointments partially out of distrust of career bureaucrats. But as you read about Reich's experiences of being nominated, getting confirmed, and transitioning into his new job, you may question whether the American fear of career bureaucrats justifies the current process of political appointments.

January 5 Washington

I'm cramming for my Senate confirmation hearing on Thursday, helped by several coaches including the lawyers who investigated me and several Democratic staffers from the Hill. I feel like a prize-fighter getting ready for the big one.

This evening we do a mock run at the home of one of the lawyers. My coaches play the parts of Senators on the committee. I sit facing them. They try to be as difficult and nasty as possible.

"Mr. Reich, you've had absolutely no experience managing a big organization, have you?"

"Mr. Reich, do you believe that employers should have the right to permanently replace striking workers?"

"Mr. Reich, what will you do to end silly nit-picking regulations, like the OSHA rule that prohibits painted ladders at the workplace?"

"Mr. Reich, are you a socialist?"

"Mr. Reich, should Congress require that states pay half of the cost of extended unemployment insurance?"

"Mr. Reich, have you ever had to meet a payroll?"

"Mr. Reich, do you support the proposed North American Free Trade Agreement [NAFTA], and if so, why?"

"Mr. Reich, do you believe that defined-benefit pension plans are seriously underfunded, and if so, what would you do about the problem?"

I grope for words. I babble. On the rare occasion when I actually have something intelligent to say, I give long and complicated answers.

"Time *out*," says my chief interrogator, a rotund, middle-aged Hill staffer with graying red hair and decades of experience at this sort of thing. "Let's stop here and critique your performance so far." I wish he wouldn't.

"Look," he says, stepping out from behind the table which serves as a mock committee rostrum.

"This hearing isn't designed to test your *knowledge*. Its purpose is to test your respect for *them*."

I'm confused and hurt. I feel as though I've failed an exam. He senses it.

"You *don't* have to come up with the right *answer*," he continues, pacing around the room. "You've got a big handicap. Your whole life you've been trying to show people how smart you are. That's *not* what you should do on Thursday. You try to show them how smart you are, you're in trouble."

"But I have to answer their questions, don't I?"

"Yes and no," he says. "You have to *respond* to their questions. But you don't have to *answer* them. You *shouldn't* answer them. You're not *expected* to answer them."

The others laugh. I'm bewildered. "What's the difference between answering and responding?" I ask.

"Respect! *Respect!*" my chief interrogator shouts. He walks over to me and leans down so that his face is close to mine. "This is all about respect," he says. "*Your* respect for them. The *President's* respect for them. The executive branch's respect for the legislative branch. Look: The President has nominated you to be a cabinet secretary. They have to consent to the nomination. Barring an unforeseen scandal, they will. But first you have to *genuflect*." He gets on his knees, grabs my hand, and kisses it. The others roar. "You let them know you respect their power and you'll continue to do so for as long as you hold office."

I join in the laugh, but I'm still confused. "What does this have to do with the difference between answering their questions and responding to their questions?"

He sits down again. He lowers his voice. The others in the room are enjoying the spectacle. "If you *lecture* them, they don't feel you respect them. But if you respond to their questions with utter humility, they will feel you do."

"Utter humility?"

"Have you ever in your life admitted you don't know something?" he grins, relishing the moment.

"Sure."

"But have you ever admitted you didn't know when you knew just enough to bullshit your way through?"

I'm cornered. I pause. "Not often."

He's up again, pacing. "On Thursday, whenever you're not absolutely sure of the answer, I want you to say simply, 'I don't know, Senator.'"

"Okay."

He stops and points his finger at me. *"Practice saying it. I . . . don't . . . know, Senator."*

"I don't know, Senator."

"Good! Again!"

"I don't know, Senator."

"Again!"

"I don't know, Senator." The others applaud.

"Fine." He looks toward the group. "I think he's catching on." Laughter.

Then back to me again. "And even when you're absolutely sure, and you have it all worked out in your head, I want you to give a *simple* answer. One sentence. Two at most. Simple *and* general. No specifics. Don't show off what you know."

This is going to be hard.

"And"—he brings his face closer and looks me dead in the eye—"as often as you can say it without it sounding contrived, I want you to tell them how much you look forward to working with them. *I look forward to working with you on that, Senator.*"

"I look forward to working with you on that, Senator."

"I don't know, Senator. But I look forward to working with you on it."

"I don't know, Senator, but I look forward to working with you on it," I say.

"G-o-o-o-o-d." He smiles and is up pacing again. "And whenever you can do so without sounding like your nose is completely up their asshole, I want you to *compliment* them. Praise their leadership on the issue. Tell them you will need their help and guidance. Mention their years of diligence and hard work."

I rehearse. "Senator, you know far more about that issue than I do, and I look forward to hearing your views in the months and years to come."

"Wonderful!" he beams, and points at me. "And remember, if they ask anything personal—about your writings, your political views, even your friendship with the President, whatever—*don't* take it personally. They are not interested in an answer. They are interested in *how* you respond."

"How I respond?"

"Deferentially. Good-naturedly. If they are nasty, don't be nasty back. If they are sarcastic, refrain from sarcasm. *Never* get angry. *Never* lose your balance. *Never* take the bait."

I feel like a child learning how to ride a bike. It looked so easy. It's not.

My interrogator puts an arm around my shoulder and addresses the others. "He'll do just fine, won't he?"

They say encouraging things, but they're not convinced.

The session ends. We'll try again tomorrow. I wish the hearing were two weeks away instead of two days. . . .

January 15 Washington

My first visit to the Labor Department. It will be a week or so before I take over officially, but I want to meet with [outgoing President George H. W.] Bush's Labor Secretary. I don't expect a formal orientation—just, perhaps, some guidance. I'm desperate for it. And there's no better source of guidance for how to do a job than the person who's just been doing it. Party affiliation doesn't matter all that much. Most of the job of managing a large department like this is the same regardless of political party.

The Labor Department occupies a whole block of Constitution Avenue near the base of Capitol Hill, in a monstrosity of a building. It was constructed in the neofascist style of many public buildings in the fifties and sixties—huge horizontal slabs of concrete piled high on top of one another at intervals of about twenty feet, stretching from one end of a block to the other. Forget the graceful Greek colonnades and pediments of New Deal office buildings and their appeal to classic republican virtue. This building doesn't try to be anything but what it is, with relish. It virtually screams: This is a giant bureaucracy. If you think you're gonna be heard through these thick walls, forget it.

The front door is three times my height. Inside is a vast, silent space. My footsteps echo on the hard marble floor. In the far distance I spot a security guard behind a desk, reading a newspaper.

"Excuse me, sir." He looks up with a surprised expression, as if I'm the first person he's seen in several weeks. "I'm Robert Reich and I have an appointment with Secretary Martin."

"Up the elevator to the second floor." He returns to the paper.

The elevator opens onto a windowless corridor, twenty feet high and twenty wide, brightly lit by fluorescent lights in the ceiling. It seems to run the length of the building. Its walls are white and bare, and the floor is white and spotless. I can see other doors opening off it, but no human beings.

Directly before me is another set of giant doors, and over them, in large black letters: "Office of the Secretary of Labor of the United States." A reception area is carpeted in blue and paneled in laminated pine.

"Can I help you?" asks a small woman with thick glasses who sits behind a high counter. I can barely see her, but by now I'm grateful for any human contact.

"I'm here to see Secretary Martin. Robert Reich."

Her smile broadens. "Oh, *yes!*" The little woman springs up as if propelled from an ejector seat. "She's *expecting* you. May I take your coat?" I give it to her and she flutters off to hang it up and then returns in seconds. "*Please* follow me." She leads me swiftly down another corridor, into an outer office. Cardboard boxes are piled in one corner. The walls are bare. Framed pictures and documents lean against the boxes.

The little woman rushes through another door and then pops out again, holding it open. "*Please* enter." She smiles and her eyes twinkle.

It's the largest office I've ever seen. Two sides are floor-to-ceiling windows offering a postcard-perfect view of the Capitol. The two other walls are covered in finely textured beige hemp. On them hang elaborately framed oil paintings from the National Gallery of Art. A tasteful puce sofa occupies one corner, surrounded by soft armchairs covered in crimson felt. The carpet is blue-green. In another corner: a king-size mahogany desk and credenza, and the outgoing Secretary of Labor.

Lynn Martin stands to greet me. She has been Secretary of Labor for two years. Before that, a congresswoman from Illinois. She's thin and angular, with spiky red hair. Her friendly face disguises a fiercely partisan Republican who spent much of last fall blasting Bill on TV.

"Well, congratulations!" She approaches, extending her hand.

"Thanks." I shake it. An instant of mutual recognition: She knows I know that she despises much of what I stand for; I know she knows that I despise much of what *she* stands for. Yet our relationship is not entirely symmetrical. We won. Her side lost. In a week this office will be mine.

"Please, sit down," she says breezily, gesturing to one of the crimson armchairs. She sits on the sofa.

"So . . ." I begin awkwardly. "Any advice for me?"

"Advice?" She seems taken aback.

"On being Secretary of Labor."

"Oh, you'll like it here." She smiles blandly.

"Anything to . . . er . . . watch out for? Keep an *eye* on?"

She pauses. "Just one thing," she says, suddenly quite serious. "Don't go home too often."

"Sorry, I don't understand."

"Where do you live?" she asks.

"Cambridge, Massachusetts. But the family will be moving down here in a few months. Why?"

"I'm from Chicago. I flew home at the taxpayers' expense once too often, and the press raised a real *stink* about it."

I try to look sympathetic.

"Just watch your travel," she says intently.

"Anything else I should know?" I ask.

"No. Can't think of anything. You'll do *fine*. The people who work here"—she makes a long sweeping motion with her arm, as if to take in all 18,000 employees of the department—"they're mostly Democrats. They'll *love* you."

She stands. My orientation session obviously has come to an end.

We silently walk to the door, across the broad expanse of blue-green carpet.

"Good luck," she says with a dismissive smile, extending her hand once again.

"Ah . . . thank you. And good luck to you too." We shake.

As I walk out of her office it suddenly strikes me: I'm on my own from here on. There's no training manual, no course, no test drive for a cabinet secretary. I'll have to follow my instincts, and rely on whomever I can find to depend on along the way. I'll have to listen carefully and watch out for dangers. But mostly I'll have to stay honest with myself and keep perspective. Avoid grandiosity. This is a glamorous temp job.

The small woman in the reception area flashes me a huge smile. "Good *luck* to you, Mr. Secretary! We're all *very* excited you'll be here!" She flutters to get my coat.

"Thank you," I say as she hands it to me.

"Aren't *you* excited?" She beams.

"Panicked would be a better word," I say. I walk back out of the monstrous building into a cold, clear Washington day. Thus the passing of power in our remarkably enduring system of government. . . .

February 1 Washington

I interview twenty people today. I have to find a deputy secretary and chief of staff with all the management skills I lack. I also have to find a small platoon of assistant secretaries: one to run the Occupational Safety and Health Administration (detested by corporations, revered by unions); another to be in charge of the myriad of employment and job training programs (billions of dollars), plus unemployment insurance (billions more); another to police the nation's pension funds (four trillion dollars' worth); another to patrol the nation's nine million workplaces to make sure that young children aren't being exploited, that workers receive at least a minimum hourly wage plus time and a half for overtime, that sweatshops are relegated to history.

The Department of Labor is vast, its powers seemingly endless. With a history spanning the better part of the twentieth century—involving every major controversy affecting American workers—it issues thousands of regulations, sends vast sums of money to states and cities, and sues countless employers. I can barely comprehend it all. It was created in 1913 with an ambitious mission: *Foster, promote, and develop the welfare of the wage earners of the United States, improve their working conditions, and advance their opportunities for profitable employment.* That about sums it up.

And yet here I am assembling my team before I've even figured it all out. No time to waste. Bill will have to sign off on my choices, then each of them will be nitpicked for months by the White House staff and the FBI, and if they survive those hurdles each must be confirmed by the Senate.

If I'm fast enough out of the starting gate, my team might be fully installed by June. If I dally now and get caught in the traffic jam of subcabinet nominations from every department, I might not see them for a year. And whenever they officially start, add another six months before they have the slightest idea what's going on.

No other democracy does it this way. No private corporation would think of operating like this. Every time a new president is elected, America assembles a new government of 3,000 or so amateurs who only sometimes know the policies they're about to administer, rarely have experience managing large government bureaucracies, and almost never know the particular piece of it they're going to run. These people are appointed quickly by a president-elect who is thoroughly exhausted from a year and a half of campaigning. And they remain in office, on average, under two years—barely enough time to find the nearest bathroom. It's a miracle we don't screw it up worse than we do.

Part of my problem is I don't know exactly what I'm looking for and I certainly don't know how to tell whether I've found it. Some obvious criteria:

1. *They should share the President-elect's values.* But how will I know they do? I can't very well ask, "Do you share the President's values?" and expect an honest answer. Even if they contributed money to the campaign, there's no telling. I've heard of several middle-aged Washington lawyers so

desperate to escape the tedium of law practice by becoming an assistant secretary for Anything That Gets Me Out of Here that they've made whopping contributions to both campaigns.

2. *They should be competent and knowledgeable about the policies they'll administer.* Sounds logical, but here again, how can I tell? I don't know enough to know whether someone *else* knows enough. "What do you think about the Employee Retirement Income Security Act?" I might ask, and an ambitious huckster could snow me. "I've thought a lot about this," he might say, "and I've concluded that Section 508(m) should be changed because most retirees have 307 accounts which are treated by the IRS as Subchapter 12 entities." Uttered with enough conviction, bullshit like this could sweep me off my feet.

3. *They should be good managers.* But how to find out? Yesterday I phoned someone about a particular job candidate's management skills, at her suggestion. He told me she worked for him and was a terrific manager. "Terrific?" I repeated. "Wonderful. The best," he said. "You'd recommend her?" I asked. "Absolutely. Can't go wrong," he assured me. I thanked him, hung up the phone, and was enthusiastic for about five minutes, until I realized how little I had learned. How do I know *he* recognizes a good manager? Maybe he's a lousy manager himself and has a bunch of bozos working for him. Why should I trust that he's more interested in my having her on *my* team than in getting her off his?

I'm flying blind. . . .

April 29 Washington

"The White House wants you to go to Cleveland." Kitty is sitting next to my desk, reading from her daily list of Things to Tell the Secretary.

"Why?"

She sighs. "Because we're hitting the first hundred days of the Clinton administration and the President along with his entire cabinet are fanning out across America to celebrate, because Ohio is important, because there are a lot of blue-collar voters out there, and because you haven't been to Ohio yet."

"What'll I do out there?" I feel bullied.

Kitty is glancing through the rest of the list while she reels off the obvious. "Visit a factory, go on local TV, meet the *Plain Dealer* editorial board, plant the flag. It'll be one day. No big deal."

She is about to move to the next item on her list, when I stop her. "*Who* wants me to go to Cleveland?"

Kitty rolls her eyes. This is going to be another one of those days. When will this guy learn that he has to be a cabinet secretary? "The White House. They called this morning."

"Houses don't make phone calls. *Who* called?"

"I don't know. Someone from Cabinet Affairs. Steve somebody. I'll schedule it. Now, can we move on?" She looks back at her list.

"How *old* is Steve?"

She puts down her pad and stares blankly at me. "I have *no idea* how old he is. What *difference* does it make? They want you to go to Cleveland. You're going to Cleveland." She picks up her pad. "Now, I have a whole list—"

"I bet he's under thirty."

"He probably *is* under thirty. A large portion of the American population is under thirty. So what?"

"Don't you see? Here I am, a member of the president's cabinet, confirmed by the Senate, the head of an entire government department with eighteen thousand employees, responsible for implementing a huge number of laws and rules, charged with helping people get better jobs, and *who is telling me what to do?*" I'm working myself into a frenzy of self-righteousness. "Some *twerp* in the White House who has *no clue* what I'm doing in this job. Screw him. I won't go." Kitty sits patiently, waiting for the storm to pass.

But the storm has been building for weeks, and it won't pass anytime soon. Orders from twerps in the White House didn't bother me at the beginning. Now I can't stomach snotty children telling me what to do. From the point of view of the White House staff, cabinet officials are provincial governors presiding over alien, primitive territories. Anything of any importance occurs in the imperial palace, within the capital city. The provincial governors are important only in a ceremonial sense. They wear the colors and show the flag.

Occasionally they are called in to get their next round of orders before being returned to their outposts. They are of course dazzled by the splendor of the court, and grateful for the chance to visit.

The White House's arrogant center is replicated on a smaller scale within every cabinet department. (The Washington hierarchy is, in fact, less like a pyramid than a Mandelbrot set, whose large-scale design is replicated within every component part, and then repeated again inside the pieces of every part.) The Labor Department's own arrogant center located on the second floor, arrayed around my office. The twenty-somethings Tom and Kitty have assembled regard assistant secretaries with the same disdain that White House staffers have for cabinet officials. And each assistant secretary has his or her own arrogant center, whose twerps treat the heads of regional offices like provincial bumpkins.

"You'll go to Cleveland," Kitty says calmly. "The President is going to New Orleans, other cabinet members are going to other major cities. You're in Cleveland."

"I'll go *this* time." The storm isn't over, but I know I have no choice. I try to save what's left of my face. "But I'll be damned if I'm going to let them run my life."

In fairness, arrogant centers do serve legitimate purposes. They have a broader perspective than the view from any single province. And it is also occasionally true—dare I admit it even to myself?—that provincial governors go native, forgetting that their primary loyalty is to the crown, to the president, rather than to the inhabitants of the territories with whom they deal every day.

But I still hate those snotty kids.

Kitty is about to discuss the next item on her list. I interrupt again. "Next time when the White House gives me an order, find out how old he is. If he's under thirty, don't talk to me until you've checked with someone higher up."

"Yes, boss." Kitty is amused.

ARTICLE QUESTIONS

1) What advice does Reich receive from his "chief interrogator" while cramming for his Senate confirmation hearing?

2) Reich asserts that no other democracy and no private corporation would operate by replacing all high-level managers when a new president starts. What does Reich include in his description of what happens every time a new president is elected?

3) What is included as part of Reich's "obvious criteria" for selecting his chief of staff, his deputy secretary, and his assistant secretaries? What are his concerns about being able to properly screen for each of these criteria?

4) Based on the excerpts you have read from Reich's experiences, what concerns do you have about how the U.S. bureaucracy functions?

Chapter 16

The Judicial Branch

The courts in the United States wield an unusual amount of influence—far more than courts in most other nations, perhaps too much in a modern democratic society. At the same time, there are clear limits to judicial power; federal judges are appointed by the elected branches and the courts must rely on other political actors to execute their decisions. The restraints placed on the judicial branch have led some scholars to refer to the "constrained courts." Other scholars emphasize judges' lifetime appointments and judges' independence from public opinion to argue that the courts possess "judicial supremacy" over the other branches and possess "judicial finality" when interpreting the Constitution.

How can such widely diverse theories of judicial power simultaneously exist? Perhaps both theories reflect elements of reality. Most scholars do not see the courts as wholly constrained or completely supreme. Here is one way to balance these views: The United States has independent judges but a dependent judiciary. Federal judges are independent because of their lifetime appointments, but the court system is dependent on others for resources and execution. On a deeper level, the role of the courts in a democracy will always be vexing for the simple reason that the courts are designed to serve as a check on "We, the People."

Note that our readings focus on the federal courts. Each state also has its own court system—and in 37 states, the voters elect their judges. Federal judges, on the other hand, are nominated by the president and confirmed (or approved) by the Senate.

The first three readings in this chapter examine the judiciary's dependence on other political actors and the courts' shared role in interpreting the Constitution. Louis Fisher, in excerpts from *On the Supreme Court: Without Illusion and Idolatry*, asserts that the authority to interpret the Constitution "is not exclusive" to the courts but "is part of a joint exercise" that includes "the elected branches, the 50 states, and the American public." According to Fisher the meaning of the Constitution—as is appropriate in a democracy—is the culmination of a continuing dialogue among the courts and other political actors. The next two articles expand on this theme. Ryan Emenaker, in "High Court Not Final Say on U.S. Law," provides examples of how the federal courts' power to interpret the Constitution is constrained by the elected branches. The editorial was written just before the Court announced its opinion on the constitutionality of the Affordable Care Act (ACA or Obamacare). Emenaker's editorial ends by noting that no matter how the Supreme Court ruled in the case, it would not be the final political decision on the ACA.

The *National Public Radio* story "Supreme Court Appears Divided in Cross Case" reports on another continuing constitutional dialogue. In this case, Congress maneuvered around several Ninth Circuit Court of Appeals rulings requiring the removal of a cross on federal land. At the time of the news report, the Supreme Court was deciding whether its interpretation of the First Amendment would be consistent with Congress's or whether its interpretation would rebuff a Congress that had resisted rulings by the Ninth Circuit.

Donald F. Kettl, in "Why States and Localities Are Watching the Lower Federal Courts," notes that federal court cases rarely make it to the Supreme Court (even really important ones). According to Kettl, this has two repercussions: (1) the interpretation of federal law usually happens in the lower federal courts, and (2) there are more than 900 federal judges below the Supreme Court who decide most federal law; thus every president has a chance to remake a large portion of the judiciary. The final reading, "In Conversation: Antonin Scalia," is an interview by Jennifer Senior with Supreme Court Justice Antonin Scalia—the longest-serving and often most engaging opinion writer on the Supreme Court. Scalia is an arch supporter of using originalism as a method of interpreting the Constitution. As the article explains, an originalist interprets the Constitution based on what he or she thinks the Framers meant when the Constitution was drafted. This interview seems like a departure from the other readings in the chapter, and in a sense it is. The first four readings analyzed the courts from an institutional perspective. This article reminds us that federal judges are human beings with their own biases and worldviews. Studying the actions of the courts from the perspective of the biases of the justices (often called judicial behavioralism) became the dominant way of studying judicial politics at the end of the twentieth century.

All of these articles place the federal courts within a system of politics (rather than outside of it). Judges are political (not just legal) actors, and they cannot make any decision they want. They are restrained in what cases they can hear, and they are restricted by who will execute their decisions. As you delve into the five readings in this chapter, reflect upon how each author approaches the biggest question animating the study of the U.S. courts: what is the proper role of unelected judges in a democracy?

CHAPTER QUESTIONS

1) In what ways do the federal courts check the power of other political actors?
2) How do the federal courts serve as a check on "We, the People"?
3) In what ways are the federal courts constrained by other political actors?
4) Why do other political actors follow Supreme Court opinions?
5) Should judges be elected? Should judges have lifetime appointments? What other reforms, if any, should be made to how the federal courts function?
6) What is the proper role of unelected judges in a democracy?

CHAPTER READINGS

16.1) Louis Fisher, "Preface" and "Conclusion" from *On the Supreme Court: Without Illusion and Idolatry.* Paradigm Publishing, 2014, pp. ix–xiv, 221–228.

16.2) Ryan Emenaker, "High Court Not Final Say on U.S. Law," *Times-Standard*, April 12, 2012.

16.3) "Supreme Court Appears Divided in Cross Case," *National Public Radio*, October 7, 2009.

16.4) Donald F. Kettl, "Why States and Localities Are Watching the Lower Federal Courts," *Governing*, October 2010.

16.5) Jennifer Senior, "In Conversation: Antonin Scalia," *New York Magazine*, October 6, 2013.

16.1) "Preface" and "Conclusion" from *On the Supreme Court*: *Without Illusion and Idolatry*

Paradigm Publishing, pp. ix–xiv, 221–228

LOUIS FISHER

> Louis Fisher's book is an effort to correct a familiar error: teaching about the courts in isolation from politics. Fisher expresses a familiar concern about the proper role of unelected courts in a democracy: he argues it is impossible to have popular government if the Supreme Court has "the last word on constitutional issues." But he argues that the courts do not have the last word. The Constitution grants the *courts restricted power*. In the preface to his book, Fisher boldly states that "the Court is neither infallible nor final" and that "the elected branches have the capacity to change constitutional doctrine" after the Court rules. He provides examples of the elected branches modifying Court decisions throughout the book; some of them appear in the conclusion, which is also included in this reading. As Fisher points out, if other actors can and do modify court decisions—and court decisions are just one part of an ongoing dialogue—we need not fear judicial power. Instead Fischer sees constitutional interpretation as "part of a joint exercise" that includes, not just the courts, but "the elected branches, the 50 states, and the American public."

Preface

[T]he Supreme Court shares statutory and constitutional interpretation with the elected branches, the fifty states, and the American public. Judicial review does not mean judicial supremacy. Contrary to what is often claimed, the Court's role is not exclusive and detached. It is part of a joint exercise. Over the last five or six decades, however, the Court has been described by scholars and the media as supplying the "final word" on the meaning of the Constitution. Increasingly the Court makes the same claim. It was never the intent of the framers to vest that authority in the Court, it has never functioned in that manner, and it is incompatible with democratic government to assign such overriding political power to the Court.

As with other branches of government, the Supreme Court has had its highs and lows, contributing to individual rights and freedoms in some cases while undermining them in others—strengthening democracy at times, weakening it on other occasions. In its most candid moments, which are, unfortunately, increasingly rare, the Court will look back at a particular decision and publicly admit it was poorly reasoned and damaging to the Court and the nation. All three branches benefit from institutional reflection. The Court is a human institution fully capable of making human mistakes.

We should not study the Supreme Court in isolation. Yet it is now common practice for textbooks on constitutional law to concentrate almost entirely on decisions issued by the Court. The focus is primarily on case law, with little attention to the important contributions by nonjudicial institutions at the national and state levels. The result, as noted by one law professor, is the absence of a "comprehensive course on constitutional law in any meaningful sense in American law schools."[1] Political scientists used to supply a broader, richer, and more realistic view of constitutional interpretation. Over time, they have moved toward the law school model as well.

Those who teach in law schools and political science departments may find it more convenient to study celebrated Court decisions and ignore the contributions of Congress, the president, and the states. That approach, however, poorly serves students, the public, and our constitutional system. It places upon the Court an expectation it cannot meet. Lord Radcliffe advised in a legal essay that "we cannot learn law by learning law." The study of law must be "a part of history, a part of economics and sociology, a part of ethics and a philosophy of life. It is not strong enough in itself to be a philosophy in itself."[2]

To infuse law with dignity, majesty, and perhaps a touch of mystery, it is customary to make entirely unrealistic claims about the power and authority of the Supreme Court. Those who speak accurately about the Court's role are said to threaten judicial symbols and mythology. Scholars began to draw an arbitrary and imaginary line to separate law from politics. In 1914, when legal philosopher Morris Raphael Cohen began describing how judges made law, his colleagues warned against his research. The deans of major law schools advised that his findings, no matter how solidly based on evidence, might invite even greater recourse to "judicial legislation." Cohen rejected their counsel. He had "an abiding conviction that to recognize the truth and adjust oneself to it is in the end the easiest and more advisable course." He denied that the law is a "closed, independent system having nothing to do with economics, political, social, or philosophical science." If courts were in fact constantly making and remaking the law, it became "of the utmost social importance that the law should be made in accordance with the best available information, which it is the object of science to supply."[3]

In a perceptive essay published in 1969, political scientist C. Herman Pritchett explained that the disciplines of law and political science drifted apart for semantic, philosophical, and practical reasons: "Law is a prestigious symbol, whereas politics tends to be a dirty word. Law is stability; politics is chaos. Law is impersonal; politics is personal. Law is given; politics is free choice. Law is reason; politics is prejudice and self-interest. Law is justice; politics is who gets there first with the most."[4] These are stereotypes, of course. At different periods law can be a dirty word, chaotic, personal, a matter of free choice, based on prejudice and self-interest, and a game of who gets there first with the most votes.

Under popular government, the Supreme Court cannot have the last word on constitutional issues. Judicial rulings about speech, press, religious liberty, and other values should not be left to five unelected justices of the Court. Their decisions merit respect, but the finality of Court rulings does not depend on some claim of superior and unchecked power. It depends on the quality of legal (and political) reasoning. Decisions that fail in judgment are necessarily temporary in nature, to be changed by subsequent courts and by other institutions and public pressure. Some may regret that nonjudicial forces compete with, and prevail over, the Court, but this historical pattern is clear and needs to be understood. That is the purpose of this book. In studying the reversals and modifications of Court decisions, we can appreciate how they regularly serve the interests of the nation and its aspiration for democratic rule.

In 2006, Chief Justice John Roberts and Justice Samuel Alito agreed that constitutional interpretation is not a judicial monopoly. Alito said that "all public servants, not just judicial officers, play a role in shaping our law, interpreting our Constitution." It would be a mistake, he said, for "any public officials to ignore questions about the bounds of their authority in our constitutional system and simply say that the courts will sort that out for them." Roberts presented a similar theme: "The great gift of the founding generation was the right of self-government. We shouldn't give it up so easily to think that all the important issues are going to be decided by the Supreme Court."[5] Important points, but both Roberts and Alito in the 2010 *Citizens United* decision claimed that the Court could override elected branch policy about campaign expenditures by corporations and unions. (*Citizens United* is explored in Chapter Four.) Two years later, in a case involving the Affordable Care Act, Roberts deferred to policy enacted by Congress and the president. Alito did not.

This preface concludes by comparing two extremes: (1) the claim that the Supreme Court is indeed the final word on the meaning of the Constitution and (2) the counterargument that it is not. Interestingly, both arguments were once made by the same person in the same year: Justice Robert H. Jackson. In a sentence rendered almost hypnotic by its elegant phrasing, he said in 1953: "We are not final because we are infallible, but we are infallible only because we are final."[6] The historical record demonstrates overwhelmingly that the

Court is neither infallible nor final. That same year, in an address delivered at a conference, Jackson denied that the judiciary carries out its duties isolated from politics: "Let us not deceive ourselves; long-sustained public opinion does influence the process of constitutional interpretation. Each new member of the ever-changing personnel of our courts brings to his task the assumptions and accustomed thought of a later period. The practical play of the forces of politics is such that judicial power has often delayed but never permanently defeated the persistent will of a substantial majority."[7]

As explained in this book, Jackson considerably understated the interaction between law and politics. Successful challenges to Supreme Court decisions on constitutional issues need not await changes in personnel. The elected branches have the capacity to change constitutional doctrine in the same year that the Court decides a case. Specific examples of this democratic and constructive dialogue are provided.

Conclusion: A Broad and Continuing Dialogue

In a religious liberties case in 1997, the Supreme Court claimed to possess the last word on the meaning of the Constitution. It begins with this general perspective: "Our national experience teaches that the Constitution is preserved best when each part of the Government respects both the Constitution and the proper actions and determinations of the other branches." A fair and acceptable generalization. However, it then adds: "When the Court has interpreted the Constitution, it has acted within the province of the Judiciary Branch, which embraces the duty to say what the law is. *Marbury v. Madison,* 1 Cranch, at 177." The citation to *Marbury* is pointless and empty. Obviously it is also the duty of Congress and the president "to say what the law is." *Marbury* stands for many things, but it offers not the slightest support for judicial supremacy, nor did the case ever make that claim. The decision in 1997 concludes that when a conflict occurs between a Court precedent and a congressional statute, the Court's ruling "must control."[1]

Contrary to the Court's position, nothing in "our national experience" justifies the claim that when the Supreme Court decides a constitutional issue, its ruling is final and binding on the elected branches. In the examples offered in this book, major Court rulings were more fluid than fixed, frequently overturned either by the Court or by statute and public opposition. Some decisions, such as *INS v. Chadha,* met with substantial noncompliance. In the yarmulke case of *Goldman v. Weinberger* (1986), the Court rejected Captain Goldman's plea for religious liberty. Within one year, Congress operated under its Article I authority over military regulations to pass legislation that protected the religious rights of members of the military.

Rulings by the Supreme Court are subject to challenges not only from the elected branches but also from the public at large. *Dred Scott,* in 1857, helped precipitate the Civil War and led to a constitutional amendment to nullify the Court's opinion.[2] *Plessy*'s "separate but equal" doctrine in 1896 met increasing resistance from Americans, leading to lawsuits that chipped away at its foundation until federal courts from 1954 through 1963 rejected the doctrine.[3] The Court's "liberty of contract" theory in *Lochner* (1905) divided the judiciary and the nation until discarded in the late 1930s. Public opposition to the Court's flag-salute decision in 1940 helped convince three justices in the majority to shift their position within two years. The addition of two new justices produced an opinion in 1943 that reversed the earlier ruling.[4] The Court's trimester framework in *Roe v. Wade* (1973) encountered strong critiques from liberals and conservatives, resulting in a 1992 decision that jettisoned this judicial overreach.[5] The Court's school busing decisions provoked such intense congressional and public opposition from 1971 into the early 1980s that the Court abandoned its policy.[6]

Respect for the judiciary does not mean blind deference and an unwillingness or incapacity of nonjudicial actors, including the public, to think independently and critically. Each branch needs informed, penetrating evaluations. From that level of scrutiny no branch should be immune. The aspiration for self-government and democracy cannot coexist with the doctrine of judicial supremacy.

No one doubts that Congress, like the Supreme Court and the president, can reach unconstitutional results. Justice William Brennan said in a 1983 dissent: "Legislators, influenced by the passions and exigencies of the moment, the pressure of constituents and colleagues, and the press of business, do not always pass sober constitutional judgment on every piece of legislation they enact."[7] It's a fair point, but the Supreme Court does not always pass sober constitutional judgment either. If we count the times that Congress has been "wrong" about the Constitution and compare those lapses with the occasions when the Court has erred, often by its own later admissions, the results make a compelling case for legislative confidence and judicial modesty.

Here are some observations to explain why the Supreme Court is not the last word on the meaning of the Constitution.

First, the fact that the Court upholds the constitutionality of a bill, as when it sustained the U.S. Bank in *McCulloch v. Maryland* (1819), places no obligation on the elected branches to agree with that judgment. Congress was later free to discontinue the bank. If it passed legislation to renew it, presidents (as Andrew Jackson did) were free to veto the bill on constitutional grounds. The elected branches were at liberty to exercise independent judgments. If they decided the bank had constitutional problems, they could abandon it. Over that decision the Court had no control. Similarly, the Supreme Court in 2012 upheld the Affordable Care Act, but no one should assume this ruling ends the constitutional debate. Congress and presidents will continue to rethink and most likely modify parts of the statute.

Second, a decision by the Court that a certain practice is not prohibited by the Constitution, such as the use of search warrants against a student newspaper in *Zurcher v. Stanford Daily* (1978), did not prevent the elected branches from passing legislation to abolish search warrants and adopt the less-intrusive subpoena power.[8] Rights unprotected by the courts may be secured by Congress, the president, and the states.

Third, when the Court concludes that an activity has no constitutional protection in federal courts—for example, distributing petitions in a shopping center, as in *PruneYard Shopping Center v.*

Robins (1980)—states are not inhibited from protecting those actions by interpreting their own constitution.[9] Decisions by the Court may set a floor, or minimum, for constitutional rights. States may exceed those rights by acting through independent decisions under their constitutions.

Fourth, the Court generally announces broad guidelines: "undue burden," "compelling governmental interest," "narrowly tailored," and "all deliberate speed." It is left to elected officials, jurors, and members of the public to apply those general principles to particular disputes, many of which will never reach the Supreme Court. The Court defines the edges. Nonjudicial actors fill in the vital and important middle. For example, the Court provides general guidance on what constitutes obscene materials (e.g., "prurient interest"). It is up to jurors to decide whether a book, movie, or photographic exhibit belongs in their community. The last word is there, not with the Supreme Court.

Fifth, through threshold doctrines (standing, ripeness, mootness, etc.), the Court often sidesteps a constitutional issue and leaves it to the regular political process. Article I, Section 9, of the Constitution requires that "a regular Statement and Account of the Receipts and Expenditures of all public Money shall be published from time to time." However, the Central Intelligence Agency and other agencies of the intelligence community received covert funding for decades. By invoking the standing doctrine, the Court refused to decide this constitutional question.[10] Years later, in 2007, Congress passed legislation to make public the aggregate budget of the intelligence community.[11] Many other constitutional issues have been settled outside the courts.[12]

Sixth, decisions by the Supreme Court are not pure creative acts, producing something out of nothing. They depend on precedents and values established by other actors, both at the national and state levels. Long before *Gideon v. Wainwright* (1963), many states had decided that due process required that attorneys be appointed to represent indigent defendants.[13] The Supreme Court of Indiana in 1854 stated that "a civilized community" could not prosecute a poor person and withhold counsel.[14] In 1859, the Wisconsin Supreme Court called it a "mockery" to promise a pauper a fair trial and tell him he must employ his own counsel.[15] Congress in 1892 passed legislation to provide counsel to represent poor persons.[16] Not until 1963 did the Court announce its judgment.

Finally, states have substantial discretion under their constitutions to flatly disagree with the U.S. Supreme Court. In 1968, the Court held that a New York statute permitting textbooks to be "lent" free to students in grades seven through twelve, including children attending private and religious schools, was constitutional. The Court upheld the statute by concluding that the benefit extended to parents and children, not to the schools.[17] A number of states, looking to their constitutions that specifically prohibit the use of public funds to assist private and religious schools, rejected the child-benefit theory.[18]

In 1982, the U.S. Supreme Court collided with a state court but came out the loser. The Supreme Court of Washington in 1980 held that a university police officer had invalidly seized incriminating evidence in a student's dormitory room. It determined that the evidence had been obtained illegally and could not be admitted at trial.[19] The U.S. Supreme Court reversed. Relying on its "plain view" doctrine, it said the police officer was in a place he was entitled to be (in the hallway outside the student's room, with the door wide open) and could see drug paraphernalia. Therefore, the evidence could be introduced at trial.[20]

The case returned to the state court for "further proceedings not inconsistent with this opinion." Sounds like judicial supremacy for the U.S. Supreme Court. No. The Supreme Court of Washington rejected the "plain view" doctrine. No such doctrine existed in the state. Whereas its 1980 decision had cited several federal decisions, this time the Supreme Court of Washington based its reasoning "solely and exclusively on the constitution and laws of the state of Washington." It concluded it was right the first time and excluded the evidence.[21] Final word.

In her book *The Majesty of the Law*, Justice Sandra Day O'Connor offered conflicting positions on judicial finality. At times she described the judiciary as "the final arbiters of the constitutionality of all acts of government," even citing language in *Marbury* on the Court's authority "to say what the law is."[22] Elsewhere, however, she showed an appreciation for the mix of judicial and nonjudicial forces that constantly shape the Constitution. She spoke of the "dynamic dialogue between the Court and the American public" and understood that no one could consider *Roe v. Wade* as settling "the issue for all time."[23] More generally, she said that a nation "that docilely and unthinkingly approved every Supreme Court decision as infallible and immutable would, I believe, have severely disappointed our founders."[24]

A judicial ruling is not fixed and binding for all time simply because it has been issued. It is controlling if sound in substance and reasoning. In 1849, a dissent by Chief Justice Roger Taney urged the Court to keep an open mind. In his view, an opinion by the Court "is always open to discussion when it is supposed to have been founded in error, and . . . its judicial authority should hereafter depend altogether on the force of the reasoning by which it is supported."[25] Also in dissent, Justice Louis Brandeis observed in 1932: "The Court bows to the lessons of experience and the force of better reasoning, recognizing that the process of trial and error, so fruitful in the physical sciences, is appropriate also in the judicial function."[26] The Court, as a creature of the Constitution, is an experiment as well, to be judged on the basis of its performance and respect for self-government, not on some abstract theory of judicial finality.

NOTES

Preface

1. W. Michael Reisman, "International Incidents: Introduction to a New Genre in the Study of International Law," 10 *Yale J. Int'l L.* 1, 8 n.13 (1984).

2. Lord Radcliffe, *The Law & Its Compass* 92–93 (1960).

3. Morris R. Cohen, *Law and the Social Order* 380–81, n.86 (1933).

4. C. Herman Pritchett, "The Development of Judicial Research," in Joel B. Grossman &

Joseph Tanenhaus, eds., *Frontiers of Judicial Research* 31 (1969).

5. Robert Barnes, "New Justices Take the Podium, Putting Personalities on Display," *The Washington Post*, November 20, 2006, at A15.

6. *Brown v. Allen*, 344 U.S. 443, 540 (1953).

7. Robert H. Jackson, "Maintaining Our Freedoms: The Role of the Judiciary," delivered to the American Bar Association, Boston, Massachusetts, August 24, 1953.

Conclusion

1. *Boerne v. Flores*, 521 U.S. 507, 535–36 (1997).

2. *Dred Scott v. Sandford*, 60 U.S. (19 How.) 393 (1857); discussed in Chapter Three.

3. Discussed in Chapter Five.

4. *West Virginia State Board of Education v. Barnette*, 319 U.S. 624 (1943), reversing *Minersville School District v. Gobitis*, 310 U.S. 586 (1940); discussed in Chapter Five.

5. *Planned Parenthood of Southeastern Pa. v. Casey*, 505 U.S. 833 (1992), reversing the trimester framework in *Roe v. Wade*, 410 U.S. 113 (1973); discussed in Chapter Four.

6. Discussed in Chapter Four.

7. *Marsh v. Chambers*, 463 U.S. 783, 814 (1983) (Brennan, J., dissenting).

8. 436 U.S. 547 (1978).

9. 447 U.S. 74 (1980).

10. *United States v. Richardson*, 418 U.S. 166 (1974).

11. Louis Fisher, *Defending Congress and the Constitution* 65–69 (2011).

12. Louis Fisher, "Separation of Powers: Interpretation Outside the Courts."18 *Pepp. L. Rev.* 57 (1990); http://www.loufisher.org/docs/ci/460.pdf. Accessed Feb. 19, 2013.

13. *Gideon v. Wainwright*, 372 U.S. 335 (1963).

14. *Webb v. Baird*, 6 Ind. 13 (1854).

15. *Carpenter v. Dane*, 9 Wis. 249 (1859).

16. 27 Stat. 252 (1892).

17. *Board of Education v. Allen*, 392 U.S. 236 (1968).

18. *Fisher & Harriger*, *supra* note 8, at 600–03.

19. *State v. Chrisman*, 619 P.2d 971 (Wash. 1980).

20. *Washington v. Chrisman*, 455 U.S. 1, 6 (1982).

21. *State v. Chrisman*, 676 P.2d 419 (Wash. 1984). See Louis Fisher, "How the States Shape Constitutional Law," 15 State Legislatures 37 (August 1989).

22. Sandra Day O'Connor, *The Majesty of the Law: Reflections of a Supreme Court Justice* 243 (2003).

23. Id. at 45.

24. Id. at 45.

25. Passenger Cases, 48 U.S. 283, 470 (1849).

26. *Burnet v. Coronado Oil & Gas Co.*, 285 U.S. 393, 407–08 (1932).

ARTICLE QUESTIONS

1) In his conclusion Fisher offers seven "observations to explain why the Supreme Court is not the last word on the meaning of the Constitution." What are these seven observations? Which of these arguments do you find most and least compelling?

2) Do you agree with Fisher's claim that "under popular government, the Supreme Court cannot have the last word on Constitutional issues"?

3) If the courts do not have the final say on the meaning of the Constitution, are fears that the federal courts wielding too much power unfounded? Why or why not?

16.2) High Court Not Final Say on U.S. Law

Times-Standard, April 12, 2012

RYAN EMENAKER

Ryan Emenaker is an Assistant Professor of Political Science at College of the Redwoods. His studies focus on judicial politics and separation of powers.

> "High Court Not Final Say on U.S. Law" appeared as an editorial in the *Times-Standard*, a small newspaper in northern California, just before the Court issued its opinion in *National Federation of Independent Business v. Sebelius* (2012), which was a constitutional challenge to the Affordable Care Act (ACA). In a surprising 5-4 decision, written by Chief Justice John Roberts, the Court ruled that the ACA was a constitutional exercise of Congress's taxing authority. Despite that ruling, there have been numerous efforts by states and by some members of Congress to repeal or modify the ACA. These postjudicial review activities underscore the final claim of the editorial that the Court decision should not be "expect[ed] to be the end" of this political struggle.
>
> Ryan Emenaker uses the Supreme Court review of the ACA as an opportunity to argue that judicial finality—the concept that the Court has the final word when interpreting the Constitution—is a myth. The editorial begins with some classic critiques of judicial review, and as the editorial progresses it points out that the legislative and executive branches have the ability to delay or prevent court decisions. The reading provides a classic argument of judicial dependency and provides some historical examples of the elected branches bending the federal courts to their will. Perhaps the most important contribution of this editorial is the citing of empirical data to emphasize how common it is for Congress to pass legislation overriding the Supreme Court's interpretation of the Constitution.

As a professor of political science I have followed the spectacle surrounding the Supreme Court and the Affordable Care Act with great delight—this is an educational opportunity. We in the U.S. tend to be woefully ignorant of our political institutions. According to a 2010 FindLaw national survey, only 16 percent could name the chief justice of the Supreme Court and only 1 percent could name all nine justices. A survey of RealClearPolitics.com over the last month shows a number of articles focusing on the court. Sadly the content of these stories, and comments posted on-line, display a misunderstanding of the court's political nature—this lack of knowledge is more concerning than an inability to name justices.

In recent articles discussing the role of the Court there is near universal acceptance the court has the final word interpreting the Constitution. Even President Obama came forward to defend judicial finality stating "the Supreme Court is the final say on our Constitution and our laws." As a matter of constitutional law and practice, judicial finality is a myth. Contrary popular belief the power of judicial review—the power of the Court to strike down actions of the other branches, as well as states, for violating the Constitution—is not granted in the Constitution. Judicial review was granted to the court by itself, a power it simply announced it possessed in *Marbury v. Madison* in 1803. Thomas Jefferson decried judicial finality for turning the Constitution into "a mere thing of wax in the hands of the judiciary." After appropriating this power in 1803, the Court failed to strike down an act of Congress until 1857. The decision in this case drew the ire of Abraham Lincoln who responded by resoundingly rejecting the concept of judicial finality. In a speech soon after the *Scott* decision, Lincoln argued court decisions were binding on the parties in that specific case, however these decisions need not set constitutional precedent for the president or Congress; as separate branches they retain independent authority to interpret the Constitution.

Alexander Hamilton wrote in Federalist 78 that the Court is the "least dangerous" branch as it "has no influence over either the sword or the purse."

Hamilton acknowledged, in a way we fail to today, that this lack of power makes the Court dependent. This dependency translates into the court rarely striking down acts of Congress. An examination of all congressional acts struck down by the court from 1803 to 2010, shows the court has invalidated less than one congressional act per year.

We may have independent judges with lifetime tenure, but we have a dependent judiciary. When the court gets too out-of-line with the other branches, the court has little power. After the Civil War, Congress worried civil rights legislation would be struck down, so Congress simply took away the Court's ability to hear appeals on the issue—Congress controls the court's appellate jurisdiction. Throughout history Congress has raised and lowered the number sitting on the court to control decisions. These are only a couple of constitutional powers Congress has over the court.

Justices seem to be able to read the Constitution well enough to know it provides the other branches power to control their institution. The Court has only struck down 167 acts of Congress in U.S. history. In many of these, the court's decision was not final. In four cases, the Constitution was specifically amended to get around the Court's decision. In other cases Congress simply passed laws to override decisions. An original dataset I compiled examined the 41 acts of Congress struck down during the Rehnquist Court (1986–2005); 12 of those decisions were overridden by Congress. That means in 29.3 percent of those supposedly final interpretations of the Constitution, Congress simply passed legislation changing the outcome. Another study that looked at 1954–1997 noted that in 48 percent of cases, Congress acted to restore policies the Court invalidated. These studies directly challenge judicial finality.

The Court is one step in a constitutional dialogue among the states, Congress, and the executive branch. Separation of powers is the game that never ends. The Court will most likely announce its decision on the ACA in June—don't expect this to be the end!

ARTICLE QUESTIONS

1) What were the concerns that Lincoln and Jefferson expressed about judicial review?
2) According to the editorial, how many times has the Court struck down an act of Congress?
3) What methods does Congress use to limit the independent power of the federal courts, according to the editorial?
4) What are the potential concerns with Congress being able to modify Court decisions or being able to punish the Court for decisions it doesn't agree with?

16.3) Supreme Court Appears Divided in Cross Case

National Public Radio, October 7, 2009

This piece from *National Public Radio* (NPR), "Supreme Court Appears Divided in Cross Case," provides another example of a continuing dialogue between the courts and the elected branches over constitutional interpretation. According to the article, in several instances Congress maneuvered around the Ninth Circuit Court of Appeals' determination that a cross on federal land had to be removed because it violated the First Amendment. When NPR reported on the story, the Court was deciding whether its interpretation of the First Amendment would be consistent with Congress's or whether its interpretation would rebuff a Congress that had resisted implementing the Ninth Circuit's rulings.

In addition to the separation of powers struggle between Congress and the courts, the case also brings up debates about religious liberties and religious pluralism. This means we can debate both the outcome of the decision (should the cross be removed?) and the process for making that decision (should the courts or Congress decide?).

The Supreme Court appeared divided along philosophical lines Wednesday as justices heard arguments in a long-running legal battle over a cross built as a memorial to U.S. war dead on federal park land in California's Mojave Desert.

The Obama administration argued that Congress removed any constitutional questions over the separation of church and state when it transferred ownership of the land where the cross stands to a private owner. The approach appeared to have some traction with the court's conservative justices.

Justice Samuel Alito asked, "Isn't that a sensible interpretation" of a court order prohibiting the cross' display on government property?

But the more liberal justices seemed to agree with a federal appeals court that invalidated the transfer, saying Congress was trying to maneuver around the First Amendment.

Opponents of the cross have argued that the presence of a Christian symbol on public land violates the First Amendment's prohibition against the government favoring a particular religion. But those who want the cross to remain say it's a historical symbol that is intended to honor all war dead.

The cross has stood on an outcropping of rock in a remote part of the California desert for 75 years. It was originally erected in 1934 by the Veterans of Foreign Wars without the permission of the government and been rebuilt twice since then.

In 1999, a Buddhist asked the National Park Service for permission to build a Buddhist shrine near the cross, but the request was refused.

That led a former park service employee, Frank Buono, to challenge the presence of the cross, saying it was unconstitutional to have a religious symbol on public land. The U.S. Court of Appeals for the 9th Circuit in San Francisco has sided with Buono in several instances and ordered the cross removed. Each time, Congress has intervened, and for now, the cross stands covered with plywood.

In addition to transferring ownership of the land, lawmakers have also prohibited the park service from spending money to remove the cross, and later designated the site a national memorial to those who died during World War I.

On Wednesday, Obama administration attorneys contended that Buono did not have legal standing to file the suit in the first place because he's a Christian and was not harmed by the cross' presence.

Veterans groups are on both sides of the case, *Salazar v. Buono*. Some worry that other religious symbols that serve as war memorials might be threatened if the court sides with Buono.

Some Jewish and Muslim veterans maintain that the Mojave cross honors Christian veterans.

ARTICLE QUESTIONS

1) What action in 1999 led Frank Buono to file a lawsuit challenging the presence of the cross?

2) What are the three specific actions reported by the article that Congress took to prevent the Ninth Circuit Court of Appeals' rulings to remove the cross?

3) Do you think Congress would have taken the same actions to protect a Jewish or Muslim religious symbol that was erected on federal parkland to memorialize U.S. soldiers?

4) Do you think Congress would be just as likely to maneuver around a Supreme Court ruling to remove the cross as it was to maneuver around the Circuit Court's decision?

16.4) Why States and Localities Are Watching the Lower Federal Courts

Governing, October, 2010

DONALD F. KETTL

Court cases rarely travel up to the Supreme Court, so lower courts are often the last stop for controversial cases.

> Donald F. Kettl's "Why States and Localities Are Watching the Lower Federal Courts" turns our attention away from the Supreme Court and redirects it to the federal courts. As Kettl notes, most federal court cases do not make it to the Supreme Court (even really important ones). The Court only hears about 80 cases a year, while the 13 U.S. Courts of Appeals (which are one level below the Supreme Court) hear about 60,000. The Supreme Court has almost complete discretion over which cases it will hear. About 9,000 cases are appealed to it each year; thus the Court selects less than 1 percent of eligible cases to review.
>
> Kettl draws two important conclusions from the fact that the Supreme Court only hears about 80 (of the more than 400,000 federal) cases per year. One, the interpretation of federal law most often occurs in the lower federal courts. A decision by one of the U.S. Courts of Appeals is likely the final decision in that case. The other conclusion is that it is important to follow all federal court appointments. There are just nine Supreme Court justices, but there are nearly 1,000 federal judges—all of whom are appointed by the president and confirmed by the Senate. Presidents are lucky to nominate one or two Supreme Court justices in a term but they have the opportunity to nominate more than 200 federal judges. This allows a president to remake the federal courts without even nominating a justice to the Supreme Court. In President Obama's first term, he successfully nominated 218 federal judges—only two of them to the to the Supreme Court. The obsessive focus on Supreme Court appointments misses a major dimension in making public policy.

Within the federal judiciary, the Supreme Court of the United States (SCOTUS, for short) undoubtedly captures the big headlines. In the last term, the SCOTUS ruling that opened the way for corporate political contributions led to an icy face-off at the State of the Union address between President Barack Obama and Chief Justice Roberts.

While SCOTUS gets most of the ink, the lower courts do most of the judiciary's work. In 2008–2009, the last year for which official numbers are available, the Supreme Court heard 87 cases. One step down, the U.S. Courts of Appeals dealt with more than 57,700 cases. The U.S. District Courts, the first level of the federal system, handled nearly 276,400 civil cases and more than 76,600 criminal cases. The odds that SCOTUS will decide a case first filed with a district court are tiny—less than three in 10,000—so the lower courts are the last stop for most issues.

In the process, the lower federal courts are making landmark rulings. Because the makeup of those courts is very much up for grabs, Obama could have a huge impact on the judiciary and the vast majority of cases that never make it to SCOTUS.

In June, for example, U.S. District Judge Martin Feldman halted the U.S. Interior Department's moratorium on offshore drilling in the Gulf of Mexico. Feldman held that the freeze on drilling was too broad. He ruled that the feds couldn't shut down all of the wells because one rig failed, and "no one yet fully knows why."

Oil producers—and Gulf workers on their payrolls—celebrated while the Obama administration hastily redrafted its response to the fallout from BP's Deepwater Horizon drilling disaster.

In July, federal Judge Susan R. Bolton blocked Arizona's tough new immigration law, which required police to investigate the legal status of every person they detained. That, she said, would increase "the intrusion of police presence into the lives of legally present aliens [and even U.S. citizens], who will necessarily be swept up" by the policy. Bolton found that the Arizona law conflicted with the federal government's laws and policies. Her ruling broadcast a warning to other states considering similar laws.

In August, Vaughn Walker, U.S. district court judge for California's northern district, struck down the state's Proposition 8, which banned same-sex marriages. Walker wrote, "Proposition 8 fails to advance any rational basis in singling out gay men and lesbians for denial of a marriage license."

California Gov. Arnold Schwarzenegger applauded the decision, but legal observers wondered whether proponents of same-sex marriage would be able to find five votes if the case reached SCOTUS. [Note, In June 2015 we learned that the answer was "yes" when the Court ruled, 5–4 in *Obergefell v. Hodges* that the right to marry was a right guaranteed by the Constitution].

We all know about separation of powers from high school civics and college political science courses. We learned that the founders gave the courts independent power because they didn't fully trust democratic rule. When decisions like these come down, however, they always strike like lightning bolts at the heart of typical battles between elected legislators and executives.

And we all know that the judiciary is independent of politics. But the lightning bolts are always political—they are launched by judges who bring to each case their own reading of the Constitution and law, and the judges were put in place by elected officials who hoped that those readings were right.

Before Obama, Republicans held the White House for 28 of the past 40 years, and their lifetime appointments of federal judges have made a deep mark on the bench. Obama's election sent shivers through those who closely follow the federal lower courts, for they knew that Obama would have many appointments to make.

One judge, J. Harvie Wilkinson III of the Fourth Circuit Court of Appeals, appointed by President Ronald Reagan to a circuit viewed as the nation's most conservative, warned in a January 2009 *Washington Post* op-ed article that Obama's election would bring a "takeover" of the lower courts. In the Senate, some Republican senators have been sitting on Obama's nominees for the lower courts to try to prevent this from happening.

In a 2009 study, Washington attorney Eric R. Haren wrote that conservatives held the majority on most of the dozen federal courts of appeals, but he argued that "these courts are up for grabs, and Obama's impact on them could be sweeping." Some analysts have concluded that Obama had already tipped two appellate courts to a majority appointed by Democrats.

By the time his first term ends, Obama will have had the chance to reshape many more federal appeals courts—perhaps every one if he serves two terms in the White House. That could bring an impact even larger and more lasting than whatever will happen to SCOTUS.

Huge policy battles with deep implications continue to brew in the states. We surely haven't seen the last of cases like offshore drilling, immigration and same-sex marriage. With the lower courts, the last stop for more than 99 percent of all cases, Obama's ability to reshape the judiciary beyond SCOTUS could well prove one of his most quiet but lasting legacies.

ARTICLE QUESTIONS

1) What are some of the landmark rulings the article cites as being made by the U.S. District Courts and the U.S. Courts of Appeals?
2) Does it undermine the public's trust in court decisions if the justices are seen as being appointed through a partisan political process?
3) In what ways, if any, should the judicial appointment process be modified?

16.5) In Conversation: Antonin Scalia

New York Magazine, October 6, 2013

JENNIFER SENIOR

On the eve of a new Supreme Court session, the firebrand justice discusses gay rights and media echo chambers, *Seinfeld* and the Devil, and how much he cares about his intellectual legacy ("I don't").

Jennifer Senior's "In Conversation: Antonin Scalia" is a very lively interview with Supreme Court Justice Antonin Scalia. Scalia was nominated to the Court in 1986 by Ronald Reagan and is the longest-serving justice on the current Court. He is known for his engaging and sometimes acerbic opinions. As Scalia explains in the interview, he is an advocate of interpreting the Constitution based on the meaning ascribed by its drafters. This principle, known as originalism, has gone from obscurity to mainstream thanks, in large part, to Scalia.

Scalia states in the interview that he is a Catholic who believes the Devil is real; he feels out of touch with pop culture, and he avoids news from sources he describes as "shrilly liberal" such as *The Washington Post* and *The New York Times*. As political scientists, our interest in the lives of the Supreme Court justices is about something more than celebrity gossip: this interview reminds us that federal judges are real people with individual biases and worldviews. Studying the actions of the courts from the perspective of the biases of the justices (a method known as judicial behavioralism) became the dominant mode of studying judicial politics at the end of the twentieth century. Judicial behavioralist scholars argue that you can accurately predict how judges will rule in a case by knowing their personal preferences. Scalia argues that interpreting the Constitution through an originalist lens keeps his personal bias out of his decisions. Many court watchers admire Scalia and his approach; others charge that his rulings reflect his deep conservatism. Based on what you read in the interview, do you think you can predict how Scalia will rule in upcoming cases?

On September 26—a day that just happened to be the 27th anniversary of his swearing-in as associate justice—Antonin Scalia entered the Supreme Court's enormous East Conference Room so casually that one might easily have missed him. He is smaller than his king-size persona suggests, and his manner more puckish than formal. Washingtonians may know Scalia as charming and disarming, but most outsiders tend to regard him as either a demigod on stilts or a menace to democracy, depending on which side of the aisle they sit. A singularity on the Court and an icon on the right, Scalia is perhaps more responsible than any American alive for the mainstreaming of conservative ideas about jurisprudence—in particular the principles of originalism (interpreting the Constitution as the framers intended it rather than as an evolving document) and textualism (that statutes must be interpreted based on their words alone). And he has got to be the only justice to ever use the phrase "argle-bargle" in a dissent.

You came to Washington as a lawyer during the Nixon administration, just before Watergate. What on Earth was that like?

It was a sad time. It was very depressing. Every day, *The Washington Post* would come out with something new—it trickled out bit by bit. Originally, you thought, *It couldn't be,* but it obviously was. As a young man, you're dazzled by the power of the White House and all that. But power tends to corrupt.

Then you served in the Ford administration. That must have been an awfully lonely time to be a young conservative.

It was a terrible time, not for the Republican Party, but for the presidency. It was such a wounded and enfeebled presidency, and Congress was just eating us alive. I mean, we had a president who had never been elected to anything except . . . what? A district in Michigan? Everything was in chaos.

It was a time when people were talking about "the imperial presidency." I knew very well that the 900-pound gorilla in Washington is not the presidency. It's Congress. If Congress can get its act together, it can roll over the president. That's what the framers thought. They said you have to enlist your jealousy against the legislature in a democracy—*that* will be the source of tyranny.

But weren't you just saying that you learned from Watergate that presidents aren't incorruptible?
What, and Congress is? I mean, they're all human beings. Power tends to corrupt. But the power in Washington resides in Congress, if it wants to use it. It can do anything—it can stop the Vietnam War, it can make its will felt, if it can ever get its act together to do anything.

Had you already arrived at originalism as a philosophy?
I don't know when I came to that view. I've always had it, as far as I know. Words have meaning. And their meaning doesn't change. I mean, the notion that the Constitution should simply, by decree of the Court, mean something that it didn't mean when the people voted for it—frankly, you should ask the other side the question! How did they *ever* get there?

But as law students, they were taught that the Constitution evolved, right? You got that same message consistently in class, yet you had other ideas.
I am something of a contrarian, I suppose. I feel less comfortable when everybody agrees with me. I say, "I better reexamine my position!" I probably believe that the worst opinions in my court have been unanimous. Because there's nobody on the other side pointing out all the flaws.

Really? So if you had the chance to have eight other justices just like you, would you not want them to be your colleagues?
No. Just six.

That was a serious question!
What I do wish is that we were in agreement on the basic question of what we think we're doing when we interpret the Constitution. I mean, that's sort of rudimentary. It's sort of an embarrassment, really, that we're not. But some people

think our job is to keep it up to date, give new meaning to whatever phrases it has. And others think it's to give it the meaning the people ratified when they adopted it. Those are quite different views.

You've described yourself as a fainthearted originalist. But really, how fainthearted?
I described myself as that a long time ago. I repudiate that.

So you're a stouthearted one.
I try to be. I try to be an honest originalist! I will take the bitter with the sweet! What I used "fainthearted" in reference to was—

Flogging, right?
Flogging. And what I would say now is, yes, if a state enacted a law permitting flogging, it is immensely stupid, but it is not unconstitutional. A lot of stuff that's stupid is not unconstitutional. I gave a talk once where I said they ought to pass out to all federal judges a stamp, and the stamp says—*Whack!* [*Pounds his fist.*]—STUPID BUT CONSTITUTIONAL. *Whack!* [*Pounds again.*] STUPID BUT CONSTITUTIONAL! *Whack!* STUPID BUT CONSTITUTIONAL... [*Laughs.*] And then somebody sent me one.

So are there things in the Constitution you find stupid? I remember Judge Bork saying that there were few people who understood what the Ninth Amendment meant, as if it was partially covered by an inkblot.
You know, in the early years, the Bill of Rights referred to the first eight amendments. They didn't even count the ninth. The Court didn't use it for 200 years. If I'd been required to identify the Ninth Amendment when I was in law school or in the early years of my practice, and if my life depended on it, I couldn't tell you what the Ninth Amendment was.

Do you think there are flaws in the Constitution?
The one provision that I would amend is the amendment provision. And that was not originally a flaw. But the country has changed so much. With the divergence in size between California

and Rhode Island—I figured it out once, I think if you picked the smallest number necessary for a majority in the least populous states, something like less than 2 percent of the population can prevent a constitutional amendment. But other than that, some things have not worked out the way the framers anticipated. But that's been the fault of the courts, not the fault of the draftsmen.

What about sex discrimination? Do you think the Fourteenth Amendment covers it?

Of course it covers it! No, you can't treat women differently, give them higher criminal sentences. Of course not.

A couple of years ago, I think you told *California Lawyer* something different.

What I was referring to is: The issue is not whether it prohibits discrimination on the basis of sex. Of course it does. The issue is, "What is discrimination?"

If there's a reasonable basis for not letting women do something—like going into combat or whatnot. . . .

Let's put it this way: Do you think the same level of scrutiny that applies to race should apply to sex?

I am not a fan of different levels of scrutiny. Strict scrutiny, intermediate scrutiny, *blah blah blah blah*. That's just a thumb on the scales.

But there are some intelligent reasons to treat women differently. I don't think anybody would deny that. And there really is no, virtually no, intelligent reason to treat people differently on the basis of their skin.

What's your media diet? Where do you get your news?

Well, we get newspapers in the morning.

"We" meaning the justices?

No! Maureen and I.

Oh, you and your wife. . . .

I usually skim them. We just get *The Wall Street Journal* and the *Washington Times*. We used to get *The Washington Post,* but it just . . . went too far for me. I couldn't handle it anymore.

What tipped you over the edge?

It was the treatment of almost any conservative issue. It was slanted and often nasty. And, you know, why should I get upset every morning? I don't think I'm the only one. I think they lost subscriptions partly because they became so shrilly, *shrilly* liberal.

So no *New York Times*, either?

No *New York Times,* no *Post*.

And do you look at anything online?

I get most of my news, probably, driving back and forth to work, on the radio.

Not NPR?

Sometimes NPR. But not usually. . . .

It was recently reported that the justices don't communicate with one another by e-mail. Do you go online at all?

Yeah. Sure, I use the Internet.

You've got grandkids. Do you feel like the Internet has coarsened our culture at all?

I'm nervous about our civic culture. I'm not sure the Internet is largely the cause of it. It's certainly the cause of careless writing. People who get used to blurbing things on the Internet are never going to be good writers. And some things I don't understand about it. For example, I don't know why anyone would like to be "friended" on the network. I mean, what kind of a narcissistic society is it that people want to put out there, *This is my life, and this is what I did yesterday?* I mean . . . good grief. Doesn't that strike you as strange? I think it's strange.

I've gotten used to it.

Well, I am glad that I am not raising kids today. And I'm rather pessimistic that my grandchildren will enjoy the great society that I've enjoyed in my lifetime. I really think it's coarsened. It's coarsened in so many ways.

Like what?

One of the things that upsets me about modern society is the coarseness of manners. You can't go to a movie—or watch a television show for that matter—without hearing the constant use of the F-word—including, you know, *ladies* using it. People that I know don't talk like that! But if you portray it a lot, the society's going to become that way. It's very sad.

And you can't have a movie or a television show without a nude sex scene, very often having no relation to the plot. I don't mind it when it is essential to the plot, as it sometimes is. But, my goodness! The society that watches that becomes a coarse society. . . .

Has your personal attitude [toward homosexuality] softened some?

I don't think I've softened. I don't know what you mean by softened.

If you talk to your grandchildren, they have different opinions from you about this, right?

I don't know about my grandchildren. I know about my children. I don't think they and I differ very much. But I'm not a hater of homosexuals at all.

I still think it's Catholic teaching that it's wrong. Okay? But I don't hate the people that engage in it. In my legal opinions, all I've said is that I don't think the Constitution requires the people to adopt one view or the other.

There was something different about your DOMA opinion, I thought. It was really pungent, yes, but you seemed more focused on your colleagues' jurisprudence. You didn't talk about a gay lobby, or about the fact that people have the right to determine what they consider moral. In *Lawrence v. Texas*, you said Americans were within their rights in "protecting themselves and their families from a lifestyle that they believe to be immoral and destructive."

I would write that again. But that's not saying that I personally think it's destructive. Americans have a right to feel that way. They have a democratic right to do that, and if it is to change, it should change democratically, and not at the ukase of a Supreme Court.

The what?

U-K-A-S-E. Yeah. I think that's how you say it. It's a mandate. A decree.

Whatever you think of the opinion, Justice Kennedy is now the Thurgood Marshall of gay rights.

[*Nods.*]

I don't know how, by your lights, that's going to be regarded in 50 years.

I don't know either. And, frankly, I don't care. Maybe the world is spinning toward a wider acceptance of homosexual rights, and here's Scalia, standing athwart it. At least standing athwart it as a constitutional entitlement. But I have never been custodian of my legacy. When I'm dead and gone, I'll either be sublimely happy or terribly unhappy.

You believe in heaven and hell?

Oh, of course I do. Don't you believe in heaven and hell?

No.

Oh, my.

Does that mean I'm not going?

[*Laughing.*] Unfortunately not!

Wait, to heaven or hell?

It doesn't mean you're not going to hell, just because you don't believe in it. That's Catholic doctrine! Everyone is going one place or the other.

But you don't have to be a Catholic to get into heaven? Or believe in it?

Of course not!

Oh. So you don't know where I'm going. Thank God.

I don't know where you're going. I don't even know whether Judas Iscariot is in hell. I mean, that's what the pope meant when he said, "Who am I to judge?" He may have recanted and had severe penance just before he died. Who knows?

Can we talk about your drafting process—

[*Leans in, stage-whispers.*] I even believe in the Devil.

You do?

Of course! Yeah, he's a real person. Hey, c'mon, that's standard Catholic doctrine! Every Catholic believes that.

Every Catholic believes this? There's a wide variety of Catholics out there. . . .

If you are faithful to Catholic dogma, that is certainly a large part of it.

Have you seen evidence of the Devil lately?

You know, it is curious. In the Gospels, the Devil is doing all sorts of things. He's making pigs run off cliffs, he's possessing people and whatnot. And that doesn't happen very much anymore.

No.

It's because he's smart.

So what's he doing now?

What he's doing now is getting people not to believe in him or in God. He's much more successful that way.

That has really painful implications for atheists. Are you sure that's the Devil's work?

I didn't say atheists are the Devil's work.

Well, you're saying the Devil is persuading people to not believe in God. Couldn't there be other reasons to not believe?

Well, there certainly can be other reasons. But it certainly favors the Devil's desires. I mean, c'mon, that's the explanation for why there's not demonic possession all over the place. That always puzzled me. What happened to the Devil, you know? He used to be all over the place. He used to be all over the New Testament.

Right.

What happened to him?

He just got wilier.

He got wilier.

Isn't it terribly frightening to believe in the Devil?

You're looking at me as though I'm weird. My God! Are you so out of touch with most of America, most of which believes in the Devil? I mean, Jesus Christ believed in the Devil! It's in the Gospels! You travel in circles that are so, *so* removed from mainstream America that you are appalled that anybody would believe in the Devil! Most of mankind has believed in the Devil, for all of history. Many more intelligent people than you or me have believed in the Devil.

I hope you weren't sensing contempt from me. It wasn't your belief that surprised me so much as how boldly you expressed it.

I was offended by that. I really was.

I'm sorry to have offended you!

Have you read *The Screwtape Letters?*

Yes, I have.

So, there you are. That's a great book. It really is, just as a study of human nature.

Can I ask about your engagement with regular pop culture?

I'm pretty bad on regular pop culture.

I know you watched the show 24. Do you also watch *Homeland*?

I don't watch *Homeland*. I don't even know what *Homeland* is. I watched one episode of—what is it? *Duck Dynasty*?

What?

I don't watch it regularly, but I'm a hunter. I use duck calls. . . .

Did you just stumble on it by accident?

No! So many people said "Oh, it's a great show" that I thought I'd better look at it. Have you looked at it?

No. But there are three books on *The New York Times*' best-seller list about *Duck Dynasty*.

Is that right?

Yes. Three. Did you watch *The Sopranos? Mad Men*?

I watched *The Sopranos,* I saw a couple of episodes of *Mad Men*. I loved *Seinfeld*. In fact, I got some CDs of *Seinfeld*. *Seinfeld* was hilarious. Oh, boy. The Nazi soup kitchen? No soup for you! . . .

. . . I feel like Washington has been playing a pretty high-stakes [poker] game lately. You've seen more Congresses than I have, and you've seen this nation go through more turbulent events than I have. But now seems an especially acerbic moment.

It's a nasty time. It's a nasty time. When I was first in Washington, and even in my early years on this Court, I used to go to a lot of dinner parties at which there were people from both sides. Democrats, Republicans. Katharine Graham used to have dinner parties that really were quite representative of Washington. It doesn't happen anymore.

True, though earlier you expressed your preference for conservative media, which itself can be isolating in its own way.
Oh, c'mon, c'mon, c'mon! [*Laughs.*] Social intercourse is quite different from those intellectual outlets I respect and those that I don't respect. I read newspapers that I think are good newspapers, or if they're not good, at least they don't make me angry, okay? That has nothing to do with social intercourse. That has to do with "selection of intellectual fodder," if you will.

When was the last party you went to that had a nice healthy dose of both liberals and conservatives?
Geez, I can't even remember. It's been a long time.

Is that true on the Court as well? Are things tenser in this building? Were there ever more harmonious groupings of justices than others?
No. Everybody I've served with on the Court I've regarded as a friend. Some were closer than others, but I didn't consider myself an enemy of any of them. Now, that hasn't always been the case. Frankfurter and Douglas, the Harvard Law professor and the Yale Law professor, hated each other. They wouldn't talk to each other. Imagine being on a committee of nine people where two of them won't talk to each other! But it's never been the case since I've been on the Court.

You were asked this summer about the most wrenching case you've decided, and you answered, "Is Obamacare too recent?"
[*Laughs.*]

Is that true?
No. Probably the most wrenching was *Morrison v. Olson,* which involved the independent counsel. To take away the power to prosecute from the president and give it to somebody who's not under his control is a terrible erosion of presidential power. And it was wrenching not only because it came out wrong—I was the sole dissenter—but because the opinion was written by Rehnquist, who had been head of the Office of Legal Counsel, before me, and who I thought would realize the importance of that power of the president to prosecute. And he not only wrote the opinion; he wrote

it in a manner that was more extreme than I think Bill Brennan would have written it. That was wrenching.

That sheds new light on your famous odd-couple friendship with Ruth Bader Ginsburg. Do you think it's easier to be close to a colleague who is so ideologically different?
There may be something to that. If you have low expectations, you're not disappointed. When it's somebody who you think is basically on your side on these ideological controversies, and then that person goes over to the dark side, it does make you feel bad.

Who was or is your favorite sparring partner on the bench? The person who makes or made your ideas and opinions better?
Probably John Paul Stevens. There are some justices who adopt a magisterial approach to a dissent. Rehnquist used to do it. [*He turns his nose up theatrically, flutters his hand in dismissal.*] Just, *Don't even respond to the dissent. This is the opinion of the Court, and the hell with you.* I am not like that. I think you should give the dissenter the respect to respond to the points that he makes. And so did John Stevens. So he and I used to go back and forth almost endlessly.

Are there any lawyers who you also consider really formidable?
That's one of the biggest changes on the Court since I've been here. When I arrived, there really was not what you could call a Supreme Court bar—people who appear regularly. But now we have people who appear four, five times a term. What has happened is the big law firms have adopted Supreme Court practices. I'm not sure they make money on it, but they get prestige from it. So we get very good lawyers. Many of them ex–solicitor generals.

How does that change your job?
It makes my job easier. We are dependent upon these people who have lived with the case for months—in many cases years—to clarify the facts and to clarify the law. I come to the thing maybe a month beforehand. These lawyers—the reason to listen to them is that they presumably know more about the subject than you do.

Another change is that many of the states have adopted a new office of solicitor general, so that the people who come to argue from the states are people who know how to conduct appellate argument. In the old days, it would be the attorney general—usually an elected attorney general. And if he gets a case into the Supreme Court [*pumps his fist*], he's going to argue it himself! Get the press and whatnot. Some of them were just disasters. They were throwing away important points of law, not just for their state, but for the other 49.

Let's talk about your opinions for a second. Do you draft them yourself? What's your process?
I almost never do the first draft.

How do your clerks know your voice so well?
Oh, I edit it considerably between the first and the last.

How do you choose your clerks?
Very carefully. What I'm looking for is really smart people who don't necessarily have to share my judicial philosophy, but they cannot be hostile to it. And can let me be me when they draft opinions, can write opinions that will follow my judicial philosophy rather than their own. And I've said often in the past that other things being equal, which they usually are not, I like to have one of the four clerks whose predispositions are quite the opposite of mine—who are social liberals rather than social conservatives. That kind of clerk will always be looking for the chinks in my armor, for the mistakes I've made in my opinion. That's what clerks are for—to make sure I don't make mistakes. The trouble is, I have found it hard to get liberals like that, who pay attention to text and are not playing in a policy sandbox all the time.

How picky are you about which law schools they come from?
Well, some law schools are better than others. You think they're all the same?

Now, other things being equal, which they usually are not, I would *like* to select somebody from a lesser law school. And I have done that, but really only when I have former clerks on the faculty,

whose recommendations I can be utterly confident of. Harvard, Yale, Stanford, Chicago, they're sort of spoiled. It's nice to get a kid who went to a lesser law school. He's still got something to prove. But you can't make a mistake. I mean, one dud will ruin your year.

While your opinions are delectable to read, I'm wondering: Do you ever regret their tone? Specifically, that your tone might have cost you a majority?
No. It never cost me a majority. And you ought to be reluctant to think that any justice of the Supreme Court would make a case come out the other way just to spite Scalia. Nobody would do that. You're dealing with significant national issues. You're dealing with real litigants—no. My tone is sometimes sharp. But I think sharpness is sometimes needed to demonstrate how much of a departure I believe the thing is.

Especially in my dissents. Who do you think I write my dissents for?

Law students.
Exactly. And they will read dissents that are breezy and have some thrust to them. That's who I write for. . . .

Wasn't it Stevens who said to Souter, "Tell me when I'm losing it and need to retire?"
No, it wasn't Stevens. I think it was Holmes who asked Brandeis.

Oh, so I got it completely wrong.
[*Smiles.*] Completely wrong.

But how will you know when it's time to go? It doesn't seem like you have anything to worry about at the moment, but it's interesting to hear you even flick at that.
Oh, I'll know when I'm not hitting on all eight cylinders.

Are you sure? All these people in public life—athletes in particular—never have a clue.
No, I'll know.

What will the telltale sign be?
One will be that I won't enjoy it as much as I do. I think that's the beginning of the end. I was

worried lately about the fact that the job seems easier. That I really don't have to put in the excessively long hours that I used to. I still work hard. But it does seem easier than it used to. And that worried me. You know: *Maybe I'm getting lazy.* You know, I'm not doing it as thoroughly, or whatever. But after due reflection, I've decided the reason it's getting easier is because so many of the cases that come before us present the issue of whether we should extend one of the opinions from the previous 27 years that I've been here, which I dissented from in the first place!

Yet today, you're a conservative icon, and federalist societies abound on university campuses, and originalism and textualism are no longer marginal. Do you feel like you're winning or losing the battle for constitutional interpretation?
I don't know how much progress I've made on originalism. That's to be seen. I do think originalism is more respectable than it was. But there's still only two justices up here who are thoroughgoing originalists. I do think things are better than they were. For example, I truly thought I'd never see an originalist on the faculty of Harvard Law School. You know, everybody copies Harvard—that's the big ship. There are now three originalists on the faculty, and I think I heard that they've just hired, or are considering hiring, a fourth. I mean, that's amazing to me. Elena Kagan did that, and the reason she did it is that you want to have on your faculty representatives of all responsible points of view. What it means is that at least originalism is now regarded as a respectable approach to constitutional interpretation. And it really wasn't twenty years ago, it was not even worth talking about in serious academic circles.

An area where I think I have made more progress is textualism. I think the current Court pays much more attention to the words of a statute than the Court did in the eighties. And uses much less legislative history. If you read some of our opinions from the eighties, my God, two thirds of the opinions were discussing committee reports and floor statements and all that garbage. We don't do much of that anymore. And I think I have assisted in that transition.

Fifty years from now, which decisions in your tenure do you think will be heroic?
Heroic?

Heroic.
Oh, my goodness. I have no idea. You know, for all I know, 50 years from now I may be the Justice Sutherland of the late-twentieth and early-21st century, who's regarded as: "He was on the losing side of everything, an old fogey, the old view." And I don't care.

Do you think you're headed in that direction?
I have no idea. There are those who think I am, I'm sure. I can see that happening, just as some of the justices in the early years of the New Deal are now painted as old fogies. It can happen.

Wow, it's amazing your mind even went there. I ask about a triumph, and you give me another answer entirely, about the possibility of failure. I was expecting you to end on a high note. Do you want to try another stab at a heroic decision?
Heroic is probably the wrong word. I mean the most heroic opinion—maybe the *only* heroic opinion I ever issued—was my statement refusing to recuse.

From the case involving Vice-President Cheney, with whom you'd gone hunting?
I thought that took some guts. Most of my opinions don't take guts. They take smarts. But not courage. And I was proud of that. I did the right thing and it let me in for a lot of criticism and it was the right thing to do and I was proud of that. So that's the only heroic thing I've done.

As to which is the most impressive opinion: I still think *Morrison v. Olson.* But look, we have different standards, I suppose, for what's a great opinion. I care about the reasoning. And the reasoning in *Morrison,* I thought, was devastating—devastating of the majority. If you ask me which of my opinions will have the most impact in the future, it probably won't be that dissent; it'll be some majority opinion. But it'll have impact in the future not because it's so beautifully reasoned and so well written. It'll have impact in the future because it's authoritative. That's all that matters, unfortunately.

ARTICLE QUESTIONS

1) Scalia asserts he will know when it is time for him to retire from the Court. Should it be up to the justices to determine if they are still competent to serve?
2) Do you think it is desirable for justices to keep their biases out of their decisions? Do you think it is possible for them to do so?
3) Does choosing to advocate originalism display its own type of bias?
4) Is it possible to derive one original meaning from the Constitution (or any of the amendments), given that the Constitution was the product of many minds and the drafters of the Constitution disagreed among themselves as to what the words meant?

Index